To the Buckleys
Christopher & Hunter
1973, 3 November

in memory of two
trout

Hugh [illegible]

Law, Language and Communication

By

WALTER PROBERT

Professor of Law
College of Law
University of Florida
Gainesville, Florida

With a Foreword by

Harold D. Lasswell

Professor Emeritus
Law and Political Science
Yale University
New Haven, Connecticut

CHARLES C THOMAS • PUBLISHER

Springfield • Illinois • U.S.A.

Published and Distributed Throughout the World by
CHARLES C THOMAS • PUBLISHER
BANNERSTONE HOUSE
301–327 East Lawrence Avenue, Springfield, Illinois, U.S.A.

ISBN 0-398-02477-4
Library of Congress Card Catalog Number: 70-190334.

With THOMAS BOOKS *careful attention is given to all details of manufacturing and design. It is the Publisher's desire to present books that are satisfactory as to their physical qualities and artistic possibilities and appropriate for their particular use.* THOMAS BOOKS *will be true to those laws of quality that assure a good name and good will.*

Printed in the United States of America

CC-11

To Barbara

FOREWORD

WALTER PROBERT's novel exposition of "the law" can be profitably read by many different audiences for many complementary purposes. The largest potential audience is composed of the rather literate members of the body politic. From the standpoint of an observer of world affairs every individual belongs to a body politic that expands in ever-widening circles from his immediate vicinity, and passes through metropolitan and national areas until the entire world community comes within its domain. Our lives are shaped within the constraints of the authoritative and controlling norms that are commonly called "the law."

This book is about "the law." It re-introduces the reader—who may be a lawyer, a student, or a layman—to the fundamental characteristics of law in life by examining its most distinctively human dimension. This dimension is communication. The book deals with communications *of* and *about* law.

Few competent observers would quarrel with the proposition that "the communications revolution" is a dominant feature of the world transformations of our time. Until recently, however, our ways of thinking and talking "law" were highly resistant to change. It was customary, for example, to refer to law as a "body of rules" that somehow hovered over and transcended the everyday routines of life.

The most radical initial efforts to change this tradition have not been successful. Early "behaviorism" tried to de-mystify the conception of law by reducing the indicators of a legal pattern of behavior to "bodies" described as "moving" in relation to "things." It was, of course, possible to observe and record vehicles as standing, passing, or crashing; or to report "dollars" given in exchange for pieces of paper called "checks." The idea of reducing law to "'nothing but" specific behaviors was suggested by the success of physicists in observing physical particles and movements. However, primitive behaviorism proved to be too clumsy and unwieldy to provide a serviceable account of legal process. A distinguishing feature of such a process is the flow of distinctive forms of communication, and behaviorism was at a loss to classify and predict the significance of the words employed in controversies, whether uttered by those who pressed a "claim" or who made a "decision."

A more sophisticated attempt to "reduce" law to one set of partial indicators also failed. "Information theory" admitted and indeed stressed the importance of communication. It tried to "save objectivity" by introducing a new set of restrictions. The only phenomena declared eligible for observation and recording were the physical media employed in a sequence of communication. Not words but sounds; not written statements but black marks on paper; not meaningful gestures, but changes in body movements: these were the "bits" of early information theory. "Bit analysis" proved disappointing when applied to summaries of evidence, argument and opinion. The number of letters in a legal brief could be counted, but the same number of characters or of spoken syllables did not elicit a predictable number of printed or spoken items by "judge" or "jury."

The merit of primitive behaviorism and of information theory was that the precision of their procedures of observation was self-correcting. It became increasingly apparent that the critical feature of a communication sequence—message content—was left out. The bits described the signs utilized in transmitting a message. They did not describe the events referred to by the signs, as perceived by communicators who shared a common language, for example. A comprehensive theory of communication calls attention to message content, as well as to the message initiator, carrier or recipient; and explores the causes and consequnces of an act of communication in terms of the shaping and sharing of the values affected.

Walter Probert's re-introduction to law can be used by

citizen, student and practitioner as a self-help textbook or refresher course on the subject. We must at once admit that it doesn't look like the traditional casebook so widely employed in legal education. It doesn't have snippets from appellate court briefs and decisions, and it lacks a rat-a-tat-tat of citations. Nor does it look like a textbook, although the resemblance is closer. And it doesn't fit the austerities of a treatise. So what is it?

In this instance the ambiguity of form is part of a battle plan. Probert is searching for means of winning a "game" in which some professors never engage. The object of the exercise is to arouse students, teachers, practitioners and laymen to join in rethinking the "obvious." The point of an unconventional form is to encourage unconventional thought.

The question can be asked whether the goal is worth the effort. Are not contemporary human beings—especially students—sufficiently unsettled and disturbed as it is? Is "unconventionality" a legitimate end?

Probert is willing to disturb the peace. He has no doubt that independent thinking, if not an end in itself, is at least part of a composite set of ends that are worthy of pursuit. Most of us say that we believe in the dignity of man and therefore cherish freedom of inquiry and expression. Once these things are said, it is evident that expositors of law are committed to challenging, though not necessarily to changing, traditional wisdom.

Perhaps so. But is a case to be made for treating lawyers as exceptions? If lawyers are to man the courts and to serve as members of the bar are they not bearers of a special responsibility? Do they not stand for the rules of the game? Is it not important to cultivate a frame of mind that renders some thoughts unthinkable—or at least unacceptable? If the complexities of a science-based technology spread diversity and alienation, can it be argued that it is incumbent on those who acquire legal knowledge to stand committed to the verities of the established system of public order?

Whatever our position may be on this issue, we are tacitly recognizing the importance of basic conceptions of law, and therefore of professional or public education in law.

No doubt Probert agrees that orthodox education has had a remarkable effect on growing minds. It is not difficult to demonstrate that traditional legalism leaves its heel print on the thoughtways of all who survive its cases, courses, quizzes and exams. In the American system, at least, propositions treated as authoritative are magnetic fields that warp fact-form statements into rigid patterns. Are not the lawman's "facts" what the decision makers say are facts of a case? Do not these final judgments depend on the polarization of specific claims and general justifications in arenas of official controversy?

The traditional law student learns to pursue facts, not for the light they throw on the processes of man and society, but for their estimated usefulness as means of influencing decision makers to respond one way or another in a contest. This is not training in the pursuit of enlightenment. It is drill in acquiring skill in the manipulation of words (and word equivalents) to obtain previously defined results.

Probert is introducing a far more subtle conception of language than has prevailed in conventional legal education. He is trying to equip students with a contextual technique for exploring the place of linguistic statements in the legal and social process. The everyday "meaning" of a string of words is multiple. There are the "preferential" or "volitional" commitments of the statement maker. There are the "fact-form" meanings: events are designated in time, space, and figure. There are "syntactic" arrangements of statements: for instance, some are more abstract, hence inclusive, than other statements. And statements affirm or imply that the statement maker is, or is not "identified" with the individual or group with which he communicates. Moreover, the role of the statement is sometimes "causal"; it is also a "consequence." And so on and on.

If human beings are capable of facing a fundamental

question it is less than human to deny them the opportunity. Opportunities must be extremely complex to enable individuals who have been exposed to very different social environments to comprehend the issues. And this calls for ingenuity in inventing teaching techniques that circumvent the built-in blindspots.

Probert may not have been completely successful in solving the pedagogical problems involved. But his courage and creativity will make it much easier for others to do as well, and perhaps better. This is no pedestrian performance.

HAROLD D. LASSWELL

PREFACE

THE RECORD NEEDS some detailing: To explain how a law teacher can claim to be contributing not only to legal theory but communication theory as well. The further claim is made that the materials are not just theoretical but a teaching device for sensitivity training in words consciousness. How so?

Blame it on the likes of F. S. Cohen, Jerome Frank, and Messrs. Lasswell, McDougal, Northrop, and Rodell, all at Yale Law School in 1952 when it all started, the turn-a-round (and round and round). Each manifested words consciousness of one kind or another. Then there was Korzybski, in print, causing a switch from a doctoral thesis on life insurance law to law and general semantics—and involvement in sensitivity sessions before they were discovered, in the mid-fifties.

Responsibility for teaching Jurisprudence provided a good mechanism for application not only of theory but also techniques. Even better was a seminar arrangement beginning in 1964, with a supportive and innovative colleague, Walter Weyrauch, and co-leaders from the Psychiatry Department, wherein psychoanalytic theory was infused into the mix, with helpful suggestions from Drs. Jay Katz and Andrew Watson. In "permitting" a comparatively unstructured dynamics, theory was being examined and assimilated into the teaching of communication. It was a laboratory in small group behavior. Later on came solo efforts in law-and-communication seminars, the first time with law students and graduates in communication theory jointly. Some of the insights were tried out in more structured courses on legal counseling and techniques of interviewing.

There have been several (other) research projects contributing along the way. There was a joint effort with Reed Lawlor and his fact computer for predicting judicial decision, funded by the National Science Foundation. The Law School Admission Test funds supported a study of freshman law student tolerance to ambiguity. Work with sociologist Gresham Sykes in exploring the "professionalization of law students" provoked reflections about the possibilities of enriching not only law research and teaching but also sociology and anthropology with communications theory and techniques.

The University of Florida supported work at Oxford in fall, 1968, to see what was doing with "linguistic philosophers," including some time with H. L. A. Hart. Asked what was happening, he said, "Chomsky," and he was, in a seminar with Strawson pursuing depth grammar and the Oxford approach (very deep indeed). One particular discussion with Warnock threw open the doors wider to the epistemological tensions under the surface of Wittgenstein's and J. L. Austin's efforts. Special insight came out of a seminar with Anthony Kenny, Fellow in Philosophy at Balliol, in a seminar on Morality and Intent, not because he was one of the "linguists," but because he was not.

The National Foundation for the Humanities helped in the exploration of Oxford and its philosophers and too with some time off from teaching in the winter and spring of 1969.

And ah, yes, there are the legalists I have known! Some have been students, of course, but there have been others in higher places in teaching, administration, on the Bench and in the Bar. A very special experience let me see the interplay of brands of legalism, as the law member of a University disciplinary committee. One sees there, if he can be both participant *and* observer, how rules (can) get used. It is in that unwritten sort of experience that one can feel the interplay between media of rules-communication, especially the way the group encounter processes rules.

Along the way came some cross-country sessions with Lou Brown of USC, doing a joint article on the "jurisprudence of lawyering," and appreciation of the possibilities of translating from one perspective to another without the need for either loss of face or principle.

Finally, special thanks are due to those who read all or part of the developing manuscript: Richard C. Allen, Wilfrid Rumble, Alfred G. Smith, and Walter Weyrauch. Most of all, of course, deepest thanks to those students who have explored the text and other materials with me, sometimes unwittingly it is true, but often enough as willing pioneers. There have even been some legalists who changed their stripes in these ventures.

WALTER PROBERT

INTRODUCTION

Preparing for Experimentation

IF THE MAJOR FUNCTION of an introduction were to tell you what is coming, it could not be done. If it could be done, then there would be no need to go beyond the introduction. (But see Directory, p. 332.) In the case of these particular explorations, a pre*view* would not involve so much telling as showing. While communication, particularly from academic sources, usually is of the telling, here-I-am-giving-you-facts, kind, that is only one of the kinds involved in these explorations. But we will rather glide into those variations. Probably that is what an introduction is supposed to do, break some ice, establish a relationship, prepare the way. In our case of dealing with communication, it is a matter of getting on the right channel.

Maybe, since we are dealing also with law, we should set up some rules. State some facts and apply the rules. But that would be to satisfy the very sort of expectations that are going to obstruct some participants in this set of communicative interplays, the ones who believe facts to be things that can be stated and law to predominate with rules that need merely be asserted, they also fully believe they should merely have to read and be informed. Of course *we* do not believe that, but I worry a bit that some readers may not quite *fully* realize that the workings of words, in law or out, cannot be adequately appraised in merely traditional academic forms and styles.

There could be some irritations and frustrations with some of the material ahead. There are several reasons why, including resistance to probes beneath the surface functionings of words, especially of law and other order words. Overriding everything are those expectations, those psycho-linguistic habits. Each kind of communication depends upon certain set forms and styles. One cannot communicate a law in a song, for instance. While verbal communication is not as dependent upon grammar as some purists would have us believe, still there are certain limits on the feasibility of breaking those rules, and pretty clearly you do not communicate to the purist if you break his rules.

When McLuhan said the medium is the message, he only dramatized what every anthropologist and every would-be explorer of language in depth must soon learn. Form and style (kinds of media communicatively speaking) are invisible controls of thought and action. They are particularly important in the structuring, the *ordering* of law words, or what we will stress as law talk. To explore the workings of words, in and out of law talk, we must examine the machinery, take it apart, and look at it. It will not be possible to do that job without stepping outside of the expected, accepted forms. Then one may come back to the required forms with a new consciousness, what we may call simply a words consciousness. What we may then do is use familiar forms in new ways.

The point is well illustrated by an experiment I understand was conducted at M.I.T. some years back as preparation for a course in creative engineering. The control situation was that a group of students were brought into a room in which they were confronted with an upright pipe-like cylinder fastened to the floor. Inside, at the bottom of the pipe was a ping-pong ball. Their job was to free the ball from the pipe which was of sufficient length and small enough in diameter that the ball could not be reached with one's hand. There was also a bucket of water in the room. Well, the control groups solved the problem easily enough by pouring water into the pipe to float the ball to the top where it could be plucked out.

The experimental situation involved the same pipe but there was no bucket of water. Groups of students who had not gone through the control situation did not solve this one. They were inhibited by their acculturation. They could not see the solution right at hand. Along one side of the room was a long, finely laid banquet table, the best linen, silver, china, crystal goblets, and all. Goblets filled with water! One would not think of using that water for such a purpose. How one sees a situation, how he thinks, how he acts, is controlled by his expectations and his habits. So it is, especially, with words. In allegory, the words are the water, every bit and more fluid, the law the crystal goblets on the banquet table all implicit with rules of behavior.

Of course it is even more complicated in the case of law talk. Rules of law are asserted by means of words which themselves are asserted with implicit interweaving rules on the way words must be put together (form, style, grammar) and other subtle rules and expectations concerning the situations in which all of these things are blended.

Show Me A Rule

You are invited now to step out of this introduction for a demonstration. If you will, turn to the dialogue called Show Me A Rule, Exhibit I in the Appendix. And think of this: A dialogue is a familiar enough form, but it surely is not regarded as entirely appropriate as a *form* for scholarly presentation. Yet, even if all of its messages do not now come across, they will before we are through. It "says" things that cannot be readily, certainly not simply said in the usual declarative style. Think further of this: One reads this dialogue, we may say, yet it is not reading in the same sense ("read" is ambiguous) as reading of this paragraph. One is placed in a different communications perspective. He reads in order to witness. The structure of that reading situation is different from this one. One is involved in a very different way. One more think: How that reading-experience hits you is a test of your words consciousness as well as a vehicle to promote it. It has been much used out of these particular pages. It has worked, in some cases producing insight in the sort of flash that other techniques of verbal analysis may fail to light. A number of other techniques are explored in these materials. They all are, of course, to be "read" in one sense or another, but the involvements vary.

Has Anyone Seen A Fact?

"Show Me A Rule" is actually a mixture of dialogue and narrative, as well as a mixture of different words that are look alikes. The covering form is the spelling as "rule." We explore more deeply into this word-form as we proceed. The second Exhibit in the Appendix is pure dialogue, exploring the word-form "fact," also more deeply explored anon. "Has Anyone Seen A Fact?" more clearly than the first Exhibit involves not only words consciousness as such but the inter-involvement of words and things. It is a vehicle to demonstrate and promote communications sensitivity. One ought to read it now, not looking for philosophical implications, of which there are many, but to see how much of a feel he may already have or may begin to obtain for the verbal level of communications as it relates to and yet remains distinctive from the non-verbal levels of experience.

The Right Way

There is one other Exhibit that might be read now, The Right Way (No. VI, Appendix) but maybe only by those fairly familiar with writings in legal theory. Its form and style is rather traditional although at times its tone is not. Experience has demonstrated, as odd as this point will sound, that there is a sense in which this piece is "tougher" reading for scholars well-versed in legal theory than for the untarnished novice. Of course it can be turned off as effrontery or maybe even a bad joke. Yet, somehow the point has to be made, some law theorists are resistant to words *consciousness*. For these scholars, if there is "toughness" in this reading, it certainly is not a matter of intelligence or capacity. Maybe like the legalists we shall be talking about—in and out of the law profession—they have a psycho-linguistic investment in their definitions and the power that can come from controlling how things shall be said, as well as a certain security. We find a similar sort of phenomenon shutting off one discipline from another. The invitation to words consciousness can be a threat to disciplinary lines. Well, it is.

For lawyers, our probings of legal concepts could on first blush seem to promote practicing without a license. Maybe they will worry about an undermining of the stability of law. That is a problem and we grapple with it. Legal theorists have reason too to be concerned about law and order in ways we shall discuss, but less reason than say judges to insist on preserving a closed and camouflaging rhetoric.

Put it this way: Playing with words can actually be a creative and constructive pursuit. We all do it. We do it unabashedly here and there in these pages, as what is thought to be a valid method of exploring the very guts of language and communication. Above all, philosophers in and out of law do it. They should be encouraged to do it.

But considering the impact they often ultimately have in the market place of law, they should perhaps not take the *play* as seriously as they do, as least amongst themselves.

An *inescapable* philosophic task, not the exclusive task certainly, is analysis. While Anglo-American legal theory has skirmished on the surface of words-conscious analysis, it still remains quite stubbornly resistant to the sort of contemporary deeper communications analysis which is available for the talking. One aspect of this possible new approach is to examine the relationships between the arts of different kinds of analysis on the one hand with the vicissitudes of framing a persuasive rhetoric on the other.

While a band of pragmatist legal theorists well pointed out this sort of distinction for the judicial process, the distinction between the judicial solution of a litigational conflict and the judicial rhetoric in a formal opinion, it is really impossible to find anyone who will admit such distinctions for the doing of legal theory. Now what kind of a business is that? At any rate, that sort of focus interplays with the analysis of the word "right" in The Right Way and provides a pervasive theme throughout all these materials. Indeed we go an even more significant step further to explore the relationships among analysis, *interpretation*, and persuasion, three key communicative tasks involved in the use of law talk and legal theory.

No truly contemporary and relevant theory of law can develop without at least conscious sensitivity to these tasks. Most of the contemporary theorizing lacks persuasiveness for failure to acknowledge these dimensions.

Words Consciousness and Beyond

Above all, these explorations are meant to provide learning experiences for the reader-participant. In one way or another, every chapter and most of the pieces in the Appendix involve or come out of the application or use of well-developed premises of communication theory. All of these premises are stated in one place or another. (And see summaries in the Directory, p. 332.) The premises could all be plucked out and stated seriatim, in rather short space at that, or they could be elaborated didactically. Of course there is actually much of that. But communication premises as such do not really teach much of anything by themselves.

Take this premise oft repeated ahead: No matter what one says, he is always doing something else. That premise was partially applied to judicial opinions back in the twenties and thirties by some legal pragmatists. It sound rather Freudian, and it was in the way it was applied back then. However, in communications analysis one looks not just under the surface but at both what is said and done. Merely saying that does not bring much of the full ramifications into view. Much more comes of it if I not only tell you about these two "levels," but show you, involve you in them so that you do not just think about it but become involved in that phenomenon and literally feel it and experience a surge of insight that you will never forget. (Later!)

Take another, so easy to state: Words are pervasively ambiguous. What does that *do* to you? Again, something of this premise was partially applied to the analysis of judicial opinions. It sounds Wittgensteinian, and it is now, but it was applied before he wrote his fantastically significant-for-communications-analysis called Philosophical Investigations. But I have to *show* you, maybe because you either have not read Wittgenstein or have not applied his premises in the way I want to demonstrate. There are things about the phenomena of ambiguity that I cannot adequately tell you, but I can show you and involve you in it, if you will let me, if you will come into it with me, explore it right with me, feel it, *turn on to it.* To do that, especially in Chapter V, you must not read merely for the sake of information.

There are a number of other fundamental principles of communication which are articulated, applied, and demonstrated. Rather a fair number of them are articulated here for the first time anywhere. Merely stating them is not enough. Take this one: A rule is a function of the communication situation in which it is applied. Sounds good, abstract enough to be good theory, esoteric enough to be academic. It is demonstrated in two different ways in Chapters VI and IX. When one reaches an appreciation of that statement he has a feel for what goes on in the process of interpretation that cannot be exactly articulated. (But more systematic articulation is explored in Chapter X.)

This is not mysticism or non-rationalism. Another new premise has to do with the way hypothetical-fact assertions are used in rational argument, including among other sorts, legal and philosophical. Here is how it is said in Chapter VI: ". . . the hypothetical assertion . . . completely by-passes the communicative processes that are involved in getting from dynamic happenings to frozen facts-statements." To appreciate the full significance of that premise, not only for analysis and for rationality, but also for techniques of rhetoric, one must relate written forms of communciation to the sorts that are involved in face-to-face communication. (Ditto as to the premise about rules.) Somehow I must try to get you to feel the interaction of these kinds of communication as you are involved in them.

That is not easy to do in writing. Nor is it easy to do orally. So, how to do it? This need to relate written forms to oral (and thought) dynamics provides the key clue for one who wishes his reading to be in familiar forms and styles, the key clue as to why things are the way they are in the following pages, why the variations and playing, not only with form and style, but punctuation even, and the words, and even paragraphs (not to mention parentheses). These are rolled up applications and extensions of the likes of Wittgenstein, J. L. Austin, Korzybski, and McLuhan.

And let us be clear right now that we are very much beyond mere semantics in these pages, much beyond mere verbal analysis. We are involved in words and language and interpersonal communication, seeing words as not independent entities any more than are laws or rules. To see how words function in language, communication and law-in-process, in law talk and similar kinds of talk, rule talk of whatever kind, fact talk of whatever kind, we must see them in the full dynamics of communciation, not just flat on the page. (Neither you nor I are flat on this page!)

We need to see with the early Wittgenstein and his ingenious elaborator Alfred Korzybski how words are not things and yet see with the later Wittgenstein and his competitor analyst J. L. Austin how very much inter-involved words are with things and actions, in the way they are developed and used, behaviorally, in the dynamics of communciation which are hardly limited to any particular written form or to the written forms at all. That sort of thing requires liberation from the captivations of the written forms as well as the grammatical forms on the surface of all verbal communication. That takes us down into deeper grammars, again with Wittgenstein and Austin, but also our own Noam Chomsky.

Words consciousness is liberating. One must be in the process of being liberated in order to heighten his words consciousness. If that sounds like *Catch 22*, it is no coincidence. Rossarian discovered that the only way out of combat duty was designed to keep him there. He could be discharged if he was insane. All he had to do was to say he wanted to go home. But then that would prove him sane, so he could not be sent home.

The major obstacle to words consciousness is intolerance to ambiguity. Tolerance can be increased by training in words consciousness, which includes conscious sensitizing to ambiguities which one pushes out of sight because he cannot tolerate them.

Imagine the heightened anxiety for beginning law students who may be especially intolerant of ambiguity in law. In order to pass their examinations they must be quite skillful in working with ambiguities. Yet they may be responding to professors who themselves are skillful with ambiguity manipulation in their law talking but not conscious of it so that it is taboo right where it is most practicable to talk about it. The demands of the rhetoric of the advocate are that it be dogmatic and admit to no ambiguity in its *conclusions.*

The greater the intolerance to ambiguity, the more the student *suffers* in a law class which is not structured, either by an outline type lecture or a clearly directive Socratic discussion. He thinks he is not learning law if there is mainly discussion with no underlined assertions. Indeed, many students suffer if there are a few questions left open, even if classes predominate with black letter assertions. Such a student might not like either dialogue in the Appendix, but he would prefer the one on "fact" to the one on "rule" because it does have a dogmatic assertion pervading it, whereas the "rule" piece seems to end up straddling the fence.

Chapter V may make such a person angry, at least at first go round (and there may never be a second). Chapter X is much more apt to be his sort of meat, being rather traditional in form and style and laying it all out to boot. There are simply many different kinds of explorations. For that matter, Chapter X could be read before Chapter V. There is purpose in the order of these explorations, there are building themes, and yet there is an independence in them. Certainly that is true of Chapter II on rhetorical definitions. Still, seeing how rhetorical definition works helps to sensitize one to the subtler ambiguities and the metaphoric process of growth of word-forms into families. It is rather like a spiral staircase but the top leads to the bottom and vice-versa. (See summaries in the Directory.)

If Chapter V is going to stand in the way of other insights, let it be skipped, or delayed. It constitutes a sort of test of one's level of ambiguity-tolerance, as well as one's potential for being receptive to forced confrontation with multiple and sometimes seemingly clashing messages. Chapter VI will attempt to show the merit of such confrontation, and could be read before Chapter V. There is a way in which Chapter V *can* communicate which can only be suggested.

A distinguished colleague of mine confirmed, just hours ago as I write, what I had told a seminar group who have been reading this manuscript and interacting with me these last two terms. I had said to the seminar, this business of being words conscious is a matter of "turning on." Just when one will be capable of doing that or just what will induce him to it is not predictable. Motivation, willingness, readiness, all are involved. I warned them, although they may have thought I was kidding, that there was a bit of a risk involved, for one could get high in the process. My colleague called right in the middle of reading that Chapter V. He wanted to give me certain impressions he was having before they faded. He actually said that he felt "high on words."

We might speak of the elation of insight. One can be talked into it, he can *write himself into it.* I strongly recommend as indispensable to this sensitizing process trying out some of the techniques displayed, with other people, by one's self, at various times and places. It does work. It is worth it, although again I warn of another risk, the frustration that can come from not being able, really, to communicate such insights to others who have not experienced them. Thus, this book.

There are a number of other techniques used here. Consider using the dialogue technique, for instance. Pick some key word-form, even "rule" or "fact" or "right," or some one of your own choosing. List some of the senses of the word on a piece of paper, including some you will not find in the dictionary. Then write a dialogue. It can be, will be, once you get the knack, quite insightful (and fun). Should you ever read some of the words of J. L. Austin, you will realize there is a relationship between this technique of analysis to gain familiarity with the complex of a word-form, the family members as Wittgenstein put it, and the Socratic *monologue* method of analysis which Austin used. Some of the Austinian technique is more closely replicated in Chapter VI in the analysis of the concept of intent.

Three Books

A major communications premise not only repeatedly articulated but demonstrated in these pages is that communication takes place on more than one level *simultaneously*. Having tested out these materials I know they work, on more than one level. But I know too that for a particular reader, the levels may come across as jumbled. This is exactly the phenomenon that takes place in a communications sensitivity-training seminar. Participants come in prepared to be taught, to get substantive level information. Some catch on sooner than others, but slowly participants can tune in to the dynamics of interaction of "teacher" and "students" as they discuss substantive matters. But they have difficulty, at first, doing both. They can get excited about getting involved and levelling with each other (generally the stuff of group encounters, but this is not our main purpose), still, it is hard for them to see that there *is* information coming across also—concerning whatever subject we happen to be discussing. (It takes t-i—m——e to develop capacity to work on both levels at once.) And I also ask them and push them to become words conscious as well. They say they do not know what I am talking about on more than one of these levels—although a few do pretty quickly—but it is happening. It happens to most of them, but of course in different ways and at different levels of "achievement," but it happens. They get started, that is. How much can you do in one seminar? (Or in or with one book?)

In a sense this is three books. There is here a full blown book on communication theory to which law illustrations need be seen only as an incidental theme. My hope is that it makes a significant contribution on that level. But the legal theorist can see this—if he will look this way—as a fully developed component of legal theory. Sooner or later the bulwarks will fall on this level! Going around the circle, it is a sensitivity-training book. That is, I believe persons who are neither law nor communications-theory trained can use this vehicle to develop general words consciousness as well as a feel for law and/or rules talk. I believe it would be a rare reader who will tune in on all three levels the first time around, or at least right off. And of course there will be those who will not tune in on any level. Still, one level at a time is something. If, for instance, Chapter V were merely received on a sensitizing level, that would be great. (Come back and get the theory later!)

A radio set cannot pick up a TV video signal, an AM set cannot pick up FM; a monaural receiver can only make it monaurally. But I sincerely believe that most humans who would be likely to cross the paths of these explorations have tuning capacities that will allow reception on one or more levels, sooner or later. The signals are there and I can do no more with them. The receivers may need to do some special tuning from time to time. For that purpose, also for the participant who wants to choose his own order of reading, or if further pre-view is desired, or when summaries are wanted, see the Directory. Sensitivity trainees should use as a guide.

CONTENTS

Law, Language and Communication

Chapter I

SHADES OF LEGALISM: SOME PROBLEMS

Prelude*

LAW WITHOUT WORDS. Try to imagine it. Yet maybe it is harder to visualize law *as* words. Marshall McLuhan sees a decline in the cultural significance of the printed word and perhaps in all forms of verbal communication. But that sort of communication is indispensable to our law(s). Yet how little we have considered the communications dimensions of the interinvolvements of law(s) and words.

As usual, legal theory is lagging. At the cultural level, we just may be entering an era grand in increasing awareness and consciousness of the levels or dimensions of communication. The best known psycholinguistic studies are called "semantics," but words operate in ways untouched in those studies. Even McLuhan seems to have failed to appreciate that words are not just media sorts of phenomena. Nor do they just mediate interpersonal relationships. In McLuhan's sense of media, words do act as extensions of man, but not just that. They are also often part of his behavior. Most analysts have failed to look at words in that way, not just as behavior, but often at least that, and always behaviorally involved.

Still, there has been in the last seventy years highly significant attention given to the words of law and of legal theory. As a result, there has been some increase in words-consciousness in the arts and ways of the profession, perhaps more in theory level analyses, but surprisingly less in scientific and behavioral studies of law, legal process, and law-society relationships.

---

* See Directory for comments directed toward each chapter.

AMBIGUISTS VS. PRECISIONISTS

Roaring out from the acidic speculations of Oliver Wendell Holmes came the legal realists, wreaking their ways through the ambiguous holes of the common-law covering, in what amounted to a direct attack upon the bastions of the judiciary. They cut this way and that with semantic sorts of analyses, applying and, in a way, developing what we now would better call primitive beginnings of communication theory. Law has not looked the same ever since, at least not in this country.

Before the iconoclasm of these ambiguists could do much more than threaten the precisionistic faith on the English side, H. L. A. Hart led a rhetorically brilliant thrust on behalf of legal positivism, at the same time shoring up the shaky antique facades of their analytical traditions. He bore down with what *seemed* to be the full power of contemporary linguistic sophistication. In purveying what in fact was a merely restrained version of the "language philosophy" of his Oxbridge environment, attempting at least to effect a restoration of the image if not the edifice of law, he worked in the light of an apparent paradox. He accused the ambiguists of an absolutistic faith, confessed to an upper layer of ambiguities, and displayed *through* this disfocus which had served the ambiguists so well, a supposedly deeper, stronger, even more realistic level of precision in law talk and legal theory. Much of our attention in the coming pages will be given to this sort of paradox.

Participants in both movements have naturally claimed to be revealing fundamental truths about the way(s) law(s) work(s). These revelations come out of rather differing empirics or views of what is real. The legal positivists seem generally to have believed that certain realities were, in some way, mirrored or captured in words, that things "out there," for instance, were not the only kind of reality. "There is more to law than people!" They have shown, for theorists with a supposed empirical bias, an excess of the *kind* of faith in words which give the sort of power to words which is needed for law(s) to function.

Their arduous efforts over long years have implicitly displayed what they themselves cannot see: the difficulty of separating words from mere lawyers' or theorists' rhetoric. "But rules are real!"

The legal realists, on the other hand, moved toward a behavioral sort of empirics which somehow tries to exclude words, purporting to reveal more tangible, or what they believed to be the only realities, under the camouflages of law talk. Their explorations in verbal analysis were more or less incidental to that and other goals. Their greater interests seemed to lie in the direction of major reforms to be accomplished by upsetting the complacently perpetuated responses of both judges and academic professionals. For that matter, the legal positivists have tended mostly to defend the accepted and traditional stabilizing mechanisms of legal process, under the cover of esoteric, descriptive-sounding justifications.

While many observers regard legal realism as dead and legal positivism as irrelevant or obsolescent, these approaches are worthy of exploration for several purposes. Their trials and errors bring insights to theories both of law and communication. Brief summaries may produce caricatures, but even in these extremes there are reflections of views commonly held, not only within the legal profession, but among laymen as well, and not just in law situations. As with law-communications analysis generally, the debates of these legal theorists bear insights far beyond the arenas of law. There are legalistic personalities, for instance, to be found waving their rules around almost any sort of decisional corner, doing battle perhaps with some opposite number whose skepticism or rebellion would lay the rules to waste.

Most legal positivists share the common view that the core, or at least an essential component, of law is rules (and laws) which can be and usually are stated with adequate clarity and precision. Ambiguities there are, but not in the predominant number of situations. These rules control and obligate the members of society as well as the officialdom who must work, not above, but under and within them. The counter view is that legal rules are highly suspect if they exist at all. The supposed body of rules is multi-fractured, hopelessly riddled with ambiguities, so that declared rules serve not as determinants or controls, but at best as guides and mostly as rationalizations for decisions or actions pursued on other grounds.

Probably no one could abide by either of such opposing views steadfastly. But most anyone's verbal-epistemological rule-profile would place him somewhere along the spectrum defined by these extremes, with, very probably, a majority falling on the precisionist side. Within the profession, the ambiguist position is more used than displayed, especially as a means for the advocate to discover the weakness in his opponent's case. Most theorists now deny the ambiguist premises, if for no other reason than it "just cannot be so." In this country they also deny the precisionists' view for its simplistic rigidity, lack of comprehensiveness, and certainly for its obstructiveness either to desired reforms or to recognition of what *our* history readily reveals to be a dynamic interplay in the politics of legal structure(s). In any event, from a communications analysis perspective, it is misleading, if not more, simply to deny these views out of hand.

Separations

Naturally, from all of this it is possible to extract differences in points of view about law(s)' verbalisms. And note how easy it is to assume there *is* a language-of-law, or even to take the view that law is separate from words and language somehow only *using* them. What the realists and positivists have split apart, we may yet profitably join together. In that pursuit, we will speak of *law talk,* not just law here and talk-about-law there.

The positivists have a penchant for separating and structuring by means of constructing verbal maps which seem only analytical mirrors. They thus fashion, not a moving, dynamic model, but one frozen in ways which serve their socio-legal views. The model at least implies the possibilities of a language of law or a system of words-in-law which operate separately from behavioral dynamics, for law purposes somewhat in the manner of a logical or mathematical system of symbols.

There are other separations in this analysis (often shared in the unarticulated theory of the actors and participants in legal process), such as the slicing of law(s) away from facts, and from morality, policy or values; or rules from the dynamics of litigation or from social behavior. Such "realities" seem to be abstracted out of the socio-legal flux by analysis much in the way that physical observables are, couched in verbal modes which add persuasively to this appearance of a reality close to the physical kind. ("The law is so and so, does so and so . . . .") In this respect, their theory is supported by the way most law professionals and the vast majority of the citizenry talk about and no doubt understand these *aspects* of life's whole events.

In all of this there lies an implicit faith in the way words serve as the medium for rules and laws, or in effect if not perception, how words *do things* to people. The implicit stress is on the inhibiting, conditioning side of words and language.

The legal realists (so-called) had reacted, perhaps over-reacted to legalism, at one time almost the trademark if not the caricature of the profession, what Llewellyn called the "formal style," but put less charitably what was a dead(ening) style. The "realists" observed not the independent body of rules that others saw transcending even the words in which they were supposedly carried or reflected; rather they saw people and people talking and acting. They saw not law but people (judges, etc.) using rhetorical techniques to do things to other people; what others could see in advocates as strategies, but not in judges and other officials.

They objected to the over-separation of legal vocabularies from other vocabularies. In so doing, they, too, in a sense implied some sort of separate system of legal language in operation, by seeming to admit that separateness is possible. They objected that such lego-linguistic balkanization had come to lack social relevance. (Familiar?)

Some "realists" may have realized that law talk was, in operation, just as freewheeling as everyday discourse. Law could be postulated (idealized?) as containing set propositions, but laws in action were something else again, capable of being subtly manipulated in the *dynamics* of law talk, as exemplified in judicial opinions, lawyers' and classroom argumentation, and in professional commentaries. At least law(s) were being used restrictively against democratic goals. Things were not being "told like they are."

Realists and Law's Rhetoric

Probably the realists are most remembered or cited for their anti-rulism (anti-legalism), although deeper down was an antagonism to repressive judicial authority. Their intellectual radicalism is, no doubt, exceeded by today's revolutionaries or even the exuberant activism of militant lawyers (e.g. Kunstler). But those who would simplify the realists as merely anti-rules pick out what may merely have been symbolic of their scorn of the terms and doctrines parlayed in law talk, *the whole rhetoric.*

There were a number of key terms they saw to be vague, weaselish, and little more than emotive; not only terms like "due process," "reasonable," and "substantial," as in substantial performance of contracts, but many, if not most, of legal terminology, when seen in dynamic interrelationship. They found a high degree of ambiguity that was seldom openly admitted in the profession and less recognized outside. They saw courts interpreting statutes by attributing a certain meaning to key words when a conflicting meaning could have been given. What was true of statutes was even more frequent regarding common law rules. Conceptualism at various turns: Sales cases turning on "title" that no one could see or locate, and similarly with duties, causes, facts, and so on and on. Legislative intent was another thingification. Conceptualism merged with fictionalizing and even cliches. Key concepts were often used in circular fashion, short circuiting more elaborate reasoning that might and ought to be given in socially related decision-making.

At the next level came words in combinations, in rules and larger collections and complexities of definitions, axioms, principles, and so on. But many purported rules were not really rules, as for instance the reasonable man rule which was simply a decision-allocating device, as between trial judge and jury and, in turn, the appellate courts. But consider statements that look more like rules. When it came to applying the correct rule from the whole body of rules, one was confronted with a situation of circularity. A judicial opinion did not within itself show the circularity, but an observer who knew his way around the problem area could see it because he knew there was another rule or doctrine which could support the opposing result.

Much more subtle were the various available characterizations and definitions which seemed to give decision-makers complete discretion. Then there was the business of analyzing cases for their precedent value. There were no controls to determine what interpretations should be made, what cases should be put together in what combinations, or at what level of generality analogies should be made or rules or principles derived.

And even more subtly, they exposed the muddling of perspectives which is still the most deceptive aspect of law talk. The communicative tasks were not being differentiated. For instance, courts would assert laws, engage in reasoning, and give justification all in the same vocabularies and style. What was worse, criticisms of the product were couched in the same way. It was as if one could adequately appraise a painting by merely cutting it apart and putting it together again, or worse, as if that were the way to paint in the first place.

Verbal Power

Communicatively, it is important to see that the realists began, or their analyses tended to take them, outside of the psycholinguistic influence held by the courts. They were like loyal opposition, not identifying with the authority figures or their coalescing patter(ns). Part of the image and effectiveness of law has been dependent on human authorities somehow being felt as submerged in the power and wisdom of law. Law, not people, is in control: The Rule of Law. Those who believe would object to any discussion of law as words. But if one is not caught up in that sort of mystical faith, as today's rebels are not, as the realists were not, then they see the puppets, not as officials controlled by words, but as law words which are being used to put on a show. There is definitely need for faith in laws, law words, and some forms of law talk, if law is to work. Yet it is possible to have an excessive faith, a blind or naive faith, at times amounting to self-deception. Of course it is possible to be excessively skeptical and distrustful of laws, words, and people, making discussion at best painful. Those whose faith is excessive tend to play with words without knowing it, generally falling into a compulsive play and manipulation which has been styled as legalism. The legal realists helped to expose this phenomenon, providing insights that ramify beyond law or law talk. It is, writ large, a psycholinguistic phenomenon that may be found anywhere that forms of language are used. Lawyer's legalism is but one kind, although ranking high among psychopathologies along with its legalistic cousin found in lay attitudes toward law.

There is high risk of legalism in the legal positivists' camp. Hart's version is supported by certain tenable socio-legal values, as I shall attempt to explain, but while he shows an artistic mastery with words and a deeper consciousness of socioverbal mechanisms than most observers, he skirts the edge of over-verbalism. Yet it is difficult to be anti-legalistic, like the legal realists, without building premises that would reject altogether the power of words. There are cultural patterns in word use that support Hart, at least this side of legalism.

Beneath the Forms

These patterns have been referred to by linguists as depth grammar to counteract the older fascination with the surface grammar. But it is true that legalists tend to be fascinated by surface patterns of word-use, the kind that have much to do with verbal etiquette, i.e. grammar and style. The surface relationships between nouns, verbs, adjectives as predicates, and so on, camouflage deeper dynamics. The root cause, from a psycholinguistic point of view, of conceptualism—legalism writ large—is insensitivity to subsurface ambiguities. It is through analysis of these subsurface variations—dynamics—that one becomes conscious of a richer complexity of patterns that cannot possibly be perceived in terms of old-fashioned grammar.

Word-meanings could not have just burst forth full blown, after all, although in a sense they did for each of us as we moved into the culture linguistically. But originally they must have developed through *use* by individuals in varying situations. This sort of development is still, constantly taking place, concealed under the surfaces of dictionary entries and grammar book rules. But there are patterns of word use that exist separately from any one individual, patterns that have developed in strikingly similar fashion to the *stare decisis* patterns of common law, patterns that no one of us could possibly change or legislate away. We speak against the backdrop of these patterns of verbal use-precedents. So there are patterns of word-use in constant process of developing new patterns in socio-linguistic ways. The dictionary is the *digest* of precedents, not the code book, certainly. One can be "legalistic" by over-reliance on a dictionary, for failure to recognize that a dictionary cannot possibly capture the marvelous complexity of verbal dynamics, with upper level patterns restraining but not strictly binding the verbal dynamics of a particular situation.

Insensitivity to the relationship between surface grammar and depth grammar is one of the factors that makes it difficult to see what has been called the normative ambiguity of law statements. A law statement uses the surface grammar of a fact statement, but much of the time they cannot be verified in the same fashion. "He has just been hit" and "He has just been battered" look much alike, but the psycholinguistic permutations are quite different as we must explore. "There is an ought factor in every law statement" is the way some would put it, to brevify the matter for now.

The legal positivists seem totally oblivious to this communicative phenomenon, partly because such an admission would weaken the rhetorical influence of dogmatic assertions of law, but perhaps partly too because of an almost fatal passion for conceptuals, as with the insistence on the independence of law and morality. This sort of separation raises communicative questions which they have never seen let alone explored. But it is interesting that the main support to the argument of separateness of law from morality is a procedural one, for instance that the way legal sanctions are imposed differs from the way that moral sanctions are imposed. (Hart's interest in "appropriate procedures" goes further.) Surface grammar is the procedure of language, the way one is to talk. Many of those outside of legal circles fail to understand for failure to know its procedures, true enough, but over-concern for procedure is a legalistic sort of symptom. We are much involved with matters of form-alism.

There is a form-al aspect to stare decisis, but in the United States one does not get so readily caught up in one form of stare decisis, not as a lawyer, because of the diversity of jurisdictions, and further because of the diversity of decision-making mechanisms in this country. Since the relationship between the stare decisis of language and that of common law is no coincidence at all, it is no doubt easier for our legal professionals to become more conscious of the way words work.

Spontaneity vs. Fixity

But there is more to understanding words-work than grammar, even at depth (and we shall explore). There is the question of the relation of words to things and situations. Korzybski's major premise was that words are separate from things. There is a verbal level and a non-verbal level. That seems a matter of common sense, much emphasized in the linguistic approach of such legal realists as Holmes, Felix Cohen, and Jerome Frank. But what seems so sensible poses immense problems in efforts to understand law-words-in-process.

Culturally speaking there is no *a priori* mandate or norm that a member of society must refer to or describe something observable in some fixed way. Things do not come with labels attached. There come to be conventional names for things as well as people, but even people are not known just by their given names. While there would be *some* conveniences in having a fixity of word-thing relationship, we would find ourselves without the creative side of word use.

When it comes to the greater complexity and dynamism of events and situations which make up the stuff of legal regulation and control, if we see rules and laws as *ways of talking*, or even as potential labels for situations, we see they are not automatically applicable. In routine situations, convention will do, just as conventional word applications work for casual conversations. But the situations leading to appellate litigation, the object of study of the legal realists, show someone's unwillingness to have them treated routinely, at least one of the litigants, no matter how conventionally the judicial rhetoric may later make the situation appear.

Recall that one of the major lines of attack of the realists was that rule application could not really be a matter of syllogistic or deductive logic, stressing that each "case" was a new situation, in some respect uniquely important at least to someone. To just apply a rule to the new case was to beg the question, logically speaking; was to make a value judgment, ethically speaking.

Laws are general; situations are unique, not only in the raw, sense data respect. Even on the verbal level any situation can be distinguished from another. The application—or extension—of rules to situations involves a characterization process. In everyday affairs, the characterization of events, things, and situations, often occurs so spontaneously that it seems perfectly natural. And that is often the way law talk proceeds as well. Characterizations can be debated, until someone with authority pronounces the final word, the final controlling characterization. One who has (or ones who have) control of the characterization of either facts or law, via *interpretation*, can fit laws and facts together, with finality. The power is all the greater if the body or entity has control over both kinds of characterizations, as is true say of a trial judge without a jury.

There has to be authority somewhere in society to make the controlling characterizations. We appreciate the need for the "last say" power with respect to fact-finding, but not so readily regarding law-characterization. The power of judges is tempered somewhat by the last say of juries, especially in criminal cases.

I am stressing here the overlap of the ways of law talk with those of general communication. Compare the communicative problems which arise in conflict situations out of court, where law has no say or even relevance, e.g. marital spats. If one looks at some such familiar happenings, he takes a perspective similar to the one taken by the legal realists in looking at the stuff of litigation, *at the point of conflict before resolution by decision.* Who has not experienced some situation (s) where understanding between the people (or groups) seems impossible? One person speaks in terms that ordinarily would be clear enough. But somehow the other person finds an ambiguity. Back and forth it goes in that way. (An interesting game for experiment, for the insights it gives.)

There is always what the lay person regards as "quibbling" room. Lawyers need skill of that sort, certainly when advocates, although it gets in the way in attempted negotiation. There is always something else to be said, always an ambiguity to widen. Conflicts that involve breakdowns in communication do not necessarily lack clarity or precision but, usually, lack rapport or desire to reach agreement or understanding.

Psycholinguistic Magnets

But then again. . . . While it is evident that things and words are separate, in another way, at another level or in another dimension, they are not. There is a great drive in philosophy to determine *which* way it is, but Gestalt psychology, for instance, works on the premise of dynamism in the relating of foreground to background. Wittgenstein probed such alternatives in word-thing relationships. He had in his first great tract proven that language works like a map to picture the way the world is. That was what Korzybski called a structural correlation potential between language and reality—the map-territory figure—what Northrop called an epistemic correlation. That language had this sort of communicative potential was important for the development of science and its languages of mathematics and logic. Everyday language has such a capacity. But to Korzybski's distress, to the distress of precisionists in law talk and legal theory, to those who would make law somehow more logical if not rational, everyday talk will not keep itself in the shape of good maps, and law talk is so confused with everyday talk.

However, it might be ideally, and logic is in that sense idealistic, there is a person-word-thing interinvolvement. In some *psycholinguistic* ways words are not separate from things, and do not evolve by a process of convention *just* to guarantee and promote the informational kind of communication. One comes to understand his world in learning to talk and vice-versa. He becomes acculturated in this way also, so that in some ways, value-words are ways of "understanding things," hard to distinguish from "true" fact characterizations.

One acquires cultural values by learning to talk. A law student, for instance, acquires legal valuations by *learning to talk law.* That is another reason why the iconoclasm of legal realism can be upsetting to a legal positivist whose deeper drives involve an ideological divergence from the legal realist, as it often does. If one does not accept a certain way of talking law, then he is not indoctrinated, and then maybe he gets the idea that maybe he can change things by being a lawyer. And the law forum in just not supposed to be a battleground but a peaceful way of resolving disputes in accordance with accepted patterns—rules.

Analysis can help probe this dimension and actually help to determine when stability is more important than change. The legal positivists tend to stop short of this sort of probing, apparently on the grounds that change is in the hands of officials, not such quasi-officials as lawyers and certainly not within the discretion of laymen. And in Hart's kind of positivism the appropriate officials hold legislative offices. Our legopolitical history knows no such fixity, "strict constructionists" to the contrary.

I have said that application, invocation, and interpretation of laws (and we should add facts) are not automatic. But it can seem to be. There is the rub. To say that decision is not just a matter of logic or that it is a value process, or that it involves policy questions, or underlying moral issues, are some of the ways of pointing out that in a psycholinguistic sense, in the ways that words can be used, there is a choice. But to the person who is not aware of the psycholinguistic possibilities or who in a given situation is convinced, conditioned, threatened, or maybe insensitive if not intolerant to ambiguity, there is no choice. *That-is-the-way-it-is* and the other way does not make sense, is not reasonable, or is even absurd.

The Neutrality Dilemma

So these are *some* of the psycholinguistic dimensions to consider. The route to appreciation of such matters has to come about through an approach that is not popular with people who are advocacy oriented, like litigational or otherwise partisan lawyers, reformers, law and order people, and others too numerous to detail. Words and communications consciousness requires a stage or kind of noncommitment, a stage of attempted neutrality. There is almost a cultural bias against neutrality, at least in a polarized society. Socratic approaches can be threatening, as many law students have discovered, if there are no final answers, only alternatives and further questions. But it is only a *stage* in a process!

Analysis that merely reveals without taking sides is thus often regarded as obnoxious, as not enough. It may not be enough, but then some other approach without such analysis may not be enough either. Of course what appears as such neutral analysis may not really be, and even truly neutral analysis may expose more weaknesses in one side of an argument than another. The weak side or the set side will regard such analysis as destructively critical rather than constructive. The legal realistic kind of analysis can have such neutral aspects, but if it exposes issues without choosing sides that expose it better to counterattack, then "it is not constructive." (The most common complaint to be heard against it.)

Maybe they had it coming for being overzealous. They attacked judicial opinions as not being neutral when they could not be. A decision involves a choice and so is side-taking. The justification cannot be completely neutral. It does not mean some prior analysis *was* not or that objective-neutral analysis is unapproachable. But it is not spread out in the opinion in that form, only muddled in (if it was ever there at all) with the justification and the promulgation.

How To Tell A Legalist . . . (. . . but not what)

> Legalism "is the ethical attitude that holds moral conduct to be a matter of rule following, and moral relationships to consist of duties and rights determined by rules." It includes not only "the dislike of vague generalities," but also "the belief that the (established) rules are 'there'."
>
> Shklar, "Legalism"

Judges are particularly vulnerable to the malady of legalism, but maybe less than administrators. Judges almost have to listen to both sides of an argument, so many may only talk like legalists because the rhetoric of judicial justification permits it, maybe requires it. But officials who make decisions under some cloak of authority of laws, rules, or regulations may too readily believe they are acting as they must, because of those rules (out there). The lower the level of authority, the more the need of legalism *to build and conserve power*! If one has authority to make or shape the rules, why pretend? If one is a legislator, why be legalistic, until it comes to pressuring others to follow the rules, maybe to expect judges to be "strict constructionists."

There is a hook-up between legalism and *literalistic* reading of regulations, statutes, and constitutions, as well as almost any set of written rules, guides, or suggestions, even on how to bid in a bridge game or the way-to-write law review articles. There is a hook-up between the attitude that rules do not allow for interpretation and that a certain rule is necessarily *the* one for any situation that arguably could fall within it. (All this as if meaning was "out there" in words.)

There is often a hook-up between legalism and verbal naiveté.

Law teachers cannot create legalists out of verbally sensitive people. On the other hand, some law teachers have been able to take a little bit of legalism, every person has some, and build it into a professional illness; an easy process when the illness serves an ideological provincialism. One who is hung up on moral, ethical, or religious rules, for instance, may be particularly susceptible to legal educational manipulation. Then there are those who are especially submissive sorts of individuals, who have been conditioned "properly," who need to be ruled, maybe who feel generally insecure in the give and take of the hard world of reality.

Yet something about these times makes legalistic conditioning more difficult in law schools.

Or take the person who aspires to power but who has doubt about his own skills of politics or persuasion. He may be especially submissive to higher authority but autocratic when looking *down* the line—authoritarian in two senses. He is apt to be intolerant to ambiguity from above and to ambiguity-sensitivity from below, but not necessarily precise in his own locutions. These tendencies are so easy to observe in the complex structures of law-authorities—authority of persons and of rules and of words.

It is a mistake to believe that this malady is one only of *rule* compulsion, and even as to that, legal rules constitute only one sort from the myriad kinds of rules that surround us, including those of language. What a complex interlocking! Justice Black, for instance, seemed hung up on Freedom of Speech. Any this-is-the-way-it-has-to-be posture is a symptom, although it can be merely a specific pathology. Automobile drivers may suffer the illness only behind the wheel. Procedural hang-ups are symptomatic. Or compulsiveness about etiquette or protocol. Not that rules should never be followed, far from it, certainly on the road, at the table, and in the mass media. But if it comes to *allness* . . . either for others or even for one's self . . .

I know legalists who are radical legal realists!

They are not complete legalists, but hardly anyone is out of an institution. One can rebel against law for the sake of some other set of postulates . . . or attitudes. Very subtle. One who believes in natural law as controlling over man-made law may be flexible about law's rules until they rub against his absolutes. It is merely a question of locating one's absolutes. But they may not be articulated. A sociologist, psychiatrist, or political science behaviorist can damn the myopia of law (yers) because his own current truths are not being followed.

Is it paradoxical to suggest a legalism about Black Power advocates. Or is it just that the rhetoric is legalistic? Maybe it is important to be able to be legalistic, while knowing when and where. If one can choose, then there is no pathology. Revolutions make for legalism. Current conditions exert such pressures. Only an old-fashioned liberal was capable of complete non-legalism.

But even he might be looking for the *right* rules, out there. Hart suggested that of the legal realists: Where, oh where are they, the proper controlling rules that are *supposed* to be part of law?

Merely because one has absorbed the law-iconoclasm of legal realism does not free him, either attitudinally or psycholinguistically. He may criticize the Warren Court, not for reaching the wrong result, but for not justifying it in neutral principles, or more subtly in policy. But which policy? Or in rationality of some kind. His policy, which he can almost touch. His rationality. And that-is-the-way-it-must-be.

But Justice calls for rules, general consistency, nondiscriminatory applications. Legal Justice settles for the going system to be non-discriminatorily applied within the established classifications. Social Justice calls for an attack against *that* legalism, in favor of a more comprehensive set of values, classifications. But these can be compulsive in turn.

Of course one should not confuse legalistic rhetoric with legalistic personalities. You cannot necessarily tell one by his words. The legalistic personality may have to be met with his own devices if not with his own terms. The legal realists proved that a rhetoric of rules was not the same thing as some inexorable set of rules. Still, the rhetorical dialectic of rules (asserting rules that actually are not binding) may be backed by a set of fixed attitudes that are all the harder to combat because they are camouflaged. One must unravel the rhetoric first.

Judicial behaviorists believe the way to discover the controlling attitudes is to ignore the rhetoric. But as I shall explain, they do not really take that route so long as they move to their results via the words in judicial opinions. Those who look only at the fact statements are looking at part of that rhetoric. One can be legalistic (conceptualistic) about law facts or whatever facts he takes if he is not in direct contact with the litigational dynamics rather than the judicially rhetoricized reports. If all judges were legalistic, then the behaviorists would maybe be taking the only possible route, because one who is unconsciously manipulating legal (or other) rules makes them transparent. It doesn't follow that he can be manipulated, except in the direction of his bias.

But the one who manipulates the rules consciously and only looks like a legalist? What to do about him? The legal realists seemed to believe that most judges were of that ilk. So they tried to do away with the rhetoric altogether. But what I am trying to say is that even if you do away with the sort of rule rhetoric they were facing, then you inevitably get some other way of putting things that can lead to the same problems. For instance, one of the arguments against the rule-talk was that there was always a rule available to justify either side of the conflict. Now that is quite unavoidable. Well, then, it is not right to call them rules because they are not in themselves determinative. So the answer is to call them principles and to balance them in light of appropriate policy.

But there are in the nature of things appropriate policies on either side, i.e. tenable, arguable policies that would allow a result on either side (in these cases that come to court). So a *sophisticated* legalist will pick his policy and say: "I've balanced principles in this and that way and this is the way it must be." It is not just if a statement is called a *rule*, and put out there that counts, although that is the leading form of legalism. The others are more subtle. It is possible for a very, very clever manipulator to damn the rules so that he can the more readily exercise his sort of legalism by manipulative exercises that bamboozle someone else who has been persuaded that rules make no sense at all. So you cannot avoid some such tangle of rhetoric.

The heart of the common-law-process-in-courts is not rules but rhetoric! It needs to be explored.

I am not maintaining that legalism is just a matter of psycholinguistics, that the cure lies in semantic therapy. It may, in some instances. There are semantic hang-ups of the kinds that Korzybski explored. They can be untied often. Still there is no casual way of finding out if the hang-up is semantic rather than deeply ideological. But many a law student has had his words opened-up through Socratic law retraining. That does not necessarily lead to the sort of words *consciousness* I am advocating, but to a words-skill.

But this I believe: Somewhere, sometime, one meets the rules-principles-attitudes that he will or must follow. To be open with words is not to be chaotic with them. Not forever. But the route to words-consciousness may be through a seeming anarchy, a mobbery, where there are no binding rules for word use. (See how very much that would bother a true legalist who believes so much, or needs to believe so much in some set of rules. He will almost inevitably believe in word-rules to a naive degree. That naiveté gets reflected in his interpretative approach, as we shall discuss.) To get the deeper feel for words, one needs to enjoy a period of not being controlled, at least to see what it is like. Then out in the world again, at least in the legal part of it, he must make a readjustment.

So if we look at some of the rhetorical devices in an open-ended way, see it not just as skepticism or iconoclasm, but as exploration and invitation to words-consciousness.

CHART #1

A. LEGAL THEORY AND LEGALISTS

LAWS
WORDS
RULES

1. LEGAL REALISTS

(a) Regarded as illusory or camouflaging of the ambiguities involved in decision-making.

(b) Part of the dynamics of decision. Judges' talk as rhetorical, i.e., subjective. Open access to morality (values, policy, etc.) as channel to social dynamics and sociological research and commentary.

MORALITY

2. LEGAL POSITIVISTS

(a) Independent realities, viewed as of time of commitment or decision.

(b) Saw as separate from LAW because of 2(a), and because morality was rhetoric; i.e., subjective, etc., and thus subversive of LAW AND (ITS) ORDERS.

3. LEGALISM

(a) All out warfare. Realists' assault on lawyers' legalism.

(b) Close tie to legal positivism. Positivistic theorists working out optimal view of legal system, but with stress on legal syntactics, encouraged legalism.

(c) Work-a-day legalists more compulsive about rules of law and less obviously, about rules of word use.

(d) Not consciously sensitive to sub-surface ambiguities.

(e) Kinds of legalism:

(1) Law—closed off *re* rules of law.

(2) Morality—treat moral rules like law.

(3) Rule-ists of all kinds; e.g. in Univ.

(4) Others: at least a little bit in everyone?

B. COMMUNICATION THEORY

1. WORDS-THINGS

(a) Only meaningful verbalisms are those verifiable in "reality" of non-verbal world—then not purely subjective. — LOGICAL POSITIVISM

(b) Look for referent of word, either a thing or emotion (or values of utterer). — SEMANTICS

(c) Verbalism as maps to be correlated with non-words; otherwise illusory. — GENERAL SEMANTICS (Korzybski)

(d) Would agree with G.S. that words not things, but contact with reality tied up with rules of word-use—verbal analysis revealing. — "LANGUAGE PHILOSOPHY" (Wittgenstein, Austin, et al)

2. WORDS-WORDS

(a) Surface grammar, but more than etiquette. Words defined in terms of and bound to each other. *Cf.* 1+1=2; A dog is not a fact; A battery is an intentional touching. — SYNTACTICS

(b) Verbal operations of good maps should borrow from ideal of math, logic and science; but philosophers and Joe-on-street thought to work with false maps, resulting in "unsanity." *Cf.* view of legal realists. — Korzybski

(c) Analysis of these relationships essential. Families of words in word-use. — Wittgenstein, et al

3. WORDS and PEOPLE

(a) Inter-involvement and discoverable by study of behavior. Words media of interpersonal relations. — PRAGMATICS

(b) Words control people, via conditioned response *a la* Pavlov. — Korzybski

(c) People do things with words. Analysis revealing a real world: of speech acts (onto communicative behavior). — Austin

(d) Ditto Austin, but glimmerings of significance of form(s). — Witt.

4. CROSS CURRENTS

A. McLuhan: Medium is the message! Printed medium said to be on decline. (But we apply his theory to that medium anyway)

B. Rhetoric (kinds):

(1) Use of words to persuade and influence.

(2) Ways of putting words together that typify particular group or people generally—Style.

C. COMMUNICATION—can be independent of words and never completely dependent.
Verbal: involves more than sending message, or using words to refer to things, or to each other.

D. LANGUAGE:

(a) Body of rules regarding word use.

(b) Coming out of and the source of understanding culture, including (")LAW(").

Chapter II

AN ASPECT OF LEGAL RHETORIC

Introduction of Rhetorical Definitions

HIDDEN IN THE form-webs of linguistic process there is a mechanism whose subtleties have only comparatively recently come to be appreciated. It is the *rhetorical definition.* It is involved wherever conventional forms of language are used, as they are in law (talk), where exploration of its ways are especially insightful. Rhetorical defining works because it plays on emotions, biases, prejudices, predispositions, predilections, and attitudes. But more subtly it depends upon habits and attitudes concerning words and language, the very ones which not only make verbal communication possible but support the excesses of legalism as well as the everyday patholinguistics such as conceptualism.

Whether it is being used persuasively, manipulatively, or creatively, it may be but usually is not with particular sensitivity, let alone full consciousness, of the subtle ambiguities of its key word-contents. It is because of these ambiguities that language works so well; but, as I shall explore more fully in a later chapter, while learning one's way around with language involves a capacity to cope with these seldom noticed ambiguities, there seems to be a high degree of intolerance to talking-about-them; an intolerance that at least promotes the persuasive-manipulative potentials of their use.

The more obvious rhetorical definitions make use of loaded words, but the skillful mover seldom comes so close to being explicit. Certainly he avoids calling attention to the fact that he is in effect redefining some word(s), or loading them, either emotively or conceptualistically. The key to perception of this technique or process is high sensitivity to those subtle ambiguities and what I have called the depth grammar, the almost invisible "rules" which make these ambiguities controllable. Of course verbal manipulation-play is not all that is involved in persuasion. I am not suggesting that if one just masters the technique he can go out and also master the world or even that he will never again be manipulated verbally. Among other factors that play into persuasion are the status of the talker, his relationship with his audience, their faith or dependence upon him, his experience, authority, and personality, their knowledgeability, expectations, and so forth.

Strangely, since in a sense the legal realists helped to reveal it, it has been only recently that commentators have come to look to the rhetorical aspects of law. One might think that in doing that he is not so much talking of law, but about the way people communicate within the dynamics of the various parts of the legal process and how people talk about law matters outside of its formal boundaries. But *communicatively* speaking, what else is there to say either about law—or *in* it?

When analysts look for the "rhetoric" of this or that area of discourse, they look for special usages and styles. And of course judicial discourse, for instance, has that. But what I am trying to explore tends to be hidden by that aspect of lawyers' rhetoric. Of course we know now that what lawyers say to judges, clients, or one another, or what judges write, or how they all reason is far from scientific or formally logical, although it may have its special strains, such as the way law-fact are interwoven in a dialectical manner, or regarding the use of analogy, and certainly in the way (s) in which generality levels and specifics are "worked" into each other. Whether it is actually possible for analysis, interpretation, or reasoning in law-involved situations to be (legally) objective and not involve some persuasive directiveness, it very, very often is slanted.

After all, law, as a process, is meshed into politics and that sort of dynamics, to what we might call the morality process which hooks them together at least in the guts of interpersonal involvement, and of course to the socio-cultural process which somehow (s) brings interplay (s) with customs and what we like to call social values. So it simply cannot luxuriate in the *impersonal* forms of logic or science, which are expecially artificial in relation to the sort of complex communicative factors which are involved in all of this. Law(s') communications intertwine in all sorts of ways with the non-law kinds, partly because of social changes and pressures for changes in laws and the very system of law. For these and many other reasons, rhetorical analysis is important to understanding of the processes of law as well as those of society generally. We are here dealing with what is an aspect of law(yer) rhetoric and at the same time a communications hooking-up mechanism with, to put it simply, society.

To speak somewhat more technically, the generality of statutes, regulations, rules, principles, and such, together with their normative dimensions, make some sort of definitional process inevitable, whether or not it is to be called rhetorical. We can, as law's apologists used to do, speak of its generalities as if they are deductively applied, or as some theorists would like now to do, we could translate these generalities into logical symbol-systems where deduction would indeed take place. But neither decisions nor interpretations in law seem to develop in a deductive way so much as by a process of correlation or association of law-generalities with the lesser generality or specifics of some situation. (Not the raw, sense-data specifics, but the verbal specifications which are at some level of generality!)

So we might better think of extension. The legal realists rightly explored the circularity involved in saying that laws were deductively question-begging, but an extension can hardly be that, although it may in given instances be unjustified—or even uncomfortable. When it is comfortable, it may seem like *application*, as we say of rule to facts, as if one were covering a baby with a blanket. But some sort of mutual evaluational accommodation between generality and specific—even in the routine situations—takes place as redefinition, either in the terms in the "given" generality or in the characteristics of the situation, or more likely *both*. Thus is the novelty of each situation in its existential uniqueness sloughed off and the openness of the generality closed for the situation. A summary name for all of this is *law-fact dialectic.* We are exploring that process in this chapter and in other ways in later chapters.

We are about to explore some comparatively simple examples which could cause the rapidly reading sophisticate to think he is watching the dissection of a dead horse. After all, the classical rhetoric of earlier days is dead. We speak more openly now, rather than just in terms of the "black letter" of this or that area. We do not so much pretend to inherent meanings *in* statutes and hardly at all regarding judicial utterances. (But then we hear much of "strict construction.") But the technique or pattern of rhetorical definition still (must?) operate(s) pervasively. Whether we speak in terms of rules, principles, or policy, there are expectations about law that keep the rhetoric fairly close to an *image* which displays general controls and guides that operate with some degree of non-discrimination. Law and its officers are *expected* to be as much as possible above personal feelings. Laws are somehow *supposed* to transcend specifics.

While there is a great deal of current skepticism on these matters, the image seems likely to survive, at least as an ideal (else why be skeptical about what may actually be happening?). The impersonal sort of rhetoric will surely continue and be encouraged (as it is in many other areas of discourse or wherever law's analogues are involved, where rules, principles, policies, etc., are involved). There can be no place for apparent motive in the laws part of law. So these simple examples will serve well the purpose of revelation.

Moreover, the classical rhetoric is not really dead at all, but simply not so widespread. It has tended to fade in the critical evaluations of law, but not nearly so much in its assertion, and it operates extensively in some areas, such as the "technical" one of tax law. (Tax law rhetoric is most legal-realistic when it is being used to pierce some avoidance effort!) And the call to "strict construction" may mark the swing of the pendulum to a reinvigorated formalism, if in the Supreme

Court, surely elsewhere where its model is followed. (Hardly anyone has dealt with this aspect of the Warren Court.) But even such dramatically developing areas as torts, involving new notions of how to allocate the costs of harms coming from various group and social enterprises, as well sanctioning-regulatory mechanisms, show much use of classicism, especially as the novelties mature and the categories crystallize.

Whether stability, continuity, or change is being promoted, the rhetorical definition thrives. It may only be all the harder to recognize or admit if one's fancy is being served, because then the words sound so sweet. Of course change is inevitable, even when slow. In olden days, fictions did much to smooth the process and stabilize the image. Today we see less of that, but the job is just as nicely borne by metaphor. One who appreciates metaphoric creativity will all the easier recognize the mechanism-technique of rhetorical definition.

Perhaps it is most readily spotted by the skeptic, or by one who has motivation to be skeptical in a given situation, like the lawyer-advocate, as he moves almost instinctively in his counter-defining, unloading, and reloading. A call to this kind of skepticism is not to further deepen what some may regard as a dangerous rift of disrespect for judges and law. It is not so much skepticism that is encouraged here, except against legalism, but increased respect for the power of verbal mechanisms. Detection of the technique is important to avoid being unduly influenced as well as to increase one's capacity-skill in counter-rhetoric. But in the long run, as a part of the inevitable progress in knowledge-awareness, it is not only a scientific *sort* of goal that is served but a matter of common sense to push this exploration. It is indispensable to promote the causes of sound interpretation (strict or otherwise), and analysis, as well as all the communications tasks. If it does make sense to look for rationality, to refurbish the image of law and promote the causes of Justice, then this definitional process ought to be better understood. Actually, somewhere in these very webs may lie the kind of rationality which makes for law and its improvement.

Some Kinds of Definitions Compared

Why not just speak of rhetoric or persuasive techniques rather than rhetorical definitions? After all, definitions are used to give meaning, or to explain or clarify, not to persuade in some more restrained reflection of the old Fourth-of-July process. Or, a definition can be a substitutional sort of process, as in the dictionary sort of reference which involves looking for synonyms, like discovering that "utilize" means "use." (We hardly notice that actually we choose among many synonyms, relating to the different senses of the questioned word, so that a proffered or selected synonym may be subtle persuasion or manipulation.) Or one may define by stipulation or fiat, for instance, "Whatever 'rule' may mean to you ordinarily, I mean to use it to mean a general proposition whose prescription is absolutely binding." This is a way to legislate, at least for some special purpose, and indeed statutes (or formal instruments) may contain complex sets of stipulative definitions to *create* technical or special usages.

But one does not have to provide a verbal equation whenever he defines. He may demonstrate by some sort of behavior. A common way is to point: "You don't know what the word 'partridge' means? Why there is one over there in that pear tree." That is a usefully common way to teach a child the meaning of words, to talk, by holding or pointing to an object and repeat a word as if it were a name for the object.

It is appropriate enough to think of these definitional techniques as ways of giving an accounting, setting the record straight, or maybe even as ways of giving information. But they are all used just as often to move someone to think a certain way, to *see* things "properly." They may be used to indoctrinate. There is a sort of unfortunate indoctrination involved even in teaching a child as if objects had given names, for he may with this kind of training become habituated to that way of thinking-seeing, not being able to discern the somewhat arbitrary aspects of so-called common usage (we will explore this matter much more deeply). It is this very sort of indoctrination which sets us all up later on to be manipulated by rhetorical definitions.

A stipulative definition may have an attitude-shaping impact. One might say in a disarmingly straightforward manner, "Look, I know 'rule' has varying meanings, but I intend to talk about rules which are binding. When *I* say 'rule,' I mean the binding sort." By this process he may then subtly urge some reader into thinking that at least some rules are binding (musts) and that certainly the speakers rule-statements are. If this be an extreme example of verbal hypnotism, lesser forms certainly are common and the analyses of legal theorists are completely dependent upon this technique in conjuction with rhetorical definitions.

Teachers of law who follow the pattern of defining legal terms as if they were must-names for kinds of situations are persuading-indoctrinating their students to think that way, to see those situations that way. We speak of that now as being doctrinaire, and it is not limited to stipulated definitions of single words. Relating particular rules to particular situations may be doctrinaire. But usually such teaching is not mostly in the explicitly defining form. What one does is to take recorded (and stipulated-hypothetical) fact situations and say that a certain rule was (would be) applied by the court. If the student is submissive, as many are in that situation, then his whole thinking process can be conditioned. Then it becomes harder to avoid being gullible if one has already been conditioned to such a process of verbal knot-tieing. A true rebel cannot take that sort of training, but he can survive it, as a game, or if he sees it as a skill to be learned. One would think that Bar Examiners would realize that most everyone now sees their testing in this sort of thing as a game-obstacle. Why not test in more sophisticated kinds of analysis?

So it is that the obvious kinds of definitions involve some degree of conscious recognition that one is dealing with words. But the more subtle kinds involve acting as if the words were not there, as if they were transparent. Indeed it is common to say that words are symbols, that they stand for "something" in the non-verbal parts of the environment. It often seems true for many people that even when they are researching words in dictionaries they do not think of themselves as dealing on the *verbal level,* as actually *involved in linguistic analysis.* (Brood on that a while, anti-linguists!) This sort of looking through words may be even more likely when the synonym-meaning of a word is not taken from a dictionary but sort of pulled from the air, as in this example: "What does 'utilize' mean? If I utilize something, I use it. If I utilize my intelligence, I use it, put it to best use." (Why ever utilize 'utilize'?)

More subtle is the definition that does not seem like one, e.g. "A motion to dismiss is a procedural move in the early stages of litigation. It is the motion which the defense lawyer files to raise this or that point of law concerning the adequacy or validity of plaintiff's petition for relief. Here is such a motion I filed in a case not long ago." Of course that behavior is not *just* definitional, but it is there. The listener is being taught how to use the phrase or to understand what it means or how it is being used or is to be used. And note the phrase is being exemplified as standing for something.

The next stage in subtlety involves the definitional use of words not to refer to some observable thing, but to a more complex piece of behavior or situation(al complex). Again the naming process seems to be involved: "Did you see Jones grab hold of the package Smith was holding? That was a battery. He committed a battery. You don't have to hit a person to be liable for a battery." Is it a battery? If the speaker is an expert and the listener is not, how can it be denied? He seems merely to have described the situation much as one would describe a robin feeding its baby. But definition is involved. (As it may be in description itself!)

Form, Style, and Other Such Factors

So, the technique of rhetorical definition involves the use of words in dogmatic or authoritatively expressed fashion, as if it were perfectly natural, *the* way to put those words together. ("It's the best movie you will ever see.") It is appropriate to call it definitional because it involves words-in-use, and definitions come from word-uses. Such rhetoric is highly dependent for its effectiveness upon psycholinguistic habits, insensitivity to words as words, an attitude that they are referring outside of themselves, and *not* the feeling that they are part of the behavior of the utterer, an emanation of his personality.

The form usually is impersonal, third person, pointing away, whether concrete or abstract, and in the descriptive or assertive mode. Obviously evaluational words may point too much to the utterer ("It was a damned lousy opinion."). The developing evaluational rhetoric of legal criticism does not have to appear at all personal. We speak of policy and values as if *they* were out there. Of course there are situations where an audience can properly be influenced by an expression of feeling clearly personal to the author (jury trial), but supposedly not by the definitions used in legal analysis.

It may help to point away from the situational setting where attitudes are being swayed. While at times the trial lawyer, for instance, will work with obvious here and now factors (the visible injuries of the plaintiff), much of the time his questions or arguments will be pointing outside of the courtroom, even though he is dependent upon the here and now factors to aid in the persuasion, such as the charisma of a particular witness, or his own. After all, "facts are being proven," (there's one) that are supposed to be outside the courtroom, even though the persuasive factors are *all* inside. The spell can be broken by calling attention to that reality. (So, consider the strategy of defense participants in the trial of the Chicago Seven.)

The very word "law" seems to take one outside of himself, out of his situation. Compare the effectiveness of a judge ordering on the basis "that the law is . . . " thus and so, as opposed to, "My sympathy is with the defendant, so . . ." By and large, acceptance of the judicial opinion is bolstered if there is an abstract, impersonal absorption of the situation at hand. The fact statement seems concrete, but even it is only remotely, abstractly related to the raw, dynamic, original happenings, and it best serves its rhetorical function by being a link in an ascending spiral of generality and abstractness. When a court tells us what a battery *is*, and then absorbs its factual characterizations *into* that definition, it well exemplifies the process (as we shall see in greater depth). Any number of such definitions can be found in cases, arguments, teachings, and commentaries, today, right now. Some leading scholars claim that "actual cause" in negligence cases is a question of fact, it just *is*. And what is a trial lawyer doing, in court, when he argues that? It sounds like a rule maybe—and despite all the scorn cast upon legal rules, court lawyers must know their rule-rhetoric—but even more like a *truth.* A truth is more binding than even a rule.

Note the stress of the words "is" in the preceding paragraph. It plays an important part in rhetorical definitions along with other ways of asserting (or negating) *existence,* being. A fiction or metaphor may be effective in legal argument, but usually not if its "non-beingness" is focused. According to the form required for argument, usually, the rule is not argued, it exists (or does not exist): "The rule is . . ."

Not that these devices work automatically. The definitions have to be tenable and in a context that helps or pushes toward acceptance, and then toward certain attitudinal or behavioral results. If the lawyer argues that "causation is a question of fact," he is trying to move the court to let the jury be involved in some part or all of the decision, but in terms of argument that "it *is* the appropriate body." If I tell you that "law is not rules, but what judges or other officials say it is," I am not *just* giving you information, probably, but perhaps trying to make you more conscious of the behavioral components as opposed to the merely verbal, and maybe beyond that to get you to pay less attention to a certain opinion, or to be less literal about it, and so on.

Of course a definition may be vast in its implications, comprehensive in its purported coverage. The theory of logical positivism turned on a definition of "meaning," distinguishing meaningful words with empirical significance and words which "were meaningless" because unverifiable. Felix Cohen transported this kind of analysis into common-law criticism to try to discredit the classical-traditional forms of law talk, maybe a little bit in the way the Establishment gets discredited today.

So, key words are transported from one context, maybe where the use is familiar and comfortable, or maybe from some sophisticated and respected forum, to be used in another context in a sort *of analogical or metaphorical* fashion, or in barely disguised epithet, as "Natural law rhetoric *is* legalistic" (or meaningless). How damning to say that certain conclusions are unscientific (where it matters), say those of psychoanalysis or maybe even a legal analysis (or . . . "That was not a rational argument. .").

Descriptive vs. Emotive Words

The loaded words provide the most familiar examples of persuasive-manipulative definitions. All degrees and valences of emotional or attitudinal charging are available. Consider this range of seeming descriptors: boy, kid, child, minor, offspring, youngster, infant, teenager, or brat. Some are obviously loaded in any context, but others go by unnoticed, until placed together for comparison. (One can ask, now why did he use that word instead of one of the others which were available?) Or see this conjugation to accentuate the chargings: "I use rational argument, you use rhetoric, he manipulates." Defendant says, "I took hold of his arm." Plaintiff says, "He yanked it." The cynic speaks of the "arbitrary" action of judges, someone else perhaps of "a necessary range of discretion."

While the more subtle style of persuasion uses seeming fact-words, the more clearly emotive or evaluative terms often work surprisingly well. Maybe it is because words like right-wrong, good-bad, correct-incorrect, and a host of others seem to imply standards for judgment (and do often enough to give the terms their persuasiveness).

Thus, consider debates whether dictionaries should act as

guides for "good" usage. Teachers of English debate whether children should be taught how people speak in varying situations and levels of society or whether they should be taught good grammar. "While it is increasingly popular to say 'Who are you sending it to?', good grammar requires 'To whom. . .' ." There is a standard involved, no doubt, but whose? (Incidentally, this sort of debate may be a part of the picture of difference between the legal realists and legal positivists.)

Even obvious evaluators fitted into the descriptive-categorizer mode work surprisingly well. "He's a communist" still has a lot of mileage left. Despite all that has been said about their shortcomings, "conservative," "liberal," and "radical" find wide usage even in sophisticated audiences. And note that this conjugation provides illustration of the way that words can change in their loadings. Today "liberal" may be the nastiest of the lot, signifying "wishy-washy noncommitment": "But open-mindedness used to be a virtue."

"In the old days," it used to be appropriate to refer to Jerome Frank and Fred Rodell as "radical" legal realists, but that did not mean "militant revolutionaries." No doubt they were "subversive" of the "Establishment," but some people today regard them as no longer "relevant." I believe that the insights and viewpoints to be found all along the spectrum of legal realism have important "theoretical" and "practical" significance for all ideologies. ("Now there is a bit of old-fashioned liberalism.") But they do have special significance for the strategies of "activist" lawyers who are working to promote the "rights" of the deprived," and to create new ones as well.

Semanticists deepened the distinction carried in the word "loaded" by contrasting descriptive terms with emotive. Today it is more popular to use the term "evaluative" rather than "emotive." (Is "emotive" emotive?). Korzybski maintained that all words are evaluative in the sense that when a person used words, even to describe, state "true facts," he was evaluating, not just reporting. The significance of that insight has not yet penetrated even the world of scholarship. But while "emotive" is vague, it still is useful in a way that "evaluative" is not. (These words are differently loaded.) Some words do appeal directly to the emotions, as we can easily see in our social polarizations, but in law rhetoric as well.

Emotive and Affect Terms in Law

Lawyers still pride themselves on objectivity and rationality, but laws' terms have high emotive *potentials*. They can be loaded in various ways. In and out of the profession, law and order involves emotions, as we well know today. Such an emotive dimension is far from apparent in scholarly works like those of H. L. A. Hart. His pleas for clear talking about law and for acceptance of the obligation implicit in valid laws are not to be confused with those of the "law-and-order" crowd. Still, like any other law or jurisprudential analysis, it is filled with emotive terms in the semanticists sense of "emotive." The very word "law" has inescapable emotive-attitudinal involvements. One cannot use the term, by and large, without conveying *feelings* about the way law or the legal system or some part of it ought to operate.

After all, even "scientific" rhetoric can be used in what Felix Cohen called a crypto-idealistic fashion. (Theres' one.) Take the argument that therapeutically curative methods of medicine (psychiatry) should be used with even chronic social deviants, instead of law's traditional punitive techniques, because they are sick, not criminals. There is some aspect of this argument that is not scientific or provable as a fact. (To some extent psychiatry and law are competitive systems of evaluation and handling. "And that's a fact.") There is some element of fact/belief which may be based in turn on some hard ground of immutable reality—but not all the way.

Of course there are more obviously emotive-loaded terms in use in law talk, attitude words backed by little in the way of empirical reference. "Substantial" performance in contracts, "proximate" cause in torts, and "reasonableness" in all corners of law talk are typical. Maybe not quite so obvious are words like "direct" ("indirect") and even "relevant," although the anti-Establishment cliche-ing of that term could finally prove how very un-objective its uses have been in law. ("But it is so useful.")

Law terms may be used almost anywhere, even in courts, to sway emotions and attitudes. That should be apparent with terms like "freedom of speech" and "due process." (Not saying that is their only use!) Or "fault." That is hardly an empirically based term, although it is still treated as if it were, by competent scholars. But note this, we can give it some syntactic precision: One is liable for damages he causes if he is at fault, i.e. if he causes it intentionally or negligently. ("Fault" in terms of "intent" and "negligence.") But now how about "intent?" That seems fact-descriptive. It may be, but it is misleading to think of it purely as a state of mind (much more elaborate analysis later). More often its reference is to external behavior. If one man hits another with his clenched fist, we say "He intended to hit him," although we have no way of seeing what he was thinking or of knowing his motivations. As obvious as that may seem, that shift of reference (a little example of the subtle ambiguity involved in rhetorical-defining) goes by unnoticed making it easier to make another "little" shift and use the term as a way of making (or expressing) a judgment on the propriety of a certain piece of behavior.

"Intent" and "cause" are much alike in this attitudinal-shaping-expressing involvement. All torts experts/commentators admit that about "proximate" in the expression "proximate cause" but it is still "in" to speak of "actual cause" as essentially a fact question. No objection if that is to say that jury *discretion* is permitted. And there are clear (easy to agree upon) cases of causation, and of fault too, as when one man hits another with his clenched fist *without justification.* But when intent or cause are in question, there is not the *kind* of fact question there might seem to be ("fact" is ambiguous). "Intent" and "cause" are not merely truth reporter-descriptors (one sense of "fact"), but also fault-ascribers. So, to define "fault" in terms of those words involves one in the persuasive-manipulative (maybe creative) syndrome. (Not saying this is bad stuff.)

Furthermore, in law talk, "intent" is not used *just* to allude to fault in any popular or socially conventional sense of the term fault. Thus consider the cases of the trespasser or converter said to be liable for an intentional tort even though quite innocent of any desire to do harm, or any knowledge of its probability.

"Well, still there is legal fault." So say the commentators. But what does that say? What we have is a fictional or perhaps metaphoric use of the word "intent" and/or "fault." Usually when a seeming truth-describing term is being used in a predominantly attitude expressing/shaping function, there is a fictionally involved or a metaphorical kind of communication!

The list of lego-emotive terms could be extended at great length, of course including "right" and "property" and correlate terms like "possession" and "ownership," "rule," and even the word "fact." Actually any legal term or proposition or doctrine, no matter how technical has the emotive-use potential. Such potential is maximal whenever there is doubt or uncertainty or wherever discretion may be exercised. (Or as it *may* be because the terms are used.) Of course some terms have greater emotive potential than others. Terms and propositions at the level of principles or policy have a high attitude potential. And for that matter, propositions which are called (defined as?) rules or doctrine (or laws) may have the same sort of judgment-allocating function as those terms or propositions which are openly called principles or policy-statements. Whether a proposition *is* a rule or whether it *is* a principle (or policy-statement) is very often not an empirical matter but one of definition; i.e. a matter of persuasion/manipulation/creation.

I am not saying that law and para-law terms are *just* used emotively. They can/may be. But all these terms have somewhere in their history of multiple use-sense-meaning development a factual, descriptive *sort* of base. Even terms like "good," "reasonable," and "arbitrary" are used in circumstances where the standard or criterion of judgment are fairly well fixed, and so with "intent," "property," and even "right" and "fault," clearly so with "fact" and "science." Indeed there must be *some* such base somewhere in the history of development of a given term (proposition, doctrine, etc.) for it to be susceptible of the sort of rhetorical defining we are exploring. The greater or more established the empirical history, the more subtle the rhetorical potential!

Nor again is it just a matter of using words any way one wishes. The definition(s) must be tenable/acceptable. It is not just a matter of psycholinguistics. As times and conditions change, what is acceptable or potentially persuasive varies. Even then, one has to know his audience.

How is it feasible, for instance, for Marcuse to say that violence against the Establishment is justifiable because the force behind law is often itself violence? Some may think the definition does violence to "violence," but one's attitude on the social/moral propriety of the use of force is clearly what determines whether it is acceptable. Certainly there are times when policemen act lawlessly, beyond their authority, improperly. Is the beating of a campus radical who is unarmed (but not untongued) lawful? May it indeed *be* violence? Surely these are not empirical questions. Surely verifiability lies in the attitudes. Still, we need not say that every application of the definition is purely emotional, although it has high emotive potential. To say it has emotive potential or involvement is not to say it may not carry a worthwhile insight.

How one is *moved* by words is not ever *just* a matter of rationality. That is not to say that rationality is only a facade (or that "rationality" is *purely* an emotive term). The rhetoric of the radical must be sufficiently rational to communicate. That he communicates differently to different people is obvious. But such communicative variability is unavoidable in the kind of rationality that must be involved in law-communication(s).

Relating Beliefs to Attitudes—Spelling It Out

Both attitudes (emotions) *and* beliefs are involved or shaped by rhetorical definitions, which is why fact-*type* words having attitude valences loom important. Action can be precipitated by information (or what seems information), letting the emotions, feelings, attitudes, biases, prejudices . . ., do the rest. Of course the attitudes (etc.) can be altered, but maybe not so readily as one's beliefs (what he knows or thinks he knows, information). Take a nonverbal illustration. You want me to drink from a cup. You know I like tea but not coffee. If I am alert, I will almost certainly drink from the cup only if it contains tea, because of my attitudes (likes and dislikes). It is possible that you could change my attitude, but if just one sip would serve your purpose and you had only coffee, you might do the job by attempting to shape my belief, by saying, "Have some tea." (A definition added.)

Smith knows he does not like radicals because of radicals he has known or observed. Lawyer Jones knows facts are decided only by juries. He feels too that courts should not consider extra-legal principles in reaching decisions. If one has information about Smiths and Jones's of such kinds, he has a starting point for shaping a persuasive message.

Because legal decisions and analyses involve application of rules, principles, norms, and policy to facts (beliefs), law rhetoric is particularly dependent upon fact-type words to shape/involve attitudes. To illustrate, there follows a detailed analysis of the uses of the word "foreseeable" as it has been used in negligence-talk.

The basic rule/principle of negligence law is that one person is liable for unreasonable conduct which causes foreseeable damage to another person. Whether the harmful conduct was reasonable is measured by what was foreseeable under the circumstances surrounding the situation in question. If two people play catch with a stick of dynamite, an explosion and bodily damage or death is foreseeable as a consequence. Let a child play with matches and fire damage is foreseeable.

The word "foreseeable" definitely has fact (experience) involvements. Future events *are* foreseen. Some happenings are foreseeable in the sense of that word which is synonymous with highly probable, such as rain in Miami in the summertime or snow in Buffalo in the wintertime, or some are as certain as anything can be, like the setting of the sun. A great number of future happenings are predictable or foreseeable with considerable precision, such as the movement of the stars or the television schedule for the day. Life would be (or is) difficult if many of one's expectations were frustrated. One's actions are geared to what he foresees, though he does not articulate it, but only "expects" it (note several senses of "foreseeable").

Of course the degree of precision that is needed varies depending upon the circumstances. Depending upon the nature of the gamble, one's foresight is adequate if he foresees that one football team will beat another, but at another occasion only if he predicts a win by so many or more points. By and large, a cook need not be quite so precise as a chemist in measuring ingredients. This spectrum-variability in precision needed is carried into the way "foreseeable" is used in negligence law. A chain of events need not have been foreseeable in all its precise details in order to hold an actor accountable. Actually, in the relatively uncontrolled circumstances in the human arena, laboratory precision-foresight is often impossible. If one drives his car in a well-traveled area without at least average care in watching the road ahead, it is foreseeable that he will hit a pedestrian or a car. To be accountable he need not have been able to foresee precisely the exact person or even his sex or age, or the make of the other car. Although bodily injury is foreseeable, the exact details obviously cannot be and need not be. Death may be foreseeable, but the sort of details that would interest a physician need not be. We need merely say that bodily or property damage is foreseeable to explain why we think the driver is negligent and why he will be financially accountable—and maybe criminally.

Now suppose one is riding with such a driver. It may be sufficient to say to him, "You are not watching the road."

Perhaps it would do to say "You may run into somebody," that is, that such a happening is foreseeable. The statement of prediction is set against the expected attitude of the driver that he does not want or intend such a happening. Under this and many other circumstances, to say that this or that is foreseeable is also to call attitudes and values into the picture. They are not articulated, but certainly implied or implicit. Thus "foreseeable" may have an attitudinal as well as a factual relatedness. A further kind of attitudinal involvement is possible. To say that something is foreseeable is to say that it could have been foreseen and *should* have been. It is something that one might have foreseen if he had taken certain precautions and such precautions are par for the course. I say that I did not realize the young lady would take offense if I winked at her. If my friend suggests it was foreseeable, this seeming mere piece of information implies that if I cared I should have known better.

There is another way that seeming information is so used as to have attitudinal significance. It comes in through the variability we necessarily permit in all kinds of factual characterizations. Indeed, this whole analysis of "foreseeable" is applicable to the word "fact" itself as well as any word that has a factual relatedness. We can properly say we are describing or reporting an event, no matter at what level of generality or abstractness, whether, for instance, we say we saw a vehicle on the road, or that it was a red Chevrolet, or instead, a 1970 Chevrolet, coupe, red, white sidewalls, and so on. Likewise what is or is not foreseeable may be characterized at various levels of generality or abstractness. I have already noted that precision in foreseeability is only a relative possibility. But there is an additional indeterminacy in foreseeability beside that involved in its descriptive abstractness. We can say that something is foreseeable whether the predictability is high or low. These varying senses add to the manipulability of attitudes in its name.

Suppose I tell you that a father left his loaded rifle readily accessible to his ten-year-old son who one day took it out in the yard to play with a friend. If I say he accidentally shot his friend, you would doubtless agree that was foreseeable. What if I say the bullet first ricocheted three times? Well, the result is foreseeable in one sense of that term but not in another. Attitudes regarding father's carelessness will aid in persuading a jury to hold him liable. One need not foresee precisely how the injury occurs. The gun might have been misused in a number of ways to produce injury *of the kind which in fact occurred.*

"Of the kind," that is the hook-up. By this sort of reasoning a number of happenings have been regarded as foreseeable which in their details add up to the bizarre: A man with a peg leg breaks his good leg when his peg leg gets caught in a hole in a street while he is trying to help tow away a stalled vehicle; a large metal milk container is carelessly tied onto a truck and when it falls off, the top of the can blows off and arcs through the air to hit a man on the head. To elaborate the latter event, one can say, "It is foreseeable that someone will be injured by means of the can falling off the truck. What did happen is the *kind* of thing that was and should have been foreseen by the person loading the can on the truck." Should he have foreseen that the injured man's wife would hear his anguished scream and come running out of their camper to see his head covered with blood, thinking he has been attacked, and suffer great psychic distress and a consequent miscarriage?

Well, surely in the fact-prediction sense, such a thing is possible. And we have been told they happened (in judicial opinions). This *kind* of thing is even likely, given the injury to the husband. But we are dealing with a different kind of judgment if we consider whether such happenings are foreseeable in the attitudinal sense that such possible prescience should affect how a man ties a can onto a car, or in the sense whether it seems fair to hold a man liable for one kind of carelessness that leads to this sort of happening.

The value judgments that come into play in determining if such uncommon events are foreseeable (see how the subtle unapparent ambiguities enter) are affected by what *seems* a fact-belief sort of reasoning. Of course sophistry is possible and experts in tort law are coming to see the term as at best fictional, at worst emotive, But there is more to it, much more. In some of its uses it *is* emotive and/or metaphoric. In some others, however, it is as meaningful in an empirical sense as the word "predictable." Any word that has empirical relatedness may be and will be used in *varying shadings* that somewhere along the way move it into metaphor or even fiction, at the same time involving it in varying levels of attitudinal subtlety.

There is no term in the legal lexicon that is not amenable to the *sort* of rhetorical variations just exemplified. True, "foreseeable" is a rather notorious example. One can move with facility toward facts in one direction (as it seems) or in the other toward law. This term was especially suitable for analysis because it also illustrates what I have called the law-fact dialectic. There are many law terms that have this mixed law-fact capacity (we say that "foreseeability" is a mixed question of law and fact). Terms that seem to be pure law are defined *into* terms that seem pure fact by means of these hybrid terms, as well as by other means. For instance, in the negligence doctrine where "foreseeable" plays its prominent part, "duty" is such a pure law term (duty is a law question only) and "cause" is said to be a fact term (for the jury). "Foreseeable" is one of the terms by which they can be woven together. The various ways in which laws and facts are woven together (or pushed apart!) include rhetorical defining of fact-terms, as expert trial lawyers do so well. But other kinds of lawyers who have little notion of the psycholinguistics of their skill become expert at this sort of thing, in negotiations, hearings, committees, or lawyer-client interviewing, advising, and counseling.

While law words do not function in the same way as fact words, they may seem to because of the mode of asserting them. We say such things as, "There was consideration to make the contract binding"; "He is a murderer"; "The statute was violated"; "He must give restitution because he was unjustly enriched"; "The money received is taxable because it is income"; and so on. Assume if you will, that the relevant law words and phrases start out on a firm law base, in some way similar to the firm factual base which supports words like "foreseeable." Lawyers know what law terms validly serve to characterize the clear situations in their areas of expertise. Smith knows a battery or a case of fraud when he sees a clear one. His associate knows when certain contracts are valid. An expert on Constitutional Law recognizes certain clear invasions of freedom of speech. As advocate he is free to use these terms with their clear, valid base to persuade, via persuasive-rhetorical definitions, the relevant decision-maker to his side of the cause. But at some prior stage of attempted objective analysis, he needs to be careful not to mix his skills.

So, in a sense, a lawyer's odds are doubled. Not only does he have the lexicon of the layman at his disposal (fact talk) but also the subleties of law parlance. (We can think of his *translating*, back and forth.) The technical law terms provide the potentials for loadings and definitional strategies even more complex and more difficult to uncover than terms of ordinary discourse. His odds have been lessened somewhat by the verbal skepticism of the legal realists, so that the more blatant doctrinal manipulations are generally passé. Yet so long as law talk retains its descriptive-assertive style, the definitional rhetoric will remain an odds-on favorite.

Syntactic Definitional Complexes

Thus far in this chapter, the *emphasis* has been, partly for the sake of simplicity, on the definings of single words. It has not been as confined in that respect as it might seem, however, if one turns off the sharp light and looks around the single words, to see that we have at the same time been exploring how a word may be *varied* from some base of reference in its history by the way(s) it is related, associated with other words, always trying to remember that just out of the glare of analysis, but very much in the picture, was the *situation* in which the permutation was taking place.

But even in the definitional sort of focus, blocs of words are involved which may be analyzed at that level, as with the argument, an opinion, an essay, article, or message, or as in sentences, paragraphs, or sections. The permutations are not just of single words. There will be an interinvolvement of several key words, making matters all the more complicated for the unraveling analyst. Our illustrative word "foreseeable," for instance, will when used with some of the senses it has for negligence syntax (a different set of "games" from others where it may be used) be played into and out of such words as "duty," "causation," "negligence," "risk," "facts," and so on.

So it is that attitudes and beliefs are affected, shifted, reworked, parlayed, or manipulated by means of complexes of verbal combinations. Some of these combinations have a sufficient periodicity to be identifiable and in a sense definable, *almost in the way of single words*. After all, a slogan is like that, or even a Constitutional phrase like "freedom of religion" or "due process," or such other phrases as "human rights," "academic freedom," "the law of a case," or "jury discretion." A whole judicial opinion may simlarly be defined, as when its precedent value is assessed.

If one thinks of legal discourse as being made up of smaller discrete bodies of law talk, he sees further into the complexities of definitional rhetoric. The fields of law that go to make up the traditional or basic law school curriculum correlates as well as reenforces the rhetorical power available in these bodies of discourse, analysis, reasoning, and justification. We have torts, property, contract, procedure, constitutional law, income tax, and others. In these areas we have what can be called developed or developing doctrine, what might as well be called specialized syntax.

"Doctrine" is a word that has a negative loading, equated with the "black letter" summaries or oversimplifications found at the beginning of each section of some law textbooks or throughout such encyclopedic chiché collectors as Corpus Juris Secundum. But something on the order of doctrine is apparently difficult to overcome in the same way that road maps are hard to ignore, not only in strange territory but in home country as well. Doctrine is not inherently bad, it simply gets abused. There is skepticism concerning it because manipulations of it have become more obvious, but the scorn tends to sweep up the more legitimate efforts at persuasion and *creation* along with the manipulations. Like any codification, whether legislative or otherwise authoritative, or that of a Restatement of Contracts, or the highly prestigeful analysis of a leading scholar, doctrine needs periodically to be revised to keep pace with what takes place in its constituency.

While I want to illustrate syntactic rhetoric in terms of the more familiar doctrine, I must stress that its negative definitional abuses are not peculiar to it because syntactic defining is impossible to avoid. We are discussing the relationship of words to each other. In the previous discussion, this aspect was present, but not so much in focus. But to the extent that older doctrinal bodies of law terms and phrases become cliché-ridden and fiction infested, newer bodies of legal syntax may be used to avoid the sins and promote needed development in law, although observers should realize that such newer bodies may also create new camouflages.

There is a feature of legal doctrine and syntactic combinations which give them special rhetorical potential. It has to do with the way, as it has been mentioned, that words and such combinations of words as rules, principles, and so on, come to be defined or tied to each other. Words generally are defined not only in the context of acting and interacting and in observing and relating to tangible things, actions, and events on the one hand, and in the context of feelings, emotions, and attitudes on the other, but also in the context of words. If you wish, we have *at least* a sort of three dimensional involvement.

Dictionaries provide the most obvious illustration of the ways in which words have syntactic relationship, but those sources do not go far in even showing how words are conventionally associated together, unless the researcher goes further than the usual entry shopping. You cannot put together the words "dog" and "person" just any old way, although the license varies, say to call a dog a person. As varied and ambiguous as words are, there are limits placed by the way their uses developed, not only with respect to things in the world, but with respect to each other. Legal doctrine provides the easiest examples, as witness the strangeness of talking about offer and acceptance to explain the state of law in a personal injury situation.

This webbing of relationships among words creates a sort of net. Situations can be trapped in doctrinal nets. It happens outside of law, say where a person characterizes a situation in a certain way and has difficulty *seeing* the situation in any other way. In law, characterization of a situation in doctrinal or fairly firm legal syntax may in itself be a creative bit of rhetoric, but even then it is usually offered to inhibit the thought process of the audience, to keep out other characterizations, other ways of seeing and feeling about the situation.

Suppose, for instance, a University student is convicted of using LSD in local court. Then suppose he were being confronted with a disciplinary charge in the University. The attorney might argue double jeopardy. Maybe some day the argument will be accepted in court as it increasingly is being accepted in academic settings. Still, it is an appeal to the "emotions" in the beginning, to attitudes concerning fundamental matters of "due process." It is a waving of the Constitution. By this process the lawyer also routes his audience into Constitutional law syntax and doctrine, where other favorable analogies may be available. This example is not fanciful at all, for Constitutional metaphors have been used creatively with considerable success in the process of changing the attitudes of University administrators away from one of "paternalism," from the "in loco parentis" approach. Here is an example where legal syntax serves not necessarily to create a belief that one is bound by the law but that one ought to emulate it. An argument of a general kind concerning one's rights often has some such double or triple allusion. But if it is a matter of exerting the force or threat of law, then it is a matter of changing the audience beliefs, not regarding facts, as we were talking at first, but regarding "what the law is."

Arguments in terms of rights can be inhibiting, not only for the audience but for the one who is thinking that way. One can be trapped by his own rhetoric. Martin Mayer has aptly described this phenomenon. He referred to the obstacles which well-meaning lawyers working in legal aid or neighborhood law offices may create in their own thinking and actions. For example, when such a lawyer is considering how to help slum tenants, if he thinks in terms merely of what legal rights they have, then he may find himself trapped in some traditional syntax, in seeing the situation the way it appears when colored and packaged in the lore of law, rather than bursting out of that syntax to use law *to change* the basic situation. Of course a layman like Mayer cannot quite appreciate how the "rhetoric of rights" can be itself used creatively, as witness the effort by Charles Reich to characterize welfare payments, for instance, as "property" so that individuals under welfare would be afforded the familiar protections constitutionally afforded to owners of more traditional forms of property.

To those not beguiled by it, one of the more notorious examples of inhibiting syntax is that regarding the relationship of a land occupier to one who comes upon that property. The net is becoming frayed under the pressures of changing social conditions and attitudes. Under this doctrine, one who comes upon the property of another must be a trespasser, licensee, or invitee. Depending upon which one of these he *is*, the obligation of the occupant of the premises varies as to how he should act or maintain the premises, whether to make it safe(r) for the entrant. One of the strange classifications under the syntax has been the way it computes a social guest to be entitled to less protection then one who comes to somebody's house on mutual business, the latter being called an invitee, the former a licensee. The duty to the invitee is greater in scope than the duty to licensees. ("Duty" is thus played into the classification-characterizations—with law-fact ramifications—of "trespasser," "licensee," and "invitee.") That is, definitionally speaking, these terms are frozen in relationship with each other, as well as with other key concepts in negligence syntax, in such fashion as to trap most judges in attitudes regarding such matters that in many ways are not reflective of contemporarily developing principles and policies of proper risk allocation. Whether the policy involved in the syntax is or is not defensible, trapping does take place.

Of course one may ask, "Well, what are rules for anyway?" And there we have one of the biggest nets of all.

One way to avoid a particular trapping is to offer another net. The rhetorical definition may be in terms of a whole doctrine. A good illustration of that sort of shifting comes from the products liability cases. California, for instance, defined liability for personal injuries stemming from defective products completely out of contract syntax by means of a reverse lateral with the word "warranty," maintaining that in this sort of situation it was not a contract term, but to avoid confusion of "warranty"$_1$ (contract) with "warranty"$_2$ (tort) the term warranty was dropped out in favor of "strict liability."

There are many other examples but one that ought to be pondered are the possibilities that lay in damning "doctrine" altogether in favor of "policy." A policy net is not necessarily larger gauged, but gauged it is, net it is, destined with the potential of crystallizing syntactically into doctrine.

What it may amount to is that one can see better what fish he is catching with a policy net.

CHART #2

RHETORICAL DEFINITION AND STRUCTURE

WORD ← surface form → FORESEEABLE

WORD

Partial analysis

(1) word$_1$: a unit of language consisting of one or more spoken sounds or their written representation that can stand as a complete utterance.
(a) come (yes) (b) The (no)

(2) word$_2$: as in #(1), but also representing an indivisible concept: Law? Foreseeable?

(3) word$_3$: as in #(1), but having a single referent:
(a) (This) tree? tree (?)
(b) Tom (?) Hitler (?)

(4) word$_4$: as in #(1), but representing an indivisible feeling: (a) Ouch (b) foreseeable$_1$ (yes) foreseeable$_2$ (no)

(5) word$_5$: a part of speech:
a word in print?

(6) word$_6$: as in "word of praise."
(for one minute's duration?)

(7) word$_7$: "I'd like a word with you." I'd prefer "tea" if I may (pun R/D on word$_{5,7}$)

FORESEEABLE

Definition in terms of meaning, loading, syntax, and use

(1) Referring to happenings:
(a) degree of predictability
(b) verifiability
(c) imaginable
(d) metaphoric
in various degrees of generality

(2) Attitudinal chargings
(-) .... (+)
(a) did not foresee but should
(b) need not foresee but did
(c) "you must foresee such things."

(3) Law: Negligence syntax:
(a) Duty: to take reasonable precautions against foreseeable hazards (Rule) Determination of scope–court
(b) Breach: "fact" whether fell short of standard
Atty–argues to jury
Judge–instructs jury
(c) Proximate Cause:
1 kind of harm
2 details of harm
3 result foreseeable?

DICTIONARY AND RHETORICAL DEFINITION

1. Any word can be analyzed into dictionary sorts of definitions: beginning aid for getting sense of meanings.

2. But the word does not have just meanings:
   (a) Above senses of "word" come from various different sorts of uses. So, a word is not either one or another of these meanings, but "word" can be fruitfully used in one or more of these ways, *inter alia.*
   (b) Any word also has attitudinal chargings, coming out of general use (e.g. "bad"), or specific context (e.g., "foresee" in negligence law talk) Even "word" can be used in R/D: e.g. "A word must have a specific referent (word$_3$). " 'Foreseeable' does not, so it is not a word." (*cf.* strict semantics: "Well, not a good, solid word.")

From Meaning to Discovery

(a) Many words overloaded like "foreseeable." (See chap. 6)

Others are too little analyzed, like "word."

(b) Seeing how they have actually been used with the aid of R/D tracing, throws light on those words and the whole dynamics of communication.

3. History and growth of words traceable through subtleties of R/D's

Chapter III

WORDS AND COMMUNICATIONS CONSCIOUSNESS: LEVELS OF AWARENESS

Beyond Just Talking

THERE IS MORE to communication than words. But even expertise-in-words involves more than a keen eye and ear to rhetorical techniques. We are not just exploring words! (And yet there are only words on these pages.)

The last chapter was a sort of two-dimensional analysis. Now to add another dimension. There is a leap to be made when one would move from just talking, from that plateau of involvement to another level of talking about talking (to improve the communications-observer skills).

The non-leaper may prefer another metaphor. One is on the outside of a fog bank and he can see nothing in there. You move in and you see what you did not see before. And then the fog lifts, but slowly, and you see more clearly.

Still, one does not just walk into that fog bank. Yes, even then he must leap.

The analysis of the last chapter is the sort that has prepared some people for the leap. That sort of analysis requires a degree of words consciousness and of value sensitivity. But it is a chicken-egg matter. One seems to be dealing just in words, but it is in a way flat, not dynamic, until that leap, until he can look not only through the words (as we do!) but *at* them at the same time, feeling how the words relate to the communications dynamics. Beyond words consciousness is communications consciousness, and beyond values sensitivity is role-perspectives sensitivity (key variables in a scientific communication theory).

There is a relationship to what has been called sensitivity-training.* One is supposed to get involved with his group, as he ordinarily might, but yet try to be more than usually aware of his own involvement. There are people who will say, "Well, I can participate and really get involved in a group discussion. *Or*, I can sit back and observe what is going on. But not both!"

Not so. They talk of participant-observation in anthropological research, or in the clinical involvement of psychoanalysis, of "listening with the third ear." That sort of sensitivity can be a part of reading even, an aspect of interpretation, as future pages will demonstrate.

Some one will say, "You cannot talk about talking unless you use a special language." Again not so. A meta-language simply could not involve a person in his world the way that his ordinary words do. His ordinary words somehow are involved with his contact with reality, even if just *his* reality. Everyday words can and do get in the way, and yet . . . if one is going to explore communication, he has to involve himself with those words, start with those words, because that is where *he* started, so long ago, when he was learning to talk, which was when he really got started in appreciating his (and our) world.

That was the track English philosophy took when it undertook analysis of some terms that had become important in philosophy by looking to see how those terms were being right then used in everyday speech. Critics sneered, scoffed, and snorted. What does the man on the street, the fellow who uses those words, know about such things as philosophy? But those critics missed the track. The people who were having hang-ups with words in philosophy were working with words they learned before they ever dreamed of being philosophers. Wittgenstein (and J. L. Austin, for instance) used words to explore the

---

* Directory shows ways in which this and other chapters are "sensitivity" oriented.

way(s) one's words involved him in his world, so that what seems verbal analysis *also* involves lifting layers of camouflage off one's consciousness. This sort of exploration ramifies in all sorts of directions (including empirics).

So many of the terms of law cannot be "pure" law terms, as if a meta-language, because they grow out of the words of everyday discourse. You cannot take a term from the public domain, stipulate a definition for it, and thus disassociate it forever (partly because rhetorical defining glides you back in). Students come into law school ready for technical training, right enough, but say you push them into the morass of proximate cause. The professor can pretend that "cause" is just a legal term, but he can only *build on* what has gone before. But if the professor is realistic in realizing this, and tries to get them to review what they already know about "cause," and right into the way(s) they use that term here and now, he may create some problems, because they think they are supposed to be learning law, not studying English, or grammar, or whatever.

Philosophers have also resisted such probing because it did not seem like philosophy (Wittgenstein suggested it was therapy, as did Korzybski). Well, what *is* it? How shall we *define* it? (How we define it—verbal analysis, psychoanalysis, science, etc.—depends where we are going.) Jurisprudes in this country have resisted with all of their might, preferring just to spew out the words. That has been the malady that lawyers and philosophers hold in common. Korzybski noted that lawyers (he had given up on philosophers—unfairly) were overly "verbal," (dependent on talking, insensitive to communications dynamic, too analytical, etc.).

There can be resistance to probings in the psyche, naturally enough, to removal of the layers of verbal-abstraction defenses. (Maybe not in the younger generations, not so brought up on words.) The defense-resistance is not just phychological (Korzybski said psycho-logical), but psycholinguistic. Korzybski had seen how twisted-up people were with their words. People mistakenly see his theory only as word-involved. He was trying to get his audience un-worded, to get them *conscious* of words so they could *see* better what was being covered by the words. Borrowing from Einstein he coined the expression "general semantics" because he felt he was dealing with a generalized phenomenon of communications in which words were only a special example. (Special semantics.)

("Oh, come on. We know semantics is just playing with words.")

He was interested in non-words equally much, to get individuals to the *feeling* level. He had them leap from the verbal level to the non-verbal level and back and forth. The word is not the thing. The map is not the territory. Whatever you say about *it* does nothing to *it*. And so on.

Wittgenstein wrote two philosophy-shaking tracts. He thought the understanding of language was a (the?) key to understanding reality. Both tracts followed that theme, but they were radically different studies of language. In the period in between, he discovered something about his own verbal hang-ups, and passed the discoveries on, not so very long ago in his "Philosophical Investigations." It was cathartic, probably, but also philosophically exploratory, written as a sort of Socratic monologue. (Austin, another philosophy word-shaker, used that device also—no accident, because the style unfolds in a way that other styles do not.) Whereas Korzybski stressed the distinction between words and non-words, Wittgenstein seemed to explore the *behavioral* involvement of words one used. This is a way of making the leap. All roads lead to the same cliff.

But it is not a matter of religious conversion.

Maybe one goes through the jungle before he makes the leap. (Wittgenstein had said that when you went through his analysis, you could leave it behind.) One who looks at Wittgenstein or Austin for the first time may see a jungle of words, all twisted up and snarled and interlocked in such fashion that it seems impossible to get through them. But he cannot see through it to determine if he wants to go that way. If he could only fly *over* it. But no, that would be the very leap which cannot be made without getting *into* it. (Alice drank something, or took a pill to move into the land of wonder.)

Maybe some people are destined to go in there, but others not, others who create the brambles and the thickets, like lawyers, and legal philosophers, for instance. Lawyers are very skillful with words if they are good lawyers (Socratic case approach chiefly responsible—what when that goes?). But in another sense, most lawyers seem to be rather naïve about words, in this lack of words and communications consciousness. And law is so much involved with words: What are laws, constitutions, statutes, regulations, rules, and principles made of, after all? And what do lawyers work with, in court, in negotiating, drafting, interpreting, counseling, and all the rest? These tasks and roles do not involve just words, but to the extent that laws are involved, those words get used in different ways from the way the other words get used.

Part of the problem is for a lawyer to keep his rules and tasks straight, to get that role-perspective sensitivity, which is harder than words-sensitivity, and tied up with it. When we teach law from cases, we muddle it up. We take this or that language in an opinion, or some synthesis-analysis, and we throw these words around, rarely keeping it straight whether we are exposing the student to the role of the advocate, judge, critic, prophet, or what. Some teachers solve this by sticking to but one role, some as advocate-promoters, others as social critics (policy-oriented), etc. But you get to talking about "the law" and the roles get mixed up, inevitably. I think these matters can be unraveled, just as word-uses can be.

Who Needs It?

What kinds of people in what kinds of roles can best make use of words consciousness? Certainly the poet. He does not tell the reader how to understand his work, for that would destroy the poetry, but it helps the reader to discover the poet's perspective(s) if he too is words and feelings conscious, past the point where he is self-conscious, to the point where he can appreciate "what the poet is saying" without much fuss, as a connoisseur of fine wine knows what is fine, because the subtleties are part of his experience. Compare the comedian. He plays upon words and communication in the double meaning, the twist of meaning, the fertile pause, the look. He does not explain himself, but just does it. He knows what he is doing, but does he think about it anymore than one is constantly thinking of the way to spell all the words he is writing? That would get in the way, but one has to learn sometime, to have the feel for the spellings. (As the comic learns to play with words.)

Well, of course with respect to law, there are all sorts of people who should have this consciousness who do not. Any behavioral or social scientist who studies the process(es) of law ought to appreciate the subtleties we are exploring. One might want to say that we are exploring with the tools of a special behavioral science and that only a communications-scientist need have this sort of awareness. He should, but not only he. These matters simply cut across all disciplines and approaches, just as it is clear that Wittgenstein's "philosophy" is *also* linguistic, behavioral, empirical, etc. No one classification will do for Korzybski's kind of work. He called his work Science and Sanity, meaning Science followed by Sanity. (If we use that word "science" too much, someone else will turn off.) Freud was a contributor to the techniques of communications analysis. Can there be any doubt of that? The psychoanalyst is supposed to learn to go "beneath" the obvious, the surface levels, to see the clues, to search within himself as he is listening, to increase his evaluational skill. No reason why that kind of observer-interpreter skill should remain his sole province, and it has not. No reason why lawyers should not be taught such skills, but so slowly is that potential developing.

All kinds of lawyers ought to have these added dimensions of awareness, but someone might want to say that the advocate cannot afford to be thinking or worrying about what he is saying, what its implications may be, and all that, because it would get in the way, like spelling worries would overly fret the author. Reisman, the lawyer turned social scientist, raised the related question whether training lawyers in psychology might make them too conscious of their actual social roles so that they could not perform those roles properly anymore. Well, actors know they are acting but that does not seem to get in the way when they are doing it. Even the great ones need to rehearse. Great musicians practice. We speak of lawyers and doctors practicing while they are doing their job, of all things, but there is something to the thought, constantly learning while doing. It takes a special consciousness. And remember this, even the trial lawyer great is not always in *that* advocate-actor role. He interviews-talks to the client, and there he needs this sensitivity especially. Really, it is a matter of sense of timing and of role, of keeping the roles straight. It is a matter of roles perspectives sensitivity.

(Legal theorists, by and large, have done the worst job of keeping role-perspectives straight, even yet, despite all that Messrs. Lasswell and McDougal have done to aid them. Those gentlemen are especially aware of these dimensions, although not each in the same way.)

It is finally happening, but only comparatively recently have trial lawyers come to see the possibilities of the "semantics" and "non-verbal communications" bandwagons. Despite the level of intelligence and the inventive zeal of these lawyers, they do not go for mind-bending. There has to be a practical payoff, the increased chances of winning a settlement or a trial, the opening-up of a tactic or strategy that will put them one-up, now or later, some time, some place. But they have finally come to see that it is not just theory, although, in talking about it all, one is engaging in what surely looks like theory. (One really cannot talk without engaging in theory; it is a matter of the familiar and the unfamiliar. Law students will say that Jurisprudence literature is theoretical, but that judicial opinions are not, or the rules of law are not. Not true.)

Yet there is a certain respect in which to talk about these things seems mere gamesmanship (as speaking of the advocate as actor, in metaphor). But play we must too, to get this feel, to feel comfortable when it is "for real." One's sense of principle and idealism can get in the way (legalists are usually overly serious) of seeing what it is all about. Some law students have dropped out when exposed to the iconoclasm of legal realism. Are some of today's youth dropping out because of some such exposure to the realities of life? But one can build a fun house in the jungle as a sort of base for getting through it. Skepticism of words, say at the level of recognizing rhetorical definitions, does not require cynicism. And even skepticism need not be sour or bitter. It is a matter of awareness of the limits of words and of communications dynamics, and thus to see all the better their potentials. Practice in verbal play, communications play, can be helpful in getting that necessary consciousness, that values and perspectives sensitivity. Values! That can lead to a deepened sense of one's responsibilities as a lawyer, no matter what his task.

Communications analysis can be threatening, especially to the dogmatists among legal theorists, scholars, and researchers. Law tends to compound the problem because dogma is the going style for its assertion or argument. So is it for much of what passes as behavioral or other kinds of science, *because much of it is advocacy*. The observer-researcher who would look through the advocacy needs special spectacles, but that would be true for the observer of the advocacy itself. Yet if there is some other aspect to law than advocacy, if the search be for or in the name of objectivity, neutrality, or rationality, there is no choice but to push through that jungle. (To see if there really is anything on the other side. Remember Columbus? Maybe we will just drop off . . . .)

What about the lay public? Should they be educated via this route about law(s)? One should pause here. How much of the iconoclasm of the legal realists can the public take? (We can say to them, "Just Kidding.") What happens to law-and-order? Well, maybe this sort of explorations-understandings is needed as defense against the law-and-order crowd, or at least those (legalists?) who abuse the Rule of Law. It just may be that we are working our way, painfully, through a development of some new workable image for lego-political processes, where law-as-rules will appear just a little silly. We need to be ready.

Furthermore, there is nothing any one of us can do to prevent these sorts of insights from spreading. This is simply an era of ever-increasing communications consciousness, and as part of that there looms the danger that with some people words are losing out in their previous relative importance (see McLuhan) *because of their abuses.* Then what would law do? Can one imagine law without words?

Multi-Dimensionality

What lies on the other side of the jungle? Where is one after the leap. Maybe it ought to be enough to say that one obtains a better understanding of communicative processes and their interrelation with law. But there is more. As it is now, there are a number of sensible distinctions to be drawn which do not make adequate sense to those avoiding the jungle and the leap. Some have already been mentioned, but the general reference is to the multi-dimentional aspects of communication. The still somwhat viable distinctions of some of the communications theorists was in terms of semantics, syntactics, and pragmatics: i.e. word-thing, word-word, and word-behavior relationships respectively.

As it is with any analysis (a point we must bear down on repeatedly) this particular triadic slicing separates the inseparable. It really all happens at once. It is like locating a crossroads by its map coordinates. We speak of its latitude and then its longitude. But there is only one crossroads there. It is there all at once.

In communication there is always more than one "thing" happening. Some of what is going on is appreciated fully (consciously), but often some large part of it, or strands of it, are not a matter of full awareness. You see someone who is angry, but you do not say, "He's angry"; you just know it. Or it may not be obvious, but there is something about tone and nuance. It *comes through* and you react appropriately, without necessarily being aware of what has happened. (Of course there can be a complexity of misread clues which ought to be raised to the articulate level for correct interpretations.)

The split-screen movie technique shows that one may watch

and appreciate even more than two episodes occurring simultaneously; even more than one conversation at a time, although not so readily. Advertisers have taken advantage of this "discovery" to give novelty to their TV and even radio pitches, but maybe to give added dimension, more reality. (When will we do something with the really hidden dimension of the private verbal-thought process going on all the time, affecting what one hears, sees, and how he interprets?)

But even in one conversation, one piece of writing (this one, for instance), there is more than one message, maybe many, coming through simultaneously. But some get blocked off, for lack of possible awareness, or lack of adequate attention. (How does speed reading affect these matters?)

I have been deliberately involving the reader with cross currents, mainly through the parenthetical device. Someone would say, "Put them in footnotes." But why? Readers can take them, for they do it all the time.

This matter of multi-dimensionality is the most important point to try to get across about communication, and certainly about law-communication. I want to present an illustrative analogy, but it is at the same time *more than that.*

Suppose a professor in a classroom. He wants to demonstrate and then talk about "the human act," or "what an act is." So he holds up a book and lets it drop. He asks the class to describe what he has done. If we were there and were watching, we would have seen *one* event, we might say. (We could get philosophical about that right off.) But what might be said: (1) He dropped a book. (2) He held up a book and dropped it. (3) He let the book drop.

But there could be different slicings: (1) He opened his hand. (2) He made a sound. (3) He startled someone.

Maybe he damaged the book.

And hasn't he "opened up a hornet's nest," in exploring how people may talk about such a happening (or should I say act?). If he were not to say anything about the various answers, how many would get that latter message? Yet it is there, among others.

And now . . . What have I done? Here on these pages? (There is at least an important linguistic factor that has not been articulated, but it will be, in due time.)

Part of this business of communications-observing depends very much on what we say or think or believe, either by articulating in some particular way, or by thinking in a particular way because of previous verbal-seeing conditionings.

We can talk about a statement as one of facts, but is it ever *just* that? If one calls "Fire!" in a crowded theater, he is not just giving information. We distinguish between fact words and value words, but really, words are not just one or the other. Not to say that this analysis (fact-value) is not useful, but it can be misused to misstate (understate) what is going on. It would be a mistake here to use communications analysis to pick out some previously unnoticed factors and put it forth to exclusion of others which had been noticed or which also arguably are there too. An advocate for one theory or another may want to do that, as they have done with the word "law" for instance (as I shall explore). In that sense, a judicial opinion is "doing" a number of things, or might be, not only presenting the law, but also justifying, and advocating, and . . . . How can it be otherwise when you get to thinking about it? But we work so hard to pretend otherwise, in the business of oversimplifying.

Another point that needs further exploration is this: If one can report or assert the law, and teachers, commentators, and editorial writers . . ., purport to be doing *only* that very often, he is doing something else besides; i.e. it is unlikely that he is just reporting. It often is worthwhile to look for the other dimensions. We have come to see more in judicial opinions. Formerly it was: What law was involved? Now: What impact? Seeing that, the judges are asked also to look at that, not only decision-impact, but opinion-impact. We ought also to look for hidden dimensions in the criticisms of judicial opinions (for instance). And if someone says that *the* important aspect of the judicial process is decision-making, and impact-policy consideration, can't we realize there is some slanted describing going on? If the professor startled someone, do we have to say that he did not drop the book because there is only one act there?

Does it maybe make sense to suggest that no matter how much one spells out what he is doing, he thereby introduces factor(s) which he will not or cannot spell out!?

That may be an important insight, but it would not justify being simplistic. Word-meaning analysis can be simplistic, merely two dimensional, so long as it goes only in the semantic direction, *or* the syntactic, *or* the pragmatic. Word-use and communication-task analysis adds some other dimensions. Compare what you see when a pebble is thrown into a stream with the picture we can imagine of the broadcasting of a radio signal, especially if it is in stereo, or the TV audio-visual complex, especially when it becomes three-dimensional. The radiations from the pebble *seem* to be on a plane, but that certainly is not true of the broadcast signals. And the dimension of time can be added to this metaphor, a factor which is too often disregarded in communications analysis. Thus, when does a statute speak, or a constitution, or a will, or a contract? As we place ourselves in this multi-dimensional, multi-coordinated picture, we realize the considerations are not the same with respect to the time of drafting as compared to the time of interpreting. And it makes a difference to the interpretation where the interpreter places himself in that picture-situation. An interpreter needs some of the observer skills we are exploring. (And is there anyone who is not an interpreter in the process of communication? Interpreting involves tuning-in the right or desired signal.)

We are moving in these pages to an exploration of law talk, aimed toward multi-dimensionality. Out of these ways comes later consideration of what people can or may *do* with law talk, which is quite a different perspective from a discussion of "what the law is." (But remembering the professor and the book, this switch-leap does not preclude going back to that other plateau from time to time.) Felix Cohen did much to support another theme involved in these explorations, and that is that despite his sort of explorations, law talk has been and still is a communicative mechanism which camouflages values, especially when the authority aspect is emphasized to put values out of focus. ("I saw the professor drop the book, but I did not see what else he did.")

Not to play favorites, even though Cohen and many others have done much to rip off the camouflage, realize it is just possible to produce from that "activity" another sometimes more deceptive camouflage. (Who would guess that someone ripping off a cover is thus covering something else "in the act?") But one may do that in using values synonymously with morality or ethics, or more simply in the sense of good or bad. (The new dogma may be preferred.) The analyst who says that law talk is really a cover for morality talk (crypto-idealism) may be putting himself into a position of authority-expertise to challenge some commanding law talk. (See later, The Right Way.)

That is, it seems quite reasonable to say that a person is always taking some sort of stand(s) when he attempts to communicate. His stand cannot be located by just two coordinates. That is why speaking only in terms of values is not enough any more, as helpful (I want to say valu-able) as that has been. We can now go into further dimensions, just as we can go beyond words and semantics to understand and use communicative mechanisms that seem only to involve words (as here on these pages).

There is yet another vision observable beyond that jungle. We talk about seeing the way people use words, and so how they use law *talk*. We should be able to talk about the way laws are used. That is less jarring if we say use of law talk, but laws can be and in a sense always are used in some tactical or strategic way. That was clear about the Black Civil Rights movement. It ought to be clear enough by now in the instance of political trials in Chicago and elsewhere.

Well, law as a process can be described in a number of relevant ways: as a rational process, a power process, a dispute settling process, a value-conflict resolution process, and so on. All these dimensions are involved—all at once, although one may be predominant at a given moment, more in focus, more a matter of concern.

(So, can I say that the preceding was not only a piece of communications analysis but *also* of jurisprudential theory?)

CHART #3

WORDS
CONSCIOUSNESS

LAW

a. dictionary of common usage
   (1) the principles and regulations established by a government and applicable to a people . . .(2) any written or positive rule or collection of rules prescribed under the authority of the state or nation as by the people in its constitution. (3) the department of knowledge concerned with such rules: jurisprudence. (4) a system or collection of such rules . . . . .Etc.

b. dictionary of jurisprudential usage:
   (1) an authoritative set of words in an accepted system of law (2) what judges do (3) a statute (4) a norm for behavior promulgated in accordance with established rules and practices (5) a system of authoritative rules . . . .Etc.

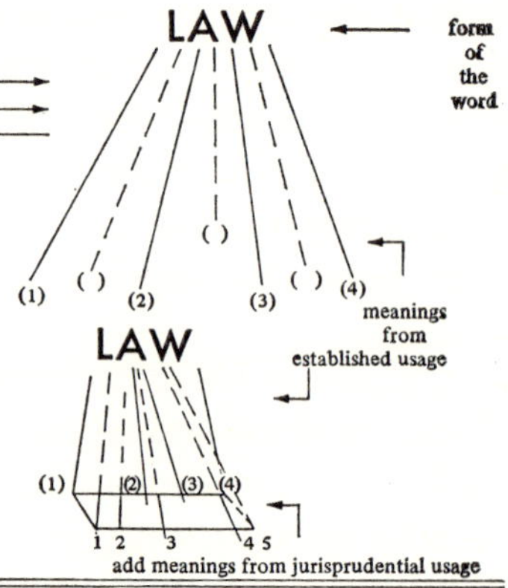

WHAT IS LAW?

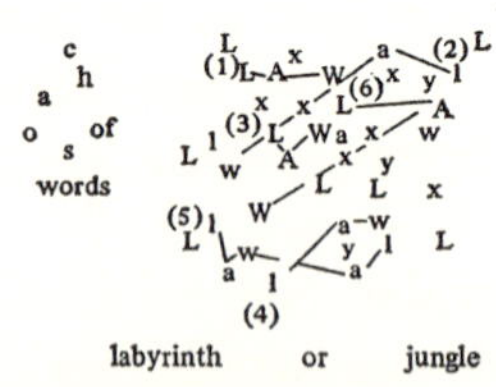

words consciousness – into jungle and beyond. See above figures in perspective

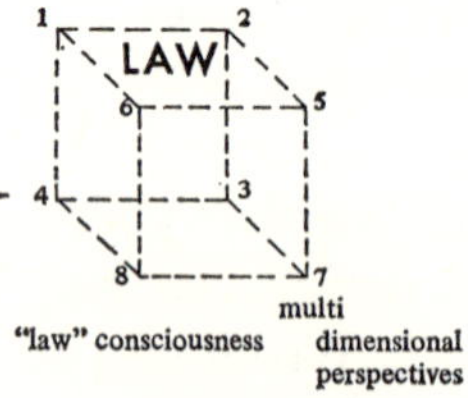

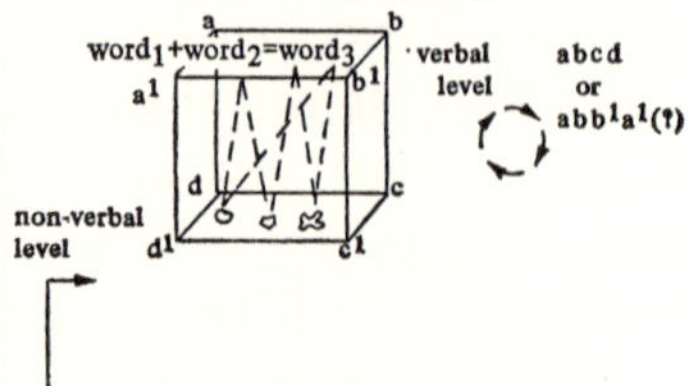

KINDS OF CONSCIOUSNESS

(1) sensations, feelings, sense perceptions, etc. non-verbal; not dependent on words.
(2) of things, actions, etc. non-verbal. (a) without articulating or thinking words (b) stimulated by here and now articulations; e.g. see this page!
(3) *as if* of absent things, etc.
   (a) without words
   (b) completely or partially dependent on words.
(4) consciousness of words: the forms, structures behind forms, interrelations, etc.
(5) consciousness of communications dynamics because of consciousness of words

visual models of aid: e.g., planes of interinvolvement of words and things, not fixed, changing.

Chapter IV

FROM LAW TO LAW TALK

Prelude

WHATEVER I SAY, or think I say, I *do* something else also, at least given some communicative potential, if I am trying to communicate. (The professor and the book.) When law is being talked about (or as we are going to say, when law is being talked), this multi-dimensionality seems particularly camouflaged in formalism, as if there were some sort of magic there. It seems very probable that there is a tie-in with the expectations regarding interpretation and meaning *in* words. Not that one is always thinking about interpretation when he hears of law(s), maybe not enough, but when one does think of interpretation, or when some question is raised about a law, then there is a tendency to strike a meaning attitude. And that moves toward a uni-dimensional focus. Just as it is natural to look for one characterization as the proper one when asked just what the professor did when he dropped that book. As when someone asks what law is. Or when the word "law" is used. In such circumstances, if one is habituated to think of rhetorical definition, then he realizes there is some sort of selection from a number of possibilities.

The best illustration of this interpretation-meaning learning occurs when there is some question about a statute, which seems to sit on the page and beg to have its *meaning* understood. But that is not enough, for there is a communicative package there. Today's tendencies to ask what the legislative purpose may be may have the opposite effect of suggesting that meaning of words is not relevant at all, and that is not valid either. If we relate the professor and the book example, we see that either meaning or purpose approaches are going to be especially inviting because they seem to get us down to the one appropriate answer, as asking "what the professor did" could. (But did not since we pressed it further.)

So we see a conflict between the present task of trying to open up to the full range of potential messages in the communicative act and the ever pressing "practical" goal of deciding what particular thing to say or do. It seems to me that we should not try to do both things at once in these explorations, but is important to try to make it clear that the goal is not to say that we can never really know for sure, as we move ahead in exploring multi-dimensionality, indeterminacy, ambiguity, and relativity in words and other communicative dynamics. What is risky in law communication is not so much that authoritative interpreters do not reach decisions, but that they give the appearance of reaching them too soon, or of not having explored the range of possibilities *from which* the appropriate meaning or purpose or what have you can be selected or derived or constructed. And we will have occasion to consider this latter sort of problem.

Words in Talking: Two Dialogue-Analyses

We have already touched on a feature of words which is important to both of the preceding tasks, one of seeing the full range of potentials, and two of selecting from them. There is no one way of characterizing this feature, but I have put it in terms of subtle ambiguities, in connection with rhetorical definitions and in connection with characterizing a non-verbal act (the professor *example*). On the one hand there is the lack of fixity of a given word to *have* to be used in a given way and on the other the freedom that actually exists to take a given thing, event, or situation and characterize it in a great variety of ways. In talking at this stage or level, we are exploring the *potentials* of relating words and things and trying to stress that just because certain words have been situationally affixed does not establish that they have been affixed in the way that a first blush reaction assumes. That sort of stress is carried through into the distinction between meaning of words and use of words, which in turn is carried through in distinguishing law from law talk.

The "Show Me a Rule" dialogue has bearing here. There are a number of ways a person could go wrong in interpreting that interplay. In that respect, it is interesting to consider the dimensionalities of interpreting a dialogue and what may *seem*, perhaps because of form and style, to be a uni-directional narrative or exposition. The situation confronting a jury is somewhat analogous. Jurors may get caught up in one or another dimensions, maybe at one instant concentrating on what the witness is saying and forgetting they are listening to a dialogue which the questioning attorney is trying to direct. He is talking to the jury through a dialogue, yet he also has to talk to and with the witness in a way that makes sense to him. But the jurors ought to ask themselves repeatedly what the attorney is trying to do. Often he is trying to do more than one thing at once, and he is communicating on several levels whether he always remembers it or not: talking to the witness and the several jurors simultaneously, to the trial judge, and potentially to the potential appellate court via the record of the case that is in the making as he acts.

If one reads the Show Me A Rule dialogue wondering what the right or true meaning of "rule" is, then he will not get the messages. They could be spelled out in narrative form, but it would not say or do what the dialogue hopefully does. It is possible through that dialogue to learn something about the word "rule" and some of its variations, and so in the process, something about rules. One could become more expert in dealing with rules-talk when he next gets in that situation. (Rules-talk is not restricted to the oral form and one is involved in it, for instance, when he is reading a judicial opinion which asserts certain applicable rules.) The dialogue itself is not rules-talk because it clearly is not one of the ways in which people ordinarily talk (or talk about) rules. We might call it rules-talk talk.

Ordinarily, when people engage in rules talk, they do not examine the word "rule." But they could, and to attempt to move people into *that* posture (making the leap), the goal is to encourage at least those people to be "appreciating" what form of rules talk is being used on a given situation. (So there is some aid-to-interpretation goal here after all, although it certainly would not seem so on a first reading of Show Me a Rule.) So, it is quite possible to have the kind of sensitivity to the word "rule" which is shown or demonstrated in the explicit dialogue whenever one hears it in rules talk or even if rules talk is going on when the word rule is not even articulated, as when someone asserts a statement or proposition where it is rather clear that he is thinking rules or talking in that vein. Rules-talk talk is, then, preparation for communicative participant-observation during just plain rules talk.

The "Has Anyone Seen A Fact" dialogue is another matter. It too is meant to be preparation for facts talk and more generally, as with "Show Me A Rule," to promote words sensitivity as to other words. But in this case, while there is a dimension of exploring some of the ambiguity of "fact" (we must do more with that word and with "rule" because tolerance-skill does not come easily), here there is more of a focus on the relationship of "fact" as a word with other words. This is an even more subtle feature than with "rule," and it is explored a bit in "Show Me A Rule." Actually "fact" may be subject to a greater diversity of uses than is "rule" which is why it may be interesting and insightful to show how the syntactic involvements of "facts" are rather tightly limited, to show that despite the quite generally unappreciated subtle and pervasive ambiguities of all words, there are some rules or conventions in their use after all. There are some rules or conventions of other kinds that relate to help one to know, perhaps unconsciously, often, but not often enough, which one(s) of the many variations of the word is being offered on a particular occasion; as Wittgenstein put it, which "word game is being played."

These two analyses ("rule" and "fact") are not exhaustive by any means, nor are they of the form which either Wittgenstein or J. L. Austin (or anyone else for that matter) have offered, but they can open up similar insights. They have.

And they may demonstrate possibilities of verbal analysis which are not just tedious. It has proven interesting and instructive to some law students to try to write some such revealing exploration of a term. On ahead there are a considerable variety of ways of analysis demonstrated, maybe some a bit tedious, but there is a necessary time for that just as there can be benefit from play with serious goals. (Compare the possibilities of role-playing.)

Working out rhetorical definitions is a technique of verbal analysis. But there and in the two dialogues it would be disappointing to think that some reader(s) might think that only the particular words analyzed are being analyzed. We are drawing implications for all words and for all communication, and it seems necessary to see those messages at least dimly in order to be benefited in the narrower concerns of "rule(s)" and "fact(s)" and rules talk and facts talk.

Exploring the Uses of "Law"

Well, of course the word "law" needs to be appreciated. There has been quite a bit of exploration of that word in jurisprudential literature, and the arguments still can be heard as to whether it is worthwhile to try to define it or explore it. On the American side there is an antipathy to either effort, but to his credit, not for H. L. A. Hart. Any teacher of a Jurisprudence course who abstains from this sort of exploration is doing his class a disservice not to mention missing some entertaining possibilities to boot. So let's have a bit of a go at it, for otherwise talk of law talk may seem fanciful. There is some flexibility needed here.

1.1 What sorts of insights might be gained from discussing the word "law"? If I ask what is law, there is a hidden linguistic dimension, although maybe it is not quite so hidden as asking what the professor did when he dropped the book. Asking what is law is not so much different from: *What and/or where is/are (a) law(s)?* This latter oddity is several questions, but so is "What is law?"

1.2 There are some other such questions: "What is a rule?" or "a fact?" "What is a battery?" "What is intent?" Just think what on the *surface* seems to be asked. Of course such questions are invitations to conceptualism. It might be better to ask, "When is a battery?" Or better, when is it appropriate to use the word "battery"? Or having a given situation, "Is it all right to speak of this as a battery?"

1.3 What is not so easy to see is that in everyday life, if a child were to ask, "Hey Mommy, is this a ball?" (what child would?), he is asking his mother for a ruling, the way a lawyer would be doing if he went to court and said, "Hey, Your Honor, is this a battery?" (Except the lawyer would say, "This *is* a battery.") But both the mother and the judge are faced with interesting linguistic questions. If the child is holding a fragile Christmas tree ornament, she had better be careful with her answer. And the judge knows that he is free to call the situation something other than a battery, probably. (Compare in this respect our exploration of "foreseeable" in the section on Rhetorical Definitions. "When is an event foreseeable?" That is partly linguistic, but so is the lawyer's argument to the jury that a certain happening was foreseeable.)

1.4 So when someone says the law is so and so, he is exercising jurisdiction over the definition of "law." Take the most general *sort* of lego-political defining in use: "The law is the complex of governmentally authoritative rules by which a society governs (itself)." One could deny the statement easily enough, or counter it with another one. *But one could not disprove it empirically*. Nor is it grammatically wrong, although it is grammatically correct, which is not to prove it is required, just acceptable, for some purpose(s). If someone were to argue that the test is one of usefulness, and that he sees little usefulness to it, then I would remind him that *we are making use of it*. (This is a major point!)

1.5 Suppose someone tells me that A promised to take care of B's yard for a certain amount of money, that A simply did nothing in furtherance of this legally binding contract and that B has suffered considerable damage to his yard as a consequence. That someone now asks me if A can be sued for negligence in causing the damage. Suppose this response: *"The law does not impose an obligation in tort for failure to perform a contract; maybe for contractual misfeasance, but not nonfeasance."*

1.6 "The law does not . . ." is rather tricky phrasing. Consider the difference in my saying it, a lawyer saying it to his client, and a judge writing it in his opinion. The word "law" is actually being used in more than one way *simultaneously*. (see *infra*) How we view the word depends upon whether we are interested only in the rhetorical force of the sentence, whether we want to see in a more analytical sense what the word "law" is referring to, and so on. (Not to mention the communicative significance of who is saying it to whom, under what circumstances, for what apparent purposes.)

1.7 In 1.4, in talking about law, I seem to be describing some phenomenon, something that could exist, a body of rules. (Let's not argue about that for the nonce.) Beyond that, I am defining the word "law," via rhetorical definition. If we think in terms of socio-legal processes, we realize there is more to it all than rules-governing, but if there is that component, why call *it* law, or why restrict the scope of "law" that way. Yet to restrict its scope that way for that time and place is not to restrict it for another time and place when we are, in Wittgenstein's metaphor, playing a different game with "law." (This is so hard for some people to see, or to take seriously, or if they see it, to realize the implications. Nor am I saying, well, use "law" any old way you wish.) If we investigate the socio-semantics of the term "law," we realize that it *has* been used in many different ways (as have "rule," "fact," "foreseeable," "is," "ball," "intent," "love," "you," "etc."). But not all words have the great drawing power of LAW. While it has a great variability in use and reference, there is an overriding symbolism that makes it harder to see the subtle variations in *use.*

1.8 You cannot use the word "law" in describing (or supposedly describing) some aspect of social phenomena without defining it in some selective way, and using it in some way. (Can you pick up a hammer and not use it. How do you define "use?"). You cannot use the word "law" in talking law (now we are using the little "l," specific laws, specific states of the law; the law in this case is so and so, etc.) without defining it in some selective way, and this is harder to see. Stating what the law *is* in such and such a situation is also saying how to use the word "law." That is not only rather interesting, but very important to know.

1.9 One might think the term is too ambiguous to be meaningful, but that is not so. In any event, you cannot be a lawyer without using it a great deal. One could try getting along without it as an exercise, and it would be interesting to see what other words popped up in its place. It's a great word!

1.10 The English commentator Blackstone said that law involved rules commanding what is right and prohibiting what is wrong. Many years later Felix Cohen objected strenuously to that statement. I object to it! But something of this sort of definition of law is spreading across the land. Whether it ought to be, whether children ought to be conditioned to it (but turn off the TV) is a very important question. The objection from this quarter ought not be that this is a linguistically incorrect use of "law," but that it is bad propaganda, and that it might take *advantage of* linguistic naiveté.

1.11 Cohen pointed out that there was an oughtness implicit in such definitions as Blackstone's (as there is in any assertion of (a) law). That is, if this is a way of viewing law, ought one to view it that way. Should he be persuaded? Cohen's disagreement with Blackstone concerned the attempted compulsive-compulsory drawing power (we must go into this sort of thing more later on) of that sort of *talk*. Someone might want to say the compulsory aspects of law, but I am trying to get us to looking at talk, trying to bridge the chasm between ordinary thinking of LAW (where: out there) and a communicatively valuable new way of looking at the phenomenon of *law talk* (compare: 1. Where is law? 2. Where is law talk?). Clearly enough Blackstone's definition was authority-oriented (Establishment-oriented). Obey law, right or wrong. It is not yours to question, but to conform. Surely this is one of the burning issues of *our* time and there is a great deal of verbal ignorance involved in the fires.

1.12 We should be careful not to confuse, however, the issue Cohen was raising with today's burning socio-legal issues, although they are related. Cohen was a skeptical idealist (sound familiar?). Thirty-some years ago he was not encouraging disobedience but critical thought and assessment and reform. So, he was right in intimating that Blackstone was legislating. One may want to obey law and still be able to feel it is a bad law. What sort of contemporary absurdity is it to suggest that law is right because *it* (?) is law, especially when we remember the power of definition! This is a fantastically complex sort of question that people all so blithely answer off the ends of their tongues, including most lawyers and a lot of law teachers who ought to know better.

1.13 It is not *just* a matter of words or definitions, but much more than almost anybody realizes or is ready to admit, especially dogmatists (or in one's dogmatic episodes. "Who, me?").

1.14 At the end of 1.4, I stopped the glide through a point by saying it was major. It is fair to ask in relation to that point, what am I doing on-in-through these sections? Possibly I am doing more than meets the eye (like the professor and the book). Lest anyone think we are just exploring words, realize that for someone who has not thought about law in the way we have in these sections there could be some socio-legal insights. All those people in Jurisprudential literature, including H. L. A. Hart, who have stipulated this and that definition of law in talking about law were adding in various ways to man's understanding of his environment. In exploring their comments, we could get some of that. In exploring the word "law" we can get some or all of that insight-information, eventually. (Now another major point that might glide by.) It is hard for some people to realize that in communciation's explorations one is engaged in more than verbal analysis. It is, for instance, an empirical technique.

1.15 Wittgenstein and J. L. Austin and their colleagues have been called "language philosophers" in a way that is disparaging. They came along in the evolutionary development of an empirical theory that has been very important to our scientific age. There is a new empiricism here that few have yet seen. So-called linguistic analysis is re-search, bringing to the surface what one has learned (and socially, what man has learned) and *buried*. It has to be or at least can be uncovered. This is one of the insights that can come with the leap! ("Oh, it's just semantics.") And in saying that, we are facing some facts about words in general, not just the word "law." (But not just research, also discovery.)

2.1 Consider the italicized piece of law talk in 1.5. Suppose I utter that in a speech. Does the statement refer to a rule or some set of rules? It could be to some particular law, or maybe without really thinking about it, both sorts of references. It sounds authoritative. Is it? Oliver Wendell Holmes said such a statement was really a prediction of what a court would do, thus giving a provocative rhetorical definition involving his overriding view of law, or interest. If I have in mind rule(s) in uttering that statement in 1.5, then the statement manifests a differing overriding point of view (or special argument?). The dogma of the statement seems to preclude Cohen's and Holmes' sorts of qualifications. If I were trying to indoctrinate or influence someone's behavior, then I would not welcome either kind of their skepticism. (If a lawyer were saying that statement in 1.5 to a client in an appropriate situation, he might be trying to influence the client.) What of a judge who wrote that in an opinion for a court majority? If we took the approach that a word is defined by its context, then we would have to say that "law" refers to the court itself, not to some "brooding omnipresence in the sky" (Holmes) because as the legal realists said, law is what judges do, not what they say.

2.2 Why not both what they say *and* what they do: law talk and its consequences.

2.3 Any assertion of the this-is-the-law-in-this-situation kind involves some, all, or more, of the socio-linguistic implications raised in 2.1 and 2.2.

2.4 So what is a law teacher doing when he teaches law? (Anyone saying "imparting rules of law," off to jail without passing Go.)

3.1 John Chipman Gray said that statutes were not law, but merely sources of law. When we get to thinking of statutes, consider the verbal-linguistic dimensions, and put them together with Gray's rhetorical definition. There was a valid interpretative insight in his re-definitional, metaphorical refocus, because there *is* an interpretative act between the statute on the books and its invocation, implementation, application, or other use-strategy. He was probably thinking of judicial interpretation as the last say, as a way of asserting judicial supremacy. Still, someone may have to interpret that statute short of court (police?). It does not just speak for itself. Someone interprets the statute and then probably says, "The law is thus and so . . . ," pointing to the statute. Gray would have said that the interpreter was pointing to the court, or if not, then the interpretation failed for not taking the courts into account.

3.2 Gray was not empirically right or wrong, although he may have been abusing a propagandistic license, but if we take account of all the possible interpretations that stand between the statute and whatever action that is taken in *its* name, then we realize something of the multi-dimensionality of the statute-in-action, a complexity of which other written forms are functions, like constitutions, regulations, and so on. Then consider judicial rules that are not really written down in that form or way(s). (And in all of this, whose "strict construction" shall we take?)

Law Talk Explored

There are analytical aids, models, and metaphors available to one who wishes (they may be needed) to turn on his words consciousness and/or to engage in communications analysis. Years back, Korzybski used the map-territory analogy to compare *a* relationship between words and things. Words are words and things are things. That seems as if it must be true, but it is basically an anti-conceptualistic figure of speech. It helps one to jar himself loose from *seeing* (literally seeing) things and situations in certain ways just because he has learned to talk *about* them in certain ways.

Or take the formulation of operational definitions. That is an empirics-relating aid for the theory of science. It is related to the distinction the logical positivists drew between meaningful and non-meaningful words. (Having to do with verifiability.) And see how both of these analytical aids are related to Korzybski's word/thing slicing. These seem to be ways of talking (or talking about) things in order to bring one closer to them, or to non-verbal operations. Related is the distinction between descriptive words and emotive/value words. From all of this comes awareness of rhetorical definitions.

All of these "notions" are models, metaphors, figures of speech, maybe rhetorical definitions, to allow one to see, feel, and hear the multi-dimensionality of words—in communicative behavior, transactions, and situations. Also important is Wittgenstein's metaphor of "language games," to bring out the way a word (or better, word-form) breaks apart into a family of words (species of the genus) that are related to each other, but serving a variety of roles along a spectrum, or maybe around a circle, depending upon the word-game being "played" (metaphor). Some observers object to the metaphors of Wittgenstein but we shall explore their usefulness along with his and J. L. Austin's use-of-words approaches (How to Do Things with Words"). The use theory helps to get some people off the meaning-in-words kick. It helps to think of or see words *in that way* (at least sometimes). For one thing it makes it easier to see how words can be *used* to explore words and communication, a rather marvelous potential. So, for instance, in the preceding section we were using the word "law" to explore multi-dimensionality and to get us to "law talk." If we were stuck with "meaning" (some of whose members are metaphors. Think of that!), then we would have difficulty getting off those planes or levels.

Relevant or useful models need not even be verbal. To talk in terms of planes or levels is verbal, but it is a way to *affect* visualization (!) and feelings. Korzybski is but one who believed that communication relationships should be "seen" in structure. He was said to have used his hands a great deal to "describe" (circumscribe?) and simulate the levels separating the verbal from the non-verbal and in turn to show structure in verbal relationships. (As the word "fact" stands above, so to speak, the words to which it refers, and what those words refer to—see further discussion of Has Anyone Seen A Fact, *infra.*) There is some relationship to my figure of "leaping" from one level of appreciation to another.

No words can say it all. Word-bound critics over-objected to McLuhan's *picturesque* efforts to jar readers free from literalism and verbalism. He suggested that today's generations were growing up with less word-bindingness. Maybe he did overstate. What else can you do with metaphors? He said the written forms were losing out. But they may lose their relative significance, a wondrous if not awesome spectacle for law and lawyers. It may explain not only the generation gap but the credibility gap of law. Well, it does not have to be one form *or* another, but extensions into new forms which affect the way(s) the old forms communicate. That's all. ("That's all?")

So let us now explore a bit with an analytical model or metaphor which has until now been mostly an allusion: law talk. Consider, for example, a statute, a prime form of law. Look at the statute through this perspective locator rather than as (*through*) just law. (Or in relation to law talk.)

A statute sits there in a book, the official code. I may copy it on this page and then write and/or talk about it, but it remains there in the code-book. Still, putting its copy on this page may involve more than just copying. Or it may involve an illusion. If I talk about a tree on this page, you have no illusions about seeing the real tree. Is printing the statute here akin to putting a picture of the tree on this page? Really, it is more than that. It is rather like putting the tree on the page.

What if I put *part* of the statute on the page? That may influence a reader (especially as I add some words of my own) to think he sees all he needs to see, something like, *but more than* quoting out of context.

See the statute as something more than just a command, as an interesting sort of tool. Compare the various uses of a statute with the use of a hammer. The hammer is somehow independent of one's uses of it, especially when it sits in a tool box. Yet a part of the hammer does not seem subject to use in any analogous ways to parts of a statute. If I cut the hammer in two, I might use the separate parts, but I have lost my hammer. But we do not act as if that were the case with the statute. So it seems. It just sits there in the code-book, no matter what I do with it here.

Do only word-analysts play with words. What shall we say

of the judge or lawyer or newspaper columnist who cuts a statute into two or more parts? Perhaps a statute lies more in its cutting (if we do not lie with its cuttings). At any rate, there is some sense in which the statute is carried into what seems talk of or about the statute but actually is talking with it, or in which the statute talk supersedes the statute.

We like to say that we interpret, apply, or enforce a statute. But these are also general ways of talking about the uses of statutes.

The man who said that a statute is not law but only a source of law was making a useful cut with his analytical knife. Surely somewhere in the totality of human talking "of" or "about" or with parts or all of a statute lies its significance, wherever the "law" of it begins or ends. Within this communicative dynamics is statute talk, a species of law talk (thinking, interpreting, etc.). We could call it law-in-action, this totality. Or maybe even *law!* But I have no desire to manipulate, no need, I think, at this point.

Lawyers have learned to law talk in the classroom and in student sessions and by reading and arguing in various sessions, just as they learned other kinds of talk earlier. You can recognize rather readily much of that student's efforts with law talk. (Not just doctrine!) A piece of talk is not always pure law talk nor always filled with technicalities. Laymen can talk law too, certainly newspaper columnists, as with talk of The Constitution.

There is nothing unusual about giving names to verbal activities that are distinctive. Remember "Twenty Questions" and other talking games? Compare a lecture with a discussion. Interrogations are distinctive. Law talk is not of one kind either. There is an interesting sort that is not analogous to doctors' medical talk and even distinctive from lawyers' talking shop, or from weather talk. Maybe weather talk does not presently exist in this sense of law talk, because you can do nothing about the weather by talking *about* it. But sometimes lawyers (certainly judges) are doing more than just talking *about* law when they engage in law talk. Wittgenstein and

Austin spoke of philosophers *doing* philosophy, their very talk-analysis being that, an activity. We might thus speak of doing communication while talking "about" it. *Sometimes* a doctor may *do* medicine (therapy) by talking. We do not *see* lawyering as law(ing) in that analogous fashion to the psychotherapist. Compare talking about a verbal game and playing the game. Think of lawyers talking law while negotiating or drawing up contracts. Maybe even an advocate in appellate courts is not just arguing. He is having an influence and a shaping. *The lawyer advising his client* and "talking about law" *may in a sense be doing law.*

To speak of law talk in this latter sense is certainly not just to call attention to lawyers' jargon. Lawyers' law talk is by no means restricted to legal doctrine, although that tends to be the most noted species. It is only one way of talking law, just as there is law talk with no doctrine at all. And distinguish this law talk analytical metaphor/model from that of "language of law," which does not suggest the situational dynamics of "law talk." (Not that it is useless.)

To speak and think of law talk is to *see* some things differently, *if not just parroted,* to slice law dynamics differently from the way we do in talking in terms *of* law. It aids in structuring and with less torturing than some of the rhetorical definitions of the past.

We could say that law is what people say and communicate in certain sorts of contexts. Ehrlich distinguished "living law" from lawyers' law, thus stressing the social patterns of behavior which preceded and in a sense outranked the technical law (technical from a layman's view). So there is law-in-action, what people generally do, maybe because they are conditioned by laws (or are conditioning laws?), but not necessarily. Shall we say they are conforming-to-laws or simply not-breaking them? These slicing-variations have consequences. But if people behaving can be law in action, then certainly what lawyers do has some distinctive possibilities for characterization: law-in-action; doing law; talking law; livening the law; lawing; lawyering; legalizing; in law process; processing law.

The legal realists wanted to move the emphasis from laws on the book that just sat there, and from the slicing that judges were just applying law from the books (as if common law rules were like statutes). So they de-emphasized the judicial metaphor of law out there by saying that law was what those judges did, not what they said. That is a very useful slicing (rhetorical redifining, note). But notice what we can do in saying that a judicial opinion contains judicial rhetoric! What if we call it law talk? As to lawyers, it is not just what they say that might be regarded as law in action, but what they say and do. And if we realize that people communicate in a complex of words and *other* behavior, then we would need better to say law behavior. But since too many people are too anxious to ignore the verbal-talk part and naively fail to appreciate talk as behavior, I better stick for now to law talk. (You know what I mean.)

Compare "laws" with "law." It is laws we tend more to see out there (or, a law), separate from society, and that may only be because we can state them in a way that asserts some independence to the asserting—as when statutes and constitutions are in writing, over there ("to be strictly construed"). But they get worked out of there in processes of communication that are distinctive from the kind of communication which is involved in asserting them. Remember (pity our legalistic literalists), what you see there in writing is only a communication. To say that a statute is law, the law, or a law still makes its own sense: the official, authoritative base of reference. The way to start talking from which you can move only *so far.* But just because we speak of "a cow" and see it there does not mean we should get all mixed up in any further analogy just because the way we say "a cow" and "a statute" are in writing look-alikes (bad mapping). And of course we have to take account of this convention (e.g. statute = a law) when we are speaking conventionally. But why should convention require us to be always thinking and perceiving in those terms also?

Consider this point of view generally in regard to rules. A

rule is a function of the particular communication situations into which it is transported. (If you were to try out the Basic Rules, to be talked about, you would see that. You cannot get this by just reading. It takes *participant-observation.*) They are *transported* (communicated) into judges' chambers, law office conferences, lawyer-client situations, law classrooms, articles, books, a man's head. Because of the way we talk about rules, the conventions, and that includes the *surface* grammar (subject-predicate), one is apt to visualize rules as merely being carried about from situation to situation, unchanged, unaffected by the media. To see rules as interspersed in interpersonal dynamics, sometimes submerged, is quite different. The law-talk model/slicing helps, not as an either-one-or-the-other, but as a way.

Take the statement: "This will is invalid because it lacks the signatures of two attesting witnesses." Someone will say that *is* (or sounds like?) the application of a rule of law. But consider it from the law-talk perspective. It could be stated in a judicial opinion, by a lawyer in court or in his office with a client, or even by a mere mortal to his wife. Its seeming invariant form (having taken these several statement-in-context's and coalesced them into one statement: "a rule") is *de*-ceiving (compare *per*-ceiving). If it were stated in the true-rule form—"A valid will must have two attesting signatures"—then we would want to argue the first form was obviously the application and the rule did remain unchanged, but that is a "cop out." In any event, the first statement, typical of technical law talk, serves a different function in each situation, respectively a decision, persuasion, advice-counseling, and maybe complaint. Those are some of the ways the rule-form statement or the less formal law-talk variation may be used. They are both species of law talk.

Will someone say, "Well, you are getting away from verbal analysis, from meaning and that sort of thing. You are talking about the consequences of the rule." But for one thing, meaning has no significance in a non-communicative vacuum, for it is a function of the full potential of situational-uses! And more generally, there is no communication without some sort of consequence, with some use-goal involved in the utterance. The rule just sits there, until someone communicates-with (uses) it.

It could make a difference in law teaching and curricular planning if legal educators appreciated these dimensions of law talk. Law(s) might be seen in some larger portion of the total situations in(to) which they may be appropriately (or inappropriately) transported and used (or abused). There is still, almost astonishingly, almost no attention paid to law(yers) talk with laymen. Such talk with clients ought to be considered relevant, not only regarding advice techniques and strategies, but the subtler aspects of psycho-legal counseling. But it is relevant in matters of "public relations," writing for the mass media, speech-making, public education, and many other areas.

One can almost feel the tension in a faculty meeting. Someone will say, "But that is not law you are talking about." That sort of protective, restrictive rhetoric-slicing was quite clearly one of the targets of the legal realists, most of whom were law school teachers, but even in this post-realist era, the specific example given would be resisted by many a sociologically oriented, or even social-conscience-oriented individual, because in such an area (for example) the old images still prevail. They literally might not be able to *see* how this sort of thing was dealing with law, whereas they would see that old-fashioned law rhetoric ought not to stand in the way of needed reforms. (And then, "Who would teach it?!")

Not even in a legal theory class would it be regarded as appropriate, where law talk is not the common commodity, as it would be in some substantive-law course (e.g. contracts, taxation.) But to talk about this sort of thing is in some way to talk about legal process, if not law, and about talking-about-law and *of* law talk. How people, including lawyers, *talk law* has everything to do with "its" impact. What shall we call it?

There is not yet even sufficient appreciation of what difference it makes to look at a judical opinion in this light. A judge there asserts law, talks about law in the midst of other sorts of statements, reasonings, justifications. But in another sense it is *all* law talk, because it is in the opinion!

Talking law is not just reciting rules, doctrines, principles and all that. It involves certain way(s) of sizing up problems, characterizing events in ways that mesh with slicings contained in law talk. And it feeds into perception, cognition, and non-verbal "evaluation." (After all, it is a way of behaving.) A lawyer sees an automobile accident differently from a doctor, and talks about it differently, at least when in his lawyer-role (preconceived partly on the basis of law-talk training). And law-and-order people see things differently too, because of their talking-views. Not all lawyers are law-and-order types (although they may believe in and have loyalty to law-system), nor are they, even most of them necessarily restricted in their visions, except maybe when enmeshed in the nets of doctrine and other close to doctrine law talk, because for one thing, they are not forever talking law even when dealing with problems within their province. It is not law talk that is *per se* restrictive, but what is done with it, and it is often certain kinds of people (legalistic personalities) who use some of its forms.

But it is a definite mistake to go so far as to say that lawyers should be taught to be scornful of law talk. They should be taught the hows and the variations, be able to talk and think like a lawyer, as they say, but that should mean imaginatively and creatively when appropriate, and maybe legalistically when appropriate. But it is not just gamesmanship any more than talking to a three-year-old is always a game, or knowing how to talk to persons in other social-strata or groups is a game. It is a matter of knowing how to communicate. (And why shouldn't laymen be taught to talk law properly too?)

Researchers and various sorts of scholars have had real trouble with law talk. They seem not to know what to do with it, so they tend to ignore it or even ridicule it, even when they have no idea whether they are dealing with legalism or not. ("Well, you know lawyers.") Of course they see quite legitimately that specialized vocabularies can be a way of perpetuating group or professional power or snobbery. That attitude may have as much as anything to do with the extreme approach taken toward law talk by certain judicial behaviorists among the political scientists (such as Glendon Schubert). Following the lead of some of the legal realists, *who also were involved in a power-authority battle* (you would think political scientists would see that), they dismissed as mere rhetoric what the "establishment" said was legal reasoning.

Even to analyze judicial opinions for the rhetorical definitions they contain is not to dismiss it all as "mere rhetoric." Of course mere rhetoric is suspect, but rhetoric is not (the word needs conjugating into its various family-members). But even "mere rhetoric" is, like uttered words of all kinds in all places, some aspect of behavior that cannot be usually, let alone totally, ignored.

Schubert also abjured the lawyers' favorite model which divided the stuff of lawyers' concern into law and facts. It is true that this is an oversimplism and it ought to be better understood by lawyers, but it will not likely be discarded any more than love. ("I mean, really, just what *is* love?") When you study the tribe, you need to know their way(s), including how they talk. But these behaviorists who scorned judicial rhetoric and the law-fact model had to have something to study, so they focused on the facts of cases to plot them against decisions to discover what attitudes unfolded into what patterns to prove what regularities of behavior they could discover. (The Real Rules?) If you are going to use judicial opinions as the source of data, you are not going to be able to ignore *all* the words.

But a skilled interpreter (can behavioral scientists somehow skip over the problems of interpretation?) knows that words here and words there are often interrelated, that words in one spot are very often a sort of function of words in some other spot. (Else why all the criticism of the Joseph McCarthyistic quoting out of context?) If judicial opinions contain "mere rhetoric," it is not to be avoided in the fact assertions sections, even if they are separately stated, which they rarely are, completely. See what a naive bit of psycholinguistics this is, the belief that you can look *through* words to the (invisible) facts beyond. (See also Has Anyone Seen A Fact?) What one "sees" beyond the words is whatever the words allow to him (along with whatever illusions he may have, or suitable inventions).

The factual characterizations in opinions are psycholinguistically, dialectically, and rhetorically related to the seemingly more technical verbiage (fact-talk is easy to understand), the technicalities being what to most people was the sum and substance of the law talk. Fact statements, references to sociology, and some people think, policy assertions, are not regarded as "strictly legal." Well, why not? When someone slices them out of law, he is giving us some important information about his attitudes and preconceptions!

Law teachers of the post-realist orientation, scorned by Schubert for sticking to primitive methods of analyzing cases, have long realized that attitudes are discernible in judicial talk, but most assuredly not just in the fact-assertion part of it, although there may be some degree of correlation between the attitudinal-manifestation of the fact-assertion portion and that of the total in some instances. (The best locus for attitude-revealing behavior, the judicial conference in the chambers, is unfortunately off limits.)

Law students still receive their baptism in law talk through judicial opinions and relevant commentary, so there tends to be drilling in the distinction between law and facts. Later on, as lawyers, they become so comfortable with judgments about facts they may think much of the law they learned was unnecessary. (Personal injury lawyers are notorious in this respect.) But all one need do to test where their fact judgments come from is to compare their fact judgments with non-law trained individuals. Of course it may work the other way at times, that the events may pull and shape the law characterizations. So law-talk glides into the law-fact dialectic. *Feel them in stereo.*

But in all this the important point for our purposes is not

just to consider whether law and facts are or are not separate but to consider the part that *available* verbal characterizations *of* law may play in judgments that are made. The feeling is that one has experience and then puts it into words. It is common to hear someone say, "Well, I know it, but I can't quite put it into words." Even without respectable scholarly support from the likes of Sapir and Whorf and Gestalt psychology, it makes sense to realize that words have something to do with what we see, as do patterns of words, like rules and principles.

Suppose I lay out seven cards from an ordinary playing deck. What one sees in that lay-out depends upon what if any card games-rules he may know. Suppose an Ace, Jack and Nine of Diamonds, Jack and Nine of Hearts, Nine of Spades, and Nine of Clubs. What have we there? A poker player will see four-of-a-kind, four nines, four cards that to a Euchre player are almost totally insignificant. He instead will sort out those cards in the order Jack of Diamonds, Jack of Hearts, Ace of Diamonds, and Nine of Diamonds, as strange as that might seem to a Bridge player or a Gin Rummy fancier. What cards are important is somewhat like knowing what facts are relevant in a law-talkable situation.

"Relevancy" is an interesting word for lawyers to ponder. The tests for what evidence is relevant in the trial of a case are not at all the same as for relevancy in the "reasoning" stages concerning facts and law and how they interrelate. A trial lawyer may want to get in all sorts of evidence, such as the economic status of his client, personality, marital status, character evidence, and so on, none of which is supposed to bear on the "law" of the case. These matters no doubt may influence decisions not only by jurors but by judges, and it is when they are thought to be "unduly" influential, out of proportion, and such, that they must be ignored. Many law teachers in freshman classes spend considerable effort in training their students to separate "the wheat from the chaff" in sizing up cases, even to the point of paring out as irrelevant much that appears in the fact-assertions of judicial opinions, often missing matters, that very likely had some sort of influence (see Garratt Case Analysis, *infra*). If nothing else, and there are many other significant examples along these lines, teaching students that law is "impersonal," that variations in characteristics of people are generally irrelevant, can have *much* to do with a lawyer's attitudes toward his client. It affects what matters he regards as *his* business to consider, what it means to be a *lawyer*, and whether he finds out what the real problems of the client are so that he can handle them in some intelligently balanced way, rather than as a legalized computer. (Next case!)

Relevancy is not just a question regarding facts so far as lawyers are concerned. Whether certain kinds of moral, economic, and sociological, (and so on) kinds of principles (and data too, of course) are relevant in the application of this or that law or in law generally is still a burning sort of question not only in legal theory but in classrooms and courts and throughout the lego-intellectual community. It is not uncommon to see a judicial opinion in which it is said that "the law does not concern itself with morality," which is of course absurd, but at least it means the particular argument was noninfluential and it may mean that moral arguments should be translated into "legal terms" wherever they can. The very distinction between law and nonlaw enters not only as a rhetorical definition (not as "mere rhetoric") but also as an overlay blocking out huge areas of information and attitude forming and reflecting principles and conceptions.

It is not just a matter of rhetoric and clever wording, whether, for instance to distinguish *between* law and facts, or law and policy, law and morality, and so on, because such distinctions go much deeper than definition. (One value of recognizing rhetorical definitional patterns is to locate clues to *such* deeper configurations of attitude, vision, evaluations, predisposition, and so on.) It makes a difference how we slice these matters. The law talk model is not merely a catch expression. (It reflects very much the way *I* see things, for instance. But I am not stuck with it!)

So, whether certain statements that appear in a judicial opinion are law, or fact, or extra-legal is not just a "question of semantics." Whether a court is "talking law" or "about law" or "of law" is not either. If a particular statement is called extra-legal or non-law, we may have a *subtle* or even unconscious influence operating, or an allocation of status and influence to competing verbalisms. To call a policy statement extra-legal may be to promote a theory-position on the way courts should function, perhaps in decision-making, maybe in opinion writing.

We should note that "style" of writing enters even more subtly. When is one writing like a judge or a lawyer? Can a judge or lawyer who does not write like one know his law or know what he is talking about?

My purpose in making these points and distinctions is not to freeze lines in some new way, nor to promote some new conceptualism. Quite the opposite. And . . . it is to change psycholinguistically unhealthy attitudes, if possible. Strict constructionists will object, but that approach, like legalism, is hard to recognize or distinguish in its two forms: propagandistic or character-istic (or both).

In any event, what is law talk in the sense of what lawyers will talk with and about, what sorts of words will fly in law classrooms and in legal commentary, of what is relevant and what *in*-style and what styles there are will change as the days pass by, as they are doing now, perhaps in accelerated fashion.

Some Further Comment on Talk Talk

It sounds so very much like *just theory* (compare "mere rhetoric"): All this talk of what is law, when is it definition, when something else, law talk as something as significant as law (for heaven's sake), whether law has a separate language, do rules really exist, is a dog a fact, is "relevant" really relevant???

Still, if it is theory it is intensely practical. There *is* a lot of theory mixed in there and it may be digestible on its own grounds. Some of the established lego-philosophers may have difficulty with their digestions. But they present only extreme cases of preoccupation with their own word-spaces, relatively disabled from moving around from one area of discourse to another. (Not over the hill, just firmly anchored in the valleys.) Legal philosophy is too valuable to leave rutted, and there are developed in these pages some notions on that sort of plane.

The major difficulty in American legal philosophy today is that it is not communicatively honest! (See The Right Way, *infra*)

A major difficulty in our society today is that we are not communicatively honest. The virtue of the *ideal* of scientific method (compare the politics of science) is that it is communicatively honest. Korzybski made too much of applying science to language in the sense of rigor and structure, but he caught the underlying sickness of communicative dishonesty. So he entitled his Bible: Science and Sanity (Science then Sanity). Truthfulness, not just truth. It is easier to know when one is being truthful than when he has found truth.

Our society is so firmly entangled with mechanisms for camouflaging, distorting, or hiding-from truthfulness, our culture and its institutions (including politics, but also law) so habituated in hiding behind masks and facades, that the average individual is apprehensive of analyses that seem to tear down these facades (legal realisms and their "iconoclasms" were regarded as malevolently subversive by many established academics).

The result is that we must (with respect to communciation) attempt to communicate as best as we can behind these facades. No mere theory will change let alone sweep aside the defensive structures so deeply fortified.

Our aim here is more truthfulness than truth, on the practical theoretical premise that whatever truth is, truthfulness is the only route to it.

And it may seem strange, but the route to truthfulness is not just a matter of being serious. Those facades and other mechanisms of psycholinguistics are themselves taken too seriously, so that some of the time deliberate word play is necessary to reveal them. When it comes to rules, for instance, those who are captivated by their own persuasive-manipulative mechanisms of rule talk can hardly stand analyses that *seem* to deprive them of this major mechanism. But exactly the same sort of problem exists for those who would outright deny the validity-truthfulness of rule talk *at all.* So for different reasons (defend/attack) both advocacies will be bedeviled by something like Show Me A Rule.

But it is talk talk, that dialogue. (For lawyers it is also law-talk talk.) It may look philosophical merely if put in the style which both philosophers and lawyer like so well, some tedious form which supposedly is *per se* objective, rational, valid, and truthful because it is so firmly and dignifiedly stated. Well there is more truth in that dialogue than many people can take.

The question is not what it may seem at all. It is not whether there are rules or not, but for instance, is it truthful on one occasion to deny rules and on another to affirm them. One has to have an especial words consciousness to deal appropriately with that sort of problem. (Truthfulness, sincerity, honesty, good faith.)

Is a dog a fact? Well that must be the most theoretical nonsense since the pin-dancing angels. (How may judges can dance on the head of an opinion?) But it is not just (or even) a theoretical question. That dialogue is another example of talk talk, but even less obviously also one of law-talk talk for lawyers. It is truly a test, for lawyers of their legalism (as is Show Me A Rule) but for anyone of his conceptualistic hang-ups. Legalistic justifications are insincere! Legalistic analysis and reasoning in the privacy of ones thoughts is *self*-deceptive. (To Thine Ownself . . .) But legalism is only a special example of the larger sort of psycho-linguistic attitudes that are shared in varying degrees by every person in this society. (Whatever one may think of Hayakawa's ideological stance, he does seem to be very, very sincere. And he is hated as much for that as anything. The Warren Court was criticized by supposed friends for its truthfulness. So now, back to the insincerities of strict constructionism!)

To put the focus on law talk is at once to open a path toward some new truths and to promote sincere *analyses,* even if it has no impact on the law talk itself. But even more important than that focus is the focus on talk talk and law-talk talk. To appreciate the possibilities of law talk analyses, it is important to be able to engage in talk talk, but beyond that, in order to appreciate the dynamics of any kind of talk.

There has been and will be much talk talk in these pages. But it can seem only theoretical and confusing until the relationship between talk talk and just talk is appreciated (part of taking the leap—a means of taking the leap). Some individuals have had something of the sort of "aha" experience that is needed in the reading of the Rules and Facts dialogues. Even further probing into the multi-dimensionality of communication can be a sensitivity-training sort of group-teaching mechanism into which problems of interpretation and analysis are interjected. We will speak more of this sort of thing in connection with some experimental seminars on Law and Communication in which the Basic Rules were used in a group role-playing in a social microcosm. In this sort of situation, one must be able to use talk, law talk, talk talk, and law-talk talk virtually simultaneously. (No small trick.)

In day to day situations, there are numerous occasions when some sort of mutuality of words consciousness would help the participants in a communication transaction, and certainly that is so in the day to day business of law-talk teaching. Whatever degree of words consciousness exists among the parties can be sometimes energized by questions and comments directed toward problems of interpretation (as and if they are recognized). "Well, now, what does that mean?" or "Let's define our terms," are fairly familiar mechanisms. Another one that is less irritating, not so seemingly quibbling, might be this sort, "Let's see, as I understand it, you are saying that . . . ," during which there is a sort of translation-interpretation feedback in which words-sensitizing is an ongoing part of the transaction. Two person transactions may in one sense be ideal for this sort of effort, although larger groups promote the possibilities that some such feedback would come from someone who sees an interpretative problem. But the larger the group and/or the more formal the situation or otherwise where feedback is inhibited, or possibilities of misinterpretation increased, the less possibility there is for a casual exploration. One literally does not have time/opportunity to spell it all out. But anyone who has tried to go very far in word-sensitizing during some sort of communication transaction where that is not agreed as being on the agenda knows what obstacles there are. It is this clinical sort of data that has convinced me, for instance, that it is important here to make distinctions between talking and talking about talking. Let me spell this out a little more in a way that relates to Show Me A Rule and Has Anyone Seen A Fact.

There are a number of ways of getting into and exploring the "theoretical" conflicts raised in the debate between the viewpoints of H. L. A. Hart and the Rule Skeptics (as he chose to call that aspect of legal realism). But if there is sufficient appreciation of the Hartian viewpoint or if the leader (teacher maybe) of the discussion is sufficiently words-conscious, then one of the problems presented is discussion of the word "rule" itself. It is the very sort of problem which could be interjected into the most practical of discussions, say that between two lawyers negotiating the settlement of a damages claim. One is faced here with the conventions of word use which are buried quite deeply (although not homogenously) in the linguo-psyches of the participants, coming into conflict with an attempt to explore those conventions in a situation in which the rules of those conventional situations do not apply and the new rules of the new exploration situation have not been learned.

At the level of Hartian exploration, for instance, in order to understand his point that the legal realists were from his point of view excessive, you have to see the varied ways that the word "rule" can be used. To see a counter-criticism that

Hart is going only a little way in mixing the new game (word consciousness) with the old, you have to wrestle with the subleties of his rhetoric in merely saying that what was wrong with the Rule Skeptics was that they did not see there were several kinds of rules.

Hart's statement is not a piece of rules talk, but somewhere between that and fully sincere rules-talk talk! Atlhough Show Me A Rule is playful, it is much farther along the road to Rule-talk talk sincerity. (Maybe Hart could now afford to play the game differently. Wittgenstein was one of the most sincere philosophers, the least self-deceptive. This is *not* a reflection on anyone's good faith.)

When one is engaged in rules talk, he is playing a different game, occupying a different perspective-space, in a different role from what he needs to be in when he is playing the rules-talk talk game. Of course, in Show Me A Rule the teacher and the student are playing a game in which it is not really clear who wins, because actually there are several games going on simultaneously. And that is the way linguistic-situations usually are, although with different sorts of games. One may shift role and perspective quite rapidly without even realizing it, but pretty much within the conventionalities of shifting(s). That is why rhetorical definitions work. It is one of the conventional mechanisms! But for the student even to play the teacher's game with the word "rule" he has to gain at least a degree of capacity *and* willingness to recognize the ambiguity of the word "rule" itself. (And to appreciate the possibilities of ambiguity of a given rule. How does that feel?) But the teacher cannot lose that game so long as he is not cornered in a situation where he has to revert to the use of that very word to justify his conduct, shifting from rules-talk talk to rules talk, and then no longer teacher either, although in our dialogue he tries to recoup. The final ploy of the student to question the practicality of it all does not cause the teacher to think he has lost because he goes off into his own possible mistake of believing the student is using that word ambiguously on purpose.

But it is actually difficult to find people who are willing and able to play that game-complex. In a classroom, for instance, a student would find it difficult to follow if a teacher shifted back and forth from rules talk (judges use rules talk in opinions talking with and about specific rules), to talk about rules (in which the definitions established in rules talk are usually manipulated), to rules-talk talk (in which definitions and use of "rule" are explored in one way or another) and back around again, unless he comes to have some feel for the shiftings and/or the skill of simultaneous appreciation. A few have it. Most do not. But they can all be given it, with time and opportunity.

Some such sort of words-consciousness is necessary to appreciation of Has Anyone Seen A Fact, or that part of it asking, "Is a dog a fact?" Some people are able to see the point(s) of this dialogue in a flash, others have difficulty even after effort at explanation. Methinks this some measure of conceptualistic (legalistic) leanings, verbal flexibility, ability (willingness, freedom) to move into new word-function positions, to see how the word "facts" has a linguistic involvement of a special kind. The implications are philosophically and legally quite considerable and important, but at the moment the purpose is more modest, to promote the skill-feeling-capacity for talk talk.

There is a deep socio-linguistic convention (rule? conditioning?) that makes it quite improper in *facts talk* (compare philosophy talk possibilities? what games-conventions are to be followed?) to call a dog a fact or to hook up "dog" with "fact" (compare poetic metaphor). "Fact" as a categorizer does not sub-group "dog" under it. "Animal" and "pet" are two of many words that would allow that subgrouping. There is not that syntactic relationship between "dog" and "fact." Depth grammar says no-no. We do not learn the word "fact" that way. No one points to a dog and says "fact." One does not go to a pet shop and say "I would like a fact," and *that* is a fact. ("What is?")

Lawyers deal in facts, (what does "facts" refer to there,

and/or what use is being made of the word?) but they do not call dogs facts. An investigating lawyer might head up a memorandum by saying "Facts: defendant kept the dog on a leash . . ." He might have at the top "Facts": Then below that "Animals owned by defendant: dog, cat, and two rabbits." This is not an everyday usage, but even it ("Facts":) is not referring to the dog as a fact.

A reasonably intelligent child of eight, or maybe younger, will "know" this convention of facts talk, although he will not be able to explain it. He has learned the rules, as part of his psycholinguistic upbringing. But being able to use correctly the depth grammar of "fact" during facts talk is something quite different from engaging in facts-talk talk.

If one follows through the implications, he understands the law-fact dialectic (and other X-fact dialectics, like rule-fact, etc.). The word "fact" is actually conventionally related most immediately to verbal propositions. The word "fact" is used in various ways to aid in labeling and distinguishing one sort of proposition from another. Necessarily then it can be used in a process of rhetorical definition to route in various ways, to load in various ways, and so on.

Postscript Game: Is It All Just Theoretical? (Another bit of talk talk)

One of the major uses of talk talk is to unload rhetorical definitions, not just in emotive-attitudinal charging but in the use-meaning of a given term in more than one sense simultaneously, in taking advantage of a well-established conventional use to serve as umbrella for a perhaps metaphorical or other sort of situational adaptation. (See earlier analysis of "foreseeable" in chapter on Rhetorical Definitions.)

There have been several occasions in the preceding section when the terms "theory" (or "theoretical") and "practical" have been used. These are terms that occur in certain sorts of communication transactions relevant to our exploration, serving in rather subtle ways to reject, justify, or somehow route attitudes concerning communications analysis. They are famiiar ploys in teacher-student dialogues, and in various sorts of interchanges in the legal profession, possibly between academics and practitioners. Certainly it is legitimate to ask whether this chapter, for instance, is practical, but it is then equally legitimate in this context to ask just what sort(s) of question(s) that is.

"Practical" is, then, a term that can be loaded. (So are "fact," "rule," "etc.") It is often used in rhetorical definition to describe (seemingly describe) a state of affairs, or a technique, or a discussion. There are agreed references for the word, but the loading it gains in those situations can be used to attempt to charge some one such situation which is being "described." The opposite loading can be attempted (imposed) with its sometimes opposite, "theoretical." In some situations, the latter loader is negative with respect to what is being discussed. It rejects. One might be somewhat more sincere by saying, "What you offer is not good for my purposes" (desires, wants, attitudes). Or one might stay at the same level by saying, "It will not work in the real world." Or IT'S NOT RELEVANT! Of course in some scenes the loadings are reversed, where it is regarded as good to be theoretical, and maybe bad to be practical. ("Lawyers are just technicians.")

> As a practical matter, talk-talk is doing, not just talking. Delve into the available conventions:

By and large, it is practical (sensible, usual) for a lawyer to go swimming in a swimming suit, but not to court, at least not to argue a cause before a judge, usually. It is not practical (sensible, possible) to try to walk a mile in four minutes. Theoretically (according to law), children on your land without your consent are trespassers, but as a practical (worthwhile) matter, who is going to sue them? It does no good to theorize (*just* talk about) a problem, you have to attack it in a practical (workable) manner. Lawyers, doctors, and politicians are practical. They do things. (Compare a legal theory teacher, or almost any law teacher who just teaches. "I mean, teaching is not doing anything. The classroom is not real.") A child playing with a toy is doing something, but we would not say he is being practical. "Well, but lawyers and doctors are doing worthwhile things in ways that work." The child's playing is worthwhile and good for him, but he is no model, that's all, for anyone else but another child.

It is practical for a lawyer to go to court and argue the law of his case, but it would not make much sense to tell his four-year-old son how he argued the case, for it is too theoretical (*over his head*, beyond his capacity). To talk about Wittgenstein in court is too theoretical (even though judges are not four years old). To talk depth grammar to law students is *too* theoretical. (Why?) You can and should, if you want to, be able to show its relevancy, but first you have to overcome the slogans and the cry of resistance, the organizing of resisters, very subtly effected in a soft suggestion that something being said is not practical.

So, is it practical or relevant to talk-talk rules and facts, for instance?

(And let sincerity roll out fully: See how talk talk can itself be used to grind an axe. Is there any way around that?)

CHART #4

WORD (form) GAMES ⟶ at three levels: Level_1: Everyday talk and law talk
(wg's) Level_2: Theory talk
Level_3: Talk talk
involving communication { transactions (ct) within / situations (cs) } at each level

A. Level_1: ct_1-cs_1: two college students	HIT word-form: abstract, no meaning
1. He hit her. She hit him, causing him to hit the floor. She was a real hit, believe me. (everyday talk)	He [H] her. She [H] him, causing (H) him to /H\ the floor. She was a real (H), believe me.

(cf. hit_1, hit_2, hit_3)

Comment: the form HIT–cf. "hit"–is available for use in numerous different ways. Verbal context here easily helps identify word-game (wg) involved.

	REAL
2. He is a real nice guy, and what he did was not a real hit, really	He is a [R] nice guy, and what he did was not a /R\ (H), (R) ly.

Comment: see also "real" in #1, yet another variant. *Cf.* 1

	WORD
3. He said the wrong word to her, but I told him off before she hit him. "You gave him the word, eh?" Huh!?	He said the wrong [W] to her, but I (W) told him off before she [H] him. "You gave him the (W), eh?" Huh!?

Comment: a word can be used in more than one way simultaneously, which is yet a third use, if intended. A split-screen like phenomenon–like seeing two moving pictures on the same screen.

	IS
4. J is going. J is the girl's name. But the rule is clear. She is crazy to go.	J [I] going. J (I) the girl's name. But the rule /I\ clear. She \I/ crazy to go.

Comment: a dictionary does not catch such variations: Deeper down in the syntax, below the surface grammar.

	RULE
5. The University rule is clear enough, but fortunately there may be a legal rule which could be invoked in her favor.	The University [R] is(?) clear enough, but fortunately there may be a legal (R) which could be invoked in her favor.

Comment: the second use of RULE is different because it invokes the law talk syntax. Further it is not asserted as binding or clear. It takes much rule-wg experience to reach that capacity.

B. E↔F in $(\text{ct-cs})_2$–within "real" ct (you-me) cs. (split-screen)

1. Did she have a right to go? 2. "Well, she has a (legal) right because there is a rule of law in her favor." 3. What is that? 4. "The University rule is unconstitutional." 5. Well, if that is so, it is not really a rule.
(Try it out. What wg's, what levels? Tracing R/D's helps.) See following. Subscripts used, but same approach as above (A).

ANALYSIS:

#1. The word-form right likely used in particular way by E. If lawyer, might well mean legal right. If not, or even so, might have another sense "in mind." As it stands, a split-screen use ($\text{right}_{1,2,3}$)

#2. If F using right_1 (i.e., legal), a specific use at level_1 of law talk. Made clearer if he were to use "legal." (cf. " "=word-form) If he does not use "legal," then may be $\text{right}_{1,2}$ or right_1 or 2, etc. Whether or not F is a lawyer, "there is a rule of law in her favor" is a piece of law talk.

#3. Another piece of law talk!

#4. Ditto

#5. ". . . not really a rule." "Real" is viable at level_1 and/or 2. Can be used subtly in rhetorical definition to slip from first level of rule talk to second level of rule-theory talk. Not clear what quoted excerpt is: just as one word may be used in two senses simultaneously, so one may operate at two levels at once. A whole assertion can also be split-screen. (See chapter 8).

CF.
"The University rule is a rule whatever the law."= Rule talk@level_1.

"It is not a valid rule if contra to the Constitution."= law talk@level_1.

At level_2 of theory talk: "A University rule_1 is not a rule_2 unless it is supported by a legal rule_3." (redefines "rule.")

CF.
To break a legal R is a breach of morality. "Oh come now. L and M are separate phenomena." (theory level wg's)

Chapter V

(UN)STRUCTURING (")WORDS(")–SPLIT SCREENS

Sensitivities for Levels of (")Words(")and(")Rules(")*

IF IT WERE NOT FOR the rules of grammar, and punctuation, we could say, "(')Rules(') are ambiguous." (Well, we could not *say* that, actually.) "Rules" *is* ambiguous, and that allows for persuasive, manipulative, and creative definitional rhetoric in the name of rule. So there is a degree of freedom in the way the word gets affixed or associated.

We have the interesting problem of trying to see how the word gets used, and *for that purpose* we should be as uninhibited as possible, not asking "Is it being used properly?" or whether, for instance, the "thing" which is being called a rule, "really *is* a rule."

But then we have the other perplexing problem of looking at rules themselves, the statements which we for one purpose or another accept as rules. As one looks at each such statement, which is verbal, and tries to decide what it is good for, or how it can be (ab)used, he probably can move it around *in his mind*, and see how it might operate. Even as he moves it around in this hypothetical sort of way (and what a powerful form of manipulation that technique is) he sees there may be some problems of fit, where the words *within* the rule are not altogether clear, and so on. We could say it is ambiguous. But in moving it around in his mind in this fashion, he probably will have no appreciation at all for the problems that arise for this rule in the *real world*. Then the question comes up: does this rule fit the situation, i.e. the facts (before there

* First see comments on this chapter in Directory.

are any facts, before they are frozen, for real and certain, although he may think he has the facts in mind, thus missing the very problem of fitting.) There are very few people who can quite *see* what is being driven at.

Now in this fitting-room situation, as we have said, not only does the rule get cut to size, but so do the facts. (Everyone is so mutually accommodating.) But one who is really sensitive to words will see there is another way of putting that. Whatever we finally state as the rule here, and the facts there, is not really what we started with. (It is equally possible that what is *stated* is not what was ended-with.) The legalist-literalist will simply regard these statements as nonsense, academic pfaff. This is not something that can be readily spelled out *to see*, indeed, it literally cannot be spelled out, because what happens is rather between or behind or somewhere out of sight. (But much more will be said about it anyway.) In the material on Interpretation, where we explore how-one-deals with the written word (s), we will hit this harder, but so out of sight is the process, it could well be stated in a number of different ways and places. (That does not say "could be well stated . . .")

Whatever we start with—or end with—whatever is frozen in the written form ("The rule in this case is as follows: . . ."), or whatever is emphasized in the oral form, as the relevant rule, etc., turns the lights off the interpretative process, which may have been purely in the head of the interpreter-applier, or now lost in the flurry of interpersonal dynamics. The now out-of-sight interpretative dynamics make what is there in writing (or in $sound_1$) look ($sound_2$) different, but there is nothing there in the writing (or the sounds which are now gone) to call attention to the ways in which it looks different. (This *is* all very $sound_3$.) Is it here or there, or somewhere in between (,) the meaning of those words?

Summary: What we *call* a rule is not self-executing. It is not ever as automatic as it may sometimes seem. The interpretative process is part of whatever communications dynamics are involved in the application of that rule, and there are always some such dynamics.

So the statement we have called a rule, or *the* rule, is not operating in the way that it probably seems to be operating. So while you may show me a $rule_1$ (in the sense of a *statement* which might conventionally be called a rule—legitimate rule-talk, that is), you cannot show me a $rule_2$ (in the way it is conceived in talking *about* rules). You see, what gets in the way here is the theory about rules. In that theory-talk *about* rules, the word "rule(s)" is not used in the same way(s) that the word "rule(s)" is used when, say a judge is explaining his court's decision. That is a comparatively easy point to see, but the implications are absolutely out of sight.

PAUSE: In the last paragraph, three levels of convention get in the act. There is much of rule-talk talk, but the conventions of rule talk may get in the way, and those of theory-talk *about* rules. The word "rule(s)" was being used unconventionally relative to either rule talk or theory talk about rules. We are not playing the games, if you will, of rule talk or of theory-talk *about* rules, although we are referring to them. Reference to the conventions of the way "rule(s)" is gamed with in rule talk (of judges, and lawyers, and such) by the symbol-notation of rule is all right, but how the word is used in rule talk must actually be checked out when one is playing in those games, *if you will.* (Editor, note the pun, (")if you will(").) Thus, the word rule in rule-talk talk is not quite the same, indeed quite different, from the word rule actually used in a piece of on-the-scene rule talk ($rule_3$ v. $rule_1$).

(If any reader thinks this is hard to get, just stop to reflect how hard it was to get it in just that way.)

Then came reference to rules within the conventions of theories. I am not referring here merely to up-in-the-clouds theory, and not necessarily even to the kind of theory that jurisprudes put out. There is some time or another when most anyone engages in this theory, when he talks about rules in a different sort of game. The jurisprude is clearly playing different games with the word "rule" ($rule_2$), but so is Joe-in-the-street when he gets to saying that those "Damned students ought to be made to obey the rules." ($rule_4$) Now he is not very likely to appreciate that he is a theorist at that point, relative to the situations in which the students are located. He is using his theory-assumptions, maybe in some very practical way relative to his situation, and may come to have influence on the way rule talk proceeds in those student-situations. (Remember that we did some parsing with "theoretical" and "practical," so we are not just $playing_2$ with those words.) Joe is not aware of his rhetorical definitions, but he knows how to do it, he knows the different sense of rules, he can $play_1$ that game, that word "$rule_1$" is in his vocabulary, although he would not list it as a different word, certainly, nor as even a different sense. The dictionary will not list this sense of the word "rule" at all. It is out of sight and hearing. It is (a) non-sense, we might want to say, unless we are ready, willing, and able to engage in rule-talk talk and theory-talk talk simultaneously, so to speak (write) (right?).

The jurisprude *ought* to be able to realize that he is using "rule" in a way different from the way that even he does when he is engaging in pure rule talk, that when he is engaging in theory talk he cannot, simply cannot, use "rule" in the same way as it is used in pure rule talk, when one has committed himself to that (rule talk) action. The jurisprude's theory-talk constitutes a commitment to a different action. Now just because he cannot see that, or will not allow himself to see that, for whatever psycho-linguistic defensive sort of reason, or just because Joe cannot or will not see that, does not mean it does not happen. Korzybski, Wittgenstein, and Austin (for instance) made it clear enough (multiordinality, word-games, and doing-things-with-words, respectively). While we might excuse Joe, there is really no excuse for the jurisprude, but we can pass him by, although we cannot, of course, ignore him. And we can try to help him locate himself in communicative space-time so that he will talk a little more to the point of reality. (*Rule-skeptics included.*)

Before we started this "Pause:" we were not engaging in rule-talk, but only referring to it by "$rule_3$." Someone might want to say we were engaging in theory-talk, but it was not rule-theory talk, because we are calling attention to the different senses of "rule" in a way that just does not occur in the conventions (really so conventional, even in the radicalism of Jerome Frank and Fred Rodell and other such rule-skeptics. Really!) of rule-theory talk. We are trying to locate in a different portion of psycho-linguistic space-time, (and) *if you will* (please do) (Does that explain it, Editor?) (Editor, please note that the last parenthesis encloses a statement that refers to what just preceded and also to a previous parenthetical in the first paragraph of this "Pause":)

It can be quite fascinating (if at first numbing) to realize that one can take a word like "rule" (and what word isn't, "is," for instance) and refer to several other locations in psycho-linguistic space-time simultaneously while one is standing and doing something in his own portion of it without anyone truly appreciating what is going on. Celestial motions are like that, relatively speaking. (Certainly you get that one, Editor, meaning not the pun, but the way that this parenthetical refers to *several* previous parentheticals to help explain them and demonstrate the relativity also. That may seem quite a load for one parenthetical, but I believe I once saw a rule that carried at least as much of a load when it was being moved without seeming to, because it just seemed to sit there on the page.)

Put it this way: When the teacher plays the game of Show Me A Rule, he cannot be caught in the verbal tag game except by someone who can play at rule-talk, rule-theory talk, and rule-talk talk (which we are playing) and rule-theory-talk talk (which we are probably playing too), all at once and one at a time.

On the other hand, whoever it is that is leading the Has Anyone Seen a Fact game wants to be caught (the professor in the other game wants to be followed, of course), but seems to be trying to *avoid* fact-theory talk.

Both these dialogues have implications for and will inevitably be psycholinguistically located as jurisprudential. (I hope so, anyway, but not too soon, please, before other appropriate locations are screened out, before those screens are dimmed—Editor, do you see....)

Just stop to think of this. The word "rule" may be a lot like the word "fact" after all. The dialogue on (")fact(s) (") show that "facts" refers by way of other words or maybe *only* to other words, even though we do (and properly) say "the facts are ..." (That is a convention.) Or, "the rules are ..." (another convention). We can say that facts are out there and rules are out there, but who does say that? It is the sort of thing a rule-theorist might say or a fact-theorist or a legal-theorist. We will stress it for the sake of theory, but also for the sake of preserving rules-talk and facts-talk, and for the sake of clarifying what we are after in this talk talk. (Go ahead, it may help. When you read something like rules-talk, run your hand through a plane at about knee level, meaning an imaginary plane, of course; then for theory-talk, another plane above it, and for rules-talk talk, yet a plane above that, to get not only visualization-feeling, but also a sense of relative importance. It is of relativity importance.)

So, rules are! (from rules-talk). And rules are not! (from rules-theory talk). And they can both make sense here even without subscripts.

But the word "rules" does not have the same sort of out there reference that "facts" does, because there is nothing out there for it to refer to. But you will have trouble convincing Joe-on-the-street of that, and probably should not, for the sake of Law.

The legalist will have had trouble because this talk talk blows his absolutes out of sight. But the rule skeptic-cynic should watch out for painful splinters too. Rules do exist, as everyone knows, even Joe-on-the-street in his theory-assumptions, because of his rule talk capacity. Sure, you can "show me a rule," but not the kind that will satisfy the skeptic-idealist. But we must be concerned about this skeptic because he may miss the messages and not be able to engage in talk talk sorts of explorations and to improve his own communication techniques because he read too fast to see we were in some ways disagreeing with him. The thing for him to do is to go back over that material substituting some other word, maybe like fact, policy, values, or whatever. (Well, not "whatever," however— Dear E . . ., what can I do?) There is a place for absolutes, for everyone talks in them (absolutely everyone) when he is within his favorite kind of talk. Even in talk talk they are not absolutely avoidable.

Summary: (")Rule(s) (") is/are ambiguous (E . . .)!

Post-summary: Because I do not merely$_1$ want to confuse, let me merely$_2$ mention another important thought. We have mainly explored some of the ramifications of the "rules"-family. But the statements we call rules are themselves susceptible of movement through the planes and dimensions we have drawn-out. What we can and do (do) with single words can and is done with a collection of words. If a rule is anything (E . .), it is a collection of words.

Tolerance to Ambiguities—in Games and Metaphors—E

There has been discovery of the ambiguity of "rules" by H. L. A. Hart, but faint recognition by him of the ambiguity of rules. The legal realists discovered the ambiguity of rules, but failed to appreciate the ambiguity of "rules." Naturally, it is time that someone put these things (E . .) together.

Hart has contributed much of value and provocation to scholars of law as a result of his insight which he used but did not pass on to his audience(s) (who thus proceed to play different games on the planes of legal theorydom). One of his most important contributions has been to tell us there is more than one kind of legal rule. Professor Rawl made quite an impact by writing about just "Two Kinds of Rules." But they were not interested in overall communications insights. Not at all. In the name of Analysis (we will poke around in that some more too) they were engaging in persuasive/manipulative/creative rhetoric, justifying rules (and "rules") and certain kinds of judgments they wished to move in the name of Rules. (And they might have lost their persuasiveness if they gave away the game, if they really appreciated it themselves.)

What they were doing may be all right for their ends, but not good enough or right enough for ours.

Of course, there is more than one kind of legal rule! As Hart said, there are rules for citizens. There are rules for judges and some of different kinds for other officials, none of which apply *to* citizens as such, although there are rules that allow the citizens to invoke the rules that obligate judges, to invoke those rules against the judges on behalf of the invokers or someone other than the judges. (Although it could be done for a judge not wearing his judge hat.) Then there are rules that tell us what purported rules are valid and of what scale of priority. There are rules that invoke obligations and correlative rights. And there are rules that create powers for private citizens to use to act in this or that fashion, say to enter into a contract, and in that fashion engage in their sort of private-legislative capacity to create rights and duties among themselves in such fashion as will be re-enforced by the courts because of the rules of contract and of procedure, and so on. (E. ., do you think we need to supply the subscripts in there?)

Of course, there is more than one kind of legal rule, but does anyone notice that Hart may have tried to create some new conventions, at least for rule-theory talk, although actually he said little that has not been said before in the era of the legal realists. They were not so elegant nor so conserv-ative. (Realizing this *finally*, after several years of perplexity, I have finally seen why some of those who follow Hart and purport to be knowledgeable *re* the likes of Wittgenstein and Hart will resist seeing that these philosophers have something to contribute to communication theory and that necessarily so did the legal realists. I had naively assumed they were interested in discovery rather than just intellectual-ecological conservation. I would like to suggest that we try to know more about our communications ecology, to know what to save and how to progress. The analogy is really quite appropriate.)

Of course, there is more than one kind of legal rule! Many, many more. We have no choice in that so long as we use words-in-language the way(s) we do. And there is no choice in the latter respect either, not in everyday sorts of talk, not in law talk either. Yet these sorts of insights present problems because of the risk that we come to think of rules in just the games sense and that in the play sense, rather than the "games people (must) play" sense. We get to thinking that people ought not to play games with serious matters. Is there a better metaphor than "game," or than "rule"? (How about "talk.") Maybe we could play with metaphors to advantage. (Haven't we?)

When a metaphor comes to be seen as a fiction, it is on the way out of law talk. To call legal constructs "fictions" is to (try to) insult them (via rhetorical definitional loading). The line between metaphor and fiction is thin. "Rule" is used fictionally, but it is also used construct-ively, metaphorically, and as a model.

There is a real need to think of legal rules as real. Really! There is a compulsive sort of need for the legalist to justify his judgments, decisions, and behavior that way(s), but there is need for the sake of LAW, to be able to have a level of reality. As we have said (explored), not all legal rules (so-called) exist on the same level of reality (communicative-coordinates vary). Even the rules which might be said to be on the same plane are not all of the same kind. We have some control over the level and the kind, *at least* in the rhetorical respect(E) (,) given to the status of some particular rule offering(E). (Dear Editor, I may have forgotten to tell you that E is a sign to you that I know there is more than one message in what preceded. E = Dear Editor . . . .)

The legalist would, no doubt (E), want to have some rules to settle the matter, but since the words will not sit still, nor the rules either, he sh(o)uts *out* the diversity of reality. Some people get so bamboozled by this sort of thing they try to declare bankruptcy against the whole rule-establishment(E), throw the baby into the drink, so to speak (E). The legal realists tried to kill the baby, it almost seems. The thing to do is to kill it with kindness, when appropriate. Treat it with understanding. (E) (Dear Editor, do you suppose these parentheticals are appreciated (E)? Someone will maybe think they are diverting, without realizing that their own private thoughts may be diverting, sort of a second, but silently flickering screen, in the communicative process where the split-screen principle has always been operating (E).)

Rhetorical definitions (and metaphoring) work best with silent metaphors. "Rules," for instance, has been loaded, punned upon and sat upon. It has gone through a metaphor-misis, like all great words. It is a meta-form for all the family of words called "rule." Every word comes in families. Surely, "rule" in rule-of-thumb is not the same as "rule" in rule-of-law. (Modifiers serve as subscripts.) But even in the sometimes separate word-domain of law talk, "rule" has sired a great many offspring of its own.

"Rule" and the lega-list (E) of rules rule not only the legalist, but the norm-alist as well (,) as it can (,) try (,) as it will. (Well, of course, E. Compare: Three meat-cattle farmers, of the same father who named them each Ray, called their Texas ranch Focus because that is where the Sun's Rays Meat.) Well, how do you right that? If you spell it$_2$ out you may get it$_1$ better, but you do not have it$_2$ any more. Analysis kills the pun and the baby (if they get thrown out with the bath).

Enuf? (That sounds funny backward.)

That sort of thing may be bad but it could be worth—a great deal, believe it or not, in the realization that that sort of thing goes on in some much worse ways, but operating (too) silently. This is one of the ways to try to help prove the subtle ambiguities of "rule" and other words and word-complexes. There is need for a programmed course of instruction on achieving sensitivity and tolerance for and to ambiguities (six being about as much as the average person can take). It is funny but it is (al)most (im)possible to bring many people to the edge of sanity, (E), regarding the ways of words and rule words (E) because perhaps of the fear of ambiguity, especially in law.

Well, law talk may be ambiguity-ridden, but not law nor

legal rules. If I cannot even show you a real legal rule, then I can hardly show it to be ambiguous. Or if it were ambiguous, it could hardly be a rule. This must all prove some-thing.

(The end is in-sight.)

Coordinating Through Words

The preceding sections of this chapter may have seemed a bit unstructured (maybe even confusing?). But the purpose is to get to a level of understanding and appreciation of communciation-behavior that is reflected or maybe even concealed in the structured facades of word-and-other-forms. To use Korzybski's figure of speech, it is partly a matter of tearing up the old maps and preparing some new ones, or learning better to read the old ones.

Imagine a play in which the actors wore undetectible masks, which they exchanged with each other between scenes. It might be confusing, until some new reference points were established by voice quality or what have you.

Communication is rarely as orderly as we somehow make it out to be. Many a novel, for instance, will tell us what is on somebody's mind when he speaks or thinks (or on the minds of *all* the characters). But in real life, one is constantly guessing what is, or even who is behind that mask or the flurry of words (or crypticism). Examine the next conversation and plot out what really takes place, including all the bodily movements and all the rest, the thoughts you have, with some blank spaces for the thoughts others are having. Maybe one can draw a line from beginning to end, but then maybe he has missed something. Most of us are not as good observers as the novelists are of their characters.

The statute, a judicial opinion, what have you, look so orderly and organized as they sit there, but plot out all the other variables that enter into their uses. In a little bit we will tear at a judicial opinion, exposing the chaos within its radiations, but showing all the same how a route may be steered through it, all the better for recognizing its many dimensions and facets.

Of course, the easier method is to let one's self be piloted by the communicator, letting him worry about the navigation. That works often, yet there are many times when he does not know where he is going (let alone where he has been), or he makes it appear (maybe innocently enough) that he is heading in a direction different from the one he takes. One may still have trust in the pilot, and yet there are times and role-places and situations (say for a lawyer, a scientist, or even just an independent thinker) when blind or careless following or riding along is not enough. Not even for reading a judicial opinion—it just will not do for understanding much of anything about law except at superficial levels. And it will not do for one who is trying to improve either his observational or interpretative skills regarding all sorts of communications.

So what is going on here is simultaneously some explanation about verbal communication along with some demonstration which is aimed at promoting sensitivity (if there is tolerance) for the fantastic complexity of word roles-functioning. *The written form gets in the way* of understanding how communication with the written form takes place! (or at least the usual written forms, especially those by lawyers, philosophers, and behavioral scientists.) You cannot just say, "Be sensitive with words"; or "Well, words are ambiguous and look more closely," or, that metaphoric extension is the most common route of verbal growth.

It is very difficult to bring this sort of sensitivity into even the more realistic levels of communication, say in the conversational setting. I say more realistic because there is better chance to observe, even if one is not expert at it, in that sort of setting, some of the clues which are not so readily detectable (or are absent) in the written forms. A trainer would have to break into the conversations somewhere, although a video-tape replay makes the task easier. (We here are a bit limited in that potential.)

Maybe, just maybe, one way is to jar the sensibilities of the reader, out of the ordinary ruts. But there is no doubt in the world that anyone willing to adopt the trainee role will simply not be able to "get there" just from the stimulus of these or any other written forms which cannot, repeat cannot, duplicate for the reader his other life situations. And it is there that one must do the real practicing, experimenting, observing, testing, what have you. (He should be careful, though, lest he be thought mad, paranoid, hallucinating, troublesome, quibbling, or a lawyer.)

And it goes slowly, with only little pieces of success. But seeming frustration when analyzed may produce the real successes, checking out where communication went wrong, for instance.

Now some of the real life situations involve just reading and thinking (hopefully thinking). Or writing. The lack of feedback makes this a more difficult effort, but just consider the possibilities of analysis in the dialogue form (as demonstrated), where more than one role or viewpoint is adopted. One may think he has to be schizoid, but of course that is not so, if one will just observe himself in various settings, to see how differently he acts, what different masks he uses, what varying roles he adapts, how he is forced into these variations by the personalities and dynamics and varying goals and motivations of differing situations. Then he may recognize that even within the confines of a given situation, with its separable episodes, that he may be doing some varying. He can see that in others as well. Then maybe he can detect what is harder to detect, how he actually takes words and defines them (by rhetorical defining, metaphoring, etc.) in sometimes strikingly varying ways, partly because the use is different, but partly because the demands of the situation are different. Whether this ever involves lack of honesty or sincerity, he will have to decide for himself, but there is, after all, a "politics" to word use.

Then he comes to realize that the Wittgensteinian figure of speech regarding "word games" is absolutely accurate. So far as verbal analysis is concerned, it is the key in-sight. Along with this way-of-looking at words, goes the Austinian-based, look-to-see-what-is-being-done-with-the-word(s). This sort of thing can go only slowly, but already (,here,) there have been numerous efforts to demonstrate the reality of it, doubtless the aspect that is most confusing when it is pointed out. Korzybski's subscript device is one of the best mechanisms for keeping track. One may write out some short analysis and then go back and put in the subscripts. The revelations can be very surprising. Or one can put a "suspicious" word in quotes, even if he is not sure how to plot it out. That helps in sticking to the business of finding word loadings, and the more subtle routings. It is the habit of taking-for-granted what one sees that simply gets in the way of more careful observing and analyzing. Almost anything which breaks up the habituation is helpful, even a pun. (After all, it was good enough for Shakespeare and it is well used by judges.)

These varying pieces of sensitivity can add up into the most difficult bit of on-the-spot analysis-perception. (The hyphen device is very useful too, to show how word categorizers separate and slice wholes into parts, so that one may see with the aid of the hyphen the whole and the part both at once. It is a useful psycho-linguistic mechanism.) This involves what has been called locating one's self (or someone else) in psycholinguistic space-time. Such has been one of the functions of the preceding analysis which slices across the traditional mappings, to allow and/or promote contact with law talk and talk talk and all kinds of talk. Whether it is a basic or second level insight for such purposes, it is important to realize that a word or set of words (to the extent that they refer at all, as one possible function) do not really ever just refer in one direction or have relationships in just one direction. This is an at least *four* dimensional matter (more likely six or more, to take account also of the mind, psychic, intellectual senses). We have gone into some of that (and will do it some more) with words like "law," "rule," and "fact." These words may each have some special relational-referential involvements, but there is nothing unique about their general multi-dimensional relatedness. (Korzybski captured part of this with the notion of multiordinality of words.)

Those who are familiar with legal interpretational problems, or really any interpretational problems, will readily recognize that they must always go through some sort of coordinate locating process, not only to see where this or that (set of) word(s) sits, but to see what the implications are of its relationships with other words in its context, its history, as well as other aspects of its larger environmental context and history. Those who would suggest that somehow analysis is completely separate from interpretation fail to see that some authority's analysis of a situation involves a sort of map which may or may not be accurate, and which, in any event, itself needs interpreting. Thus, one who tells us what a particular judicial opinion "stands for " is doing some sort of a job of relating the opinion (some or all of it) to other aspects of the communications' ecology. Very often, what seems an empirical report or a description of reality, is "really" (look back in this section to see how that word has been used) a proffered map which amounts to a stipulation or other sort of large scale rhetorical defining, to serve as the analyst's interpretation by which the audience is thereafter supposed to guide itself. We are back at the question whether or not to follow this particular pilot.

Verbal Construct-ing

So being words-conscious is not just a matter of being skeptical or cynical, although it can feed that sort of need. It may just as well fit the desire for sincerity or some higher form of idealism. One might conclude that extreme words-consciousness drives one to see only marks on the page or sounds in the air. If that becomes the predominant message, then indeed it is time to turn off, although an occasional awareness of that kind may be beneficial. Sometimes that is all some words amount to. (But may we now say that the word "word" is subtly ambiguous, so that surely being conscious of words somehow amounts to much more than being aware of marks and sounds, but these aspects of "words" should not be excluded from awareness.)

There is a sense in which words-consciousness makes for

some disappearing act, causing meaning to float away, rules to crumble, persuasion to turn sour. That certainly would not always be desirable, but such risks are sometimes part of the gamble of being careful or wise. After all, there may be a given situation when one is completely skeptical of legal rules. They just are not there, but to be created or even pretended. At another time one may not feel or wish to believe in that fashion. If that somehow seems absurd, inconsistent, or dishonest, remember that it is only in this or that intellectual fabrication that words come tied together. Words are only tools. But to act as if rules were real, even if not fully believed is not an unusual sort of behavior, certainly not for lawyers, but not for life generally. (Trust and faith have *something* to do with it all.) And now once again, look at that word "real" and realize (but there *is* an insight there) the levels and gradations of reality, partly because of the way (s) in which we involve ourselves with (")reality("). Just consider the degrees that enter along the spectrum from full certainty about what one *observes*, through lessening percentages of probability to possibility to . . . (incidentally, this device is legitimate, just as Korzybski's use of Etc. after every sentence where he wanted to show there was *always* more to be said; and then he used a comma after a sentence instead of Etc.,). And consider the variations involved in describers, emotive-words, and varying kinds of abstract conceptuals, like "rule" and "fact," just for instance., In law talk and law-theory talk and even in talk talk of various kinds we have fictions, models, metaphors, constructs., There is a use of language which seems to have only a logical reality (validity, we may wish to say, to distinguish from the fact-kind of reality).

Perhaps the most notable example for consideration is the corporation. In a law talk perspective, that is accepted as a legal entity, real in that sense, talked about that way. We speak of corporate personality, but whether fiction or metaphor or model or construct (the line-classifier is not always easy or necessary to draw), there are times when the figure fades, when the "corporate veil" is pierced, as it is sometimes put. There are many other examples, but this one alone shows how law talk may have some overlap in its construction with mathematics, or philosophy, or even poetry. (Pierce the veil indeed.)

Or take the commonly accepted sort of formulation that in order to have a binding contract, there must be the following: offer + acceptance + consideration = contract. What sort of behavior will make up these components is in some way indeterminate, but the formulation seems to take on the aspects of logic or mathematics. It is not fictional in that sense, although obviously it can be fictionally used, as even logic or mathematics can be. Of course, the legal realists simply hit harder what many others were also saying, that law talk was overly quasi-mathematical. But can you even have any conception of rule which somehow binds without its having some quasi-mathematical aspects? Even $1 + 1 = 2$ is not automatically applicable, when it comes, as it must sooner or later, to determining whether the logico-mathematical operables have been operated in some "real world" correlations sense. Do an apple and an orange equal two? Well, two what . . .? But numbers are not completely distinctive from words (numbers have some word-aspects, and words have some number-aspects) and lego-mathematical or lego-logical formula can be, have been, and will be used. (And Korzybski said words were multi-ordinal, as is x in $x^3 - 2x^2 + 3 = 0$.)

It helps a great deal to be able to say when law talk is being used in a lego-mathematical or some other way! That is part of what is involved in being words conscious. Yet it ought not to be the death of an operation simply to say it involves "pure logic." Still, an exercise in pure or supposed logic ought not to be able to stand on some other base (or behind some other facade). So Felix Cohen was wrong in suggesting that any piece of law talk which could not be "cashed-in" for verifiable, sense-experience sort of data should be declared bankrupt, but right in saying that there ought to be some justification for it. For Cohen, that justification lay in the realm of values or ethics (or social policy). He did not make clear just how he was going to avoid absolutely all legal constructs, metaphors, fictions, models and . . . . Those who today opt for some completely journalistic sort of law talk where all that has to be present is some articulation of policy ground which they can accept or debate are standing at the doors which Cohen and others opened but shunning the hard job(s) of analyzing what sorts of jobs law talk must be amenable to, and what forms it ought to take.

There is just no way for law to retain *anything* of traditional forms of operation, and there is no way for there to be any kind of communication, without general propositions that somehow can be frequently used without the sort of empirical verification which Cohen required. At one level of consideration these may be rules, or principles, or . . .; certainly in law talk itself. We may want to call them something else at the level of law-theory talk. At the level of talk talk, one job is to see what is happening at these other levels. That is an *empirical* task.

When we accept that perspective of trying to see how words are being used, then the question becomes, for instance, not are rules of law just like (or much like, or barely or not at all like) rules of games, but when is the word "rule" used in law talk by way of analogy or as a metaphorical extension of "rules" in the rules-of-games formulation. Maybe it would be worth while to check out the etymological history of the word "rules" to see how it got into the vocabularies of law talk and of law-theory talk, but even if "rules" of law talk were to have preceded "rules" of games etymologically, it would not be true that these senses would not merge in some area or situation or another. (The sort of thing we shall discuss further in exploring a related sort of problem concerning the so-called law-morality relationships.) But in this process of exploration, we may discover something more about the different sorts of rules that operate in law, some being more like this sort of games-rules. Those sorts of variations are simply a self evident sort of starting hypothesis when one is even slightly conscious of the way words-in-language work. (And note the further beauty of the Wittgenstein language-games metaphor, for it suggests that there may in some of those games, if not most, be some sort of so-called rules operable.)

So we can draw out of this sort of realization that the word "rules" inevitably gets worked in metaphor-misis in law talk and in law-theory talk. (Now recognize that there are lines of communication between these two levels of talk.) We can say to the legalist, "Look, there are times when you take your metaphors too seriously." Even if we went all the way with our legalist in seeing rules or laws like (metaphoric extension) the laws of nature and the operations of those laws in the ways of science, maybe we could open up his clinchers by pointing out that a science of law simply could not be the same as any physical science, for to speak of a science of law is metaphoric also.

Words are not *just* marks or sounds, but at least that. Oh how angry some one may be to hear, "Rules are just words." But they are at least that, and . . . . We like to think of words as more than marks or sounds, at least as referring outside of themselves, to things, for instance, and of rules as more than words, as referring to, in some controlling way, situations. Still, words and rules (and laws, regulations,) refer in such ways only if people let them, for as marks or sounds no one can be forced *by them* (except he be hypnotized or conditioned) to treat them as more than marks or sounds.

We are supposed to act as if words had meaning. Well of course they do. That is the purpose of words. If "had" were followed by an E, would that be distracting? Yet there is metaphoric ambiguity there. If words have meaning, it is not in the way that a bull has horns. We follow words or *react* to them by doing something, maybe thinking only. There seems to be some sort of energizing of the cerebral-computer. (Is some other part of the human system involved too?) Whoever provides the words has done something, providing at least potential stimuli, something to react to, to think about, or think and act with., "His words indicate what was on his mind" we may want to say. But all we have are his words, and he does not retain control of them (as marks and sounds, and certainly whatever more . . .), for now we invest those marks and sounds with meaning. But there may be *clearly* more than one meaning and never only one. (Every sentence could be followed by an E.)

We should write "meaning" like this: "Meaning?" (E)

Maybe we are showing too much interest in words and meaning. We should be talking about concepts, to get away from the materialistic or behavioristic biases. After all, some words are purely or mainly symbolic, referring to things, as the expression "this page" clearly does. And if they do not do that, they refer to concepts. (No one would say that words *are* concepts, but maybe that they are backed up by concepts.) The word "page" could not refer to *a* page, not by itself, but only with the help of the reader who has in his being the page concept. We have to have page in mind (not the word, but the concept). Not "page," but page. "Page" pages the page concept. As a rule (E).

But what if we write concept like this: "Concept?" (E). (That is a destructive thing to do someone will say, distracting, and yet "concept" *is* a word and we cannot put concepts on the page here. Maybe we cannot even put words down here, if they are more than marks.)

What do we mean (E) by "concept?" (E) What sort of concept is concept? (We can avoid quote-marks by saying concept instead of word.) But only a philosopher would ask that sort of question. (What sort of talk level are we on here, what games, what dimensions?) Concept is a word *and* a concept, but apparently people have a conceptual approach to (") words ("). To think of or treat words *as* concepts is to raise the risk if not the certainty (E) of conceptualism. This may seem like playing with words, but whatever it is, if one really wants to explore, it should not be avoided, even though it may stagger the mind (?) to think about such things.

Concept is a construct, some*thing* we have constructed. It is symbolic (E) all right, but not just or even in the sense of referring, but in the sense of evoking feelings and attitudes. (As the American flag is symbolic, or the Queen of England, although not in the same ways.) One need not have "concept" in his working vocabulary in order to have that sort of feeling-response to words. Concept floats off into metaphor. Semanticists might say it is pure fiction. But it is believed. Concepts are not confined to single words. Consider: Rules! Language!

Legal concepts! The language of law! Law! Policy! Values! Facts! Morality! Words! Meaning! Principles! God (?) (E) Ambiguity? (E (tc.)) While these are meta-forms, still there *is* use of these terms at the conceptual level, to evoke feeling and attitude responses.

Nobody invented law, or morality, or facts, or rules, or policy, or principles, or rights, or duties, or society, or space, or time, as concepts. They did not start out that way, but there was a snowball effect. Even if at that massive-concept level of use, they have some sort of meaning, despite the efforts to unload them in and out of law talk and law-theory talk. Nor is it just a vague, so-called conceptualistic blab effect. They can at that level have a map-routing effect, as high level definitions, slicers and cutters of massive amounts of phenomena. So compare space-time, law-facts, law-morality, rights-duties, rules-principles; and law talk, or law-talk. These are invitations to (un) slice or (un) cut in other ways.

Socio-Legal Structurings in Theory Talk

If in law-theory talk one speaks of rules being applied to facts, or of rules or more specifically in law talk of this rule being applied to those facts, or if one speaks of law as one matter and morality another, or of the language of law, he does not invent, for the conventional uses of these words are not thus twisted in any obvious way. Yet, if we explore to see that there are other possible slicings, at least at this wide-sweeping level, yes, if we literally play with words, as a mathematician might, to see what lies hidden in his maps, then whatever assertions or slicings we stick with take on some added significance because we have rejected some available alternative slicings. That is, these high-level sort of slicings are *usually* serving some hidden or even unconscious purposes. We discover their existence even if we cannot specify them, by not merely accepting them as feeling-symbols.

Thus, when H. L. A. Hart insists on the component of rules as the fundamental basis of law (see the level), against the other cuttings of the legal realists (and if he calls them rules *skeptics* instead of legal *realists*) there has to be more at stake than meets the eye in the words(?) themselves. (But one who does not question this theory talk because he concerns himself only with law talk is not being merely practical. He puts forth a rule, and says, "Of course there are rules . . . ." But then he is theorizing in a way that he is not if he says, "Now this rule applies to those facts in this way," although there is also theory implicit in that way of talking, a set way of looking at things.)

When Hart would preserve law as largely separate from morality as against such lego-moral analysts as Lon Fuller, or as separate from policy as against practically the whole current stream of American analytic action (E), he is not just using his words to refer to things out there. (We should do more than pity his naiveté, but learn from the debate how words can be used.) He is preserving or reshaping certain metaphors and constructs, with the inevitable aid of rhetorical definitions. These ways of saying (looking at) things have importance beyond mere fussiness or even elegance.

Even though Hart and his debaters cannot be said to be empirical in the field study sense, collecting of data in tightly controlled situations, and so on, that is not the only form of research that makes empirical contributions. It is difficult for those with the data-collecting sort of bias to see the ways in which explorations at the Hartian or the so-called theory talk level have empirical sorts of potentials because at that level one is involved in metaphor in ways which may be discovery-full. There is even such potential in mere verbal play. But there are risks, other things to be done before the play is to be taken too seriously. It is necessary to climb yet again to the vantage point of talk talk to see the interrelationships.

To go further with the Hart theory-talk as an example: as is usual at such a level, there are several communicative dimensions involved. There are socio-legal stands. But there is also a stand on the way words work and how they relate to language. The very title of Hart's influential and provocative book, *The Concept of Law*, involves an important construct and/or metaphor and/or fiction. His restraint in using the approaches of Wittgenstein and even J. L. Austin, in now manifesting even deeper awareness of, or maybe tolerance to, ambiguities reflects attitudes and views on language, whether regarding the way(s) it operates generally or regarding the way(s) it ought to operate in law—or both.

Law, as a concept, requires the concept of language, and thus implicitly we must expect and look for metaphoric behavior. It seems to get us to *a* language of law, and concepts that are peculiar (E) to law. His separatism infects his words(E) and/or vice-versa. Words serve for slicing, as well as to weld, blend, stew, stir.,

We have sliced out (gouged out?) law talk, but *is* there actually a language of law? We hear of the language of law(yers), but that could be the sense of "language" that means talk or a piece of talk behavior, as in "What bad language that fellow uses." A language of law could not be exactly like a foreign language, although it doubtless sounds it to the layman, because of the specialized terminology, the words of the art of law, the special doctrines and syntaxes., But it would not be parallel to speak of the language of medicine, because there is a special separation in the construct-ion of law. (We are exploring "language" to see what it might mean to have a language of law or not.)

Could there be a language of law? There is said to be a language of mathematics and of logic, or that they *are* languages. (See metaphor at work, but not fiction.) Someone might want to speak of a language of art, or of music, or even of madness. There have been pressures and pullings toward a specialized language of law, very much tied to a belief and wish for logic or rationality and precision, as a way of doing away with the ambiguities of everyday "language." Cardozo sighed for a logarithm. Hohfeld and many others after him moved to set up a specialized language, trying to establish that "rights," "duties," "powers," and so on, be used in only legal ways in law (talk). Thus, one should not speak of a right of self defense but of a privilege. If X has a right, Y has some correlative duty. If there is no duty, there is no right, and vice-versa. He was legislating for law (yers), for *law talk,* not just for law-theory talk, and really trying to do for that talk what no one, absolutely no one can do for language, so that we might say that he had some false ideas about the way language works, and in effect, if not consciously, he was trying to set up a separate mechanism or system of law words, a separate language, but just for the sake of clear thinking, to avoid the fussiness and ambiguities of morality talk and other supposed subjectivities. And he was not just involved with those special terms to make them into only law-language terms, but starting a project for all of law language. But the implications of this effort are tremendous. And today there are computer-oriented and symbolic-oriented scholars who really have no concept-ion of the implications, for they think they are only trying to clear out those horrid ambiguities. It is utter madness! (In the sense of anger, of course.)

Korzybski wanted to mathematize everyday language. Imagine using mathematical notations. (E^2) The subscript device pointed out ambiguities. But to demand them at all times would be to inhibit the creative, metaphoric use of language. To ignore their potentials is to encourage the abuse of the metaphors of words-in-action. We are not going to be able to choose one or the other. For one thing, people, and lawyers, and theorists just keep on talking. But look out for the computerists.

Should there be a language of law?

Computer-orientation does pose the problem afresh. Do computers deal with $words_1$ (marks, sounds, stimuli) or $words_2$ (concepts)? Symbolic logic can help in moving from the ambiguities of everyday law talk into the precisions desired by Hohfeld, and maybe the computer age can force what no man could. No doubt such logic can help in analyzing, clarifying, and improving certain forms of communication. But we cannot do with it the communicative jobs we do with words—in law (talk). If ambiguity were something to be cleared out of (law) talk, then we should use symbolic logic and computers to do our talking. (E). But then we could not have (law) (concepts).

(E^6). Clearly enough we would not have $words_2$. We would have something (s) serving the function of $words_1$, and maybe a portion of the functions of $words_2$. But how could a logical (stripped) language do all the tasks? What would it look+sound+feel like?

To set law apart from facts, from morality, and policy and . . . , is to set aside and/or promote law-concepts talk here, free-wheeling facts talk over there, and morality, policy, and such talks, somehow way, way over there. There is *deliberate* balkanization for a deep thinker like Hart, methinks, but only varying degrees of awareness in those who just talk, and think, and feel that way, (as with legalists.) The legal realists wanted to destroy those boundaries. Either side (E) brings mixed blessings.

Why not both? At the same time? I believe the legal realists knew what they would do but not what they were doing.

Law(s) and Order(s)—Authorities

The way law is supposed to work, it cannot be made up just of people in authority, and therein lies further justification for the concept (s) of rule (s) (and principles, if you wish; i.e. "rules" = verbal mechanisms that are not completely within the control of the human authorities). One envisions maybe an hierarchy of human authorities, but necessarily a hierarchy of verbal authorities, whether separate or meshed in with the human structure. Here again, understanding of the way (s) language and/or words work or can be worked is important from both empirical perspective and the ideal. Once again ambiguity is the seeming enemy.

Since Hart has been one of the leading contemporaries to worry about such things, consider his views further. His and the general view called legal positivism share with the legalists certain attitudes about authority, but Hart does not go so far in a law-and-order direction, although the risks of his view running into legalism are very high.

If law is to work in an ordering way, its authorities need to be respected or obeyed much of the time. That requires an internal order(E), including clear *lines* of controlled communication, not only among the human authorities but among the verbal authorities. If words are to be usable as rules, they need not only to have a symbolic significance but also a sign(al) effect, like the traffic light or the traffic sign. To have that latter sort of impact, they need to stand out clearly when they are needed to stand out(there). Just imagine if a traffic light were always ambiguous, as in a way it is when it is yellow. Suppose the red light were simultaneously an indicator of temperature. What if the red light were merely a principle rather than the sign of authority, and the symbol of law generally as well as of a particular rule? What if one were always free to consider the morality of a red light—on a street corner, that is, or whether it might be a better policy to have it timed differently or not there at all—and to act accordingly. There are times when rules-talk must be taken just as seriously. Talk *of* rules may be another matter, so long as it is not subversive of the signal-rules.

To give up rules altogether in law would be to give up an important idea(l). Bertrand Russell said that there were no Christians because no one acted like the only one Christ. So maybe there are no legal rules in that same sense. But the world may still be better off for there having been a Christ as well as the idea(l) of rules. We just have to have legal rules(,) for Christ's sake. (E^3).

But to be sympathetic to idea(l)s of law and order in such senses is not to be legally authoritarian in all senses. The authority of law is one matter and of the human authorities another. And in all senses it is not absolute in any sense. Both sorts of authority need to be limited, for our sake. But how to do that?

We might rely on politics and democratic processes. Hart seems to believe that we need to construct the limits, build them into our constructs, or as he puts it, our concepts of law, laws, and rules. (The law-talk model would seem not to serve that rhetorical, symbol-feeling function.) It is a matter of keeping law as well as officials in their place, and the citizenry in theirs. Such limits on law(s)' authorities are necessary partly because the law mechanisms do not provide the best way(s) to solve all social problems nor certainly the only way(s) of keeping order. (Why not love and order, faith and order, truth and order, justice and order?) We say there are matters that are none of the law's business, as whether we keep our social engagements, and maybe soon whether we sleep only in our own beds. Or we say you cannot (ought not as well) legislate (certain areas of) morality. So, one might share something of Hart's emphasis on rules, not for law-and-order-crowd purposes, but to keep the powers of law and officials strictly limited. This is said to be a libertarian ideal. The less clearly the lines (limits) of authorities are set (of the rules as well as the rulers), the greater the potential for inhumane powers, as witness the Nazi sort of law and order. (Can words rule the rulers? Maybe it is not so much that they can but that they provide power to the non-authority ruled-ones to build them into a rhetoric of resistance.) If the concept(s) of law(s) or rule(s) fail in this regard, then we find other sorts of theory-talk, like natural law or concerning human rights, and so on, coming in to provide some sort of base of power for demands upon the rule(r)s.

It is not just a battle of definitions, but to the extent that it is even that, it surely is not merely academic.

Holmes objected to confusing law with morality. (Consider that sentence if "law" and "morality" are verbally analyzed.) His reasons were related to Hart's. Laws should not be immoral or amoral or iniquitous, of course, but they are still law. But it is difficult to prevent the blurring of lego-verbal authority lines with those of other verbal-authority kinds, however clearly we can keep the (E)stablished officials in sight. Morality has enough trouble keeping its own house in order. Some think it has fallen down. We do exert control and influence over one another without calling on law much of the time, and some of that authority is in terms of morality-talk (but many other kinds as well, but the problem of law-morality relationship is perhaps exemplary). Morality and other rhetorics have influence, even if the line, for instance, between moral-fact talk and moral-rule or moral-principle talk is less clearly drawn even than the membrane between law and fact. Good, bad, fair, just, wrong, right, duty, principle, and . . . , are some concepts of moral rhetoric, in everyday use as well as in professional theory.

Aye, but here's the rub. Those concepts are not exclusively within the jurisdiction of moral rhetoric. Their sounds continue to be heard in law talk, despite Holmes, Hohfeld, and Hart. But what is the measure of them. Holmes thought them open doors to the mere subjectivities of the person free to use them, unlike law talk, he seemed to think or at least hope—Hohfeld set out to purify them for law talk. They are not orderly(E). There is no way to control them. A tradition of precise, strictly legal terms would give the necessary kinds of control. Holmes view would place the control over the controls in the hands and minds of judges. And they did have the keys to the legal terminological doors. And the doors were thus tightly shut to reform through the judiciary.

So the legal realists huffed and puffed and tried to blow the doors down.

Even if they were not before, the lines certainly are rhetorically blurred today. Given the right conditions that puts power in the authorities, except where the lines of governmental human authorities are not so blurred as they are in this country. (Compare England.) So here the blurring facilitates subtle reallocations of power (grabs?), such as those we see in the lego-political dynamics between courts and legislatures in this country. No wonder Supreme Court appointments loom so important. Courts have proven they can be activist, yet we see the limits are not clearly legal, but *also* moral and political. It is doubtful that "strict construction" can do anything but make it appear otherwise.

But see how in all of this, there is still quite legitimate concern in trying to verify when someone in or of authority is talking valid law. Law talk is not *per se* valid, certainly not according to the Hartian sort of view. In the final analysis the job of validation is in the hands of the courts. But there are so many times when law talk must be measured without the aid of courts. Actually lawyers do a lot of validating for their clients and never get (con) tested. We shall explore this sort of thing further, but ultimate tests are much harder to come by than laymen or even lawyers might expect or hope. For the legalist the answer is simple and quite selfserving. It lies (E) in his rhetoric.

Validation is more a matter of persuasion than anything else, although certainly not just that. So it is that the power of lawyers may not be served by the realism of the anti-legalists, for it puts the power of persuasion wherever acceptable (as opposed to valid) talk is accepted as law talk. So, for instance, the only alternative to opening the bar-doors to sociologists outright is to make them take bar exams first ("and the more legalistically technical the better").

CHART #5

SPLIT SCREENS

(1) *word form* *wf* — Hidden lies a complex family structure. Form lulls, e.g., one-meaning, one level. wf= letters, syllables, order

(2) *surface grammar* — Sentence, clause, phrase, structure on surface, covering multi-faceted dynamics.

(3) *interactions* — (1) & (2) combined over-powering. Interpreter gets lost. (What wg's, what level 1,2. . ., etc.?)

(4) *compelling hypnotizers*

	NAME	*THING WORD*	*CATEGORIZER*
e.g.	Jones family	ash-tray cup	family cup ashtray

inFORMation form:
"This is Jones' cup."
cf. Smith using as ashtray:
Just info. imparted?

Illustration:
Hit with intent (info. form)
a. He intended to hit her
b. He had the intent to hit her
c. He had the intent to be a hit
d. The statute showed that the legislative intent was to punish it

Analysis:
No problem with "to hit:" clearly different from "to be a hit." Grammar: 1st a verb, action word; other (noun) a thing-categorizer (about to be lulled).

But 8 out of 10 people will not recognize chilling-freezing effect of grammar *qua* intent and intend. Intent= something. Carries into "d". *Four* different family members a-d, covered by grammatic function, word-form—and METAPHOR (see next chapter & Chart #6)

(5) *some other interacting structures*

Punctuation	*Syntax*
and tone, emphasis, etc	word-order go-togethers

Media	*Style*	*Definition*
print, oral, etc.	academic lawyer etc.	explicit, implicit etc.

ETC. ETC. ETC. ETC. ETC.

(6) *CF. Ambiguity:* Digging into these structures at first gives sense of chaos, until deeper structures are located or *constructed* (Things without words something else again) (E).

C. LEVELS OF LANGUAGE PROCESS

(1) on surface: word-forms, simple grammar, etc.
(2) beneath: syntax, how words put together (e.g., you cannot see a fact)
(3) further down:—variable uses of words and sentences, etc—as appropriate to wg's, ct's, cs's.

D. SURFACE LEVEL

(1) *Mapping* level--

uses of maps:
(a) to follow territorial and behavioral directions
(b) to give ditto

(c) give ORDER (E) intellectually psychologically

(2) *Confusion* level — can be misled here, into a lulled satisfaction, on the surface

E. DEEPER LEVELS—THE BIG MIX

(1) Growth of language takes place beneath surface

Cf. common law process

(2) Language grows despite *stare decisis* of word-forms and dictionaries. Surface is reaction level, deeper down the action levels.

A. LANGUAGE ← (desensitizing word-form)

e.g. (1) The language of law
(2) Language is made up of words, grammar, and punctuation and rules thereof all

B. LANGUAGE PROCESS – (a thawing phrase)

e.g., compare:

1.	2.
The Law	legal process
common law	judicial process
Facts	fact-finding
Word	word-games, word-form, word-family
Body of rules (or hierarchy)	rule process
Meaning	metaphor
Communication	Communication dynamics

F. METAPHOR

(1) Indispensable to growing language, growing society, growing law, etc.
(2) Takes place because of *surface level freezing* (hiding)
(3) Necessary in present state of linguistic insensitivity, but other techniques available

G. SPLIT-SCREENING

There for the viewing.

Chapter VI

(UN)LOADED CONCEPTS–IT'S ALL IN THE FAMILY

Pre-view from the Bridge

THERE ARE A NUMBER of recurring sub-themes along these pages whose appearance is justified mainly in their serving as illustrations of the several major themes. One major *substantive* theme carried forward in this chapter is word-concept analysis. Within this process is *a* demonstration of the ways in which analysis can go hand in hand with interpretation, in this instance, how-to-read a judicial opinion, coming out of a claim for damages against a 5½-year-old boy. We also explore further the ways in which law-fact dialectic works in law talk, the opinion being a prime example, and far from unique, leading us into the next chapter on fact talk.

There are *demonstrative* or *involvement* themes carried forward in this chapter also. These call for reader cooperation in somewhat different manner from "just reading along." The most obvious example is to ask that an opinion be read and interpreted before it is discussed and spread out in analysis-interpretation. But during that demonstration, the reader is asked to reflect on his own reactions and state-of-mind along with the author, the closest we can come to mutual involvement, to take us out of the flatness of print.

Even at a more subtle level is the reader involved. While we are stuck with our medium, in order to try to prevent the ordinary messages of the printed medium from overpowering the communication messages "within" the print, if the reader is willing he may join a sort of sensitivity-aiming effort. No doubt this is a major *demonstrative-involvement* theme. We have been engaged in it in several ways in previous pages. One that may not be so apparently demonstrative is the E device. The E merely asks the reader to look again at something which has just preceded to see that some word(s) have *more* than one sort of textual, communicative involvement; if you wish, "ambiguous" in one or more ways. It is somewhat related to the parenthetical comments which could irritate any style-purist, but they serve to demonstrate if not *prove* to the skeptic that he can and very often does take in more than one message at a time. The E then serves to suggest the possibility that often even other messages are being missed. The judicial opinion to be analyzed and interpreted contains no E's in it, but we will spot a few of the many that are at least subliminally there.

This sort of involvement-request has some relationship to communications or sensitivity sessions in interpersonal confrontation. (See other discussion of the Seminar on Law and Communication.) There is inherent in that sort of experience a basis for a rather new teaching technique (comparatively untried in legal education). It is possible, say in a law course with the usual substantive sort of content, maybe contracts or evidence, but certainly *any* seminar on any subject in the University (communication is of course an ideal subject), to work on that substantive level while at the same time actually giving communications training. One need not even be interested in that training as a major goal, merely as a way of *improving* the class teaching-learning product. ("Well, *that* is the last straw!")

This sort of involvement asks (requires) the participant to approach his situational learning on at least two levels. There is the usual intellectual or cognitive level, including anything one usually includes in class sessions. But the other level(s) calls for the participant to *see* what else is "going on" right there in *that* situation. An obvious example would be the use of loaded words to manipulate what otherwise might *seem* merely intellectual or legal issues or a taken-for-granted fact statement. (The uptight teacher would have trouble in being contested, of course, but maybe he could say, if he was the one caught, "I wanted to see if you were awake; heh.") Just imagine how law talk could be explored with such two level involvement. (This is a clinical type of experience that ramifies into all of the interpersonal involvements coming up for our embryos. It is a way of teaching participant-observation skills for, e.g. interviewing, committees, and behavioral research.)

In any event, here, the reader is being asked to interpret on these two levels (or learn to do it, if necessary). That may require separate readings until it becomes comfortable. (Just as one might listen to a tape of a class session, to get the substantive content.) It is difficult because we are exploring, certainly in this chapter, the very sort of phenomenon which helps to keep the second level out of sight.

While our substantive level could be said to be in terms of theory about conceptualism, the second level attempts to get at that partly through a technique that the style-purist would call a deviation. Style expectation is a major obstacle to communicative writing about communication. While McLuhan's style thrusts in The Medium is the Message are now comparatively pedestrian (forgive me, but he is much responsible that it is. *He* is not pedestrian), there is many a critic then and now who does not get his message because he cannot forgive him, and vice-versa, thus proving, but not to the people who most need it, what McLuhan set out to explain.

Style-expectation is not merely snobbish, even in academic circles. What shall we say, for instance, of the subject-predicate form (The leaf is green.) which has so much to do with conceptualism? It is grammar bound, but also a matter of style in the many instances where it does not *have* to be used. (Compare: I see the leaf as green.) We shall explore something of what difference it makes, but see it is partly habit. But there are those who say it goes much, much deeper, into unarticulated (inarticulable?) views on the "way *things* are." (Add: properties of things.) As a psychologically-oriented philosopher (imagine) might say, reflected (or determining) are unconscious metaphysics. If that seems too esoteric a thought, put it linguistically: This subject-predicate *style* promotes conceptualism (which is bad), although in its metaphoric aspects it is creative (which can be good). But in either event, it helps to conceal the depth grammar of words (which is not so good). If that is still too esoteric a thought, put it this way: It camouflages the way(s) words (are) work(ed). (Those are pretty bad.) (E)

Other forms of style habit and expectation go quite deeply also. We have been commenting on some of them. What has been called the language of lawyers is mostly a matter of notorious style. But it is a tie that binds. (E) Imagine a statute written chattily. (It might tell more of intent, but not commandingly enough.) It literally (E) goes to power. We explored that a bit in the last chapter in discussing lines of authority, both verbal and human(e). I doubt they fully realized it, but the legal realists were attacking judicial-lawyer style. (This sort of thing constitutes an important, perhaps major theme in this book, and again see The Right Way, where it is explored for the circle of lego-philosophical theorists.)

How can we avoid realizing that style goes to pecking order matters. That has been clearest in England, where ways of speaking are immediately communicative of "where you belong" socially. In this country these matters are just as important, although maybe even more brutally enforced. Blackness is not a matter of style, but all sorts of discriminatory (bad and not quite so bad) practices are related to the style-dynamics which *separate.*

So, style also goes to prevent if not prohibit communication, just as legalistic rhetoric has worked very effectively to keep out other viewpoints and approaches, the sort of factor that has to be the chief explanation for Glendon Schubert's not merely petulant but enraged commentaries on the "damned lawyers" and the way they talk. Let's face it, much of academic writing, and certainly the stuff of law reviews, has been downright stuffy. Who can doubt it is partly a matter of insulation. It does not do a good job of communicating out, but it also keeps otuside communications from coming in. It provides not only for internal stability but preservation.

To tamper with set style is to threaten, indeed to *be* sub*versive*(E). There is an exact parallel between the protectionism of (E) judicial styles (and lawyers' commenting thereon) and that of academica. See how unsettling it might be to tamper with law-school writing styles.

So once again, the people who intellectually and psychologically need communications sensitivity the most will resist, cannot help resisting it the most. We could shout, holler, and scream, and they would try not to see it or hear it. (So the young radical shouts, hollers, and screams. The older liberal fools (E) with style. And lawyers pour new wine into old bottles. If you are not a lawyer, a lawyer will say, "Hey, what's this, new wine in an *old* bottle!")

Be that as it may, there are some substantive level matters in this chapter relating to theories and techniques of linguistic analysis, namely, conceptual unloading. In connection with the judicial opinion analysis, the key unloading involves "intent." (Then later, and by way of carrying on, "fact(s).") As will be explained, intent-analysis has significance much beyond law, in connection with communications analysis generally. So, all the better.

It is a bit of a novelty to speak of conceptual rather than emotive or attitudinal *un*loading. (There is a deep level relationship, as suggested in the chapter on rhetorical definitions.) Critics of conceptualism say that what is wrong with it is that words are treated as things, or, as suggested in the preceding chapter, that a concept is regarded as some*thing* behind the word used, as "the concept of law." (The word "concept" is a classifier!) Linguistic and philosophic critics spoke of hypostatization, reification, or objectification. For law concepts, Felix Cohen spoke of transcendental nonsense, concepts unverifiable in sense experience. The criticism was in some respects well-founded, but it failed to comprehend the full range of functions of words. (As did logical positivism, nor more balanced in Wittgenstein, if his balance is appreciated.)

Concepts may be unloaded not only by charting the surface valences and more subtly by picking out the route of rhetorical definition (e.g. recall "foreseeable"), and equally subtly by breaking the term apart to see in a particular case what family member is actually involved in a particular situation. (Or as it may be, whether the whole blamed family is being thrown all at once, or just a bit of (b) (f)luff.) We shall do some exploring of the intent-family, both in and out of law talk.

There already have been some such earlier analyses ("law," "rule,") but *the intent analysis comes the closest to using the technique or approach of Wittgenstein and Austin,* so that for those interested it may serve as some sort of base for other such explorations. But there is more than technique of analysis, there is an empirically related sort of research. (That claim bothers the data-tapper.) Wittgenstein and company are often criticized for being merely empirical in some old "positivistic" bias and tradition. The analysis of intent will help to reveal how some individuals might come to that criticism, for there seems to be some abandonment of state-of-mind as well as of concepts. But our analysis does not involve an either-or sort of choice requirement, it merely separates the potential for such a word as "intent" to be referring, if you will, to some state of mind, maybe as an etymologically core meaning-use, but at other times to be referring and/or involved in quite different ways. What is started in this chapter with "intent" is carried further in the essay on "Intent in the Law of Crimes and Torts" where its judgmental aspects are explored a bit.

To appreciate these subtler aspects of use of such words as "intent," and "cause" for further instance, one needs to appreciate the *kinds* of loadings which can be involved with some*thing* words (related to subject-predicate style). Some other terms are more incidentally treated.

Turn it around. While it does not purport to represent a precise hsitorical reproduction, analysis of "intent" at least suggests what we might call the phylo-linguistic evolution of the family-of-words (concept-covered?), in this instance, "intent." (Consider how our E concept—big E and all the little E's—started, spread, and branched.)

In exploring in this sort of analysis, we move even further along the line of exposing the limits of a theory of meaning for either interpretation theory specifically or communication theory more generally. Meaning is not being outlawed in some sort of kangaroo effort (not yet). We do not throw it out with the water, but add the *behavioral* sort of element that is involved to see and consider what some person(s) may be doing with or by means of the words. One may utter words with meaning, either spoken or printed, but he behaves, acts, moves in some way, even if only intellectually. It is rather difficult to behave without being inter-involved with the culturo-linguistic way(s) of words, but words cannot operate without people at both ends of the communicative teeter-totter, or *whatever* sort of activity is involved. To see how such things go on with facts, we have to see "facts" as a word being used in one way or another—as well as a concept.

There is another way of looking at words, language, and situational *use*. It may help in understanding conceptualism and the debate between the precisionists (positivists, Hart, etc.) and the ambiguists (legal realists, etc.).

If you say a word, just any word, all by itself, it is abstractly indeterminate, just as the name of Kennedy denotes a family, but not the specific member, his personality, role(s), potentials, and so on. But instead of just thinking of a "family of words" (which carries along with the metaphor the implications of structure and interrelationships), think of words as sitting in a pool. That is where the legal realists or ambiguists looked. They saw that courts might have chosen other words from the pool, even of law talk (not law; they set the base for law talk, not law). They were concerned with the situation prior to decision and/or characterization—and we stress that sort of factor. The precisionists view words after the decision has been reached, after the words have been given their situational involvement. And we stress that factor. But I think the ambiguists saw better how words work than do the precisionists. These are not extremists, merely somewhat myopic.

Word-Magic Words

If word magic were doing things to people or things by merely uttering the words, that would be magic indeed. (Or if words suddenly became things.) One who thought there were people who could do such magic, or that words were things, would not be a magician, whatever else he might be; but he would be especially susceptible to someone else's manipulations of him by means of words.

Then we might wonder about the person who treated words *as if* they were things. That has been called word-magic, or maybe it should be words' magic, the magic words can work. We say that words say something, or say, "What do these words say," but really, words cannot speak. (If they did, what would they say, after all these years?) But I suppose nobody really treats words as if they were things either. Maybe we ought to say that there are occasions when, because of words, someone gets to thinking or believing in something that does not exist. But again it would not be the words working the magic, but the person who uttered them. But what if that were not his intent? Or what if he believed it too? We could hardly call him a magician. We might say they were both suffering from delusions, or maybe just faulty reasoning, or just oversimplifying the significances of words.

Of course if I tell you it is raining and you believe it even though it is not, we call that a lie. If I believe it is raining merely because I can say it, that is self-deception. (Only that?) Or a statement that asserts something that is not true is simply false. I suppose we would not want to call manipulation of people by false statements a kind of word-magic, because it is such a common happening.

But what if one can make an assertional *sort* of statement and make somebody else believe there is something or some event or situation which does, had, or can have a sensate existence, when such existence could not be. We might at least say that the manipulator was tricky with words. We might even want to say that the words were tricky, words can trick us, we can get tripped up in language. I think these things happen. Apparent metaphors are not to be fully believed. But silent ones are believed: The simile, "the dawn came up *like* thunder," is seen as comparison. Or the metaphor, "His hand was a giant claw as it dug into my throat," is merely graphic. Others may be picturesque, but not pictures; although maybe caricatures, but not true maps. What of, "He clawed at her dress?" Or, "He was green with nausea." What shade? What about "He drove her to drink." To a tavern? Or does it mean on a bicycle?

"Well, you know what he means!"

Of course. Nowadays we do. I wonder about the first time "drove" was heard in such way. Who fashioned that metaphor and how did it become not a metaphor at all but a different sense of "drove" altogether, really a separate word? Which came first, the ball one plays with or the one he plays or dances at and how from one to the other? These are clearly look-alike and sound-alike words, deserving of subscripts, as in $ball_1$ and $ball_2$. But probably the subscript is never needed, because of context. ("I had a ball.") (E)

Consider intent. "I intend to buy milk at the store." He has the intent to buy milk. That is substantiated if he buys it. One might buy milk without having planned it, however, and we would still say he intended to buy it. Of course there are not many times when a question would arise. Who would say "I bought the milk accidentally?" Yet, it could happen if someone slipped a carton into the cart, or maybe if one took the wrong package from the shelf. In any event, how do we get from intend to intent? What *is* intent, or an intent? ("Why it is a state of mind.") I just wonder if there is any word-magic involved.

Nouns are rather tricky, especially in the company of the "be" verb. Naming becomes confused with descriptive judgments, for instance. Korzybski had an interesting example regarding adjectives and the "be" verb (from things to properties of things): "The leaf is green." What color is it at night or under colors of light varying from the ones we are most used to? Well, of course, but there is no problem with that, even though we think of the greenness as being *in* the leaf. Is that word-magic? Well, how can we think the greenness is *in* the leaf if we do not think about it at all? Yes, but greenness is a function of conditions in the environment of the leaf.

My, that sounds like saying the meaning of a word depends upon the context. Meaning is like color. Meaning is color. He coloured his words. Well, not *really*. Anyway, if a leaf is green, it is green, when it is green, and not some other color. It cannot be green and not green at the same moment, simultaneously. Although what if you were looking at the green leaf without glasses and I had colored glasses that made it look brown? It wouldn't *really* be brown, would it? Someone who is on a "trip" and sees green leaves as purple is having a delusion. (What if we were all on trips?)

Now this may sound like philosophy except to a philosopher, but philosophy has no corner on crazy questions. Still, we know beauty is in the eye of the beholder. How about craziness, or greenness? These questions are relevant to philosophy though, and to law, to both because language is so important in both. (Words and what they do.) Again, there is concern here regarding the way words and things relate. Thing words (and property words). Thing words do not necessarily name only things. But there may be a sort of metaphoric, fictional, affective hangover of thing words. Call it thingifying, conceptualizing, word-magicking, oversimplifying, falsely identifying the verbal with the nonverbal, projecting, hypostatization, reification, illusion, delusion, nonsense, insanity. Maybe there is an overattachment, to words, or of words *to things;* or an overdetachment, in a world of words, *away from things.*

I say A hit B ("What is that?") It is a battery. ("You mean you can put it in a car.") No, no, a tort, maybe a crime, if it was intended and all that. Very simple, fundamental, the early, "not very important," drilling kind of lesson in one sort of freshman law course. After all, he has to learn to think like a lawyer. I believe he should know that sort of thing, and how to talk about possession, and so on. And what a wonderful opportunity to learn the ways of words. ("That is not what law is about.") It does not come that easily, the sort of sensitivity I am talking about. ("But *is* it a battery?") It *is* a battery, a battery, a battery, battery, battery, is, is, is, *is*, a battery. Here battery, here battery.

Does it have to be called that? Is that its *name?* A word sort of like a fact-word, a description? Compare saying a descriptive judgment. Battery is what I call it, for now, because . . . ,

("I say it is not a battery.") Fine. It doesn't make any difference. Here on this page, between us. You can call it a battery or not. Depends what you want to do. And that *is* magic, maybe? But not when everybody can do it and knows what is going on. ("Then you spoil the fun.")

I have a cup here in front of me. (I really do not, but strike that from the record.) Think cup. Magic? (I-magi-cination)

Compare: Gentlemen, what is the law of the matter if A hits B intending to do him a favor to keep him from doing something he wants to do? Hypothetical facts to be treated as real, because I said the words. Some very interesting magic can be done that way, by lawyers, but by other people as well, say philosophers, newspaper editors, and a few others. But more of that.

I have a cup here in front of me. I am using it to hold ashes from my cigar. Now I stick what is left of the cigar, to let it die in dignity, in the . . . in the what? Is it a cup? or is it an ashtray? Well I am using it like an ashtray, but it *is* a cup. What if there is a sign saying "Empty all ashtrays in the metal wastebasket, all cups in the sink!"? What it *is* depends upon the circumstances.

"Another great insight. Let's have some law."

Well, when is a trespasser not a trespasser? Suppose a person is walking along the sidewalk and intentionally crosses the boundary two feet into Smith's yard. Is he a trespasser? ("Of course.") What if he falls into a hole six by six by six, that has been used by children to play war, and they have camouflaged it? ("Well. Maybe he isn't a trespasser, because that could mean land occupiers could have such conditions on their property that would create unnecessary and unreasonable risks to passers by.") So he was a trespasser until he fell into the hole? ("I have it. He is a technical trespasser.") But what if he does not fall into the hole but ruins some prize tulips? ("Well, he is liable because he is a trespasser. We have no trouble with that.") And that is a good thing, to be flexible.

Look at words as having a classifying function, although not always or only that function. But if we say a dinner guest is a licensee, that means, for instance, that the host does not need to go around to see if there are any dangerous risks lying in wait for the guest, even though everyone might think such an inspection would be a reasonable sort of thing to have. How do we distinguish words that can be used to classify for one purpose, but not for another, between a flexible classification system and categorizing or stereotyping? A person's name does not in itself create a stereotype, but it can. The licensee-name for all social guests and for all situations that might arise, somehow, begins to sound like a stereotype. ("No. It is just a rule of law that is involved.")

Why not call it a principle? And put it on the scales.

"If it is a rule, it is a rule. Here rule. It binds the classifying mechanism to the situation and freezes them both in the pigeon-hole."

And that is what words are for?

"That's what rules are for."

That sounds like a rule regarding rules. Legalism. Conceptualism. Word-magic.

"Name dropper!" (E^3)

A classic example of conceptualistic word-magic concerns title in the old law of Sales. The question there was, can a person have title to goods and yet not have title to goods? If there is only one title, one owner, then there is no choice. But wait a minute, how do you move from title to owner. That would have slipped by, unnoticed, as if by magic. Title can readily be thingified, oversimplified, and so on. Title is not the handle to the goods, it is the handle applied to a *relationship,* a name, for relationships, to be applied or not. (Thing-like words and property-quality words classify, not only things, but relationships. See greenness and title as frozen relation-shippers.)

Now here we must be careful. Sound reasoning regarding

potential liability for risks to guests and passers-by is one sort of thing, security of title is quite another. If you can bounce title around the way you can the "licensee" descriptive judgment, as if you were just worrying about whether cup is always a cup, there would be no stability whatsoever. I have to know if I have title or not. If someone can come in off the street and say, look, I have your title, the way a father says to his child, "Hey, gotcha nose," where in the world would we be? Pure anarchy and chaos.

All right and true. But take a Sales case situation and not the situation of that other kind. There title is something else. A certificate of title to a car can be a tangible document of title. So can a bill of lading. But consider this sort of thing. A seller contracts with a buyer to ship him goods. Suppose the goods are destroyed en route by fire. Does the buyer have to pay for them? Suppose he paid in advance. Can he get his money back? Well, if the goods are his before they are burned, then the loss is his. The risk of loss goes with title. There ought to be a rule on that to cover that sort of situation. But does it need to be the same rule as the one to cover the situation where one of the parties goes bankrupt? The other one would rather have the right to the goods than a claim to a debt that cannot be paid. Whether he should be preferred over other persons (shall we say "creditors" or "*other* creditors?") is not the same question as asking who should take the risk of loss, the latter having something to do with practices regarding the taking out of insurance on the goods. Of course there ought to be a comprehensive contract spelling all these things out. But the problem arises when there is not.

If we say title passes or it does not, and the same for all situations, then we are saying the same *rule* covers all these situational-relationships. That seems a bit closed-minded. No reason why that should be, so long as we have some rules people can rely upon and some rules to settle disputes, and so long as they can be as fair as possible and as commercially relevant as possible. No magic words will do it. Title is not a good word.

Well, the *word* is all right. Actually, it is not just one word. (From concept to *family*.)

We can have a ball with title. Watch the bouncing ball. Who has title. Who has the ball. Let's throw a ball. Put the title on a string. Here a title, there a title, everywhere a title, title, title. Here title. $Title_1$. $Title_2$. $Title_3$. For situations by those numbers.

But we've seen the light on title (Uniform Commercial Code). How about intent? Or cause? It should be easier to see cause in judgmental use than it is to see title used that way. We can see that cause is not a *thing*. We do not treat it like a thing. Why did I say "it," then? Of course I was referring to the *word* "cause." We do not treat *it* like a thing, "cause," that is. Do we have causation in the following situation. (Have?) Suppose A invited B to his house for dinner. (We can avoid word magic by using symbols maybe.) (Could that lead to symbol magic?) B falls down the steps and breaks his arm. Did A cause B to fall?

"Well, hardly."

I forgot to tell you. There was a bad step.

"That's different."

But A did not know about it.

"Back to first base."

And I was wrong about B being just a guest. He was there to see about buying the house. Now he is an invitee and A owes him a duty to find out about that step because he easily could have.

"There is cause there then. But this is not quite fair because you have changed the facts."

No. I just didn't tell you about them.

"Double play."

No. $Ball_3$ three. $Cause_1$. $Cause_2$. $Cause_3$.

See how this $strike_3s$ you. There is a person lying unconscious in a pool of water so that his face and nose are in the water. X comes along and sees C. He could seize C out of that water. But he does not and C drowns in that little bit of water. Did X drown him, kill him, cause his death? Oh,

I forgot to tell you, C is X's little two-year-old son. Strike that. They are complete strangers. Tell me, when is cause not cause. Just as Hayakawa said, just as when cow_1 is not cow_2.

Now how about rules? We know a rule is not a cup. It is a vessel on the sea of law. It is an anchor. It containeth the blood of law, the arteries of the system. The bones, backbone, skeleton. One who breaketh a rule puts another nail in the coffin of the American Ship of State. Well, a rule is like a cup. "Rule" is like "cup." But there are more rules than cups and more different kinds.

A rule is not a thing, but "rule" is a thing-like or some*thing* word. It can be thingified. I have a rule here. Do I have to call it a rule? Do I make it a rule by just calling it one? Probably if I am a judge who drinks his judgment from it, giving himself a handle for decision. But it *is* a rule, just as a cup *is* a cup. But what if you $break_1$ a cup. It isn't a cup anymore. Broken rules are not like that. You could $break_2$ a rule by breaking a cup. How from 1 to 2?

How did it get to be a rule? If it is a rule, then does it become mandatory to call it that? Seems strange that there should be a stronger attachment here of *that* handle, than to a real *thing* like cup. When is a rule not a rule? (Of course I am just playing with words.)

What of "rule" as a relation-shipper?

Legalism Writ Large

What is being demonstrated is the deep down, subtle ambiguity of words coming about through the shifting, then metaphorical transformations of word-forms. The master form of the word as it *appears* in print or in sound tends to cover or conceal, to act as camouflage, for the deeper complexities within the dynamics of what we like to call the concept represented by the mere sound or letter. But "concept" is itself a cover. Blowing these covers off allows explorations in the mines of the mind. The treasures in the minds must be uncovered, the covers blown off, the mind blown open. No merely lazy, nor some familiar, merely dignified and covering style will do it. Wittgenstein knew it. Korzybski too. McLuhan. Bare with me.

The lowest form? Puns are not weaknesses. To be funny, they need be somewhat subtle. To be serious and even deadly, they need be hidden. The line between pun and metaphor, between either of these and deadly serious word use lies merely in the staging and the effects. Rhetorical defining is redefining for purposes that are usually serious. Rhetorical definitions are hidden and so unfunny puns. A kind of word-magic. Have I punned, rhetorically redefined, or stated truth? If a pun is a low form of rhetorical definition, what are the high forms? Does it depend upon purpose? Maybe a pun can have high purpose. To help one get high, I mean make the leap. These dynamics of word effects and affects are ordinarily subliminal. They can be blocked out or dredged up. But one can lower his threshold (heighten his sensitivity). He can, for instance, look and listen at more than one meaning-use, at multiple messages at the same time, as with the split screen or mixed-media involvement.

This sort of thing calls for not a porous but an open mind. "Legalism" is a descriptive judgmental epithet pointing to one sort of closed-mindedness. In the hands of one in authority, legalistic rationalization can be horrifying. *Conceptualism is legalism writ large.* ("Conceptualism" can also be such an epithet, but there are varying species of phenomenon related to the concept-dynamics of conceptualism$_{1,2,3 \ldots n}$, as one immediately realizes when he appreciates word-concept dynamics.)

The way (s) of law (s) simply cannot be understood, except on the surface, if the subliminalities of communications are left forever uncovered. So far as the common law process is concerned, for instance, law (s) grow in a way very much the way words grow. Lawyers speak of pouring new wine into old bottles, but there is no choice with words, by and large, although the figure oversimplifies the matter. Every time a word is used, it is used in some at least slightly new way. One is aware of this when enough is at stake, if he knows what is at stake, which he may, if he attends not only to the uniqueness of a particular thing or person, event or situation, but also to the ways of words. With respect to appellate process, one can justify saying that every case is always one of first impression, if one is impressed with what is different about the case.

But words have among others the classifying and catgorizing function, in law(s) as elsewhere. Classifications serve to discriminate as between themselves but not within themselves. To call an object a cup is to do more than name it, it is to prescribe its use and value. The "this-is-its-name" attitude can preclude seeing other uses. Other impressions are there to be poured into other classifications. If a particular law or rule is identified or projected onto a situation, then the situation is not to be seen or valued in some other, perhaps more imaginative, useful, important way.

Suppose, for instance, one person hits another person intentionally, doing some at least little bit of hurt, or being offensive. That in law is a battery. That is what it *is*, then, and for a lawyer it may be difficult to see the situation in any other way, at least if his *job* is not to see it otherwise, or if he is legalistic. Of course we recognize the proportions of the phenomenon only if we multiply the example many, many fold and beyond the bounds of lawyering. Later on I shall elaborate a few, more complicated examples. So it is a battery. And it is a battery even if one only says the fact words because one comes to recognize a battery without its name, just as with a cup. "Battery" is the name of the situation and when you are being serious, polite, and proper, you do not go around changing names. After all, that could be confusing. And battery is the name of the fact situation, the uttered statement purporting to say what really happened. So, no matter what happened, if the fact statement is substituted for the situation, the name of the map, the fact statement, is projected onto the situation to block out any other impression. It attaches *even more firmly* than nouns do to objects. The battery-rules and classifying words in them *become sort of linguistic rules as well.*

It can work both ways: (1) to brand a situation in such fashion that the rule *must* apply—it is a battery and the law *must* operate accordingly—or (2) in another situation the rule does not apply; e.g. "The situation is grievous, but since it is not a battery, no remedy can be granted. This piece of mail goes into that slot and that one goes elsewhere." We are not just dealing with words, then, nor even just rules of law, nor even with rules or habits of law and language, but of perceptions as well, and of feeling, and attitude—and yes, of policy.

Naturally, not even legalists are completely blinded by conceptuals if other words or conceptuals are thrown at them. Other classifiers or stereotypers may switch their allegiances, although of course not their biases. Or if they are too much impressed by a given classifier, whether word or rule, then something on the order of rhetorical (re)definition may serve to change the scope of the classifier, through the silent metaphor-misis process, or maybe only a slighter shift in meaning; i.e. designation of things-to-be-impressed-by in the situation. The names are changed without notice.

So the words will not stand still, not completely. They may be slowed down to a level of verbal molecular action sufficient to freeze what is around them. A marvelous fluid. But short of freezing, words go through shifts in meaning so subtle one does not realize the movement, like the entertainer who stood on the stage for ten minutes, imperceptibly moving his body through an angle of 180 degrees. There he was backward, but you could not see it happening. We could have taken pictures and have seen the movement through selected frames, or by close scrutiny of the spot where he stood-moving. But we seem to have difficulty with close scrutiny of law words, even with the faster motion discernible in a given judicial opinion. There is a sort of magic in all this.

Now I know this is so. I am not just making it up. I offer actual clinical observation in the classroom and from talking to law students, lawyers, judges, law teachers (and to John Q's). Let me offer an elaborated example. It involves a judicial opinion in the case called *Garratt v. Dailey* which I have used in courses with freshmen law students, not only the course in torts, but a course called Legal Method. Among other things, it exemplifies how one may attempt to demonstrate the magics of words (etc.) by depth analysis of opinions. The difficulty students have is not just a matter of lack of familiarity with the process of law. They have not yet learned words well. (Why not, when it is so easy, so practical, so important?)

As a *test* of one's own words consciousness, the reader might first turn to that opinion (Appendix) to see what the court *did* with the word "intent"; not, what is the legal meaning of "intent," nor what sort of intent is sufficient, (at least not merely these questions) but what was *done?* It would be interesting to know if an unsullied layman might do better than the leading experts among the commentators on torts.

Intent in Law Talk

Intent is one of the more interesting subjects to explore for communications purposes, including, but not just in, law and philosophy. After all, intent is relevant to a number of socio-behavioral matters. So, my intent is to travel down several tracks.

Many people coming into law study are rather one-tracked (although not each the same track), and so appear rather obtuse with respect to this Garratt case. It is not unfair to say there is a limited capacity. By limited capacity, I do not necessarily mean lack of intelligence or sophistication of one kind or another, but lack of capacity for *awareness.* Despite the special sophistication of today's generation, there is not an over-all communications consciousness, so it is difficult to be open to the communicative multi-dimensionality of this case (among many other cases). And it is like that at each turn, because each person has some one rule or purpose he thinks he is or ought to be carrying out, even in just reading an opinion. ("After all, it's not poetry, you know.")

The Garratt case currently appears very early in the Prosser Casebook, tort-teachings' best seller, not just to demonstrate battery rules and principles, but the nature of intent in tort law. He uses the opinion for purposes of illustrating tort-law talk of intent, not what is *done* with such talk, as it is played back and forth in law-fact dialectic. But one thing at a time for beginning law students who are, after all, only graduate students. And maybe it is true, that they are not prepared somehow, or blocked by false expectations regarding law. They have trouble reading the words without conceptualistic blinders, even in a so-called legal method course where they are supposed to be expecting some supra-subject insights.

It is true that for one hitting torts in the beginning of his law study, it may be quite a chunk to find intent being talked about in a much different way from everyday expectations. This is not the ordinary term "intent," but a special legal usage—of art. Still, that special usage is rather blared forth and legislated, stipulated and reenforced. Maybe the blaring hides the deeper subtlety cleverly, partly because of the linguistic habits. So there is a special chance to learn that game here. The name of the game is camouflage. It seems to be a legitimate game in our culture as well as our law.

The subtleties lurk beneath the ambiguities and they in turn beneath the surface dogma-rhetoric. If one were to make the appropriate sorts of marks and notations and note the puns and metaphors, all in Garratt, he might just end up with a script on the order of some of the preceding material.

That is how it is.

What the court does is to take the intent concept into legal metaphor or construct. However, the orthodox legal definition quoted from the Restatement of Torts is not regarded as metaphor or construct. Still, to the layman it might appear as fiction: "In order that an act may be done with the intention of bringing about a harmful or offensive contact . . . the act must be done for the purpose of causing the contact . . . *or with knowledge on the part of the actor that such contact . . . is substantially certain to be produced.*" (Deletion and emphasis is mine. Of course that does not change it any(?). It is like taking the handle from the cup, rather than taking the side. Actually, it is like putting a handle *on* it.) The 5½-year-old defendant Brian need not intend any bodily harm, merely offensive contact.

We should put an "E" after a phrase within the Restatement statement, "intend offensive bodily contact." Does that mean that he should intend the contact to be offensive, or that he should intend a contact that is offensive whatever he intends regarding the feelings of the victim? Or is it offense to the judge-jury who are evaluating it? Is that any better than "Focus—Where the Son's Rays Meat" in the spoken form? Is it impolite or offensive to call attention to it? Is it disrespectful to the court? Is it poking fun? No, it is a way of insighting to understanding.

If an adult had engaged in what may have been such "bad" conduct, the phrase-construct within the Restatement statement would be clear (er) with reference to him. Of course even an adult playing a trick might think (have it in mind) that the victim would maybe be surprised but take it all in the setting intended, in good sport, and all that. But trick-playing contacts are probably to be *presumed* offensive. (You cannot tell that just from these words, however.) If that is so, then maybe it is sufficient merely to intend bodily contact. The court in Garratt does not say that literally, but . . .? (Should we give the court "E"?)

Consider the parallel for an earlier statement by the court: "A definition (not all inclusive but sufficient for our purpose) of a battery is the intentional infliction of a harmful bodily contact upon another." (parentheses theirs) Yet in this case the court makes it clear that there is no need to intend to *injure*. The trial court judge sitting without a jury had made a finding of fact (which must now be a fact because it is irrefutable, irreversible, according to tradition and procedure. It is truer than true because it is a fact?) that the boy did not intend injury. The Restatement says it is enough to intend harm.

So, is the court saying it is enough if the contact is offensive, harmful, or injurious and if a bodily contact was intended? Well, I would read that over quickly enough, ordinarily. One looking for *the* rule would ordinarily strike these problems out of his thinking after he had found his rule (or reached his decision), but actually he does have to thrash his way through there, that jungle. Yet these are not really issues in this case, because much of that has been talked out elsewhere, in other opinions, commentaries, and Restatements. It is hornbook law. And yet, it is part of the rhetoric, historical justification, allaying of the shock which the decision might otherwise have. ("Gee, if it is all old hat . . .")

So we get to the *real* problem. The difference in intent in *torts*. Every law student realizes this and takes-it-for-granted, surprisingly quickly. Well, of course, if that is the law . . .,

The actor does not have to *desire* the result for which he is held responsible. In this case, for instance, it is enough that defendant (notice how emotively unloaded or maybe negatively loaded that word is. Compare "Brian, 5½-year-old, little boy") intended a contact with the body, and not even necessarily with any part of his body or from any object he set in motion. He is liable for the apparently serious physical damages the arthritic, elderly lady (plaintiff) suffered. That does not have to be his purpose or one of his purposes, the why or a why of his actions, a motivation. It need only be a result.

Not even the contact needs to be desired, purposed; or the, or a, motivation or end wanted or sought! Is this really a conservative view? But I did not say it was that! The *orthodox* view of tort law is that liability is to be based on personal, individual fault, and that the gravest sort of fault is that which involves intentional wrong. Lower down comes negligence.

Why was not this boy sued for negligence and why was he sued at all? Well, a boy that age cannot be negligent, because he is not old enough to be able to form the kinds of judgments which allow us to say that he did not act like a reasonable person. The law has been clear enough on that. But he can be liable for an intentional wrong. In California the high court ruled that a four-year-old boy could be liable for battering a baby sitter, mischievously pushing her around. Still, there it seems he wanted to push her. Children that age can have such desires.

Brian will have had the requisite intent if he had the knowledge (?) that plaintiff would hit the ground. This is based on analogy to the situations of something hitting the victim. If you trip a person with a rope, you batter him right then, but certainly when he hits the ground, i.e. when the ground hits him, because you caused it.

The court does not say that defendant Brian must know that plaintiff Ruth would come into contact with the ground, nor that he must have such knowledge, but that the act is to have been done *with* knowledge that such contact "is substantially certain to be produced."

Intent in Lay Talk

As I shall elaborate, in exploring the intent concept, there may be justification for such a legal definition of intent, but it is not the way the word gets used in lay talk. We might want to say that someone who does an act which will bring about certain results is responsible for such results. Suppose I open the window to see up the street. It is cold and windy. You are sitting nearby in the room, and the cold air hits you. Did I intend that? I caused it and I am responsible for that. But intend?

I could have, by desiring it. But suppose you said, "Hey if you open that window, you will get me cold." And I say, "Sorry about that, but I must look into the street." I know it is going to happen, but would you say I intended it. If nothing is said, we might want to *infer*, lacking any other evidence, that I had the intent to get you cold, that it was on my mind, that it was my purpose. (Do we actually *do* something when we infer, or is that a way of justifying, after the fact(E)?) But if it is seen I am doing it for some other purpose, then intent is not likely to be *there*. (What happens to you is a sort of co-incident.)

Note, interestingly enough, how one might characterize the act as thoughtless, meaning not in every way, but with respect to getting you cold. Thoughtless of me (well, about you). Nothing in mind *re* you. In everyday life, "intent" is not needed to lay blame, but it is in the Garratt Case. (See further elaboration in "Intent in the Law of Crimes and Torts"—Appendix.)

But note how I might resist blame-laying by saying, but "I did not mean to get you cold." ("Mean?" Very interesting. Do not take my conduct to *mean* that.)

At this point comes a request for a bit deeper reader involvement, to test the point just made and to explain a little bit about the implications of looking at "ordinary usage." I want to ask you about my intent in writing the words in this sub-section up to the beginning of this paragraph.

Do I intend to imply that the word "intent" *cannot* be used outside of law talk the special way it is used in the Law of Torts (as so far illustrated *re* Garratt), to refer to the awareness one may have regarding the consequences of his acts which are not those he wants or plans and are not even within the scope of his purpose(s) in acting? That implication could be drawn, and may seem even more obvious just a bit later on. It is an objection leveled against Wittgensteinian and Austinian sorts of analysis that they measured creative philosophic uses (for instance) against usages of the man in the street, to prove that the philosophic uses were absurd, because fanciful. It is true that purely invented rhetorical definitions produce that risk because they have not been approved by the courts of culture. It is this sort of risk of fancifulness (or arbitrariness in judicial courts) that brought Felix Cohen's complaints of "transcendental nonsense" against what he saw as legal conceptualisms.

But there are other implications as well in my question about what intent I may have manifested earlier in this sub-section. It gets to the question of how we ascertain intent and whether we speak of something in one's mind or "something" else.

How do you answer the question? (E)

If you consider only words that are in this sub-section preceding my asking of this question about my intent, it is rather clear that I am at pains to distinguish the everyday, outside of law, use of "intent" from the special law usage of intent which lets the Garratt Court say one may intend a consequence if he knows it is substantially certain to result from his act, even if it is not within his purposes.

But if your memory serves you well, then you have trouble keeping out of the record comments further back which stressed the subtle, shifting, exploratory, and creative uses of words in everyday talk. Certainly metaphoric uses of "intent" could embrace the law-of-torts kind.

Yet, so far as I know, if someone has used "intent" in that fashion outside of legal analysis, it has not yet become common enough to justify dictionary backing. It might be a significant use to develop, if there were need. (On this and some other related points, see further elaboration in "Intent in the Law of Crimes and Torts"—Appendix.)

But is is not ordinary usage or even occasional use. To hear its use in that vein would be extraordinary. (Such questions could be the basis of significant behavioral research.) This conclusion is based on something more than an intuitive or casual understanding, and more than an educated guess.

So there is need to distinguish between usage and usage-potential. The potential of any word is that it may be used idiosyncratically, possibly in rhetorical definition, metaphor, or fiction, in ways that do not meet the tests of the dictionary, nor even of developing usage not yet dictionary-documented. But it may reach the non-documented stage of usage, finally to be charted as "in" by an unabridged, and conceivably by less comprehensive dictionaries. (But realize that many, many senses of words never "make it.")

Whenever a word develops to any one of these usage stages, it does not mean that somehow the intent we now talk about has changed. (Just because I drive you to drink does not mean I cannot drive you to the store.) This needs stressing where it is clear because when the shadings become less distinct, the word-magician is at his best. New word usages grow out of the old (in law via the process of stare decisis and precedent-following generally. There are *stare decisis* bases in the linguistic courts of culture.) But for rhetorical definition to work, for instance, the lines will be blurred and not a matter for fully conscious discrimination, as contrasted with "Boy did I have a ball at the ball when we threw that ball around."

Well, of course, right now we have common usages of "intent" which are distinctive enough to be called family members. But they are hard to discern under such circumstances as these (but easy enough to *use*), perhaps equally as hard to appreciate as the family members of "title," in both instances because of the conceptualistic camouflage of the master word-form. (And so it is for any word you can think of. "Of?" Yes. "Yes?" Of course.) But in some ways "title" is easier to expose because we discover there is no-thing behind it, actually (in those Sales cases), whereas there seems always, to be a state of mind behind "intent" as its referent.

One might think that in law, as illustrated by discussion in and of Garratt, intent has been exposed by extending it fictionally (as related to lay use, at least) to refer to knowledge without purpose. But a conceptualistic covering remains, now over the word "knowledge," which is also a state-of-mind sort of word, what we might call one of the sub-categories running parallel with thing words. It seems to be naming *something* that exists, a something-word.

Now I have no intent to go so far as to say that it makes no sense to speak of a state of mind. I can look at the typewriter and say to myself, I am going to type the word "type," and then having done that, say that not only did I intend$_1$ to do that, but I had the intent$_1$ to do that, in the sense of a preconceived plan, one, perhaps *core* use of the word "intent." But as I am typing along do I intend to type the word "word?" Well, of course. Did I have that intent in the same sense as I spoke of having intent with regard to the word "type?" We might not want to distinguish, but there is a difference in timing, for if I had it in mind, it was *almost* simultaneously with the act of typing. Maybe this is intend-intent$_{1\frac{1}{2}}$.

If we go back a way in the script, we have a different situation. Back there I was not thinking about *typing*. It was not on my mind in the way it is even now, although even now as I am typing, the thoughts with respect to typing are not the *same* as they were back at "type," nor even at "word." Typing is in mind now, but not the words, they are just being typed. Back there when typing was not-in-mind, we would still say that I intended to type and that I had that intent, but this is a somewhat distinctive use. It seems to me fair to call this intend-intent$_2$. Compare other examples at this point in the matrix. A while back I stopped to stare out the window, and without *thinking about it* in any conscious sense of think, in the now-I-am-going-to-do-*that* sense, I picked up the cigar I had previously lit and took a couple of puffs, at which point I became more aware or attentive to the cigar-smoking experience.

Now there is an interesting comparison between talking and typing (or writing). It certainly seems true to me from an introspective, what am-I-verbalizing-to-*myself* perspective, that I can be typing along here, and it is not always clear that I am saying the words to myself even as I type, but that I am doing it all at once, think-typing. There is sometimes a clear lapse between thinking the words and typing them, and there probably is such a lapse in most instances, split-split second, maybe the micro-second sort of lapse in "time" that comes between my seeing my associates talking and my hearing them, but not enough to make any difference. The lapse is often apparent in writing with pen, and that slows me down. But when in here do I have the words in my mind? Maybe we will say always, I am not sure about that, but compare if I were talking out loud as I typed. If there were a lapse between thinking and talking, I often cannot detect it. Some of the words seem spontaneous. I am quite sure that is often the case when I am engaged in casual conversation with other people, but even in less casual situations.

Still, we would doubtless say that I intended everything that I said or typed, even without any conscious awareness of having them "in mind" first, before saying or typing. Under these circumstances, if I say (1) "I *had the intent* to type those words" is that not equivalent to saying (2) "I intended to type those words." That is, intent in the first statement plays into intended in the second, rather than vice versa. (Intent in "1" is not *mental.*)

When one does something spontaneously, we may say he intended it, or that obviously he had that intent, but if the words "intended" or "intent" refers to some-*thing*, it is not to thoughts on the mind before the doing, as when I decide to go to the movie later on, tonight. "I intend to go to the movies. I have that intent. It is on my mind." Here intended plays into intent-on-the-mind, as contrasted with the reverse movement from intent into intend when characterizing spontaneous conduct.

The distinction is too subtle? Splitting hairs? Angels on pins, and all that? But subtle is the name of the games we are exploring. There are shadings much finer than these, but some readers might not believe them. In any event, "intend" is the sly member which pairs up with, not intent-on-the-mind, but another member of the intent family. ("Well, you know, *they* all look alike to me and my friends.") What complicates it all is that there is another member of the intend branch which teams up with intent-on-the-mind (as her close friends call her). We need to get closer to these members. (Draw a little diagram. See chart number 6, end of chapter.)

Someone may want to say, "Well, you cannot talk, type, or what have you, without thought." If "thought" means something on the mind, then could we say I intended those thoughts. Or even where it is clear that "I have something in mind," to go to the movie tonight, did I intend to have those thoughts, was it my intent? This all has to end somewhere, we may suppose. The question probably does not make sense, because we have no occasion except this sort even to ask the question (Compare: What is law?).

There is no sense of "intent" to cover situations which are not based in some sort of experience or concern. (But I can day-dream about it, and use that term if I want to. It might make sense to someone. It just might . . . .)

This sort of brooding may help us to see some different involvements for "intent" and "intend" than on-the-mind. We use these words with respect to observed behavior, no matter what is on-the-mind of the purported intender.

When one person speaks of the intent of another, he really cannot be using it in the way he does in referring to his own thoughts or behavior. When I say "I intend . . .," I know whether I am thinking that way or not. (N. B. To say "I intend . . ." *is* sometimes to have the thought and to express it simultaneously.) But if I say "He intends . . .," or "He had the intent . . .," *very often* the judgmental assertion is based on nothing but observed behavior. Certainly I have not climbed into his mind. What I say about others' intents is based at best on some sort of move from introspected experience. Perhaps we want to call "his intent" on-the-mind inferred. Will you grant this distinction: "I intend$_a$ to go to the movie tonight, and she intends$_b$ to go with me?"

"How do you know she intends to go with you?"

She told me so.

"It's clear enough, then. Of course you do not have the same intent in the sense of having . . . ."

Ah, we are of but one mind.

"Stop that. But I do think 'intend' is in the same sense, referring to something on someone's mind."

No-o-o, but no mind. Suppose this. I see someone running after a bus and I blurt out, "Hey, he intends to run after that bus . . . ."

"A senseless sort of thing to say, but again it is the same sense of intend, because clearly it is in-his-mind to run after that bus."

H-mm. I wonder why you say "in-his-mind to run after that bus . . . ."

"Good Lord, it's clear enough."

About like his *saying*, "I am going to run after that bus," and then doing it. But he does not say it, and we are describing his behavior, and so, the word "intend" refers not to something on-his-mind, but to what he is doing. Very good.

"Not at all. Not at all. I'm not even sure what you are saying, but we are under these circumstances referring to what is obviously on-his-mind. (Hey, I've learned to speak in hyphens.) If you wish, we infer the intent-on-the-mind."

Beautiful, beautiful. What a circle. There he is running after that bus. I am standing there. I say to myself, h-mm, let's see, he is running after that bus. Does it seem likely he wants to do that, intends to do that, has it in-his-mind to do that? Well, now, according to the probabilities, yes. ,h.m-m, yes, I believe I can infer that. "Hey, he intends to run after that bus. . . ." No, I think not. We just look at what is going on and describe it, so to speak.

There is a use of intent that refers to *observable* behavior. "Intent" is not so easily used in that sense, except when describing historically. Thus compare: (1) "He intends to run after that bus" and (2) "He has the intent to run after that bus." Not that (2) is grammatically incorrect, but still it *sounds* awkward, more so than if later one were to say, "Oh, yes, clearly he *had* the intent to run after that bus." (Note that it is more likely in law situations, or where some sort of moral judgment is being made, that we would stop to consider such matters, *historically*. Well, and too, in talk talk situations.)

In any event, we do slip out-of-the-mind with these words, when discussing and judging behavior, under circumstances when really behavior is all we have as evidence.

One has already moved into metaphor of the silent kind. If A hits B, we say he intended it, if it is (1) pre-planned; (2) spontaneous, but seemingly thought about in the process, as in a joke, or to call his attention to something; (3) spontaneously but as an obvious emotional outburst, say in an evident rage. These are distinctive uses. Example "2" is closely related to example "1," and also closely related to example "3," but in a different kind of relationship. With respect to example "1," example "3" is more than rather distinctive.

In any of these situations, should one have the occasion to

speak or think of intent, he would have no reason to think of the others, and he would not. He would use the word "intent" in each one of these situations *spontaneously*. He has learned to use the word in these distinctive fashions and under circumstances where he does not realize it. If he were aware of the distinctions at the time he learned them, he no longer is, because it does not seem to matter. If one were examining a person's vocabulary, he would say he knows the word "intent." It is on his list. I prefer to say that he knows his way around with it, at least to this extent. He knows how to use it, how to play those "games$_{1,2,3}$" with it. These are different lists. (Compare earlier analysis of "rule.")

Note that example "3" can be pushed a bit further. If we could say the person was in a blind rage, then we might say he was "out of his mind." We might still say he had the intent to hit B. But then again we might not, depending upon whether we think him capable of carrying out *any* sort of design, let alone the one of hitting. If he is simply lashing out like a flailing machine, the purposefulness is gone. He is crazy mad, insanely mad. Even so, for tort law, intent might be fictionalized, but not for criminal law. Maybe he should pay, but not be punished. Perhaps he is even to be pitied, but not more than the man he hit.

Note here the kind of judgment being made, moral, legal, psychiatric., As is elaborated in the Appendix, Intent in the Law of Crimes and Torts, intent is a word which in one of its syndromes reflects or involves moral-legal kinds of responsibility judgments. So, it is possible that while the extended use of "intent" in law, to include consequences which are "known about," but not desired or purposed, is with respect to the intent-purpose syndrome not even closely related to the ordinary or tenable usages in lay talk; still, with respect to the intent-responsibility syndrome it is related. (That is, in this aspect, intent relates back to the user of the word rather than the person who is being judged.) It helps to see a sort of chart of this family of intent words, and further charts of the way it gets related to other words. (But two dimensions will not do it.) It really helps, to get the feel here, to think of there being different words which are named intent, under the metafor (m) of "intent." There is a loose set of relationships among these members, but not sufficiently unitary to justify merging into *one* concept. (i.e. by calling "it" a "concept.")

Now, before delving back into the Garratt Case, let me suggest again that an analysis of Garratt is only serving as a springboard. It is no accident that the intent and other state-of-mind concepts, used please note for behavior judgments (1. fact-describing function; 2. also responsibility attributing function) as well as something-words, are ideally suited for purposes of communications analysis. Stop to consider interpretation as a communicative task. We will take that matter up separately, but it is not something one does without respect to other sorts of communicating tasks, such as arguing, reasoning, or even analysis.

Quite a while ago, it seems as I think-type, but just a bit back for the speed-reading chap running over the surface, you were asked to interpret two short paragraphs on the open-the-window illustration. It was not the what-did-he-*say* sort of interpretation, but the what-did-he-intend type. These are interrelated as lawyers familiar with contract, statutory, and other sorts of interpretation know. We see by now that there are other perspectives raised than the what-did-he-have-on-his-mind, something sort. What has been said between that and this point bears importantly on searches for meaning, intent, and purpose and policy.

And not only is it true that understanding of the intent concept-dynamics bears on interpretation, but on understanding of communication generally. I speak not only of verbal communication. We judge a person's intent by his behavior, not just for purposes of tort and criminal law, but for that broader sort of interpretation which is involved in every communicative act-situation, including, but not restricted to the one right now (E) taking place. In the face to face sort of communication, there is behavior and usually, but not necessarily, words. The other person expresses *himself*. We would usually say he intends to express himself as he does, he means to do what he does. It is rare that we articulate it in terms of intent, but there is a behavior-concept correlative to the intent word-concept working in everyone's (isn't it everyone's) assumptions. If X knows or believes that Y does not mean what he says, or to look or to communicate (?) in the way he *might* well be interpreted, X takes it into account. You know I am frowning because of a headache and that makes a difference. A person may get away with saying he did not mean to frown, but an angry tone does not usually allow the self-serving statement. If you wish, he is thinking out loud, acting out loud, visibly or audibly feeling. The attitudes and the feelings are right out there. Any distinction between behavior and words is not here justified. Words can in that sense be attitudes out there. One uses words in talking and one talks in communicating and one communicates in behaving.

So, analyzing words can be, has been here, analyzing concepts which are involved in communicating which is involved in behavior which is involved in one's involvements which make up his total involvements—his being and his life. We are not just dealing with words!

Intent in Garratt

If you will remember, Brian was moving a lawn chair and Ruth claims she fell down and broke her hip because of it. He claimed he had no such purpose in mind, but the appellate court has told the trial judge that according to the Restatement of Torts, based on credible, routine common law rulings across country, he need not have any purpose to hurt her or even to cause her to fall down. It is enough to have knowledge to a substantial certainty of result X in order to intend X, from a legal point of view.

How does the court determine what Brian's intent was? The judges who share the opinion are not supposed to determine that intent, but to give instructions to the fact finder, here a trial judge without a jury, on what to look for. But we see that the trial judge has stated some fact conclusions. He has already found, and this cannot be reversed or qualified by the appellate court (so we say). He has said that Ruth came out to the back yard where Brian and Ruth's sister were. Then (E) Brian picked up a lightly built lawn chair, "moved it sideways a few feet and seated himself therein, at which time he discovered the plaintiff, Ruth Garratt, about to sit down in the chair; that due to the defendent's small size and lack of dexterity he was unable to get the lawn chair under the plaintiff in time to prevent her from falling to the ground. That plaintiff fell to the ground and sustained a fracture of her hip, and other injuries and damages as hereinafter set forth." What was Ruth doing all that time? Brian was moving as fast as a Keystone Cop and she like a TV simulated replay in slow motion. (She was arthritic!)

Did he intend for her to have contact with the ground? Here I believe the court does engage in its most deceptive wording. They quote from a comment on "clause (a) of the rule from 1 Restatement of, Torts, 29, sect. 13:" (Note the court says "rule." What is the court *doing* with this rule?)

The gist of that rule seems to be that it is not enough that the actor is negligent or even reckless in order to say that he has the requisite intent. He must realize "that to a substantial certainty, the contact . . . will result." The Restatement also refers to the section as a rule. Is the comment part of the rule? Is the court's comment on the comment part of the rule? (or of the court's rule?)

The court uses the rule-comment-comment, but does not really apply it. It affects the way an insensitive or running reader may read the paragraph which immediately follows the quoted comment, if he does not relate that following paragraph to the factual analysis, especially the findings of the trial judge. Here *now* (E) (then?) is the key quote from the opinion:

> A battery would be established if, in addition to plaintiff's fall, it was proved that, when Brian moved the chair, he knew with substantial certainty that the plaintiff would attempt to sit down where the chair had been. (E?)

So now, what did Brian intend-know-realize? What was his

intent (knowledge-realization). He must have had *something* meeting that characterization. (?) How avoid the invitation of this one of the most subtle metaphors (intent) in the legal lexicon, or rather, the social lexicon.

Is it required that he moved the chair when she was attempting to sit down or is it enough if he knew she would attempt to sit down? When? All he need know is that she wanted to sit there and she would make some effort. It does not follow that he would know that she probably could not stop her attempt (because arthritic) or that certainly she would fall down. Had he known she was arthritic? Had that in turn meant anything to him, a 5½-year-old boy? What does he appreciate or realize, this boy who cannot be old enough to be reasonable even? Yet he can intend in this most sophisticated manner. *The court does not say that he has to know or appreciate all that!* But if he does not have to have purposed body-ground contact, he has to have some sort of knowledge. It is not enough that Brian merely intended his act, or as the in-the-opinion quote from the Restatement comment upon the INTENT-RULE puts it, "It is not enough that the act itself is intentionally done . . . ." He must act with knowledge that . . . If an adult had moved the chair with knowledge that Ruth would attempt to sit down, we might not, however, necessarily say that he knew she would very probably fall down, for it depends how far she had pursued her attempt. If he knew she was arthritic, we might then say he was negligent, reckless, or even wanton. Or he did not care that she might well fall down. With the adult it is not very important to make the distinction between knowing and conscious risk-taking. If one acts with knowledge that . . . , in the Restatement sense, he does not merely take the risk that . . ., but he acts *despite* that . . . It may be negligence or even recklessness. He is liable in either event, to boot for punitive damages.

But not so far children 5½ years old. Taking the risk . . . , and knowing . . ., are distinctive attitudes, admittedly, but knowing that . . ., is so much harder to prove, so much harder, for adults, let alone children. How closely should the distinction be shaved?

"The boy is not being put in jail. She was hurt."

Careful. Careful. We can sweep over, start justifying too fast.

"Well, the boy must be covered by insurance. I'm not asking whether he actually is, because if he is not, then, plaintiff has an empty judgment. But if this is an insurance case instead of a tort case, then all this intensive analysis turns out to be a bit of a bore."

Please, please, be not so eager to make the judgment of irrelevancy. This is an activist court in this instance, no doubt of it, but notice it is not a shouting sort of activism. It made no headlines in Prosser's Hornbook. Of course he is not particularly in favor of this sort of judicial activism. (Could that affect what a man sees, how he reads?) The shouting activist, on the other hand, is impatient with this sort of history, and with camouflaging rhetoric, even though aimed in the left direction. But even when one reaches the shouting level, the metaphors and the fictions are there too. They may be shouted, but as metaphors they are silently lurking, working. Movement is relative to the cause. Consider in how many different ways we *are* moving when we seem not to be. (The world may be moving too slowly but is the earth?)

"Brian did not know all *that*. What did he know?"

The orthodox Tort view is that he must have knowledge that will enable him to know (notice, from knowledge of X to knowing that Y) that Ruth will be very likely to fall to the ground. Let us say that an adult would know that. Brian may have known$_1$ that. But he may not. How will we know$_2$? We simply cannot. A trial judge who might not believe in such sort of economic risk allocation might make his findings in quite good faith when faced with equivocal evidence.

Note that Ruth had not even testified, only Brian. What value is his evidence? One might think that surely it ought not to be held against him. A pure guessing game. But Ruth's sister testified. Evidence of trial judge bias comes in seeing that the judge accepted Brian's testimony. How weird? But how credible is the sister's testimony? The discretion on that has always been pretty much with the finder of fact. If there had not been a trial judge sitting without a jury, an upper court would be hard put to do anything about it. It would not have as much control as seen here, except to require that what it has said here must be given as instruction to the jury. But it would have to be blunter about it. Here it need not be. The court is talking to the trial judge. And as we see, he gets the subtle message. "Here is what we want. Obviously you can still rule as you did. So we cannot really order you, only very strongly urge you." What beautiful law-fact dynamics!

So now I must point out what is *really* (?) the key statement of the court. The opinion says, "In our analysis of the applicable law, we start with the basic premise that Brian, whether five or fifty-five, must have committed some wrongful act before he could be liable for appellants injuries." If this case were followed by enough other courts, the Restatement of Torts would have to come up with a new documented usage as with a dictionary which picks up a usage that has moved from the idiosyncratic through a "trend" into acceptable, at least embraceable, minority convention. That new definition would perhaps be some more glamorous version of something like this: "The actor must do an act intentionally under such circumstances that he knows that his conduct is wrongful."

After all, it *is* wrongful for even a 5½-year-old boy to move a chair away from an adult, whether she will fall down or not. *Bad manners?* Why not, when balancing *principles* of tort liability? What is wrong changes with time, although this sort of conduct has for some time been considered as bad even for children this young. What is legally tortiously wrong changes with time. (Distinguish crimes, even though most tort-batteries are criminal-batteries, this one is not, is not, No, not.) The general principle is there. There are rules to go with it. There are words to express it, although not in the way I am doing it here, for that is not yet the rhetoric of courts, although it has been already in some courts in some areas. Principles do not necessarily control rules, nor vice-versa. Legal principles—such as "liability for wrongful conduct"—are not clearly moated off from everyday attitudes of right and wrong. This is not even at the level of morality.

Law and morality are separate? Do not overgeneralize the question or the answer! Conceptualistic behavior is so tricky, but not necessarily always so bad. Wrongful. What harm? What good?

I am borne out. The court indicates that the findings of the trial judge could give rise to an *inference* (is that *something?*) that so much requisite knowledge existed, i.e. knowledge of the kind that would make Brian's act wrongful. Note, even if such knowledge can be inferred, it does not follow that Brian knew he was wrong, bad, or impolite. But, notice that in the trial judge's findings, when Brian discovered that Ruth was about to "sit down at the place where the lawn chair had formerly been," he at that time "hurriedly got up from the chair and attempted to move it toward Ruth Garratt to aid her in sitting down in the chair." Pity was, he could not make it. He knew better, but not altogether in time. Had he been thoughtless? If he knew she would attempt to sit down, he knew that it was wrong, even though he had inadequate experience at his age to know she would fall down.

So, his knowledge that Ruth might attempt to sit down is a possible inference which the conclusive findings do not exclude. Having such knowledge does not give the intent *named* (defined) in the Restatement, which is based on respectable authority, but it gives rise to an inference(?) of that sort of intent, possibly, and certainly the sort of realization that is enough to let *us* know that Brian acted wrongfully. There is still room for equivocation. The court closed the doubt: "If the court (trial court) finds that he had such knowledge the necessary intent will be established and the plaintiff will be entitled to recover." *Will be established!* A reasonable inference(?) becomes a presumption, as we lawyers say. Conclusive.

Conclusion

It is not my contention that there is that much gold in every opinion. But I believe it quite significant that leading commentators do not mine it, do not mind(E) it, do not see it. ("Of course they are looking for other things.") In the rush away from court law, following the iconoclasm of the legal realists, legal education may be rushing away from one of the most important elements of all that legal education *in the past* had to offer. The too common feeling these days is that cases were used to teach law. And now they think cases do not contain law. The bubble bursts, the bubbles in the bath pop. There goes the baby, down the drain.

But what if the cases contain law talk? And what if one gets down into the guts of legal process by way of law talk. If in the "old days," one did this by or under the cover of law and conceptualism, just because the cover is off does not necessarily mean the game is off too. Were the legal realists like a golfer who took the cover off the golf ball to see what was inside and what gave it its bounce and life? Getting that inside insight, they proceeded to try to play the game with a ball without a cover. Put the cover back on but let it be a transparent.

True, we have spent too much time with cases if the purpose be to get the law(s) *out* of them. We can satisfy ourselves with Restatement and Hornbooks for the upper layers of understanding. There is actually a valuable lesson for lawyers to be learned to see what courts do with past cases by quoting and abstracting *from* them. Prosser's cover treatment of *Garratt v. Dailey* is not wrong in that respect. The case does exemplify the Restatement definition, even if it does more. You have to know how to go that far before you can go farther.

"You have to walk before you can run."

You have to run before you can leap. Or what's a meta-for?

There seems to be no substitute for the deeper analysis of opinions if one wants to get not only a feel for but a skill in law, law talk, and relevant-to-that lawyering.

"Back to the good old days?"

Well, now that is not what I am backing at all. I want to say that if anyone has followed me to this point, I am suggesting that there is after all a faster way of getting this understanding. In the long run future it will not be a law specialty, but until general education catches up (and sh-h-h, if we lawyers want to stay ahead) we can readily train out students in communicative processes. If we are to be the masters with words we must be the masters of words. Or at least peerless colleagues with them. So far as I know, there is no substitute for the wrestling, but I believe the law talk skills can be filtered out, or distilled out, from the other ingredients of legal process, and that concentrate can be used in accelerate fashion to teach . . .,

"But the hocus-pocus too? Why that in Garratt?"

Simple. Simple enough. Look at the reactions to the relative sincerity of the Supreme Court of the United States during the Warren Era. Courts are not supposed to "legislate," well, at least not openly. It does take special skills to do what the Garratt court did.

CHART #6

INTENT
INTEND ________________(word forms)

Following sub-form table summarizes moves necessarily taken over long periods of time.

Not readily learned by child;
nor all moves simultaneously.

Distinguished moves serve varying functions, e.g., for describing, inferring, evaluating conduct.

Gives insight into ways of other words, how conduct is variously evaluated, and into communications analysis generally.

SUB-FORM TABLE:

	as of now for future	as of then for future
A. Fact of pre-minding	(he has) (I have) INTENT$_1$ INTEND$_1$	(had) (ed)
B. Not pre-minded	aware while doing	not aware
	INTEND$_{2a}$ed (had) INTENT$_{2a}$	INTEND$_{2b}$ed (had) INTENT$_{2a}$
C. On purpose	INTEND$_{3a}$ed (had) INTENT$_{3a}$	INTEND$_{3b}$ed (had) INTENT$_{3b}$
	(Also INTENT$_{3c}$ and INTEND$_{3c}$ when it is said now that it was earlier pre-minded)	

DISCUSSION OF A & B moves.

N.B. plotted only with respect to behavior manifested by actor.

ILLUSTRATION:
X does act D at moment R.
e.g., waves his hand

@moment R-1
may INTEND$_1$ to D
(also have INTENT$_1$)
if so,
@moment R
he INTENDS$_{2a}$ to D,

but clearly he does not have INTENT$_1$ to D.

(here is where metaphor begins. He is acting as if he had the INTENT$_1$ at moment R-1, as he did, but may not have, and still would very likely act same @moment R)

@moment R+1
we can look back and say he INTEND$_1$ed @moment R-1 to D @moment R, and that he did @moment R INTEND$_{2a}$ to D

Suppose he was not aware @moment R that he was D'ing. At best we can *only* say he INTEND$_{2b}$ed to D. To say he had the INTENT$_{2b}$ is clearly metaphor, a "play" on INTENT $_1$, for it was not "on the mind," not even in the 2a sense.

DISCUSSION OF C moves

Considering consequences:

These usages ("games") developed ("played") with respect to C moves arose out of situations where important to determine or wonder whether D considered consequences of his action(s).

ILLUSTRATION:

Suppose D told not to wave his hand, and yet later he does it, he may say:

"Well, I intended to do it in a sense, but not for the purpose of breaking your order (or rule, suffering your sanction.)"

Certainly he can legitimately say that if he breaks the lamp in the process, even if he knew it would happen, if his act was not directed to that consequence, to ward off a bee, for instance: "I did not intend$_3$ to break the lamp!!"

But in tort law, we say he intend$_4$ed to break the lamp, in order to *impute responsibility*. Surely this is metaphoric extension.

See Garratt case: D intend$_1$ or $_2$ to Z, but not necessarily to produce bodily contact. He acts as if he had the intent$_1$ or $_2$ of an adult. METAPHOR there, but since he is not an adult, a CONSTRUCT at his level of action

(See Exhibit V, Appendix further, on C moves.)

Chapter VII

(")FACT(S)(")

Meaningful Interlude: All Together

1. Ball. Say ball. This is a ball.

Give me the ball. Hand it to me, like this. Now again.

Roll the ball here. See, like this, roll, the ball. H-mm-m, ha, hu-h, heh, ha, yes, that's it.

No, not in the mouth, no-no. Put only food in your mouth. A ball is not food. A toy. No toys in mouth, no, give me the ball, roll it. No-no, do not throw the ball.

Throw the ball. No, not like that, not roll, heh, heh. Here. Oh, roll it.

No-no. Do not throw the ball in the house. Outside. No, do not throw it out, go outside. Here, give me that ball!

2. It occurs all together, learning to say, know, and do.

3. Gentlemen, if you will notice in the Garratt case, the court is concerned with battery and intent. Why didn't the court talk about negligence?

No-no, you cannot talk about the negligence of a 5½-year-old child.

Can somebody tell me how intent in law differs from everyday concepts? It's in the Restatement there. The law is stated there, quite authoritatively. The court is following the Restatement. Look at the section, in the Restatement. It's the law.

What had gone wrong in the court below? How had the

trial judge erred. Yes. Yes. Great! He did not apply the rule of the Restatement accurately to the facts of the case. Do you see that everyone?

Here, someone else try that. Give me the facts . . . Now again.

What is the argument for the plaintiff? Someone make it. No, not that way, *for* the plaintiff, take his side, see, like this . . . Now give that to me better.

How about the argument for the defendant? No 5½-year-old lawyers? Ha-he-hah. Well, ahrr-mmm.

From Thing Words to Something Words and Back Again

Thing words, like "cup," "ashtray," and "ball," are learned in a variety of associations and experiences with objects named and classified and identified by the words, such as a ball. One learns how to use the word at the same time he learns how to use the object (saying and doing). No wonder the *naming* feature of words comes to take hold, not just as a tentative classification, but more like an engraving, a deeply etched feature of the object itself. The relationship has been *so* intimate.

Something words are learned through a process of association with situations. Rather than being largely experiential, a matter of physical and personal involvement, or nonverbal communication, these situations may become more and more verbally involved or predominated; mental or intellectual, someone might want to say. The first experiences with thing words has to be primarily in a non-verbal way and context. Gradually learning can become highly verbal. Learning about "intent" from, say the Garratt Case, is a matter of verbal stimulus. Law-talk learning is primarily verbal. Indeed much that is learned in a schooling context is primarily a matter of word association. (At least it was for the unyoung ones.)

While the context of childhood learning about "ball" is dramatically different from one's learning of "intent" in the law of crimes and torts, there can be a carryover of associations via the forms of language, the syntax and major *kinds* of terms. So it is that the seemingly harmless and incidental words come to be important: the articles, verbs, nouns hooked to verbs and both to other nouns and to adjectives or adverbs, subjects to predicates, having affected the way one comes to appreciate things and their seeming properties (the ball is red, red, give me the red ball) may come to have a carryover meaning, stimulation, and control in situations where the significance and use may be quite different. To say "he has_1 intent" is quite different from "he has_2 the ball." "Cause" and "caused" as verbs are not so apt to mislead as the noun form, "cause" or "the cause," but in both instances relation of tense and syntactic position certainly carry-over (hangover) from action words like wash and washed, and the familiar thing words. Yet we can realize deeper down in the grammar, if we explore it, that they are different. We may say that if X caused damage, he is a cause, or even *the* cause. But we would not say that if X washed the car he is a wash or the wash. The best (or the worst) we might say is that he is a washer.

So, "cause" becomes a something word in ways more subtle than even "intent." Of course the mental-introspective aspects of "intent" give it magical potentialities of a kind different from those of "cause" and its metaphysics, in turn quite marvelous to behold. As a something term, "title" has an even different kind of subtlety. Whether the term was originally sired in the titles of royalty and their entitlements, today it is related more closely to ownership and property. These terms and concepts interrelate in ways to produce a tangibility that can cover the *relationships* that are being named, just as it is with rights. The deeper grammar reveals that one has_3 a title to or in, title-to, title-in something, property. He has a right-in, right-to something or a right-against somebody or some sociolegal entity, say a corporation or a class of people or society at large.

And yet there are amongst us those anti-semantics who criticize attention to single words. It is true that single words rarely have communicative significance in isolation. We rarely go around uttering single words. Still, they can take on a psycholinguistic transcendence that may have justified an earlier metaphysics and the later semantic emphasis in opposition to conceptualism and "transcendental nonsense." There are single words that stand out and have key significance, hiding the other subtleties of communication as in the following: (1) child, son, offspring, bastard, sibling, brother. (2) He was the cause of the accident. (3) Whatever you say, the law says otherwise. (4) After considering the commentaries, we still know that the rule is . . . (5) All opinion to the contrary, the facts are . . . (bastard, cause, law, rule, and facts respectively).

"Fact" is such a word, no doubt of that, no doubt at all, no doubt. It is not a doubting word, but one of the most dogma-oriented, fraught-with-conceptualistic-risk, words in the English language. (along with "is" and relatives) It is not merely a legal term for sure. It has many significant special legal usages, yes. But all of them borrow in one shade or another from the everyday lexicon, going off into metaphor, construct, and fiction.

Fact Rankings

One of the most significant subtleties about the word "fact" is the way it is used to give ranking, status, and value to other words. "Law" and "rule" are also used that way, incidentally. We may treat these terms psycholinguistically like something-words, but their referents very often are other words. So, we point to a statement and say it is a rule, thus giving the statement a special significance. That is a major function of the term which has little or nothing to do with the question whether rules can be proven. They can be stated and created. Part of the act of creation is through the word "rule." It is in that sense a performative term, like the delivery of seizin or the statement "I do" in the marriage ceremony. I am not saying this is the only significant kind of context or use of these terms, however. "Fact," for instance, is a term of considerable rhetorical influence via the process or techniques of rhetorical defining.

I am prepared to say that the word "fact" displays its chief values in this combination of dramatizing-and-ranking by a *naming* process, of naming other words, along with the power of rhetorical persuasion which it has come to have. In many situations it is just a matter of having the power to say what the facts are, as with the jury, exceeded in fact-power only by appellate courts who may convert facts into laws. It is a similar process but a higher power.

This function of "fact(s)" can be proven. I have summarized the proof in the previous dialogue "Has Anyone Seen A Fact?" If it were not for such quality, functions, and powers of the word, we could not have legal education, courts, or philosophy, let alone science or history, not to mention . . . , Much of philosophy has been concerned with debate and analysis concerning the significance of statements that are labelled or regarded as factual or true. ("True" and "truth" also refer to verbal statements.) It was from that sort of significant interest that science was helped to its present state. Along came semantics. The whole business of trying to see what interrelations there were between words and things, and behavior, is involved.

As I have indicated, the proof lies in probing the depth grammar of the word "fact." There are other proofs. It is marvelous to think that deep down we "know" these things. I would rather say that the knowledge is not just in *us* but in our *involvement* with language and depth grammar. This is one of many examples I would proffer to suggest the scientific potentials of linguistic and communicative analysis. It may seem like arm-chair science, but it is not, really. It is necessary to grasp these significances by a process of person-to-person involvement that I can only suggest in these pages.

What are the other proofs? Any lawyer or law student can say, upon reflection, if he has something of the sort of awareness I have been emphasizing. The facts we take as our means of learning and discussing law (law-talk process) come from judicial opinions. The fact statements are "the facts." They are read and/or translated into other statements which are said to be "the facts." They are commented upon as facts. Whatever the "original happenings," (also facts when stated), the official statements are "the facts," at one or more removal of abstraction (and permutation). As I have put it, they are the law-facts, not the original facts, however those might be stated by the uninitiated, untrained (unspoiled) observer; the verbal statements that count, for law; that are relevant. For this and other purposes they make for official law-fact talk.

Hypothetical Facts (and Rules)

But it is not just judicial opinions that provide the source. Here we enter what to me approaches an almost mystical area of communication, but presented as fully rational, the very *form* of rationality, not at all confined to courts or law classes. I refer to the hypothetical statement of facts, those facts which are assumed for purposes of decision or argument or reasoning. This technique is indispensable to law and philosophy, not to mention newspaper editorials, politicians, and . . . ,

People who are dependent upon words in the *special* ways that lawyers and philosophers have been are especially prone to the magic of hypothetical assertions. They are part of the reasoning process. Hypothetical assertion is not to be confused with scientific hypotheses, although the latter can be just as captivating, if they are treated as laws of nature, even if only "for now," tentatively (but firmly so). Scientific hypotheses, according to the myth of scientific method, can be confirmed or not. Hypothetical assertions cannot be and need not be, which is why they are so charming (E).

The magic that lies in the hypothetical assertion is this. It completely by-passes the communicative processes that are involved in getting from dynamic happenings to frozen facts-statements. What is a fact is a function of some one or more communication situations. The frozen facts (statements) of the appellate report are in that sense close to being hypothetical. It does not matter whether they are true or false. They are the facts that ground the rules, whatever they may be, that are to be derived from the opinion(s). One may, similarly, assume, and do it blatantly by admitted fiction, certain(E) facts, and go on from there. The lawyer working with a case whose facts are as yet undecided, even though he may have faith in his own conclusions, must weigh them in the process of becoming whatever they might get to be in the dynamics of negotiation, trial, argumentation, and decision ahead of him. That we have to have official ways of validating certain conclusions as facts does not take away from the magic that lies in the hypothetical, assumed, stipulated, or officially stamped facts. If we allow the power of the word "facts" to take our eyes off the statements that are thus being labelled, *to fail to see them as words*, we inevitably fall prey to one of the most powerful forms of rhetoric yet evolved.

There is an interesting parallel with rules. The parallel is therefore doubly worth comment. It was almost an accident that I had the occasion to have an experience which helped me to see the possibilities that lie in the power to assert certain statements as rules, when done in the right place and time. I refer to my first experience with a seminar on Law and Communication. It was there I introduced The Basic Rules. This was a class, realize, not just of law students, but half made up of graduate students in communication theory. My major premise in introducing the Basic Rules was that they might give the law students some common grounds with the participants from Communication. Also, I wanted to show, in maybe the only way it can be shown, that rules are dependent for their significance upon the communication situations into which they are transported or introduced. We would, I believed, make of these rules whatever substance they could have. One must experience that happening, best while it is happening, but at least in ripe reflection. I doubt that talking about it only from an uninvolved distance is quite enough. (Other potentials later.)

Now if you, who are uninvolved with them-in-that-situation, look at that body of rules, you can see that they are hopelessly ambiguous and conflicting. *How like the body of rules which the legal realists saw in law.* But it turns out you have to see this from the outside, detached, in an uninvolved way. That above all else is important to see in the legal realistic perspective. From the outside we can say the Rules do not exist. They cancel each other out. (See Basic Rules in Appendix)

But, they were called Rules, and Basic at that. They were brought in by the authority figure. (GRADES!) They *are* rules. (Compare when a teacher presents *the facts,* for discussion or examination. You cannot fight them, or better not.) There they are. They were believed. Especially were they invested with substance because some members instinctively felt or saw how they could use them to advantage in asserting their own dominance and pursuing their own ideas, by imposing them against competing individuals or blocs. And they in turn felt the threat, even though they apparently saw some of the ambiguities. That they were ambiguous gave no guarantee they would be interpreted that way. And we may note that whatever may be said of the indeterminacy of rules, they are given precision through decision. (Cases are not *decided* both ways!) So there was reality, whatever might be the view from the outside or in detached objectivity. I learned something. Hypothetical rules can be as real as anything, say as hypothetical facts.

Frozen Facts

Say it again. It must be stressed and restressed, to the point of distress. Frozen facts are a function of the dynamics that stand between them and the reference point of raw, as yet uncharacterized events. Frozen facts come out of dynamic facts. Hypothetical assertions simply by-pass those dynamics, constituting word magic of one of the most subtle sorts, providing such a shrewd way of *loading* an argument or a justification. Seeing this where in one sense the loading is clear may help to see the dynamics where they are muddled in a different sort of way. Still, so subtle is the influence of hypothetical-argument, the subtlety of movement from dynamics to freezing may be somehow easier to see. Maybe we need to look at both at once.

Whether we speak of hypothetical assertion or of frozen facts, the more embracing phenomenon is that of verbal characterization. The power to say how it shall be said is immense. This is clearest with statutes, regulations and other rules, but equally important in other power exercising situations, not just in official decision-making situations. In the extreme, there is the power of government control of mass media, propaganda, but the power of an attorney to state the issues of a case or situation carries its own nucleic energy. Stating of issues is a form of argumentation, as any lawyer knows when he is shaping them for the written brief. Courts state not only facts but the issues and the law. What control! I recall a president of a university wondering what legal education did to prepare lawyers for their prominence in the life of a community. Many people have remarked at the ability of this or that lawyer to "get right at the issues." Power over the questions that will be asked carries tremendous influence. Very often it includes the "right" to answer or determine who will answer. Lawyers are (or should be) trained to think in terms of issues and problems, and questions. This bothers the neophyte or the ambiguity-intolerant, but if only he could appreciate the importance of the skill of dogmatically stating an issue. What power lies there.

This power of loading (leading) by characterization is also seen in the analytical efforts of scholars, as the essay on "The Right Way" (Appendix) attempts to suggest. Arguments over the relationship between law and morality are *in part* arguments over "the right way" to say it, naturally giving the ones most expert in that way of saying it some considerable influence regarding the translation from the wrong or unripe way into the mature, proper, or best way. Philosophers have made much of their easy assumption that an "is" cannot be derived from an "ought" for instance. Similarly, courts determine whether an issue is of-fact or of-law, thus giving ultimate power not only over juries but over administrative bodies, although in the latter instance it is not quite so simple. Administrative bodies now have control over facts that require their special sort of expertise. And there is just too much of administrative process for courts to review. So far as that goes, trial judges are not out of the power struggle, by any means, what with their control over characterization, areas of discretion, and so on. But when it is needed, the appellate court determines the "right way," as witness the Garratt Case, as one small (boy) example.

Is intent a matter of fact? Look how the Garratt court whittled down the fact aspect to the question whether Brian knew Ruth would attempt to sit down. Given that, then the requisite intent existed. The court actually created a conclusive presumption out of a permissible inference, one of the ways that appellate judges can take control. But the intent remains a fact question.

In his essay on intent in the Law, (See intent in the Law of Crimes and Torts—Appendix) Dr. Kenny had criticized courts for allowing so-called objective tests of not only intent but of knowledge-of-likely-results-regardless-of-purpose. In the course of his essay he gave hypothetical examples where knowledge existed without purposed results: "If I open a window to look out, how do you know whether I also wanted to get you cold," or "If I say I slapped your sunburned back to kill a poisonous spider . . ." It is not only in law but in everyday life as well that we judge by objective manifestations (as they do in contract law, instead of the old "meeting of the minds"). As with an individual who does a suspicious act, self-serving statements are only part, and possibly not a very credible part, of the evidence. But in essays, lectures, judicial opinions, examinations, and many other places, self-serving statements are permitted and encouraged. After all, if I cannot have this freedom, to say, in class for instance, "now what should a court do with the following facts?" how could I train in the law-fact dialectic, or if someone could stop me by saying, but that did not really happen.

And yet . . . Not only does this technique train-in a needed dogma skill, it leads to self deceptive dogma, and it continues the complicated sort of conceptualism that is based in learning word-thing relationships in the nursery. It is not always vicious, but there is a circle there.

Key words besides "fact(s)" play their parts. Words that are or seem to be fact words, *words on their way to becoming law words*. "Intent" has been a good example. "Negligence" is another. So consider the hypothetical assertion in negligence law-fact dialectic. (Not intended just for torts fanciers)

In order to have liability for negligence, the defendant must be "found" to have caused the claimed damage. Defendant must have done something that necessarily led (or significantly helped to lead) to the damages. Or—and here it is—D must have *failed* to do something, *omitted* to do something that, had it been done, would have prevented the damages; i.e. if D had done X, Y would not have happened. Or, on the other side in trying to establish whether what he did actually caused the damage, would the result have occurred if he had not done what he actually did. Is this confusing? More: in order to determine what omissions to consider, we must ask what he should have done as a reasonable person. So, had he done what he should have done, or had he not done what he should not have done, and we can say that the damages would not have occurred, then D is a cause, or more dramatically, *the* cause.

Suppose, as is the case, a doctor cannot practice medicine without a license. (Statute) Suppose an unlicensed doctor does operate on a patient who is uninformed (*re* license). Severe damages result from his work. Lawsuit. Claim of negligence. Lack of license offered in support of claim. Is it relevant? Well, violation of statute (as here) can be called negligence as a matter of law. But there has to be a causal relation. What did the doctor fail to do? He failed to get a license. *But if he had had a license, the damages would have occurred anyway.* Therefore the lack of a license is not a cause of the damage. The doctor's negligence is not a cause of the damage.

I have not made up this reasoning. (Actual case) What beautiful obfuscation. There are better arguments for minimizing the relevance of the statutes in question, better in the sense of getting down to policy questions regarding the importance of the regulation of such practices and the function(s) of claims suits in implementing regulatory statutes, and so on. But not better for hiding the ball behind fact-form conceptualism. One need not get down to *those* issues when he is facing other issues which can seem so clearly right.

They do not seem right? What if I had called the doctor a chiropractor and had said that he had that license, but not a license of the kind granted only to MD's and required for any practice of medicine?

"The doctor's negligence is not a cause of the damage" is an E statement. Here the word "negligence" sounds like a fact word. It can be used that way, but in others as well. There is not only a pun (double meaning) but a double pun (Where the Suns Rays Meat). At least there is if you consider whether the lack of a license has any relevance to the possible lack of skill of the doctor or chiropractor. There is the tort of negligence. There is behavior which is negligent. There is an abstract quality of a person's behavior which can be called negligence. (Enuf? Spell it backwards.)

And ask yourself this: If my problem is a hypothetical, then have I somehow loaded my argument regarding hypotheticals? I think not.

Suppose A is driving at 80 mph in a 50 mph zone. A child darts out and is killed under the wheels of his car. Did his speed cause the death of the child? This is the kind of questions that courts answer, or the kind of answers that give rise to my questions. Well, we want to ask what would have been the case if the driver had not been speeding. We can assume or think that the same result could well have happened. But . . . How can we know? How can we know what would have been the case had the doctor gone through the business of getting a license? It is like going back in the Time Machine and changing a fact. But what would happen then? You cannot change facts! You can only change fact statements, fact-type characterizations.

So, there have been pleas that we try to deal with what *did* happen. Furthermore, "speed" is not something by itself but part of something. It is an abstract quality-word which seems like a thing-word because it seems a fact word and each fact seems capable of independent existence. (But facts do not exist. They are the best we can do—say.) Metaphysics? In law no less? Such reasoning is part of everyday discourse and argument and rhetoric. Negligence is not something by itself either. Compare speaking of negligent behavior. The person who was speeding was engaging in negligent driving. His driving which was negligent caused the accident. Now, should he be responsible? To say that his speed did not cause the accident is really to say that he is not responsible without considering the tougher questions. To say that the behavior caused the damage is not to solve the problem but it is to save it for more conscious consideration.

We have not even mentioned Jerome Frank's fact skepticism. But his viewpoint helps to raise questions about any dogmas concerning the finality of fact statements, however they are reached, let alone assumed or hypothesized. We are barely touching that morass, the "real world" of happenings before crucial law-fact and other sorts of judgments are made. Given the problems of perception and memory and motivation that are involved in a trial, it is no wonder that some sort of fact-dogma covering is needed.

"Fact" Functions

What I am stressing here might be called fact-word skepticism.

What is a fact? What is a fact question? When are we confronting fact, when opinion; when fact, when law; when fact, when inference? When is a word a fact-word?

These are significant questions, but recognize they are partly linguistic. There is a psycho-linguistic dimension, just as I have suggested there is in connection with the word "law" and with law-talk generally. Sorry. But that *is* a fact.

Compare my asking what has been or can be *done* with the word-concepts: fact, fact question, fact-opinion; fact-law; fact-inference, not to mention fact-value.

The dictionary is not very helpful in answering these questions. The fact family is quite complex, and some of the relationships are not entirely legitimate enough for a respected dictionary to record. (Incest. Bastardy. Etc.) When I wrote to one prominent legal scholar asking what he thought about a good analysis of the ways in which the word "fact" is used in law, he advised against it. "Why spoil a good thing?" I would not want to and I am sure I will not. The habits are too deep—and they are not all bad.

But consider this. One writer entitled a book, *Law as Fact*. I have suggested that facts have rules. Well, if there is a statute on the books, it is law and that is a matter of fact that can be verified in a typical fact-finding sort of way, (like dis-covering who said, "If it is a fact, it is truer than true" or something like that). So, this is a use, permissible if not usual. Remember the rules of facts to begin with. It is statements which are facts, not things. (Has Anyone Seen A Fact?) It is a fact "that a certain thing is." One tries to verify the statement to see if it is true (or really factual), and if the necessary correlation exists . . . Or he accepts it. Or he just asserts it.

So, "fact" fathers a family of amazing structural complexity. Fact-words do not necessarily name facts, because they can be used for many other purposes (E). Consider my earlier discussion of the cup which was used as an ashtray. In one sense it is a question of fact whether the object was still a cup when used as an ashtray. Suppose the sign on the wall to empty cups in the sink stated the words of an ordinance. Is it now a question of fact whether it was a cup or an ashtray? Well, the City Fathers certainly did not intend to have ashes emptied in the sink. But their intent (?) is not a question of fact. It is for the court to decide. It is part fact, part linguistic, part law. I had said that "intent" in tort cases was part fact, part law. But here it is not fact at all, except to determine wheher ashes were emptied in the sink, or whether a cup was being used for some other purposes.

My example is not frivolous, although hypothetical. Consider the following word-concepts: Employee, control, gift, man, communist, drug, agent, cause, insanity, reasonable, and vehicle —a few out of all possible fact word-concepts. If they are key words in a statute, ordinance, regulation, or even a contract, then they are for the court to *interpret*. Yet, in a libel suit, if defendant was charged with calling plaintiff a communist, whether he was a communist would be a question of fact. Of course whether a person is a communist under a statute constitutionally exerting some regulation over communists would probably be a fact question, under guidance from the court as to what a communist is, but such guidance (or control) of the jury would probably not occur in the libel suit. It is a question partly of time and place, and of what functions are to be served by the interacting decision-makers, under the cover of "fact."

If there are fact words, like the thing words "cup," "ash-tray" and also like action words, property words, and so on, the words that can serve as fact-words also serve other functions, just as a matter of psycho-linguistics. So courts and lawyers are just doing what comes naturally with these words and with the word "fact." But there needs to be some charting-unloading, to see if there are patterns of use and legitimacy in the patterns. Words that are used as fact-words are used to name, describe, identify, and classify. The very word "fact" is itself used this way; i.e. "Is a given statement a fact statement?" It may be with regard to verification procedures, but not for court procedures of verification—or interpretation, as I have illustrated. This is vivid illustration of what Korzybski was getting at in calling such words multiordinal (many values, like "x" in algebra). "Fact" was one of the words he named, classified, identified, and described-evaluated in that fashion. (Whether "fact" is multiordinal is a fact question?)

Let's look a bit at the dynamics. What sort of question is *said to be* a fact question in the context of a jury trial-appeal is not necessarily controlled by the same criteria with regard to the judicial review of administrative body decisions. Conceivably whether a tomato is a fruit under a criminal or tax statute would be one of law at a trial, but with regard to health control measures, it might be for an administrative body to determine, on grounds of special expertise, and so virtually unreviewable. Within the jury dynamics, opinion evidence is not admissible, unless it is given by a qualified expert. Surely these are two of many "control" mechanisms in the allocating of decisional function. Leon Green well pointed out this feature of the law-fact dichotomy and with respect to law-fact dialectic in the law of torts. Forty years ago! But many a tort teacher is benignly ignorant of his analysis and insight. And it comes hard for freshmen students, very hard. I think it requires linguistic-communicative sophistication to see it. What Leon Green pointed out for torts is absolutely true (relatively speaking) of any, literally any area or matter coming up for judicial consideration. See the Garratt case as a charming (E) example.

It is in these dynamics that indeterminacy most lies (E). I have said that the legal realists looked at legal terms and rules and principles, perhaps unbeknownst to them, as law-talk. As in everyday talk, law-talk has a spontaneous aspect. Who knows what someone will say in the next moment. What he says contains his judgments. In this the judicial behaviorists are correct in looking at the fact-talk, to see the lurking attitudes. But the facts so described, named, identified, classified, abstracted, evaluated, do not exist by themselves. To affirm a jury finding of liability against a corporation in favor of an employee is not necessarily to favor employees. It may be to determine the function of juries to be free to favor employees, among other things. Or a little of both. There are multiple dimensions in law-fact characterizations, decisional allocation among others. We might say this is what courts do with facts, but it is more what they do with fact-words and fact characterizations, and fact-law, fact-opinion sorts of dichotomy-characterizations. (Non-law researchers of judicial opinions tend to be woefully ignorant of procedure.)

But note again, that it is not just a dichotomy. Courts often speak of mixed questions of law and fact. "Intent" is a mixed question of law and fact; it is a law-fact question; it is part of law-fact talk. See Garratt! Or any case where instructions are given to juries. Look at the terms. This is the proof, along with appellate court review of these instruction characterizations, of the psycholinguistics I have been illustrating here. That is why Leon Green can say something to the effect that "law" and "facts" are words describing the functions of judge and jury. Recognize that included within that classification scheme of Leon Green are questions that everyone, practically, would agree were pure fact questions—what was the speed of the car?—and others that are pure law questions —what was the speed limit? (But. . .see later) Well, at the trial, speed limit is a pure law question—usually. There are conventions of court as well. But then there are the movements into metaphor, construct, and fiction. See Garratt!

All this consideration of court facts has not been to suggest merely that courts play with "facts" when they are being unconventional, even if using the words conventionally. That would be worth the effort, but it is only an illustration, maybe only a small one. Lawyers who never go to court engage in similar combinations and permutations. Professor-lawyer Louis Brown has well illustrated a control mechanism lawyers have regarding dynamic facts in their offices, the mechanism of freezing the facts by what he calls fact management. His theme of preventive law as a major task of lawyering depends upon this fact-management skill. Lawyers prevent lawsuits as well as engineer them, keep people out of trouble, arrange their lives in accordance with and under the benefits of the not only negative sanctioning but positive-ordering law-rules, such as those of contract and corporation and taxation, for instance. By drawing appropriate instruments freezing the negotiations at the time of contract, lawyers can therein stipulate the facts that will be relevant at trial, facts of record. Court findings are not the only records that are invulnerable to readjudication so to speak.

There is need for such finality. If courts were to admit to the control they in fact(E) have, they would lose much more authority than they can afford. Their own law-fact talk would be doubly vulnerable, not only on the law but on the characterzations they choose for the facts-statements. Such agreed starting points seem inevitably necessary as part of the ordering process of law itself. In short, a statement of facts is an agreement to "start here!" Else you get back into the morass that Jerome Frank did not invent but uncovered. (Whew!)

It is interesting that legal positivists stay out of this morass, and assume rules, principles even, on the basis of agreed, stipulated, and hypothesized facts. This is unrealistic in one regard. But it is realistic, very practical, on another level. After all, people can be trusted to reach fact-dogma conclusions, not just in courts or classrooms or professional commentaries, or newspapers, streetcorners, in the Pubs, and so on. They cannot be stopped. Law would seem to be enough to try to manage, even given these somewhat arbitrary, but human nonetheless, starting points. The starting point of the law process is the end of the fact process. Or so it would seem. So it would seem. Seem. Seem. Seem. (a seem-less web?)

If you let facts into law arguments, then you let linguistic complexity fully in as well. Then morality gets all confused with law. Then not only do the courts and the legislatures lose the control which their authorities must have, but the commentators lose theirs as well. It is the Right Way, no doubt of that.

CHART #7

An Act as Fact____ (F)ACT

ACT
FACT ←————— (word forms)

1. What did the Professor *do* when he dropped the book?
   (see chap. 3)
   word-form games

sub-forms	
Act_1	He dropped the book
Act_2	He held up the book and dropped it
Act_3	He opened his hand
Act_4	He made a sound
Act_5	He startled someone

See how different from wg's with INTENT, chap. 6

2. But–did he $INTEND_{1,3}$ to make a sound; i.e., (?) think about it & do it on purpose?

   Not necessarily, but he probably did not $INTEND_{1,3}$ Act_5, i.e., he can disclaim responsibility.

3. Did he perform five Acts? obviously not according to $level_1$ available wg's: If B asks what the professor did, A picks out one or more of above and/or others and says: "That's what he did."

4. *Cf.* at $level_2$: in philosophy, or legal theory, communication theory, etc. Not strange to say he did five acts!!!

5. In law talk, $level_1$, he did one act.

6. In talk talk? ($level_3$) Not the job to say what his act was–or what an act is. Now–at $levels_{1\&2}$–we know better what is happening, or what we can do (with words).

7. What was his act? (split)
   (screen)

8. *Cf.* Show Me a Rule–violates the linguistic rules at
   $Levels_{1\&2}$
   not at $Level_3$.

9. *Cf.* Has Anyone Seen a Fact? Shows what the linguistic rules are at $level_1$. Rule dialogue shows how linguistic rules at $level_1$ are inconsistent with linguistic rules at $level_2$.

10. Is an ACT a FACT?
    (split screen it?)
    (could use dialogue technique)

11. Thus: What he did was a fact. We can see_1 what he did. We can see_2 *that* what he did was a fact (fact dialogue), i.e., we can see the fact that . . . ., but not the act as fact, at least not at $level_1$. (maybe, just maybe, @ $level_2$.)

12. Word-form games conclusions:

    a. ACT can in one word-game be used to refer *directly* to non-verbal behavior, but in another game it can be used and restricted in the manner of FACT.

    b. When the professor says, "Watch my act, he is playing one game.

    c. When he says, "What was my act?" he is playing quite another. That game can be played only with words.

INSIGHTS

Games with word-forms
ACT
FACT
and all others

As to handiness of hypothetical facts, or better, (F)ACTS.

See what we actually do with

(")FACT(S)(")

(E)

Chapter VIII

ROLES, GOALS, AND SITUATIONAL PERSPECTIVES

Prelude

We are exploring communication mainly from the perspective of an interpreter. There is no communication without interpretation, good or bad, automatic or drawn out. As one model has it, at one end of communication is a user, a doer, an actor, or producer; at the other end a receiver. The receiver interprets in some way, whether he be on a "hot channel" in face-to-face dynamics or working over the colder stuff of history, maybe interpreting a constitution or a statute.

Of course interpretations are not all that easy to separate from other stages and aspects of communications interactions. There may be an interpretation implicit in a transmission, as there is in the statement of the "meaning" of an ambiguous regulation. In that sort of situation, the actual interpretational behavior has preceded the statement, as it does the interpretative explanations of a judicial opinion. (See Garratt) When we get into the dynamics of face-to-face confrontations, then the interpretations are often right out there to see. (See earlier analysis of intent.)

In any event, communications analysis is not restricted to the two ends of a channel (or a log). One who is observing communication, for instance, also interprets, even though he is not an intended receiver.

From that *interpreter* viewpoint, one may see various factors working on varying levels and moving in varying directions, but not necessarily with some machine-like coordination. The actor whose transmission is being interpreted may to some degree choose his medium and yet not be in complete control of it. The observer (receiver, audience, interpreter) may not feel that he can control his responses. ("If the meaning is there, what can you do?") Still there is some option, even if not exercised, as to where to "come into" the dynamics, how to view the matter, and so on. Not that the interpreter has to stick to one peephole, as we have stressed, but he may have to choose one exit or another, especially if some decision must be made. But in viewing he may at once concern himself both with "meaning" and also other sorts of significances of the communicative act or product.

Rarely is it enough to have the dictionary sorts of meanings. An interpreter is constantly involved in choosing among *implications*, of zeroing-in. Thus if you were told that a certain person "was a close friend of Schickelgruber," your informer may intend you to draw Nazi implications. Whether you do depends upon whether you translate to "Hitler," but even further whether you put "two and two together."

So, it should become clear. While we have not been involved only with them, we move away from any stress on single words. We are especially interested in this chapter in the communicative act-product, in the doing aspects of communication. Not that we are finished with verbal analysis, but here it is complexes of words that are more in focus. Thus, especially important is the relation of the conventional form of statements to their impact on the interpreter. For example, we need to compare the declarative form of law assertion with the parallel form of fact assertion: Compare (1) "The law is thus and so in this situation;" or "That is a battery."$_1$ with (2) "The facts are thus and so;" or "That is a battery."$_2$ (E)

The *implications* are revealing!

Believe it or not the declarative *form* is ambiguous. ("Oh not again.") Conceptualism on the single words level is actually parallelled on the level of word complexes, say a sentence or a whole document. Thus a rule can be used conceptualistically.

It would be easy to underplay what that last assertion implies, i.e. that the relevance of a rule (or principle, policy, etc.) to this or that situation can be oversimplified. The full implications are not easy to state. Felix Cohen spoke of crypto-idealism, Lasswell and McDougal of normative ambiguity. In exploring these matters our stress will be on the interpreter of some piece of law talk. He is to take the pains to locate the utterance in the space-time coordinates of the four dimensional communicatives mosaic. ("That's worse than 'normative ambiguity.' "). We go beyond words into a roles-perspectives analysis.

We started this move in exploring law talk. We have dabbled with role analysis in previous illustrations. But now we must consider kinds of law talk, uses of law talk, and strategies-in-use of law talk. Such analysis is indispensable in considering problems of law-and-order, law-and-morality, but even in trying really to understand how law works and is worked. For that matter, such an analysis is relevant to any discussion of moral problems, either on conventional levels or philosophical, or any place where law-like assertions are made (rules, reg's., by-laws, and so on.) So we may find ourselves complementing if not competing with some increasingly popular approaches to these areas, such as situational ethics, or running in and out of the domain of those who like to view law as a process of decision making (e.g. Lasswell and McDougal).

We also at least peek through the door to the sort of problem that plagues philosophers, scientists, and lawyers. It ought to concern the lay communciator much more than it does. It concerns the *reliability* of assertions (and their implications too). Lawyers speak of credibility of facts, philosophers of verifiability of propositions. For Korzybski, such a problem was at the top of the list, leading to his famous "Does the map fit the territory." But of course lawyers and scientists have discovered that there are degrees of reliability, not only in the courtroom but the lab.

Logicians speak of validity. Theorists including Hart would speak of validity for law, but it is validity$_2$. As we know, however, logical validity is only one of the reliability criteria of an assertion. Thus the syllogism, "All dogs are cats, all cats are spoons, therefore all dogs are spoons" gives a logically valid but not semantically or factually correct conclusion. Nor is logical validity, in any formal sense of "logic," a necessary prerequisite to the reliability of law talk. Whatever might be meant by legal validity, it is not the sole criterion of reliability for measuring a piece of law talk and indeed often would not be considered a prerequisite, as strange as that might seem to say.

J. L. Austin has had much to say about various kinds of reliability criteria for the communications analyst. You would not, for instance, want to say that an apology must be either true or false, but is it sincere ("Is he really apologizing?"). "I do" at a wedding ceremony is a performative utterance which will be effective or not, depending upon who is running the show and such. And a jury verdict is not just to be measured by its truth or some sort of logical validity, but largely by the appropriateness of procedures preceding it. There are, actually, a number of different kinds of verbal assertions, not to be recognized by grammatical form alone. ("It is raining" could be an apology.) Reliability (not to mention usefulness) comes in just as many different measures.

It may be hard to accept, but there are a great variety of criteria to measure the kinds of reliability appropriate to the various kinds of law talk!

In order to probe in some of the ways suggested in this introduction, there are some socially hot illustrations. If objectivity were possible on such issues, hardly any one whose view or attitude is rejected by such an objective analysis would see it as such. Behavioral science research, for instance, or certain kinds of analysis, are supposed to be objective (see "The Right Way"). Objectivity is a high value in law and in all sorts of communication, but it *is* a value, a commitment in and of itself, one that in social issues seems to be increasingly out of style ("old fashioned liberalism").

Maybe the word is misleading: object-ivity. How about openness, good faith, sincerity, empathy, rapport, maybe even human love? Maybe they are equally or more important for "good communication." These are the stuff of Justice surely. Tolerance is somewhere in this act, not $tolerance_1$, to be merely deferential or even deceitful in some minimally permissive way, but $tolerance_2$, trying one's darndest to understand a sharply opposing point of view or even demand. This is not just a matter of humanity in personal relationships but also a very definite aspect of any *objective,* attempt-at-science approach or task.

There will always be those who are afraid of such openness. It is simply too democratic. It *is* subversive. Christ was subversive. Science is subversive. ("So is subversion.") Of course one may be subversive merely in the name of science. In the name of law as well.

True, people do take advantage of openness, for instance of greater access to power, including the power that comes from increased opportunity for communication. Even a slight lifting of those fantastic camouflages of our lego-cultural process gives increased access and power. We are engaged in that, committed to that here. ("Spiro Agnew lifted the camouflage off the mass media!") Those who are not frustrated from being closed off by such camouflages covering naked power (it happens with law) cannot possibly appreciate or tolerate the urge to violence. But sincerity, openness, human love, and all the rest, would be the way. If not out there, why not here, for just a bit?

Such discussion has not been the main meat of our exploration. Deliberate effort has been made to avoid such issues since they impede communication at this level. The sort of communication which has been discussed does provide, however, a necessary preliminary to those more difficult confrontations. And let's face it, there are some issues where so-called good communication (polite, friendly, etc.) may not even be part of the answer.

If the brief sallies into deeper social controversy which are involved in this chapter cannot be tolerated—well, then, where are we? But we should note that for some philosophers and lego-political theorists, among others, some of the issues previously raised are quite hot. See the issues raised in The Right Way, or regarding style, and so on. There are questions raised for legal education throughout the book that might serve to deprive a probationer of tenure. (And why do law schools do such a minimal job of dealing with these all important problems of communication? Why?)

Finally, then, theory has very practical consequences. (See again The Right Way and the many other illustrations *re* the impact of "analysis" and "interpretation".) Everyone has his theories. The sort of theory on communication that is here used to explore law talk and the talk of law theorists, and the law and theory talk of layman as well, cannot remain aloof from questioning law talk patterns. Maybe most importantly, John Q's law theory talk and assumptions should be re-educated.

The vast majority of the American public is woefully ignorant on these matters. I for one hope that we who can might spend some of our time, at least, in attempting to go into the streets, the fields, and aye, the Pubs (ah, yes) to do what we can to promote better understanding.

It can be downright frightening—and yes, frustrating. Things *look* so different when communication becomes a prime concern.

(Un)Muddled Perspectives

Some of the interinvolvements of law and language are easier to appreciate than others. Comparing and seeing the intertwinings of the *stare decisis* of courts with that of word evolutions are insightful for both law and language. And one can readily see that there are no laws of language *forcing* a certain set of words to be used in connection with some situation or even familiar object. I do not have to say, "This is a page," for instance, although the case is harder for the freedom to say it is not a page. ("Well, it is a page after all.")

When it comes to law(s), this aspect of words-*use* is not so apparent, partly because of that sense of word-freezing we get from the status-invoking words like "rules," "regulations," "statutes," and so on. It helps, though, to see that a given set of words put forth in the statement of a rule, can, like a single word, be subject to a range of uses. While conceptualistic attitudes make it difficult to keep track, careful charting shows them "back of the rule," so to speak. Communicatively, a so-called rule is a function of the situation (or kind of situation at least) into which it is transported (communicated). Some sort of communicative act of articulation or interpretation is necessary to what we choose to call *their* (rules) invocation or application.

Later on, I am going to try to demonstrate what there is about interpretation(s) which often thaws what seems to be a frozen set of words in a rule, or even a regulation, statute, or constitution. (All this applies also to so-called rules or principles of morality.) So there is a relatively greater degree of freedom in the legal characterization of a situation than even most contemporary approaches give credit. Situation ethicists see that for morality, and those who would characterize law as a decisional process, rather than the application of rules and such, see that for not just courts but *all* law situations. (Such a broad generalization has to be suspect as overstatement: such potentials exist, but what one is free to do and what he feels compelled to do are two different matters.)

There are those who would have it otherwise (in the name of Justice, no less), as if we all came into the world committed to existing rules of law and morality, with no choice but to play those "games." They tend also to be committed to certain word-thing relationships. Is it just coincidence? Are there cures?

The lego-moral psycholinguistic attitudes carry the ramifications in various directions. Let a person commit one misdeed and he is branded for life. If law and morality are separate, why not be satisfied with whatever sanctions are to be dished out, and allow at least in some situations for some sort of rehabilitation? Lyndon Johnson's chief adviser commits one indiscretion in a public washroom, and . . . swish. One puff of marijuana, and . . . poof. Cheat once in a test situation, and *never* be admitted to the practice of law. Carswell displays an anti-Black attitude in 1958, and gone is his chance for the Big Bench in the Sky. Of course politics and ideology get into these perpetuated sorts of judgments, but verbal hang-ups do too. ("It's all a matter of semantics?")

There is that urge toward easy simplification, what is called the principle of parsimony in science: "Strict construction"; "he broke the law"; "the law in this situation is . . ." "What he did was and therefore is immoral"; "one bad apple . . ." (There is a parallel with what Korzybski called the allness phenomenon.) This attitude knows no ideology and is not limited to being a rhetorical technique.

Try it out. Remember the Garratt Case? Brian was ultimately held liable for having committed a battery, an intentional tort. Would the insurance company be held liable to indemnify Brian when there is an exclusionary clause in the covering contract of insurance which precludes such liability where the bodily injury was "caused intentionally" by the insured.

To say that "intentionally caused" bodily injury for the purposes of that law suit is not necessarily "intentionally caused" bodily injury for purposes of the insurance policy may seem somehow discriminatory against the insurance company. But we talk much more these days of proper allocation of economic risk in injury producing situations. Insurance, taxation, price mechanism, and so on, get into the picture when such policies are discussed. One may be against that sort of sociolegal development ("Communism, by God!"). So we cannot be sure that there is merely a psycho-linguistic hang-up in failing to see "how the very same words" can be interpreted differently.

Yet there is a choice here, at least before the court finally crystallizes the policy-choice into a rule. Previous analysis of "intent" should show several ways of getting out of the potential conceptualistic box of "intentionally caused." Until then, it is not an automatic matter one way or the other.

So, a critic of my "semantic juggling" tries one out on me.

"Suppose," he says, "that Joe Doe commits a murder. Should he be permitted entry, later on, after parole, into law school and ultimately into the practice of law?" "W-e-l-l," says I, "I think they'd keep him out as being of 'bad moral character.' "

"How so? How so?" he taunts. "Murder for purposes of criminal law is not murder for purposes of moral judgment."

I muse a bit, frown, bite my lip, squirm, but really just for his amusement. "I might be able to buy that. Just might. But I'd have to know more about this chap. My feelings would have to be overcome with some pretty strong evidence about the original case and about subsequent events." He goes off shaking his head, before I can finish my explanation.

"Murder is murder. It really is . . .", I hear him trailing off. . .

When I next see him, let me tell him that it probably matters little how open-minded I am or *might* in some rare instance be. (How many holes I have in my head.) The judgment will not be mine to make. I can predict with good odds that Doe will simply not make it. On the other hand, I predict that Brian has pretty good odds with the insurer.

Why must I be held for the judgments I think others will make? The legalist would put it a bit differently for himself: "I am just stating the law," or "I don't make the rules, you know." But even he may have a sort of unconscious appreciation of the possibility that is so often true, where law and morality assertions are used, at least in controversy-linked situations. It is so easy to project one's personal preferences, attitudes, biases, or even prejudices into such assertions. Actually it is difficult to avoid such projections even when there is no particular controversy, because of the sort of psycholinguistics which McDougal calls normative ambiguity, or if you wish, because of the "complexity of legal and ethical experience," as Northrop put it. And it is so convenient and desirable to be always on the side of the angels, not to mention rules and principles *both* of law and morality.

An attempt to unravel the multiple perspectives that are muddled together in the seeming universality of such assertion may bother even men of good will. For one thing, we risk defusing the complex rhetorics of the law-morality entanglements. Not that it is all *just* rhetoric. (E. How *do* you right that?).

Normative ambiguity? Complexity of legal and ethical experience? How put it more simply? Well, whose ox is being gored? Or, there's this story about the six blind men feeling an elephant . . . ("Well, if that's their hang-up.")

The ox and the blind men *are* relevant to this analysis. Those men did not appreciate that they were not in a position to make a sound or accurate judgment. Regarding law we get the same sort of thing, rather like the feelings of the blind men, or at least of people who forget who the decision-makers are and where *they* stand with respect to those decision-makers.

It is interesting. If I say, "I saw a good movie," there is some chance I will be understood to be passing judgment. Yet if in our Joe Doe example I agree with our critic that Doe does not have the requisite good moral character, it is not so noticeable that I am really making someone else's judgment, of the Board of Review which passes on candidates. I might try to predict them, urge them, or urge others to urge them, and there would be ways of sign-posting the role I am taking in each instance. But of course, how much easier in clouded situations to adopt a firm stance and a jutting jaw and say, "The law in this matter is really quite clear."

Remember the Garratt Case? Let's back up from the opinion to the day the event in question occurred. We are sitting up in a tree and Ruth has just hit the ground. I suddenly say, "Hey, that is a battery. That little boy is liable for battery." What is the significance and the implication(s) of my statement? Just how reliable is it at the time? The statement sounds like, "Hey, that's a little boy," but stop to consider the different sort of judgments which are involved and how one would go about checking them out, if he so desired. In making that sort of statement, *I am actually adopting some sort of role(s).*

If I had said, "What a bad boy," the subjectivity is apparent. ("Yes, we learned to recognize 'value' words from semantics.") We hear of a campus protestor, and we say, "Oh he's breaking the law. Why don't they do something about it?" That could be a similar sort of judgment. (So, the form is ambiguous, just as I said.)

But "that is a battery," or really *any* such assertion regarding the state of the law in a given situation, may have a great variety of uses, serve to support a considerable range of role adoptions, and sometimes several at once. Many games are played in the name of or under cover of this or that state of the law, by saying, to put it generally, "The law is . . ." The semantic insight distinguishing between description and valuation simply (E) does not go far enough.

Looking at the Garratt injury-producing event, to say at that time that Brian had committed a battery has almost got to be a guess (if the events went as I read that opinion), although I might have been thinking about one case that would give some support. Now that it has turned out to *be* a battery should not be the test. (When the court says it is a battery, no guess there; although actually that court only said it *could* be.) But I may not be predicting in making that tree high statement, just wishing, or maybe advocating.

Of course we all, whether lawyers or not, often argue one brief or another by purporting to state facts. But there are ways even more subtle in which an assertion of law allows such advocacy. It may be because no matter how muddied facts are, the law is often even less clear, and for that all the more dogmatically stated. (Many who argue minority rights are also "guilty" of such muddied advocacy, but with more cause and privilege, methinks.) Perhaps the added subtlety comes from the very nature of laws ("Well, of course.") Some analysts have put it this way. A law is a norm. ("How clever." Perhaps more than you know.) They have said that laws on the books, so to speak (remember that judicial laws are not so clear as laws on the book), are oughts, telling us how we ought to behave. When you say "The law is . . .", you are asserting an ought. ("I didn't know that." Think of the implications!)

What we are getting at here is the ways in which roles and perspectives may be muddled (often on purpose, often not) because of the way law is talked. The very theorists who wish to prevent *this sort* of participatory democracy, like H. L. A. Hart, seem the least able to recognize the psycho-linguistic complexities which support it, perhaps because they have more faith than American theorists in the English approach to verification. Or maybe they are more sincere and less in need of communicative skepticism.

When the average person makes an assertion of law, it is often impossible to know whether he is asserting a role of historian, prophet, advocate, judge, critic, or reformer (for instances), or maybe all at once.

Lawyers are in a maximum-potential position for this sort of role mixing.

If there is anything to the explorations and revelations of the legal realists (if not, we had better regroup), then what they revealed about the judicial role(s) applies as well to lawyers, but at least squared. If we say that judges are merely declaring law, then we can say the same of lawyers, but when we come to appreciate the decisional matrix, so to speak, that precedes the writing of the opinion, then we also realize that the language of the opinion contains other elements than mere law declaration. Even if we can be assured that there are many, many situations-not-getting-to-court in which the "law is" is sufficiently clear, there are many in which it is not. And it is still true that many a lawyer is considerably more reserved regarding ambiguity and indeterminacy, considerably less conscious of psycho-linguistics and other decisional factors than even the legal realists. The legal realists were trying to bring judges out from under their camouflage. But there are no such pressures on lawyers, generally speaking. And there may often be even more reason for them to take the position of legal soothsayer with perhaps even less justification (having heard only one side of the problem!). There are increasing pressures today to drive judges back underground. Certainly there must be many situations where if a lawyer were fully candid about his role-perspective, his client would think him indecisive, stupid, or immoral, and maybe all that and more.

But usually, the lawyer will be as candid as his consciousness allows him to be. The muddling comes naturally, because psycho-linguistic conventions encourage it, and expectations of clients and others demand it.

We need to look into these possibilities a little more deeply, but stop to consider. If there are such possibilities for judges and lawyers, what about the many, many other places where there has been little or no special training to aid in the recognitions not only of law, but of law indeterminacies, not only the various administrative offices at all levels of government, but in quasi-governmental and even private domains, where "law" is administered or somehow involved. And then there is John Q and the mass media, Finally, and maybe most important, just think what a Minister of Propaganda could do, especially if he were not labelled as such.

Law(yers') Perspectives

Suppose a lawyer plans a murder. No need to go to law school to *know* there is a law against it. An assertion of that law is fully reliable. No exemption exists for lawyers (or judges). They are under obligation, as Hart puts it, to heed the law(s), obey them, and abstain from such conduct. This law shines with equal intensity upon all persons. If the lawyer goes ahead with his plan, he has broken the law. He is a murderer.

Here is an example where conceptualism *qua* legal rules seems absolutely (E) desirable, conditioning for everyone. If only we could all be programmed against murder, rape, and ... (what else?)

But care would be needed to keep the lines clear, to confine the conceptual-programming to one's attitudes regarding his *own* behavior. Lacking such a magic pill, the requisite sort of attitude is conceptually spread by a cultural conditioning that places a social stigma ("murderer") on the violator. Surely that sort of conceptualism is what makes the law work, absent more effective programming.

Still, a lawyer ought not be so conditioned that he cannot handle the case of a person accused of murder or even of someone he is sure has committed a murder. (The availability of a champion is part of the system.)

The statute against murder helps in the conditioning process. It also serves to put a stigma on persons who are even only *suspected* of murder. (Hard even for lawyers to avoid.) He could be fired from his job or suffer any number of non-law sanctions. But we should hasten to add that the range of responses is not just due to the statute. "Murder" is not just a violation of law—and not just a legal term, actually. It is a deeply entrenched moral rule also (not just a principle), a prime example of a general social conditioning which simply cannot be referable to any one prohibiting source. Of course there are other examples of equally strong prohibitions (rape, incest, treason, public nudity in most situations, public sex acts ditto).

Even so, consider the implications of saying X violated the statute prohibiting murder. (Compare the implications of saying "X is a murderer.") Even that statute is not automatically applicable. It is a *per se* prohibition, but the legal sanction is *not in it,* only referred to verbally. It can be imposed only by virtue of criminal proceedings. Someone has to set the mechanism of legal proceedings in motion. So legal sanction can only be implied, as a prediction or maybe an ought, although maybe historically grounded.

That may sound like lawyer quibbling. All right. The lawyer must keep that in mind, that sanction is not automatic. He has to consider the implications if a person comes to his office and says he has committed a murder but he has not been charged or arrested. Should the lawyer tell him to turn himself in? Should he call the police and inform them? Maybe he should encourage it, but it can be partly a consideration of strategy. Maybe the client and even the lawyer have made self-deceptive judgments. Maybe "he is not a murderer," but one can get ensnared in criminal proceedings beyond the point of no return. Trapped! Branded for life even if acquitted.

A lawyer in the practice of criminal law, at least, cannot

afford to be, should not be anything but a rule and fact skeptic. In his role(s) as lawyer serving a client his obligations (unconceptualize) are quite different from his role(s) as ordinary citizen. If he hears the information at a cocktail party, he is not in the sense of this situation a lawyer. ("Once a lawyer always a lawyer.")

We are involved in roles and perspectives charting, indispensable for any adequate analysis of law talk, in or out of professional roles.

But compare. Suppose a man goes to a lawyer's office and says he wants to kill his wife. He says he wants advice on how best to "pull it off" so as not to be caught or convicted. Now the lawyer is being approached in a different role, not to act as a champion-advocate. The lawyer as advocate is certainly not outside the law, indeed he is *in* it in a special way. The statute against murder does not obligate the lawyer to *avoid* that task as advocate, but in the planning stage, surely there is some obligation on the listening lawyer, maybe even to call the police, or at least to threaten it ("Good Lord, man, I am not in that sort of business . . ."). Maybe he becomes a therapist-counsellor, trying to talk the man out of it or getting him into the right office for that purpose. ("Well, *now* he is not a lawyer.")

Of course there are many less dramatic examples where a lawyer may wish to divert a client from his planned path, even where criminal law is not involved. The classic example is the request for divorce proceedings. Or it could be this or that situation where the person has a right to some legal remedy. It is in these sorts of situations that it is easiest to appreciate that at least some rules and mechanisms serve as available strategies, to be put in motion or not, depending on the circumstances. Just because a person has suffered a breach of contract or defamation, or even a criminal attack, it does not follow automatically that it is in his best interests to go to court or start it in motion. As we say, the civil laws do not obligate in that way, they enable. For that matter, criminal laws do not obligate a person to "prosecute."

Do civil laws impose obligations in any way like criminal statutes against murder? Well, if a legal obligation is a legal obligation, yes, but not if legal-obligation$_1$ is not legal-obligation$_2$. ("Well, we had quite forgotten.") For that matter, not even all criminal statutes obligate in the same way. Furthermore, "criminal" laws too are used strategically. Witness the selective enforcement of this or that statute, or the use of tax-crime sanctions to put away a hood, or maybe the Chicago Seven trial or Dr. Spock.

To say, even reliably and validly, that someone "broke the law" does not end the consideration of the varying implications let alone just what the expression itself means under particular circumstances. (The moral dimensions, just for instance.)

We also see that law and morality are not clearly separate in the lawyers' offices, *whatever* is supposed to be the case in court. ("Morality=social perspectives?") e.g. murder does not have just legal implications.

Suppose a lawyer for a large business enterprise. He is told the client wants to terminate a certain business relationship. What if the only way out is to breach a contract? That would be a breach of duty by the client, an infringement of the other party's rights. Should the lawyer allow himself to be involved in that kind of "lawlessness?" Or if the answer seems too easy because we are "just involved in a business relationship," then let the client not be in business.

This is a hard one to unravel but a great example for our purposes. "Objective" analysis is difficult because of attitudes that get into this kind of picture. After all, it is generally felt that one should keep his promises even if they are not legally binding. While obviously not obligatory in the same way, one might conclude that the lego-moral involvement was akin to the murder situation we analyzed earlier, i.e. the law has come along to add its sanctions to social expectations that exist independently without such *reenforcement.* (And see how easy it is to glide off, away from any words-consciousness, just talking, reacting, deciding, going along . . . ,)

Oliver Wendell Holmes tried to unravel the strands. He said

that a party to a contract was *under the law* given the alternative, the option of performing his contractual promises or else paying damages. There are those who regard Holmes as having been amoral for reaching such conclusions. But he was trying to make it clear that he was not saying how a man should act so far as morals were concerned, just what the legal aspects of the situation were.

More broadly, he claimed that rights and duties are predictions of judicial behavior, that really any statement of law was such a prediction. But of course he was wrong, was he not?

When we are sitting up in that tree looking down on Ruth Garratt who had just fallen down and see Brian struggling with that lawn chair, and I say, "Hey, that's a battery," I do not necessarily have courts in mind. In one sense my statement is not valid if a court would not back it up, but if I was counsel for Brian's insurer, you might say my statement was a prediction we would pay Ruth some money.

What we have here is a problem of implications. Communication is very much dependent upon implications, as when I say it is raining, the implication is that I am telling the truth, or when I say, "I apologize," that I am sincere, or when I nod my head to your comments, that I was really listening, etc.

One of the implications that may be drawn from a "this is the law" statement, or one of legal rights and duties, is the sort that Holmes postulated, a prediction of judicial backing, if such recourse were necessary.

Probably most lay people feel that when one says you have a legal obligation to perform, that means you must. But of course that is not actually true. Maybe we could say this is some sort of self-fulfilling prophecy sort of rhetoric. You persuade me, or maybe I persuade myself when it is put in terms of "must." Theorists who recognize that "must" cannot actually be describing any state of affairs in the real world thus come to talk of this must as an "ought." They will say that you ought to perform, or that actually any "this is the law" statement is an ought. But do you see that rhetorically, to say that one "ought" to perform is not nearly so strong as "must?"

One is tempted to keep his law statements as dogmatic musts.

But surely it is too much to say that people must *always* perform their contracts, let alone their promises, or even that they ought always. There is not the need for the conceptualistic response that we may wish to posit in saying "Every person must keep his obligation not to murder any other person!" Just when one should perform his contract and when he should not is in one sense of "moral" a matter of private conscience, and that was just the sort of judgment that Holmes was trying to legislate out of law talk. But in another sense of "moral," in what we may call the empirical perspective, of how other people are going to react, then one may not only want to consult his conscience but his social awareness of how people are going to react to him, either for breaking a promise or the law.

Now, to get back to the lawyer's office where this question first arose. If he has any obligation, it is to be generally conversant with the risks his client takes in not performing his contractual promises, and to advise accordingly, necessarily leaving the decision to his client (although the lawyer is certainly physically free to tell his client what to do). In this the lawyer is a risk analyst and not amoral if he tells his client that he *can* breach his contract. (Although not that he can murder, even though he *can*.) But it does not follow that the lawyer ought to go around in wholesale fashion encouraging breaches of contract by his clients.

It seems to me that if communication were very good between a lawyer and his clients, the lawyer should be fully conversant not only with the law side of his client's problems, from the practical sort of viewpoint Holmes' definition opened, but also the moral side, and with respect to other sorts of considerations as well, whether, for instance, a client would lose his credit standing, or good will, or what have you, in breaching a contract.

We are exploring something of the lawyer's perspectives to see how it may be distinctive from other people's in various perspectives of their own, for appreciation of these sorts of variations is considerable aid in the interpretation of law talk.

Thus, we might add that Holmes' predictive perspective is a good one for lawyers in many situations, for social scientists under certain circumstances but not all; but that generally speaking it does not even make sense from the judicial decision-making point of view. When a judge makes a law statement, by and large he is not predicting his own behavior, although one may want to try to persuade him to be consistent with his previous statements. Of course the judge is, as official decision-maker, within the system in a way different from others. His perspective on law-applications to other people's lives has got to be different in that setting from that of the lawyer participants. It makes the *most* sense to speak of law as a decisional process *re* that judicial perspective, although it also makes sense for the person who is interested in observing what takes place in litigation.

It is important to see that these *various* perspectives are not apparent on the face of assertions of laws or of rights and duties. If we are to appreciate these other perspectives, we must see law talk for the sorts of rhetoric it is. If we are to be able to see the various way that law(s' talk) gets used, strategically and otherwise, then we must look beyond or behind the surface forms and definitions.

But it is not just in the area of civil law(s) that these varying perspectives exist. Suppose we are told that in State X there is a statute which requires non-domestic corporations to register with the Secretary of State of State X if they are doing business in the state. It is arguable that a lawyer might advise his client to ignore such a statute (especially if it be of the kind whose sanction simply was to bar such a non-registering corporation from access to the courts of the state), maybe to avoid red tape, expense, and undesired disclosure of information to public record.

Now interestingly enough, this sort of situation does not involve any likelihood of some reaction of moral indignation against the corporate client. The risk may be to the lawyer who gives such advice. ("Well, you'd better watch your step too.")

But look, any good lawyer knows that legislators are not

Gods, that there is some room for back and forth play between those law-givers and the law-receivers trying to dodge their controls. Let them pass a stiffer piece of legislation if that one does not work to accomplish what was wanted for non-domestic corporations. I do not believe a tax lawyer should advise tax evasion, but surely it is good and accepted strategy to try to *avoid* tax liability. ("How do you draw the line between murder and tax laws on the one side and whatever lies on the other?") It is in line with red-blooded Americanism to be independent of controls which are ineffectively exerted, but within limits, methinks. ("Show me the line.")

There are many laws on the books that involve this sort of interplay between the would be regulators and the would not be regulated, where some sort of discretion exists in citizens to decide how they shall act, particularly if they seek the aid of lawyers in counter-strategies. This is not communication theory but facts of life. These facts of life, however, give much support to more enlightened views in dealing with law talk. One of the strategies of control is to assert that there is no choice but to obey all laws.

Lawyers are not enforcers, by and large. There is no reason why a given lawyer should be on the side of a particular law, just automatically. (Although we might determine that he should be, as in the case of the murder statute, etc.) Of course we will always say that lawyers should be on the side of LAW, the legal system, or else resign, so to speak. But to be on the side of LAW is not necessarily always to be on the side of law and order, because there is more to the complexity of legal and ethical experience than that, for instance, just for instance, the law and justice relationship as well. (May I be able to love my country and justice too.)

The deeper we get into controversial matters, the harder it is to engage in communications exploration. But law talk is not simply representative of something outside of it, very, very often it is right in the thick of the process it purports to be describing. Surely we see that within the process of litigation. It is more difficult to see it in other areas, say in the lawyers' offices, or in the mass media channels. Of course that is one of the functions of the form and style, to divert attention from what is going on.

The trial of the Chicago Seven is as controversial as most any situation. As of this writing in the spring of 1971 to take one side or the other is to risk shutting off communication completely. To suggest something good and something bad about both sides is to take on the Pollyanna or washed-out liberal image. Of course later on, after the matter is resolved on appeal, that final word will stand as the criteria. If the defendants are all acquitted and the lawyers Kuntzler and Weinglass, as well, then we would be on the side of the angels to have supported them. (One who was anti-Joe McCarthy in the early 1950's now has trouble finding anyone who liked Joe's tactics, even though he remembers losing a good deal of blood at the time.)

There is another image that comes to mind. A man is lying on the ground, being kicked and stomped on. He mutters something about maybe changing the rules or at least taking a break and he is then kicked very hard for being a trouble-maker.

Surely it is tenable to say that all the participants were involved in an affair that was not routine, run-of-the-mill stuff. For instance, if we were to elaborate in this setting our earlier analysis of "intent" we would have to raise some very serious questions about the conspiracy theory of the statute which the defendants were charged with "breaking." Further we could reasonably raise questions about possible distinctions between "mere" criminal trials and political trials. Surely Judge Hoffman did not act the part of a "proper" judge, nor did the defendants and their lawyers play the roles they were "supposed to play."

But amazingly what so many people see is only disrespectful, blasphemous lawyers for the defense, militant revolutionaries. If they were really revolutionaries in the sense of that word in the phrase "The American Revolution," surely they would not have been involved in any trial of that sort even.

But I wonder if we can do anything but engage in "mere rhetoric." ("Good Lord, yes, you can scream it out.")

If there is anyone with an open mind on that situation, he cannot reach valid conclusions merely by looking at the situation in the way one is ordinarily tempted to look at law(s).

It does not seem fair, if one concludes that maybe the defense attorneys should suffer *some* sanction, that at the same time Judge Hoffman should be immune. There is maybe something wrong with the system, and maybe it is not at the point of that trial, but most people are diverted by the spectre of the trial itself. Maybe the prosecutors are the real "baddies"! ("Troublemaker") Why not just admit that the whole thing should never have happened and forget about it? (Members of the jury, blot everything relevant from the record and your minds.)

So the point for present purposes is that one cannot evaluate the conduct of the defense attorneys without going much, much deeper into lawyering roles. (And even then there is trouble if we take the word "role" itself at face value, meaning only the way that lawyers are "supposed to act." The word "role" is a beautiful example of normative ambiguity!)

Law(yer) Talk As Camouflage

One of the most grievously undertaught skills in legal education is what has been called "legal interviewing and counseling." The phrase is not suggestive enough because one can easily fall into the old trap of thinking about strictly law questions. But as has been suggested in the previous section, lawyers are not engaged only in saying what the law is, or doing things for clients that involve applying law, because, as was said there, saying or doing "under law" is involving one's self, necessarily, in the complexity of lego-ethical experience. (And remember we are talking about lawyering not just for its own sake, but to reflect in some way on all perspectives.)

Anyone feeling that lawyers ought to stick to being lawyers needs to reflect that it is the muddling of perspectives which allows or encourages lawyers to go down these other avenues. For instance, a fairly common reaction from some quarters is that a law school course on the psychological aspects of the lawyer client advice-counsel relationship may be bad because it can encourage lawyers to try to be psychologists when they ought to stick to being what they are trained to be. But the truth is that there are many situations in which lawyers play at psychology without realizing it. It is analogous to the lawyer playing at morality analysis without realizing it.

Of course there would be limits. ("Where are the lines?") But surely a lawyer should be helped to realize at least a bit better when he is pushing a client down the lawyer's own preferred path, in the name of an analysis of what the law is, in a situation when "the rules" are not at all clear and when, in turn, it is not at all clear what all the implications would be were "the rules" known. To be fully aware might be to risk impotency, but there are equally bad risks in being completely uninformed. These are problems not just for conservative lawyers to ponder, but militant reformers as well. Admittedly it is difficult for the kind of people who so often are lawyers to submit themselves entirely to the cause of the client, perhaps even to justify their lawyer career on such an agency sort of role entirely.

There is a gold mine of research data for observers capable of interpreting what is going on in law offices. However, the perspective they must take is not to regard law talk as merely camouflage. They must be skillful law talkers themselves, but also capable of law-talk talk and talk-talk.

The suggestion is not that there will be a lot of dirt uncovered. Not at all ("Maybe some?"). Lawyers do need to have greater sensitivity to the emotional level. The best route to that level is through training in sensitivity to communications dynamics. (Communication, psychology . . . , you *name* it.)

In a great many situations, the lawyer cannot find out how to treat (E) the client unless he is capable of making a more thorough-going analysis of the client-as-person and the totality of his problem(s), so that he knows what law strategies best apply. We have stayed away from this sort of exploration in legal education because we have been stuck with that old model of law here and facts there, rather than seeing the lawyers as participants in law-in-action, if you will.

It does not follow at all that the lawyer should feel free to do what he wants or feels is best. Charting of the "most desirable" sort of role-behavior cannot be accomplished, however, until the area is scouted and even navigated.

Doing Things With Words

Neither the man in the street nor the lawyer in his office is likely aware of the subtlety let alone the existence of the philosophical analytical distinction between the *is* and the *ought*. Like all such distinctions, it ramifies on at least two levels, the purely analytical and the rhetorical. (See The Right Way) Comparable is the distinction in semantics theory between fact-words and judgmental-words. We have seen how such distinctions have been used counter-rhetorically. They are also useful in opening the door to the multi-dimensionality of the assertive form, not only of the fact-statement assertion but the law-statement assertion as well.

Neither a science nor a merely thoroughgoing system of communications analysis could limit itself to such dichotomies. For further instance, as important as it is, the truth or falsity criterion for an assertion is only of limited value. That is one, but there are many sorts of reliability criteria. Validity is another. Sincerity may be the most important of all such criteria. (You can kill a person with all the sincerity in the world, but we are not talking that simply.)

Communications analysis does not deal only with fact-information communication. When dealing with fact-information one may be interested in knowing what the words mean, what inferences may be drawn, and whether the standard of truth (or probable truth) is met. These are important, very important measures aiding various communicative tasks, in the lab or the courtroom, for instance. Not only are they important for testing or acquiring such information, among other things, but more subtly in determining whether one is being faced with a fact-information sort of communication. Contrary to the provincial sort of empirics of logical positivism, it does not follow that a non-informational sort of communication is to be discarded as meaningless.

For that matter, truth or falsity is not always the main measure of fact-information statements. Certainly it cannot be for law-information statements. If we take the sort of implication one may draw from a fact-information statement to be what we call inferences, which are also subject to a probability test, we see that some of the implications of a law-information statement have to be talked about in some other terms. The prophecy implication may be so tested, but going to court is a more difficult way of corroborating one's law-information than suits most people's fancy. But how do you test the implication of obligation that is said to stem from (be an implication of?) a statement of law which is itself *valid?* ("Validity" is some sort of reliability test.) Even if we concluded that the obligation is automatic if the law statement is valid, the reasoning one goes through to determine what the obligation is in varying circumstances is not the same sort of reasoning used in fact-inference.

And even if the obligation is automatic, it does not follow that the sanction is. Nor does it follow that law-information statements are used merely to oblige or to sanction! As we have discussed, they might be used by a lawyer therapeutically and/or to dominate a client, or even to evade "the law."

So we see there is a sort of "What's going on" test ("Now there's a switch."). Take the simple statement, "It is raining." It makes a difference when and where that statement is made, what's going on, as to how one receives it. Said in response to a suggestion of a walk is one thing, in the middle of a marriage ceremony quite another. It may be equally true and fact-informationally meaningful, but the appropriateness and consequent impact is quite something else again.

While often automatic, the interpreter must have a sense of the situation to know how to receive fact-information, to appreciate what its significance ("meaning_2") beyond the data-aspects may be, to know why it was offered and/or what its implications may be, and to be able to decide how one should think or act upon it.

It is not usually a merely face-value matter!

("Literalists arise!")

This is why we can usefully say that the fact-form, the very *form* into which words are cast, the form itself, is ambiguous. Or if you wish, the form fathers a large family which sit in the linguistic form pool, waiting the great variety of communicative tasks to which they are necessary or amenable. One can, for instance, say "It is raining" without even trying to give fact-information, say in telling a joke, riddle, or story. And even when informationally used, there are usually (maybe always) other communicative dimensions to the situation adding to the significance of the assertion, as when "It is raining" might be used to pursue a threat, a seduction, or an apology. ("Daddy, let's play catch."—It is raining) (Intonation does it here.)

A law assertion may divert the attention of the interpreter from the other dimensions of the situation. That may be its chief function. ("Law and order") There seems to be an aspect of law which requires verbal fascination. Naturally one may take advantage of this aspect in law *talk.* (Is it valid, reliable, and what are the implications? What's going on?)

There are many situations we size up easily enough, but it helps to see their distinctiveness in order to come back to law-assertion situations and size them properly. If somebody thumbs his nose at you, probably you can take that at face value ("Ouch!"), but truth or falsity or validity are not tests. We might say sincerity, but seriousness sounds better. Compare: "Close the door!" "Thank you!" "I love you!" "I pronounce you man and wife!" "Ouch!"

Tested against truth criteria, chit-chat usually fails miserably, but it serves a great variety of interpersonal functions. "I love you" may not be as precise as "I relate to you in a special way," but it is more appropriate to the functions it usually serves. Whatever one's ideals may be, he cannot understand "What is going on?" at a trial if he measures it solely in terms of search for truth-in-facts or reliability-in-law. ("Ouch!")

Doing Things With Laws

You cannot determine on the face of a statement of law talk what is being done with the words or how reliable the statement is, even though the meaning may be entirely clear.

For a variety of reasons, some of which we have examined (and see The Right Way), legal theorists have distinguished law assertions into phases and modes, thus (1) whether historical or predictive; or (2) whether command, threat, or norm; or (3) whether involving obligation or risk, and so on. I have suggested these and others which overlap or cut across. We do have the historical was (is_1); the prophetic will be (is_2); the here and now is (is_3); here and now obligation (is_4) ($ought_1$); moralistic sort of ought ($ought_2$); rhetorical advocacy (all modes and phases); reformer (ditto plus); critic (ditto); theoretical analysis (ditto plus plus).

Another way, not entirely unrelated, is to examine more specific roles and perspectives, as we have suggested, especially stressing the strong distinctions of law-involvement regarding lawyers, where for instance, there is considerable variation in perspective depending upon whether the lawyer is acting as advocate, negotiator, preventive-law analyst-manager, counselor, rhetorical analyst (very important to see as separate task), and so on. A given lawyer may perform all of these roles at one time or another and even with respect to a particular problem situation. He must strive to keep the lines straight, even if only as a matter of habit or keen sensitivity. In these tasks he does different things with law talk!

We discussed such matters a bit when we were exploring the desirability of the law-talk formulation, so that we could see that what seemed the same rule (*re* execution of wills) had different functions and implications depending upon whether it was being asserted by a judge, lawyer, or layman. Surely it makes a difference whether a judge is merely applying or promulgating rule(s) as to how the opinion implies, and the given rule from his pen looks and feels different from that same rule (so-called) in the mouth of the sheriff. All these variations find their way into the ways that law-words are used in the great variety of so-called administrative functions. Oh, what is done in the name of administration, (as any faculty member can quickly appreciate) but especially law administration. ("Well, I really don't make the rules you know.")

In all these situations we tend to speak of the enactment, enforcement, application, or interpretation (etc.) of laws. But we can readily see how that way(s) of slicing cuts across the use of law(s) (talk) to command, threaten, warn, advise, counsel, urge, persuade, or negotiate (etc.). In so *doing* one may purport to describe, assert, deny, predict, or even hypothesize (etc.). Of course, unless we think too narrowly, realize too that law(s) (talk) can be used to teach, joke, or fictionalize, not to mention analyze, criticize, and synthesize (etc.). Whether one is amused, provoked, urged or influenced, angered, or obligated (etc.) depends of course on a number of factors, including his naiveté, gullibility, submissibility, authority-status position and on and on.

So, once again, let it be said, resaid, stressed, and restressed: Laws do not operate automatically. (If I now dare say it, on the level of talk talk, *they do not exist.* Oh, Lord, I hope that point is clear by now.) Of course laws exist but someone has to do something with them. We may not want the man in the street to crawl out from his conditioning, but really all he has to do is look around and see all those law-violators running around loose, from the Mafia Godfather to the corner embezzler. (Not to mention those "bums on the campus.")

Well, now wait a minute. Why do we say they are law violators? ("You said it." Just wanted to see if you were awake.) Very, very often to call (or think of) someone as a law violator is to exercise an option. We have discussed that. That embezzler could be called a law breaker, but we ought to realize that we could just as well say that he is *subject* to prosecution to be *declared* a law breaker. ("I don't want to say that.")

Attitudes have changed drastically in a few short (charged) years, but even in the 60's there were a lot of people, a very lot of them who could not understand why campus protestors were allowed "to get away with breaking the law" by occupying administrators' offices or trespassing upon state property. A prime example was "Peoples Park" in Berkeley in 1969. The University owned the lot in question and students along with others were trespassing. The police were called and a battle ensued. How could anyone justify the student actions? To engage in a communications analysis is to take the sort of risk involved in discussing The Chicago Seven.

Oh there are so many situations. Again in 1969, at the University of Florida, some people, including a law faculty member, were fired for refusing to sign a loyalty oath. The statute in question, passed a number of years previously, required all University employees to sign or be immediately discharged. The University President had to carry out the requirement or be subject to prosecution for a misdemeanor. The oath required the signer to affirm that he did not believe in the overthrow of the government by force and violence. It is a risk to communication to discuss this sort of thing.

Consider first a few facts of life. Suppose two people gamble in the basement of their home, or commit an unnatural sex act, or what if one of them is alone and smokes marijuana. And nobody, just nobody knows about what has happened and never finds out. Have laws been broken? Add this: these particular people are completely oblivious of any laws that might be invoked.

This sounds like the conundrum of the tree falling in the desert with no one within hearing distance. Is there a sound?

These are not just questions of semantics.

If you and I are walking along and you spy a dollar bill on the sidewalk and pick it up, is it yours? I tell you it is mine and you hand it over and nothing ever happens. Is that dollar bill *really* yours?

What if a father bloodies his son's nose. Has he broken the law?

There are certain areas of person(s)' living that is "none of the law's business." There are certain areas of activity where laws on the books (do not) (are not) applie(ed) even though they could be, seemingly. Laws simply cannot be rigidly or universally applied. We speak negatively of selective enforcement, but we mean discriminatory selective enforcement. To swoop down on my "little" poker game would be of that sort.

The University campus has been indeed a *sanctuary*. (But

why use that word with such a sneer?) But consider how many such sanctuaries there have been. The home is a leading example. Congress. The police station. Someone has to blow the whistle if the enclave is to be opened, and there are many, many places and situations where discretion is not as a matter of socio-politics in the police or in the community government. Of course the lines shift. Now governors call in National Guardsmen, to protect property, life, morals, outrage, the system, a way of life. The home is *invaded* from time to time. (Why "invaded?" Well, you know . . .) And when the whistle is blown, the discretionary aspects are camouflaged, the buck passed, if you will. ("Well, certainly John Q does not make the rules. Really, now.")

What is called civil disobedience is not necessarily. Not all rules have to be applied or impose the same kind of obligation as the statute against murder on all kinds of people. ("But a rule is a rule.") Some laws involve options. So, a call to law and order is a call for different sorts of actions under different sorts of rules and laws. Used conceptualistically, of course, it is meant to be hypnotic.

In that loyalty oath case (it has been called an "unloyalty" oath), it was claimed that the fired professor had broken the law. But another way of putting it, still favorable in rhetoric to the University, is that he refused to perform a condition to a contractual or employment relationship. Of course there was the question whether it was Constitutional. Is it valid? Is it reliable?

I said the statute "required" signing, but now we have to realize that is the way statutes talk. There are limits on legislative power, just as there are on the power of all of us. The legislature is not going to spell out its own limits, especially in some area where they are stretching to get as much as they can (as will be allowed). Holmes was dead wrong about this situation if he would insist on applying his judicial-predictive theory, for what the statute on oath-signing requires is a matter for the political hierarchy in the state of Florida to decide. By the time the Supreme Court declared the oath unconstitutional, the issue was mooted. There are a number of situations where the judicial system is too slow or where the power(s) of decision are otherwise allocated.

People's Park is more complicated. It raises the general question of property and ownership. I do not have to call the police if you pitch a tent on my property, although I may. But ownership is rather a subtle concept when it gets out of the single person situation, especially when it comes to the University where such matters have not been clearly worked out. No one had had reason previously to suggest that a faculty person could be excluded from the central administrative offices, no reason to think they belonged to the President in the way his home might, or that students could be excluded from whatever portion of the campus it occurred to another agent of the University to close off.

Could the President exclude a professor from his faculty office? Could he? What kind of question is that? Surely it is not just legal. The socio-political dynamics are not just dependent upon laws on the book, especially when those laws have not been defined into those situations. It makes no sense to say that dollar bill you handed to me after picking it up is *really* yours when there is no conflict on the matter. It is when the conflicts arise that people start jumping around to find a law that they can maneuver to call in the power of the state. We may predict that the power of the state will throw its weight in with the chancellor at Berkeley, but that puts him on the side of power and not necessarily the ideals of law. Those factors easily become separated. Law is sometimes one, sometimes the other or both or maybe something else.

In these controversial areas, or in any situation where "the law" is not clear, one must size up a number of factors, but heavy among them are the power dynamics within the various groupings of interlocking perhaps conflicting decision-makers. In the end, that is what it may come to, but before then there is the power of persuasion and rhetoric. When the smoke clears, so does the law.

In the loyalty oath matter, the President of the University

certainly acted validly, even if not ideally, within the power of his office, under a tenable interpretation which included the ploy that validity of the statute was not his to determine, only the letter to carry out. Even when the statute was ultimately declared invalid under the United States Constitution, he can still make that claim, even though he might have opted to defer the firing until the courts had acted. Then too, doubtless *he* was in jeopardy. How much is somebody else's principle worth?

And it was all quite predictable, even *if* the ultimate judicial decision was not clearly so. The battle against the loyalty oath was won but clearly the skirmish was lost. In this kind of situation, *that* is how law(s) add(s) up.

CHART #8

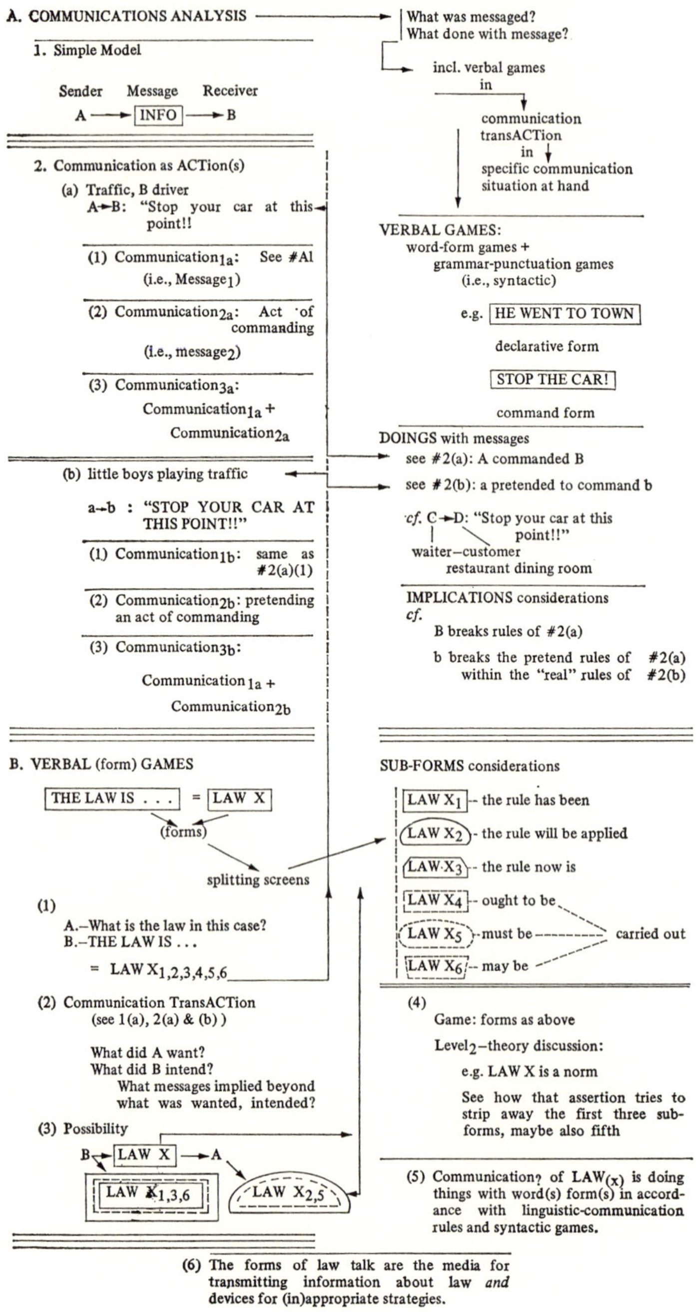
A. COMMUNICATIONS ANALYSIS
What was messaged?
What done with message?
incl. verbal games
in
communication
transACTion
in
specific communication
situation at hand
1. Simple Model
Sender Message Receiver
A INFO B
2. Communication as ACTion(s)
(a) Traffic, B driver
A→B: "Stop your car at this point!!
(1) Communication1a: See #A1
(i.e., Message1)
(2) Communication2a: Act of commanding
(i.e., message2)
(3) Communication3a:
Communication1a +
Communication2a
VERBAL GAMES:
word-form games +
grammar-punctuation games
(i.e., syntactic)
e.g. HE WENT TO TOWN
declarative form
STOP THE CAR!
command form
DOINGS with messages
see #2(a): A commanded B
see #2(b): a pretended to command b
(b) little boys playing traffic
a→b : "STOP YOUR CAR AT THIS POINT!!"
(1) Communication1b: same as #2(a)(1)
(2) Communication2b: pretending an act of commanding
(3) Communication3b:
Communication1a +
Communication2b
cf. C→D: "Stop your car at this point!!"
waiter–customer
restaurant dining room
IMPLICATIONS considerations
cf.
B breaks rules of #2(a)
b breaks the pretend rules of #2(a) within the "real" rules of #2(b)
B. VERBAL (form) GAMES
THE LAW IS . . . = LAW X
(forms)
splitting screens
(1)
A.–What is the law in this case?
B.–THE LAW IS . . .
= LAW X1,2,3,4,5,6
(2) Communication TransACTion
(see 1(a), 2(a) & (b))
What did A want?
What did B intend?
What messages implied beyond what was wanted, intended?
(3) Possibility
B LAW X A
LAW X1,3,6
LAW X2,5
SUB-FORMS considerations
LAW X1 - the rule has been
LAW X2 - the rule will be applied
LAW X3 - the rule now is
LAW X4 - ought to be
LAW X5 - must be
carried out
LAW X6 - may be
(4)
Game: forms as above
Level2–theory discussion:
e.g. LAW X is a norm
See how that assertion tries to strip away the first three sub-forms, maybe also fifth
(5) Communication? of LAW(x) is doing things with word(s) form(s) in accordance with linguistic-communication rules and syntactic games.
(6) The forms of law talk are the media for transmitting information about law and devices for (in)appropriate strategies.

Chapter IX

INTERPRETATION(S)

Prelude

WHEN A LAWYER speaks of interpretation, he usually is thinking of official, formal, printed law, the written law found in constitutions, statutes and regulations; or formal instruments such as contracts and wills. But of course the reading of a judicial opinion to see what it says, or holds, or rules, or implies for the future (each a varying perspective) involves interpretation. Actually, every communication transaction involves varying kinds of interpretative judgments for all the parties.

While writers have stressed the interpretative problems only in the area of written law, almost everything written around the issues raised by the legal realists bears on interpretative factors wherever they arise in law dynamics, that is, in every communication transaction and situation. It is true that interpretation of written law(s) involves special problems, but they cannot be fully appreciated in some sort of vacuum. We are now about to put the focus on interpretation of official and formal texts, but all that has preceded in this text is relevant, not only in its substance but as well in its challenges to the reader-interpreter.

The material on rhetorical definition, for instance, clearly bears on word use, meaning, and definition, but that perspective can also take a reader between the lines, so to speak, or below a merely literal reading (or hearing). All that has preceded attempts to open up the surface level of communication, especially, but not exclusively of certain written forms and styles. In this day of increasing lego-political stress on strict construction (mainly but not only of the United States Constitution), a contrary stress is at least figuratively, but not literally, subversive. Still such a stress is not anti-precision after all. The analysis-interpretation of the Garratt Case should prove that actually the stress of strict construction is fearfully deceptive to the extent that it plays on socio-political fears in the name of outmoded views on psycholinguistics, i.e. the communicative significance of words in certain written forms. The stress on the rubric of "strict construction" at the governmental level is propagandistic, in short, word magic promoting word magic.

Of course the rubric itself should not be taken only literally. At stake is the question of whose values and interests should be promoted through the mechanisms of legal process, and to what extent written texts can and should be seen (interpreted) as the embodiment of certain values. How is it possible to restrain the interpreter, whether an official or not, from projecting his own values and positions into the text of a written law or instrument? That is *the* question, perhaps, but it is not answered by saying, "construe strictly," or "stick to the four corners of the text," or "do what the words say," or "look behind the text only when there is a patent ambiguity."

The one who is the most likely to put his views into the instrument is the one who does not actively look for ambiguity, that is, for some other view than his own that may actually be embodied, not just in, but by means of, the written text. Of course it is just as possible to spot (create?) an ambiguity that ought not to be taken seriously. In most situations where interpretation of some written text becomes legally operable, it is as fallacious to believe you can only pay attention to the *key* words (the text) as it is to attempt to psychoanalyze the author or draftsman or the parties committed to the text. Some sort of line has to be drawn, often in the name of expedience. But the line cannot *rationally* be drawn at the same spot for all situations. It is a matter of balance of the text with the other dynamics, and I do mean *other* dynamics, for if the text is seen as a stimulus to personal and interpersonal interpretative dynamics rather than something that somehow speaks for itself, then we see interpretation for the choosing, decisional sort of activity that it is.

Explorations

1.1 It is important to know how courts interpret various texts, but the literature has over-relied on such authority. Surely judges have not proven themselves especially expert in psycholinguistics. Furthermore, the opinions do not reveal the *process* of interpretation. Rather, they display the judicial *rhetoric* of interpretation. That is a species of law talk, after all. (So much of interpretation of the United States Constitution is like that.) Of course if one does not take the rhetoric only literally, then he may get some vision of the problems of interpretation that have arisen, or at least those admitted, in the litigational context, some feel for the dynamics even.

1.2 For instance, even patent ambiguity does not in itself make a nullity of a statute or other texts, but there is no one principle or technique of resolution to cover all kinds of situations, and probably not even a finite list. And, judges do plunge through apparent surface meanings to expose ambiguities and indeterminacies that inevitably lurk around the fitting of generality to specific situation. Again, there seems no comfortable, computer-like way of predicting, for a specific situation where controversy has arisen, whether a court will take that plunge.

1.3 But odds can be calculated—and given. Lawyers are good odds-makers and wager-makers. The right lawyer may up the odds. If he goes to court, to wage his skills, he moves beyond the betting stage. He gets involved in the race, so to speak, and jockeys his mount into as good a position as he can. There is always a gamble in going to court, but a long shot may be worth while if the payoff is high enough. It is a bit difficult to see what the odds were merely from reading the results of the race. There could be better dope sheets than judicial opinions.

1.4 How often the winner looks back and sees his race as having been a sure thing all the way. That sort of confidence may be good. But the observer too? Too many interpreters of judicial interpretation-rhetoric believe in predestination.

1.5 But then, who is to say for sure, for all ways?

1.6 Assurance does not come from the questioned text alone. Law-talk-interpretation puts the emphasis there, but the shrewd calculator sizes up the whole situation.

1.7 Is it that we have to *believe*, very often, that the text tells the whole story? Of course, a well-drafted text will not be porous at the core. It is drafted to *cover* certain situations and probabilities. So, in interpreting, we can start with those paradigmatic situations. As we move away from the core, the meant-to-be-covered situations, then of course the gamble increases, as the cover thins and wavers. But to deny the possibility, nay, the probability, of clear cases is to deny communication altogether.

1.8 Postulate: No one ought to be in a position of authority to interpret, including being licensed as a lawyer, who does not believe in communication. I believe!

1.9 Postulate: No one ought to be an authority-interpreter who does not see the risks of literalism. That first reading ought never be trusted if anything of importance is at stake. Some fits are automatic, but many are not. Simply because an interpreter's semantic response is automatic does not mean he is at the core.

1.10 You cannot identify a literalist from the interpretative rhetoric. Beware the closed-minded literalist who really believes the text is the beginning, middle and end source, that what he concludes is the clear or right meaning for this or that situation was right there in the text all along.

1.11 But is he less dangerous than the one who knows better but camouflages with dogma, one who knowingly manipulates and may be less susceptible to persuasion by the counter-rhetoric?

1.12 Compare the rhetoric of interpretation with the rhetoric of analysis (e.g. The Right Way, *infra*). If the rhetoric of interpretation is law talk, then the sophisticated doing of interpretation includes law-talk talk. Or compare the statute on the books with the statute in action.

1.13 The strategy of the rhetoric which so subtly passes for the *doing* of interpretation is not to admit even the possibility of ambiguity. To admit is to be vulnerable to argument.

1.14 Previous sections of this book are not in the main aimed at the improving of the skill of that rhetoric. But there are many useful sources for that end. (Compare the dynamics of interpreting with the dynamics of persuading, and both with those of informing. One is often done in the name of another.)

1.15 So, there is more than one kind of interpretation. The clue is that the word "interpretation" has a number of senses and applications. No surprise there. Earlier portions of this text have in some senses of "interpretation" been aimed to promote the *doing* of interpretation, and the undoing of some of the rhetoric of interpretation.

1.16 Consider the analysis-interpretation of the Garratt Case. The court's interpretation of the Restatement of Torts is akin to the interpretation of a statute or a regulation. But in another sense of "interpretation" we were considering what the court had *done* with "intent." I claimed to be right in my interpretation, but no literalist would get that far. We did not stick to the text of the opinion, however, to determine how "intent" was used in the text, although key clues were in the text. (Courts give more clues than legislatures—as a matter of style and convention.) We engaged in complex *analysis*, including exploration of the intent word-form-concept, in and out of legal contexts. The final weighting might be *presented* by a literalistic rhetoric, but hardly reached by any such techniques.

1.17 Our analysis did not say the same thing as the opinion; i.e. the opinion-rhetoric was one thing, the analysis-interpretation another, on the way to concluding what were the *implications* of what the opinion *said*.

1.18 Postulate: If one is to be skillful in doing interpreting, he needs to be skillful in analysis of the kinds demonstrated and explained in the previous portions of the book.

1.19 The line between interpretation and analysis is itself an analytical line, not marked by God, or any Legislature in the sky, or even the unabridged dictionary. The families of these two words are intermarried.

1.20 But we can say this: the route to rational interpretation-analysis takes one through the swamps of ambiguities. The rational interpreter must learn to chart his way (s).

1.21 Communication involves many dimensions in addition to the transmission of information, the sending of messages. The information model is inadequate for the rational interpreter (compare the literalist). What did he/they *say* is not enough. What does it *mean* is not enough. Of course say and mean are in the picture. (One interprets a picture too.)

1.22 Interpretation (E) of paintings, plays, novels, music, casual conversation; in editorials, reviews, silent thought; appreciation, understanding, acting, reacting, re-enacting, presenting it, representing it, re-presenting it; comparing, evaluating, searching, researching, construing, construction, reconstruction, analyzing: for meaning (E), purpose, significance, USE, bearing, IMPLICATIONS: by generalizing, specifying, elaborating, applying . . . ,

1.23 Perhaps the most subtle factor: compare a faithful translation, high fidelity reproduction, with an interpretative production, trans-lating, re-lating, through my (yours, his, theirs) value field, evaluation. (How can the Basic Rules mean (E) to anyone else what they mean to me? Yet we can work them out! They had/have impact.)

1.24 To speak of "strict construction" may be a political ploy. In any event, lawyers ought to be trained in all kinds of interpretation, not just legal, not just to be literalist, although that too, and in literalistic rhetoric. To be merely literalistic is not to be objective.

1.25 And . . . intensive training in group dynamics is quite relevant to development of skills in doing legal interpretation.

2.1 There is a difference in determining what a statute *says* from what it *implies*. Consider the Garratt case by comparison. Compare what the court *did* and what the ramifications of that doing may be, in varying situations: for that court later on, other courts, a teacher of a torts course, in relation to understanding the judicial process, in considering procedural subtleties and so on. It is misleading to think only of *meaning*, in the what-did-they-say sense. One does look for meaning, among many other "things." (Compare looking for what is said with manipulating what is said.)

2.2 Are we as much concerned with what-is-said as we are with what-can-we-say-as-a-result-of-what-is-said-in-the-text? All the way from what is precisely synonymous (translation_1), to what specifics can we "include" (derive from) in some generality, on to analogues, and even what-can-we-get-away-with.

2.3 Compare interpretation(E) and translation(E). A comprehensive dictionary will tell you that translation is one kind of interpretation. Very subtle. When we translate from one language to another we like to think we are dealing with linguistic equivalencies. How many such equivalencies are there, really?

2.4 We think of synonyms and equivalencies within the same language, but again, how close. Can you ever trans-form and retain the same sense. *Semantic equivalency is not rhetorical equivalency.* "House" does not equal "home."

"They relate romantically" does not equal "They are in love". A subtly insults B and B calls him on it. A may say, but I did not *mean* that the way you took it. A way out.

2.5 Generally speaking (or should I say, specifyingly speaking?) to say what certain words *mean* is not to give natural or necessary synonyms, but to trans-late, transform, change, alter, adjust, readjust, etc.

2.6 So "interpret" and "translate" are not equivalents, not congruent; but they overlap, have equivalent senses in which one is *fairly* substitutable for another. (I am engaging in rhetorical definition.)

2.7 To say what certain words in a given text mean usually involves a most subtle form of rhetorical redefinition, what we can call an interpretative definition.

2.8 Similarly, what about the words we use in talking about a statute or piece of text. Is the statute-talk mixed in (in the pragmatics, rhetorical-impact sense) psycholinguistically speaking. How can it be avoided? (E)

2.9 Draftsmen often use explicit stipulative definitions: e.g. " 'Livestock' means sheep, cattle, swine, and goats." Rhetorical definitions are also developed, new uses, special usages, technical usages, along with conventional usages. One who appreciates the technique of rhetorical definition is aided in his interpretative tasks. But in sections 2.3—2.8 the reference is not to rhetorical definitions of the draftsman but to those even more subtle ones of the interpreter which he may not realize he is doing. Perhaps I can demonstrate with example from the Basic Rules, especially suitable because most readers will not have some emotional attachment.

2.10 Consider "intentionally" in Rule 1 (Appendix): "Any member of the class who intentionally does an act which is disruptive of a communication transaction then in process is subject to a fine not to exceed three points."

2.11 We know "intent" has a broad range of senses-meanings-uses. Is it here being used in a legal sense, as in the Garratt case? Under Rule 1, does one intend a disruption if he believes or knows it is substantially certain to happen. What if he laughs very loudly at something that has been said and breaks up the conversation, not thinking of the effect. Must one merely intend to act, or must he also intend the disruption?

2.12 There are no clues within the quoted sentence to indicate to a *layman* the legal meaning-sense-use of "intentionally," although in the whole of Rule 1 there is the word "fine" which has a legal connotation. A law trained person might in a law context have a law-sense semantic response to "intentionally." Would he be wrong? Would that be a liberal construction? (Not liberal in the sense of libertarian certainly, for the law sense in this context would work out as inhibiting of free expression.) Then it must be a strict construction? But it broadens the range of responsibility beyond the usual lay sense. Still, it would lead to a stricter class dynamics, a tighter class discipline. But in the torts sense, it would be strict liability, a viewpoint which is being used for liberal economic risk allocation in such areas as products liability, i.e. consumer protection.

2.13 You cannot trust the rubrics "strict construction" or "loose construction."

2.14 The interpretation of "intentionally" in Rule 1 is complex, but no more than most of the interpretative problems that arise in courts or in lawyers' offices.

2.15 The advantage of using the Basic Rules for illustration is that I am the only one who knows what these words really mean because I drafted the Rules. Isn't that right?

2.16 If we were to use the judicial approach, I would not be allowed to testify. You cannot ask the legislature what a statute means, not even the chairman of the committee which brought it to the floor. The testator of a will in probate is no longer available. How about the parties to a contract dispute? Hardly, because their dispute will carry right into the key words in question. They may have agreed upon the words, but not upon the implications.

2.17 When you turn words loose, you lose feedback control. You set loose (E) control over the words.

2.18 So I cannot say what the word "intentionally" means in Rule 1. Just think what control I could have if I were to have the power to say what they mean: not only to draft them, officialize them, invoke them, apply them, and then interpret them for all purposes. Too much. Enough that I have the power (if I do) to impose the risks of their interpretation upon a group of people. Compare legislation. Some such limit upon power enters into the very idea of rules, laws, statutes.

2.19 But power does fall to the *interpreter*. How seldom he admits to it. Maybe interpreters seldom appreciate the power because of a lack of full sensitivity to the interpretative process. Sections 2.3 to 2.8 suggest part of the base of the power. Today's sophisticated authorities would say that we bring this sort of problem to the surface by demanding a search for legislative purpose rather than merely meaning. Still, the interpreters end up saying that the words mean thus-and-so because of this or that legislative purpose apparent from the con-text. Purpose-defining is a subtle rhetorical technique.

2.20 What if I had said in 2.10 that "intentionally" was used in its legal sense. I could have pointed to the Preamble of Rule 1 and the following Rule of Interpretation and the full text of Rule 1 to "prove it." I could readily persuade individuals who were willing to accept my authority. But isn't that something of fiat? What if I say it was an apt translation? Isn't it adding to the text of the Basic Rules, just as if I had added another definition to the Definitions clause which *literally* carries only a stipulated definition of the symbol "CL."

2.21 Show me a judicial interpretation which does not involve some such method.

2.22 One who is not sensitive to or familiar with the full membership of the intent-family may have difficulty with 2.20! How many people know that word that well. How about other words used in legislation and other official or legally relevant texts?

2.23 But we have not explored all applications of "intentionally" in Rule 1. Suppose it had been the practice in this seminar to speak only after gaining recognition from the instructor. Suppose instructor is talking to student A. Student B suddenly utters an obscenity and rails against something instructor said right in the middle of his statement. Is there any doubt that the first sentence of Rule 1 applies? Now we do not have to determine how many senses of intentionally are apt, for the paradigmatic, clearest core meaning-use is applicable to student B. *At least* "intentionally" means that sort of conduct. If student B objected that "intentional" is ambiguous in the ways indicated earlier, the official interpreter would be justified in saying "The meaning is plain and clear" *for this situation.* Just about any text has that degree of clarity. Surely!

2.24 Is there any way out for Student B? If one considers the possibilities then he may suddenly gain insight into another interestingly subtle aspect of the interpretative-decisional process. Earlier portions of this book went into the subtlety, but it bears further exploration.

2.25 Suffice it for now to ask just who is to say that "intentionally" is the key word for the situation put in 2.23? There is considerable power inherent in the authority-right privilege-skill to characterize what *the* interpretative problem *is.* If one can be shunted, persuaded, cornered, trapped, etc., into the kind of question asked in 2.23 ("Is there any doubt. . . ."), the answer being determinative, then there is no way out for student B. This is one of the chief ways in which judicial opinions are misleading if taken as a key source for insight into the interpretative process-dynamics. At the appellate level, and often much earlier, the issues are frozen, stripped of clues to the greater multi-dimensionality-range of the full communications dynamics.

2.26 Other interpretations (E) had preceded that stage of characterization of key issues. (See the earlier discussion regarding hypothetical facts.)

3.1 Does Rule 1 apply to student B in the situation put in 2.23?

3.2 Is there any *sort* of interpretation involved in answering that question?

3.3 It has been said that the invocation or application of any fixed text, like a statute, contract, international agreement, will, etc. involves interpretation, no matter how clear or plain we say the meaning of the key words is!

3.4 Agreed.

3.5 But one can prove too much that way. The debate between the legal realists and the legal positivists involved just this very problem, a key question not just for the judicial process but for all kinds of interpretative situations, even out of law!

3.6 If 3.1 raises a question of interpretation, it is not the same kind of interpretation problem raised in 2.10—2.12.

3.7 Does 3.6 require interpretation by the reader?

3.8 Surely it does. You may want to say it does not for the person who can understand it simply by looking at the sections named. Or if everyone understood it, there would be no interpretation involved. Still, it is doubtful that many readers would readily grasp even the *surface meaning* of 3.6 had they opened the book for the first time and *read* that section. One can read without fully understanding. Reading involves some understanding. Learning to read involves learning to interpret. What is easy now was once hard. So, 3.6 is not difficult for one who is *prepared* for it, by some sort of previous involvement.

3.9 Even expert lawyers are not necessarily prepared to understand a statute, or contract, or what have you, the first time they see it. Some sort of further involvement is necessary. The words are not at first plain on their face. The layman may think otherwise, or even an unthinking lawyer.

3.10 Please turn the page.

3.11 Does 3.10 require interpretation?

3.12 Surely it does. What did you do? You may understand the words (in one sense of understand) and not do anything more. They make some sort of sense. (Compare: page the turn, please.) But if you follow through by turning the page, you have understood 3.10 in some way differently from one who does not turn the page. (Someone will turn the page!) Directive, request, riddle, illustration? It has more than one potential significance when one takes account of the implications and ramifications.

3.13 Even though "intentionally" has a minimal plain-meaning sense in Rule 1, it is actually used in more than one sense simultaneously, just as was the expression in 3.10, deliberately to call for a judgment-estimate of the situation, to prove a point. In some texts words are used deliberately in multiple senses!

3.14 Just because one's interpretation of 3.10 happened very, very quickly, it goes by unnoticed. Suppose 3.10 to be a sincere request. Could it be misunderstood? Imagine someone wanted to misunderstand, or felt hostile. He could turn the page by turning the book around, or he could tear out the page and then turn it, because after all, there is no way otherwise of *just* turning the page. Ridiculous?

3.15 Suppose a situation where I speak to you but am stuck with what you do without being able to make some corrective statement in case you do misunderstand. That is often the case, when a statute is being interpreted, or whenever any text is being interpreted in court, and so on. No feedback or interchange possible, or allowed. Just the words and the interpreter, in the final analysis.

3.16 Could "please pass the salt" be misunderstood, at the dinner table. Your dining partner picks it up and passes it like a football. The game is that you have to say it so it could not possibly be "misunderstood." He puts it on the floor and walks by it. You say, "No, give it to me." He pours it on your head. Can you do it with just one-way words? Finally you say, "You know what I mean." And of course he does when you invoke the situational IMPLIED-UNDERSTOOD conventions.

3.17 Texts are produced in conventional settings that vary, but without knowing them, we are lost. These contextual settings are not themselves in the words, the words are *in them.* There may be clues in the words, however. CLUES. But it requires cooperation. The draftsman should give clues, especially since the text is always out of its con-text.

3.18 One of these days electronic potentials may allow instantaneous reproduction of context. The statutory form, for instance, will become obsolete. That form arose in a time of greater word-magic and when it was perhaps the best form-medium available. One of its major values still is the authority it perpetuates, the status it gives. It is so permanent appearing (the statu-s of a statu-te).

3.19 So, to say that one's judgment of the words in some text is *very likely* correct is not to say that no judgment is involved, no almost but not quite instantaneous assessment. It makes sense, then, to speak of interpretation in order to keep in mind the *possibilities* of some alternate, maybe conflicting judgment(s).

3.20 To conclude that 3.1 applies to student B involves an interpretative judgment.

3.21 To say that the court in the Garratt Case used "intent" in a way that went beyond traditional legal usage surely required interpretation, even though it is almost surely correct.

3.22 One could give some answer to the questions raised in 2.11 without knowing about Garratt or its analysis. He could well believe that his answer was surely correct and say the ascribed meaning was correct, plain, and unambiguous, possibly because deeper down in his own values he felt-thought it was unfair or unreasonable to criticize or sanction a person for laughing. He might project such a judgment into *the* meaning—automatically. That sort of interpretation is common.

3.23 To say that one cannot even read without interpreting, or cannot understand, or even enter into communication: points to the subtleties of communication; implies that a person actually selects the "right" (often right) meaning from the many that are potentially there; suggests the importance of situational context; reminds how that context *may* overcome the textual context; and so on.

3.24 It is a matter of tuning into the right message. To do that, one locates the perspectives and the situational settings, to be as objective as possible. He unscrambles the signals, often automatically. He separates his semantic-response-meaning from others, sorts them out, when that is possible, by being especially sensitive to ambiguities so that he can rationally unscramble what seems otherwise TOO CLEAR, looking for clues and interpreting them. Also, he sees that statutes, for instance, are not just commands. (They are not commands at all, because they are general. A general may command but a generality cannot, generally speaking.) Statutes prescribe, direct, suggest, guide, delegate, and so on—not necessarily all at the same time and certainly not all in the same way. (So it is for rules generally.)

3.25 Compare the Basic Rules. What does each portion do? See how they vary? Statutes are like that. And note the rhetoric and the style. Those factors weigh importantly. What if they had been presented orally? And compare other texts, say a statute. A contract is styled more like a statute than a judicial opinion, but not completely.

4.1 Postulate: One with the authority to interpret should be able to appreciate what *sort* of judgment he is exercising.

4.2 Postulate: The authoritative interpreter should try to discover what sort of judgments led to the text he is interpreting.

4.3 Postulate: The authoritative interpreter should approach the text in a mood to empathize with the draftsman-promulgator. Doing interpretation, as opposed to engaging in the rhetoric of interpretation, calls for a cooperative, *submissive* attitude, at the *early* stages. That is the most important point of "Look to the legislative purpose" (not your own), for instance.

4.4 There may be some valid reason for not following that purpose-judgment of the draftsman-promulgator, but let the reason enter into the balance with the purpose, before decision, but after interpretation. Let it enter into the interpretative rhetoric *later on.* (Strategy)

4.5 In this connection consider the loyalty oath problem discussed in the preceding chapter. One may be opposed to enforcement of that legislation, but for his own sake, he should be able to *see* (interpret$_1$) that the purpose-judgment of the legislative body (its goal, want) would be to fire any state university faculty member who did not sign it. He should not fool *himself* on that point. In some rhetoric-of-interpretation (politics) effort he might be able to persuade others that there were one or more reasons for not carrying through such a discharge (or maybe some way out).

4.6 Why confuse different kinds of interpretation, if they are ascertainable and manageable? Just because I see what you want, it does not follow that I will give it to you, but I ought to be able to form the habit of seeing (interpreting) what you and others want so that I can act most intelligently and rationally. A habit of camouflaging through self deception is ultimately self-defeating. There are other judgments relevant to decision-making than the rational interpretation of what the legislative (for instance) purpose may be. But one ought to start there. That task is hard enough to carry out even when simplified in such fashion, too often impossible.

4.7 This plea does not justify automatic invocation, enforcement; because there are other questions. There is no good reason to say that a legislature, for instance, should always have its way. Life is not so simple.

4.8 The observer-analyst ought to see the political translations as something other than ministerial law application, even when cloaked with judicial authority. In the extreme, one piece of legislative legislation enables another kind via the power of interpretation which unfortunately carries with it the power of scrambling or muddling of perspectives, roles, goals, and so . . . , (Remember normative ambiguity?)

5.1 Postulate: The doing of interpretation requires a keen sense of the multi-dimensionality of communication. It is usually a mixed-media involvement. A draftsman too needs to consider these matters.

5.2 Thus, when one interprets a text he is *in* a different communicative context from the one existing at the time the text was formalized. As an office lawyer he is in a different context from that of the judge interpreting that text in the litigational setting! To say that the meaning of word(s) in the text depends upon context may be misleading because it suggests only the "four corners" approach, only that the words have a textual context.

5.3 And the text itself usually offers more than one possible internal context-figuration for consideration. Take the

Basic Rules again, to illustrate. If one considers the second sentence of Rule 1 in connection with the first sentence, he may conclude that "intentionally" means something different from what he concludes if he considers only the first sentence by itself. (Chances are the reader out there has not considered that second sentence, has taken that first sentence in the context provided earlier rather than the context in which the sentence occurs in the Appendix?)

5.4 "Any member of the class who intentionally does an act which is disruptive of a communication transaction then in process is subject to a fine not to exceed three points. He is also subject to liability to any person who has suffered harm by such a wilful or malicious disruption."

5.5 What bearing does "such a wilful or malicious disruption" have on "intentionally"? It suggests quite strongly that "intentionally" is used in a narrower sense than we have at all so far considered. A layman might not catch this clue, but a lawyer might. (For whom was this drafted; for whom statutes?). Whose semantic response is relevant? Should we say that these terms are being used in some such technical way. Such a question arises quite often in lawyer-interpretation situations. It calls in itself for an interpretative judgment. A sense of the situation provides the intellectual context for estimating the appropriate response.

5.6 If these Rules were promulgated for a law class-seminar, then it is reasonable to *assume* (recognizing it as a plausible guesstimate) that the words are used in some legal sort of sense, a law-talk sense.

5.7 But the Rules were in the first instance drafted for a mixed group of law and non-law students. At another time they were used without redrafting for other groups of only law-trained individuals. (They could be used for laymen alone.)

5.8 It makes a difference for whom they are written (or seem to be). But consider this. In a sense statutes may be written for those who are going to interpret them on behalf of those who are to be controlled by them.

5.9 As to the Basic Rules, isn't it reasonable to say that different judgments could reasonably be reached if there are different situational contexts in which they are to be applied-interpreted? What implications do the Basic Rules carry in the contexts of this book? Can we here know what they properly "mean" in those seminar contexts? (These questions will frustrate a literalist, because after all . . .)

5.10 So a statute, constitution, contract, judicial opinion, Bible, and so on, change over time, because of their "ecological" communications-environment dependency. The *implications* change and they are part of the text in a psycholinguistic sense. ("But we must have strict construction . . ." Of what?)

5.11 Well enough. But surely such considerations do not affect appropriate judgment regarding the situation posited in 2.23, the paradigmatic, core meaning regarding the student who obviously wilfully interrupted the conversation between instructor and student A. But the student who laughed (2.11) may not have laughed wilfully-to-disrupt, and certainly not maliciously. Wilfully-desiring-to, willing it, not just knowing it. (But one may be wilful without being malicious.)

5.12 If the second sentence was not meant to affect "intentionally," why add those adjectives? Could it reasonably be argued that "liability" (second sentence of Rule 1) for a disruption occurs only if there is a wilful or malicious disruption, but that a fine could be assessed for a comparatively innocent disruption? That is reversing the conventionalities of "fine" (crime) and "liability" (tort-contract) so far as lawyer-talk is concerned.

5.13 Well, such comings and goings in syntax and related situational references fairly well illustrate what goes on in legal interpretations. There is even more to consider with respect to Rule 1 and textual contexts, but no need to belabor the point. The point? A thorough understanding of the mechanisms of language and communication are quite in order for the rational, fair-minded interpreter.

5.14 And . . . interpretation is not always just chaos turned definitive by fiat. But interpretation rhetoric can be deceptively definitive (or is it definitively deceptive).

5.15 Judicial interpretation involves exploration of the words of the text by means of other words. Look to see. It is so. Compare earlier sections of this book where that is stressed.

5.16 Consider that ecological metaphor again. Disturb one significant element of the communication-environment and you affect or may upset all of it. One needs to be aware of the complexity of interrelationships.

6.1 The significance of (some) context is well known, but choice of *possible* contexts is crucial. The parol evidence rule, for instance, is said to restrict the interpreter of the formal contract to the four corners of that instrument. Any area of interpretation (contracts and other instruments, statutes, regulations, etc., the jury trial, defamation situations, fraud, and so on and on) needs some rules, principles, conventions, understandings, and such, as to what other "evidence" besides the text is relevant. That is, what contexts are relevants. What goes with (con . . .) the text? (What will be allowed to go with . . .)

6.2 Of course neither the parol evidence rule nor any other such device can operate literally the way it is supposed to operate. But the rules-principles of surface and depth grammars operate as context-switches, to push this way or that, as the above considerations of Rule 1 illustrate.

6.3 When one is interpreting a statute, there are several potential relevant contexts: the common law background-context; other legislation; so-called legislative history, i.e.

the dynamics of enactment; the socio-legal context at the time of passage, but also at the time of interpretation; the institutional context, say of a particular industry being regulated. Etc.

6.4 The words of the statute (or regulation, constitution, etc.) may give clues to appropriateness of context.

6.5 Another way of putting this: Look for clues as to which language-games are being pursued.

6.6 See Basic Rules again: Was the Professor a member of the class under Rule 1? Could he be sanctioned under the Rules? Different games are played in education with this class-ifier, as it is with all classifying, categorizing words. Teachers at all levels refer to *their* classes, not exactly as if they were *in* those classes, certainly not in those classes in any disciplinary way. Or on the other hand, the dynamics of communication separates teacher (T) from student (S): S to T: "You told the class . . ." But at some other time, "class" can be used in a different sociological way: T to S: "I'm afraid they have cancelled our class . . ." (T-S)

6.7 If we look at the context of Rule 1 in a purely classifying sort of way, "class" in a number of places seems to include the Professor. My guess would be that these verbal clues would control non-educationally involved interpreters, even though teachers are not for the purpose of authority matters regarded ordinarily as class members and even though these Rules *seem to* allocate more power to Professor. (But in Rule 1 see these words: ". . . by the class as a whole, including Professor . . .")

6.8 That latter section suggests the kind of difference that is involved between the meaning approach (what do the words say) and the purpose approach in legislative interpretation dynamics. If it were thought the purpose of these Basic Rules was to promote class discipline, then maybe Professor ought not to be included as a member of the class. But note the preamble of the Basic Rules.

Discipline does not seem to be what is of concern or interest. But more generally speaking, note that the "purpose" approach allows a shift from one internal textual context to another, or to an outside context. A meaning approach could allow that also, but since meaning tends to be a literalist's ploy, there has not been the flexibility with meaning that there could be.

6.9 The history of the group affected plays on interpretation. Remember that even judges are often part of the group being affected and legislative or other textual words will be responded to according to developed feelings. Thus, whether Professor is considered a class member by the student members of the group could depend how permissive the previous interrelationships have been.

6.10 In the seminar, contrary to most others, even yet in legal education, there was deliberate effort to decentralize classroom control, as part of the effort to promote free wheeling dynamics to serve as the very subject matter to be considered from a communications perspective. On two occasions when the Basic Rules were used, in two different seminars, the Professor was the first one charged with disruption. No question was raised about his membership. It apparently seemed obvious. (Of course there are other implications to this class action.) One might want to say that there was no interpretation here. It would only be if the action of the class against the Professor was questioned that the interpretative question would arise. But of course there was some sort of interpretation_1 by the (other?) class members, which could be challenged by another sort of interpretation_2.

6.11 Even had there been a closer contest, interpretation probably would have it that Professor was a member of *this class*. He definitely was a member of the group in a way that Professors usually are not. The interpersonal structure-dynamics get into the interpretative acts.

6.12 It is always thus. I have said it several times earlier, as to rules. A rule is a function of the communication situation in which it is being involved, dynamically (substitute laws, regs., etc.). That is why I drafted the Basic Rules for the Law-Communication Seminar to let the "class members" feel it further. It really does only a little good to just say it is so. Compare the interpretation of statutes. Judges interpret them to juries, for instance, but ultimately the interpretation is for the jury (either of the statute or the judicial instructions.) to determine, as in other *closed* communication situations. Note that the Seminars under the Basic Rules are *closed* communication-situation-structures. Compare almost any classroom. (But internal structures vary.) A lawyer's office. My head. Yours. One needs to be rather wary of his private interpretations when it comes to legal matters! Unless he has control over the communication dynamics in the setting where the ultimate interpretation will occur. But if he is the ultimate interpreter, whose influence shall he come under? These dynamics operate so subtly because while they affect the meaning of the text, we look at the text and do not see them *there*: The meaning is now clear and can be explained and it was always clear and so on.

6.13 Now—look back to 2.23 through 2.26 and then 3.1. I raised some questions in connection with the problem whether the student who uttered an obscenity and talked in the middle of Professor's exchange with another student was violating the first sentence of Rule 1.

6.14 Let me remind that I am using these Basic Rules as illustrative of some of the aspects of interpretation of statutory, regulation, constitutional, and various sorts of rule-principle writings of that sort. (And of course more than that—to explore interpersonal communication dynamics. And yet more, to explore the relationship between the written medium and interpersonal dynamics. And how subtly these factors interplay.)

6.15 (And why is not the usual essay-form being used in these explorations? The best form might be in the form of a script of a play! Re-enacting the dynamics of the Basic Rules sessions. The usual essay-form simply will not do it. A tape recording of the first session with these Rules is very revealing, for one who is prepared for it.)

6.16 Is that student guilty of a violation of Rule 1? (2.23-2.26)

6.17 See how that question is loaded? Have you stopped beating your dog? It is not merely a matter of interpreting in the sense of finding a rule which was broken, but there also needs to be a disposition to invoke the available sanctions, at least in this sort of situation. Not all situations are of this sort, but a significant number are. (See the discussion in preceding chapter.)

6.18 Does Rule 1 apply to that student (2.23-2.26)? Previously it was asked whether his conduct was intentional in the sense of the Rule and how that played back and forth with "wilful" and "malicious." But suppose now we ask whether it was "disruptive of a communciation transaction then in process."

6.19 Let's look at the situation again. Professor is talking to one student, A. Student B utters an obscenity in the middle of Professor's comments and rails against him. It may be rude, but is it a disruption of a communication transaction . . .? Is it merely a matter of finding the meaning-intent-purpose *re* "communication transaction"? These are specially used words, not everyday phrasing. Even so, one can work analogies and see that if one person is talking to another . . . . A telephone conversation ought to be a core situation under that phrase. What about Professor talking to student A? It would seem so. Would it make any difference if people did not need to raise a hand to speak? (It was stated otherwise in 2.23.) One does not raise a hand in the "real world." Still, one does not just barge in, or at least if he does, there are communicative impacts, unless he is in some special situation . . . . And if he barges in with an obscenity, then surely that vulgarity. . . . But is the rule talking about rudeness? Well rudeness does not promote communication (Unless one is willing to communicate a rudeness, on purpose . . .) "Malice" could include rudeness.

6.20 See how 2.23 was loaded. This subtle point is hard to appreciate. I regard this sort of point, raised in several different ways in this book as perhaps the key point in understanding the way that law-communication *works*, what can be done with law(s), the process of legal reasoning(s), etc. . . . (see 2.24 and 2.25).

6.21 One gets locked into the givens in 2.23, but who gives the givens in varying situations? What if the interpreter is the one who gives the givens? (And he usually is!) That is why I speak of the interpretative rhetoric of a judicial report, for the opinion has fitted statute, for instance, to facts, it would seem, but through the process of law-fact-talk-dialectic. Someone has to do it! But it does happen and in the stages of doing interpretation one is not just involved in interpreting text, but text against and into situational dynamics.

6.22 If one is going to be an objective doer of interpretation, he is not only going to have to realize when he is really interpreting some text rather than just reading, applying, etc., (see 1.20, 1.25, 4.1, 4.2, 4.3, 5.1) but *also* when he is interpreting from the other direction, from some raw, hot facts, or someone else's interpretations of those dynamics. Etc.

6.23 Put it this way. The job of interpreting the situation put in 2.23 is something quite different from being *in* that as yet uninterpreted *raw*, hot situation and having or taking the task of working text and situation together. There are so many times when it is that sort of situation. Somewhere along the way between happening-of-events and ultimate judgment (whether in court or elsewhere) that kind of situation is involved. And even the ultimate judgment-situation is more like that than it is like 2.23!

6.24 So, in or close to ultimate judgment-interpretation, as well as before, one ought to be aware-open to the levels of ambiguity and contextual involvement of the text, *but also* to those of the situational involvement of the text-interpreter.

6.25 Well, I can hear it. That is a fantastic sort of complication. We have no time for such theoretical intellectuality. But stop to consider how simple it is to interpret such phrases as "Turn the page" and "Pass the salt." One goes through a great deal of complex communicative dynamics-learning before he can carry out those "simple" instructions. It comes naturally *now*. Much of interpretation comes naturally, but if one really *wants to* understand and appreciate the happenings of interpretation of the sort of texts involved in socio-legal processes and if he wants to do more than mouth rubrics regarding "rationality" of interpretation, then he puts himself into the thick of it, even if it seems at first like starting all over again!

6.26 Not for the literalist, the dogmatist, the legalist, the autocrat, the one in power-authority, or the revolutionary either, or the lazy. (That may not leave many interested persons.)

6.27 How one might look at the raw situation which was interpreted in 2.23 obviously depends upon where he is sitting, then as a participant in the seminar, now as he reads, or imagines, and so on. Professor *might not* see it as an interruption-disruption, or if he did, another student C might not, or a sensitive observer might not. It depends upon what had happened previously, what sort of structural interrelationships had developed. In talking to student A, Professor may be talking to the whole group, showing off, ridiculing student B, what have you. (Compare an attorney questioning a witness at trial and the channels to trial judge, jury, appellate court, his client, the courtroom observers, including the press, etc.) Just who are the parties that make up the communication transaction? There are transactions within transactions and interlocking with other transactions before and after. Such is the nature of communciation (and law! And word-families). What if there had been an interplay between student A and student B just before instructor spoke, or a triangular conversation within some even larger dynamics of the whole group?

6.28 Well, of course, whatever did happen, one can always imagine other things that might have happened. But that is not the sort of point being raised. We are exploring the dynamics of determining-interpreting what happened in connection with interpreting a few words of a text. (What really happened in the Garratt situation? What really happened in Chicago? How did there come to be a "Chicago Seven" to be tried *together* for conspiracy. Whose conspiracy was it? Is conspiracy more precise than "communication transaction"? When is a lawyer-candidate of "good moral character"? Who owned People's Park? Is "ownership" more precise? How does it get to be a question? Did the professor who refused to sign the loyalty oath "break the law"? Who determines that is the way to look at it? Did the postal workers break the law in 1970? How do we get to the point where *that* question is asked?)

6.29 But ultimately such words as those of Rule 1 have to be finally interpreted. And they can be and will be. The words "communication transaction" do not in themselves give the vital clues to what games are being played, which senses are *being used*. But the phrase is all the same viable, usable, useful as a term-concept. It can be applied, reasonably, fairly. It can be worked out.

6.30 See the Rule of Interpretation and the Preamble to which it in turn refers in the Basic Rules instrument. As vague and general as they are, they could help to work out the situation. They could help to keep the group working at the problem, to see the possibility that working out this problem-situation was practical after all, a true-to-life experience, merely a special case of interpretation in *the context of interpersonal dynamics*, the context which is always there but not articulated. The text is there, the dynamics here, but . . . The magic of the written form! Maybe the canons on construction *re* statutes work in some such way, despite their internal conflicts. It is not that they are controlling prior to adoption, but that they help one to see more clearly, or to see what he would not have seen except for such a check-list for vision, for insight. They are insightful. If one wants to work it out, then such guides help. Not every text carries its own guides (maybe they should), and they cannot all be spelled out at the time, because the situation may develop in such way that they do not become articulatory until the problem arises.

6.31 Of course it *may* all work out badly.

6.32 See how ambiguity of the sorts explored *re* the Basic Rules is actually helpful for that seminar learning-situation, leaving room to move, explore, . . . There is such a technique as building ambiguity into statutes, regulations, contracts, and other texts, because gaps are inevitable, and things do change. A major function of a contract is to agree! Statutes delegate power(s) inevitably, some more than others, some on purpose. Some texts are vaguely vague. Consider "due process," "good moral character," "conspiracy," "restraint of trade," "title," and so on. Or when courts interpret such words-texts, their job may be to set the limits for some other agency's powers, broadening their own, abstaining, etc. It is not *just* a matter of meaning surely, nor of intent, nor even of purpose. And ambiguity is not evil *per se*. (Not to say that just any old ambiguity is good.)

6.33 A statute is or ought to be a polished, finished product? Yes, relative to the legislative process-program, but in other contexts it is in a sense a first draft, to be reworked!

It is often merely an agenda. See the ways the Basic Rules may work or be worked, as an illustration. They can initiate an exploration that otherwise might not take place. In a given situation they may be rejected if the time is not ripe and something else has to be tried, or they may soon deteriorate or become obsolete.

6.34 See the power dynamics in the Basic Rules. The first reaction to these Rules may be (and usually has been) general anger and hostility. They seem to be imposed, a grab of power. Even in an authority-controlled seminar they might be resented because they threaten to supersede some unwritten rules which everyone has learned to live with. (Even when shown to a group preliminary to explaining how they worked out in another situation, under circumstances where the author could not impose them, at a law school where he was involved for only one day, the whole seminar-group, including the Professor of that group, was angered and would not at first discuss them.) Then members began to see opportunities for implementing their own powers, or of gaining in ways they could not have gained, or maybe of learning about communication, and so on. These things are felt, even if not immediately articulatory.

6.35 Seeing that sort of thing is surely as important in the interpretative process as seeing 'the" meaning of the textual words: *What-they-say* plus *what-they-do* plus *what-may-be-done* plus *what-I-can-do* plus . . . .

CHART #9

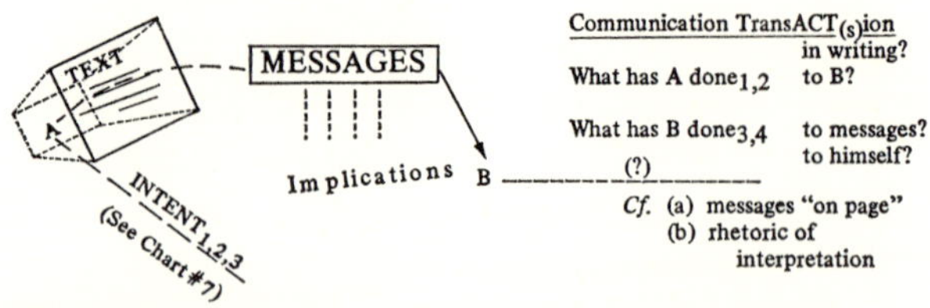

Analysis of (")INTERPRETATION(") → i.e., simultaneously the word-form and some of the family members in addition to some of dynamics of . . . .

Interpretation$_1$: Reading$_{1,2,3...}$

R_1: recognition-reading
R_2: understanding-reading

Interpretation$_2$: Analysis$_{1,2,3}$ . . .

includes: R_2

Communications analysis (See Chart #8):
inter alia, implications search

Interpretation$_3$: Translation$_{1,2,3}$ . . .

can be preceded by Analysis

Interpretation$_4$: Decision$_{(x)}$

includes Interpretation$_{(?)}$
i.e., at least R_1–and: various stages of above sorts. May or may not involve choice among consciously determined alternatives.

Interpretation$_5$: Rhetoric of justifying Interpretation$_4$
(and often confused with it, even by interpreter)

Comment on STRICT CONSTRUCTION: Interpretation$_4$ and/or 5

plain meaning — surface analysis
four corners of text

(but *can* be "liberal")

Interpretation(s) within COMMUNICATION DYNAMICS

(See diagram at top):

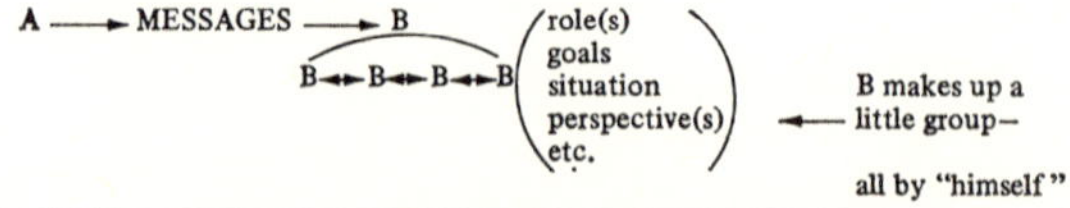

Cf. where two or more people in the transaction(s)

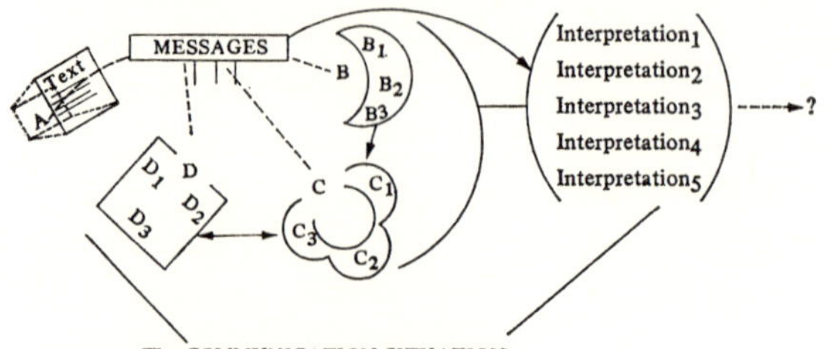

The COMMUNICATION SITUATION

includes its (")Rule(s)(")
(")Fact(s)(")
etc. etc. etc. etc.

Chapter X

COMMUNICATIONS ANALYSIS: PRELUDE TO INTERPRETATION

The Worth of a Model

THE PRECEDING REFLECTIONS were meant to be sensitizing. They were born of rigor but impressionistic in appearance. A chart would not catch it all, but some prefer the effort. There *are* analytical distinctions worth putting into a framework, as an aid to observation, a key aspect of interpretation, and too as the sort of grist preferred by many theorists.

The important question that needs to be considered goes to the degree and kind of attention that should be given as a matter of legal policy to matters of communication in official interpretations. But most commentators need to do more homework. For instance, the move to emphasize and work out the purpose approach in statutory interpretation is a considerable improvement over a mere meaning and intent model. Yet merely to speak of the meaning of words, or of the intent of a legislature or a statute, or of purpose, all of this, involves *theoretical* assumptions about communication. Few commentators evidence any deep linguistic sensitivity, and even they draw up too short.

So we shall explore a model, a framework for communications analysis, beginning with J. L. Austin's analysis put forth in his Harvard lectures, "How to Do Things with Words." We will thus be moving forward through the fields of interpretation and yet looking back at the earlier explorations of this book, articulating some of their bases, pulling a few strings together.

Caveat Interpreter! The exploration itself is a step toward

words sensitivity, but the exploration and the model are the more useful the further one is along that route, when comes a point it is no longer needed. The biggest obstacle to more realistic discussion of interpretation is verbal inflexibility, for instance someone's inability to discuss at one sitting in more than one level of communication, say what words may mean as well as how they might be and are being used. Our model can only help to aid in such a skill and to justify it. It is not itself *doing* it.

Why Start with J. L. Austin?

By the time that Austin "had got to Harvard," there was general agreement among leading experts, not so much that meaning-analysis had to go, but that it was a conceptualistic trap in need of unloading and supplementing. The shift to consideration of word *use* paid off, but it too had become overburdened and to boot the new focus shut out some of the advantages of the older word-meaning approach. Austin was to go further and yet preserve both meaning and use analyses.

Austin and Wittgenstein had moved somewhat independently from the idea-ism of meaning theory toward the behavioral dimension of communication, thus relating the written medium to the spoken, as we must even for statutes. Austin related words to speech-acts, for instance. Wittgenstein spoke of word games, clearly referring to interpersonal communication situations, not just paper games. Some critics rightly worried that this sort of move put communications analysis into a new imbalance. Words were not just pieces of behavior, but independent also, as with a novel or a statute. They carried ideas. In Ethics as well as Law, we have the normative, not only is but ought, and the matter of values. (Compare the very much related complaints against legal realism.)

Of course debates tend toward polarity, as among legal theorists such as H. L. A. Hart and Fuller. Either you separate is from ought or you do not, likewise regarding law as it relates to morality. This same sort of problem inescapably confronts us, not only in debates on interpretation, especially of statutes and constitutions, but as one engages in the activity of interpreting, even if he remains oblivious of the problem. But it is not either-or, it is both, simultaneously, or almost. It seems that Austin may have begun to see that because his analysis allows, even though not dramatically encouraging, blending right along with separation. Long ago Felix Cohen, one of our most multi-faceted geniuses, argued the realism of such blended dualism. (It need not be just two levelled.) But like Austin, his communications analysis tended at times to overdo the empirical.

Austin exhibited what Cohen did not, a proper skepticism for the very word "values." But to preserve meaning and its correlates, as he did, is to give room at least for idea-ism and e-valuation. Even an accent on speech behavior and associated word-use carries with it goal-oriented activity. But any kind of observational technique calls for skill in placing a focus on what can be observed. Sciences rest on that base. Nowadays it is realized that the "field of values" around behavior (or whatever observable) can be appreciated at the same time, and the focus shifted back and forth. Lasswell and McDougal have moved us the furthest in this direction while showing an impatience with one of the major obstacles in the path, communications insensitivity. But they are pushing value analysis while Austin was pushing communications analysis. For sound and wise decision-making we need them both, in balance. That balance requires that we see interpretation (s) as separable from as well as joinable to decision making, seeing and solving in tense equilibrium.

How It Works

Austin set up his analysis, characterizing not only in terms of words and meaning but of verbal behavior as well. Thus a speech act is to be looked at in three significantly different although interrelated ways:

1. It is first a *locutionary* act, producing words which can be observed and analyzed separately from the behavior pro-

ducing them, in ways which are related to other communication-behavior products, in terms of meaning, for instance, and in the context of language, each under the rules of grammar—and so on.

2. It is also an *illocutionary* act, word-producing behavior which can be focused as if separate. It is something one does with words, in the course of verbalizing, as a court justifies its decision while producing an opinion, as one apologizes, *performs* an apology in saying "I am sorry." An actor acts with and without words. We have a whole vocabulary available and enlargeable to *describe* a great variety of speech behavior.

3. It is also a *perlocutionary* act. We can and do describe what one has done not only in terms of his kind of behavior in the illocutionary aspects, but separably with regard to what he accomplishes *through* (per) or by his illocutionary act, as when one saves another from danger by warning him, "Look out." That is a warning kind of speech act.

These are important distinctions to make. We often focus on one aspect or another as our vocabularies show. Words like "meaning," "definition," and "ambiguity," for instance, *allow* focus on the locutionary aspects. When we translate and interpret, we may be or at least purport to be in that dimension. Then again, on the second level we speak of warning, apologizing, complaining, threatening, commanding, delegating, whether such *illocutionary* act produces the desired results or not. On the third level, while we are describing what an actor has done in saying he amused or angered someone, the focus is on some consequence beyond the actor. Note that in describing non-communication behavior the distinction between actor and recipient is usually more apparent than it is in our area of concern, as when we say "He hurt the girl," or "He hit the tree," or "He wakened his wife." We have quite adequate words to do this job in communications settings too, as we have noted, but often the distinction is muted or ignored, as it is muted in "He apologized *to* her" (compare he offered an apology), or even more so in "He insulted her" (compare saying that he spoke *to* her but she did not hear, he joked *with* her but she was not amused.)

One of the important points of this analysis is that it encourages one's skill in making the very sorts of distinctions which many of our words allow him to ignore or, whether consciously or not, to muddle or wipe out when dealing with communications involved situations. Thus, while a statute is a communication, it may not communicate *to* anyone, and furthermore, it is not *doing* the communication, some-body is, or not. One person may command another "without effect." Well, there is an effect, for instance the locution, and even a communicative effect if the words are heard as sounds or understood. We might even say the audience was commanded: "He commanded me." But if a command is "without effect," it does not have the *intended* effect, does not accomplish "its" purpose. Compare with regard to a statute. When we speak of its purpose it is often in the sense of "purpose" used in referring to the purpose of an object, such as an ashtray for instance, whereas with regard to the "purpose of the command" we are referring to the purpose of the command-er.

So, while to speak of intent or purpose will allow the vital distinction with regard to actor and recipient, it may slur it over and indeed may disregard the indispensability of the second party to any successfully communicative act. For that matter, it may even slur over the locutionary distinction as well, although reference to meaning and its families does that muddling job the best of all.

Attention to role-perspective is just as important as the distinction between language-level conventions and behavior patterns. This makes our framework all the better. It accents not only what is said. That is usually all we talk about in talking about communication. It also accents who is doing *what* (in saying what was said), and what *else* is done to *whom* else (by saying what was said, and doing . . .). We can capture every one of these distinctions with the word "ambiguity," but hardly well enough for any sophisticated theory of interpretation. What we do instead with this framework is to explore *kinds of patterns* of ambiguity with finer distinctions. (The word "ambiguous" is ambiguous.)

Thus, what one says may not jibe with what he does (in

saying . . .). That could be called a kind of ambiguity, this seeming mismatch of locution with illocution. ("I love you" said with a snarl.) Such ambiguity is the source for humor and art, but too of tragedy and pathos. Close communications analysis often reveals this sort of "ambiguity" in official law texts, hard enough to see in judicial opinions (consider analysis of Garratt, *supra*). There we have more clues than are provided in statutes. One suffers more readily under the illusion that a statute is itself what is done by the legislature, because that is all one sees.

Suppose an ordinance which prohibits "the driving of all vehicles in city parks." We can see what it says. We might say that it prohibits autos. That is what it *does*. But for a court to determine that "vehicles means bicycles too," is either for the court to be the doer *re* bicycles or else to decide that the city council intended *to do* that. The council hardly has *done* it in any perlocutionary sense. To say it is reasonable to apply the ordinance to bicycles is something quite different from saying that such is the purpose of the ordinance, unless one makes it clear that he really means intent (one sense of "purpose") of the *council.*

There are no linguistic rules to tell us how we *must* relate a given level of generalities to a lower level (e.g. vehicle-automobile), although there are reasonable implications or even presumptions (strong inferences) to be drawn. Beyond that there are conventional possibilities (e.g. vehicle-bicycle), or maybe only guesses. Investigation outside the locutionary level may reenforce the presumptions, or strengthen possibilities to probability, or maybe even guess to presumption. Yet it may some times contradict the presumption completely (e.g. a special usage).

When we are dealing with live communications, the usual locutionary aspects may not even be noticed, as when one utters an epithet more common to swearing, but with (along with?) a laugh. Is he swearing and not swearing? If one swears in French, what is he *doing to* one who does not speak French? It might seem silly, but it could help to assume that a statute is written in something like a foreign (to the interpreter) language, as if in code perhaps. We do not tell the draftsman about our practice, but then we are more likely to take account of *his* problems and the problems of illocution and other dimensions.

Taking the Observer Out of the Act

It might go unnoticed, but our model of communications analysis first puts one in the role of observer. Role awareness is as important as anything.

Suppose we are analyzing the communication situation in which the man uttered French swear words to another. As an observer we are not to take sides in the analysis. We are helped in this task by our model. If the actor A knows that B does not know French, did A swear at B? If we only say that he did, then it leaves open the implication that B comprehended, although maybe not as much as it would if we said A insulted B. If A thinks wrongly that B knows French, then he swore in the illocutionary sense, but not in the perlocutionary sense. If *we* do not know whether B understands French, then we are guessing. We slip unobtrusively into another role if we reach a conclusion reported as an observation that A swore at or insulted B. Add that the observer of the reporter does not know for sure what role the reporter is playing. This is precisely the sort of muddlement we are in when we read reports of judges even when they say they are interpreting, even more when they speak as they often do with unconsciously muddled assurance. ("The plain meaning is . . ." "The evident purpose was . . .")

There is a parallel in value-loaded descriptions of acts which do not have communications aspects. "He hit her" not only *may* leave open to implication that he intended to but that he was blameworthy, which he might not be even if he intended it. Of course communications descriptions carry such possibilities in *addition to* those we have been exploring, as in "He said . . . ."

Suppose a park director issues a memorandum, "No vehicles are to be allowed in the park." You pull into the park on a bicycle and receive a guard's raised hand, because "He said no vehicles in here." You argue. "Well," replies the guard, "that's what he meant, I know." Together the director and this guard are making the park safe, but did the director (intend to) make it *that* safe? Who *did* that?

How should an observer report? He might say that the guard did what he was told, or that he carried out the meaning of the words in the memo, or the intent, the purpose. Of the memo? The director? Or is it really only the guard's meaning, intent, and purpose? The memo had something to do with what the guard did, and in that same vein, the director might be reported to have prohibited bicycles from the park. We could cross check with the director, but not with a legislature in any parallel fashion. Whatever the desirability may be, there are times when judges and other so-called interpreters are more in the act than appears on the surface of the treatment of either a statute, contract, or what have you. One who wishes to be able to observe-analyze what is happening needs to straighten out the lines and perspectives, not only in the statute, for instance, but also in the communications that follow it—and maybe those that precede it. Interpretations of interpretations geometrically progress the muddlements.

Meaning, Use, and Ambiguity

There is bound to be objection to the esoteric terms in our model and its exploration, especially locutionary, illocutionary, and perlocutionary. For one thing there is the matter of persuading or educating someone not at all familiar with these distinctions. Well, no doubt a job of translation is necessary, and a closer look will show lesser esoterica are being explored too. Further, the subtleties of the different senses of such key terms in the mechanics of interpretation as "meaning," "ambiguity," not to forget "interpretation" itself are actually easier to see and recall under some comparatively little used labels.

One kind of ambiguity might best be called supra-locutionary. It is the sort of ambiguity which is elaborated in every dictionary when it gives more than one "meaning" for this or that word. Obviously many ambiguities of that sort are wiped out by the locutionary factors of the text itself. The word "saw" is clearly ambiguous at the linguistic level. But consider: "He saw the tree," and "He sawed the tree." No problem, subtle as the variation really is. Of course if a three-year-old child were the source, there would be. We then regard this as an illocutionary ambiguity or a potential locutionary mistake. But as we say, in the usual textual confrontations, immediate or not so immediate textual contexts provide the clues, understood intuitively, we might say. Grammar and punctuation as well as syntax help us out, although even punctuation can be ambiguous: A letter to Sylvia is thus ambiguous in this respect in saying "I want you to meet my wife, dear Sylvia," if his wife's name is Sylvia too. This could be cured by a change either in punctuation or syntax or more drastically of name.

"It is raining" does not have the locutionary clarity it might have. We might say it is vague in a semantic-referential sense in not telling us where or how hard. We could say it was ambiguous in these regards. But the difficulty could be more at the illocutionary level. It is clear enough what it "means" (locutionary), but not how it is being used. Ordinarily we may be satisfied it is being used informationally. That is an illocutionary categorization ("He informed her by saying that it was raining.") that affects the way the text is read if it is a letter, so very subtly. It need not be a piece or only a piece of information in its illocutionary or perlocutionary aspects. That would be clearest if it were a code expression, but even a straightforward piece of information can raise implications for the listener, that he will get wet, or that he is expected to take an umbrella.

How shall we describe the illocutionary and perlocutionary aspects: (e.g.) in saying the words "It is raining" she informed him. In informing him she suggested he take an umbrella (since they had often been through this before). We might not want to say only that she suggested he take an umbrella although we might say she issued a warning. It is not stretching convention to say *her words* meant he should take an umbrella, or even that *she* meant that. On some occasion he might not be sure which implications were intended: thus, he might say "Are we going somewhere?" or "I left the umbrella at the office." She might on that occasion be merely informing him: "What in the world, John?" she might well expostulate. (Enter our observer with his Austinian model to save the day.)

Thus there are various kinds of ambiguity whose resolution is actually made more difficult by the very word ("meaning") that is supposed to help resolve it for failure of the word itself to clarify which level of *its* use is involved: "What do you mean?" Well, what do you mean by mean?

It is difficult to keep the lines straight, and words like locutionary, illocutionary, and perlocutionary might help, just as might subscripts, as in $meaning_1$, $meaning_2$, $meaning_3$, so long as the references are maintained consistently.

Further, a word may have many senses even if we locate the level. Austin's suggestion of a taxonomy of illocutionary acts is supposed to be helpful in this further charting. Thus "It is raining" could be a warning, threat, apology, joke, what have you, in the illocutionary senses. The subscript helps to post the places where distinctions need to be made, but further charting is then needed.

We reach what hopefully now is obvious. If "It is raining" can be $ambiguous_{1,2,3}$ in the ways I have illustrated, it is quite true that words with the very clearest locutionary meaning can be ambiguous and indeed always are with respect to the illocutionary level, so long as we have no clues to the illocutionary level context. Words at the level of language are ambiguous with respect to use_1 at the locutionary level, and words at the locutionary level are ambiguous with respect to use_2 at the illocutionary level so long as there are no clues to the latter use. Very often there are clues at the textual level; i.e. the text is not purely locutionary! Or put another way, because of the conventions surrounding the words used in a text, implications may properly be drawn from the locutionary use as to the illocutionary sense: thus, in a letter, "John, please watch for rain." John misses the clues from his past experience if he writes back, "Why what is the rain going to do, Dear?" "Pass the salt" is ambiguous, but not at the dinner table if one attends to the situation and/or if he has the right attitude!

Well, of course there is this third level of ambiguity, the perlocutionary level kinds of ambiguity. It can be put in terms of meaning to the other party to the communication. We are led to say that meaning is relative to the observer, as Korzybski's followers have often said, "meaning is not in words but in the one who reads or hears them." That is a dramatic overstatement and a limiting redefinition of "meaning." I am not talking of the locutionary ambiguity that comes from the speaker's slip or poor composition, or from the speaker's failure to provide at the illocutionary level complete clues, or from the interpreter's failure to detect available clues. These are complexities enough, of course, and the speaker-draftsmen has wondrous burdens regarding them. He also has the additional burden of "knowing his audience," as we say. The clearest examples of this sort of ambiguity exist in attempts to communicate across social class lines, as when a lawyer talks to a jury being unaware that his conventions (locutionary and/or illocutionary) do not match those of his audience. Statutes also present this kind of ambiguity, not only for an ordinary citizen but ofttimes for lawyers too who have no way of knowing what idiom the statute is developing. All interpretation involves this level, the more subtly because the interpreter is usually blithely unaware and not concerned enough as a matter of general attitude to push for further clues and information. Whatever the burden on the draftsman, at the time of interpretation there is an equal if not greater burden on the interpreter to broaden his range of inquiry.

The problems reach another stage in permutation with regard to the one who gets his communication through the medium of an interpreter, as when one reads a judicial opinion purporting to interpret a legal or law-involved text!

Misguides Among Rules and Principles of Interpretation

There are a variety of maxims, rules, and principles which are bottomed on the assumption that a text of the kind encouraged in legal process can carry the burden of communication necessary to lead to fair and adequate interpretations. They all come out of other policies, but their solution to the problems involved prove to be misguided by these erroneous assumptions about the power of words, at least those whose power has been limited by form and procedure. Among the rules purportedly limiting one to the "four corners" of a text is the parol evidence rule. If there is no ambiguity, it says, then do not go outside the contract to produce other evidence of the agreement represented in the purportedly "final" contract (or, do not contradict the text).

The late Professor Corbin, as no doubt the leading contemporary expert in the field of contracts law and the subject of contracts interpretation, expressed in strong words that the parol evidence rule was at once a folly and a giant cover-up. He was right of course, but his chief objection that all words in a contract are ambiguous will not be fully convincing for failure to be more specific regarding the kinds of ambiguity. It is easy to rebut him at his level of objection by looking at a contract and saying, "Why look here at these words. They are clear enough." The rule seems to be going to a deserved grave, shrouded still as exceptions and distinctions, but a more sophisticated communications analysis starting with the sorts of distinctions carried in our growing model might aid in the task of developing more communicatively realistic rules and principles.

One wants to continue to put the burden on good drafting and yet use familiar clauses to cover new sorts of situations, the very sort of problem that plagues us *re* statutes. One also wants to keep the idea of a fixed agreement and disallow the quibble that an argument can always produce, in the same way that he wants to disallow evidence of a minority view in the legislature as to the meaning of the statutory words. Looking outside the contract is said to encourage fraud and perjury, as it does even more in the will probate situation where the testator cannot testify. A certain expertise is growing toward clever planting of "clues" in the record of legislative debate to affect the reading of the statute, as one might rig the record of the corporate minutes. Well, these and other problems will not go away, but just because they exist is not conclusive on the point whether they force some sort of retreat into the text where the problems prove to be worse over the long haul.

Computer storage of textual communicative debates, negotiations, and such may help, but short of that day, there is the familiar device of *presumptive* meaning, intent, and purpose, rebuttable by credible and persuasive *evidence* in the nature of clues to the various levels of "meaning" and such. So, for instance, if Seller and Buyer agree to the sale of chickens, Buyer's refusal of tendered non-tender stewers may be justified on the basis of a special usage (illocutionary) in the Buyer-Seller group of businessmen, just as in the old days courts could legitimately construe "persons" in a statute to mean men but not women, no matter what the dictionary said.

If there are to be rules and principles of interpretation, they should include distinction between a communications analysis and a decision made in the absence of adequate communications clues. Corbin is only one of many who have noted that the rhetoric of interpretation allows a muddling when he noted that courts often were really constructing additions to a contract in the name of interpreting it, just as they do in extrapolating the so-called purpose of the legislature. That is, there ought to be rules and principles not only for the doing of interpretation but for the rhetoric of interpretation as well. Of course the rhetoric feeds back into the doing, possibly more than the other way.

There should be no rule at all restricting the interpreter to the four corners of the text. Not only are there levels of communications (*supra*), it is simply impossible because an interpreter retreats into his own communicative context, the more that the search in other contexts is limited. One's reasoning and drawing of implications goes on in silent, subtle fashion to fill in what is missing. There is virtue in gong out to illocutionary and perlocutionary contexts to check out these reasonings and implications, but of course there have to be limits, not only in the name of expedience but reason and policy as well. There can be no "four corners" limiting *rule*, and there should not even be such a blind(ing) principle. We should start from the other end, if we could, if we would.

Context(s), Meaning, and Semantic Response

What one gets *out* of what he reads has much to do with what he puts *into* it, and vice-versa. So it is with interpreting. A second reading of almost any written source of even minor depth makes the source (appear to be) different in its impact. The implications change in some ways, even the meanings. Constitutions, statutes, contracts and other texts call for deep reading, and even more, active analysis and inter-involvement of the interpreter, not only with the text *per se*, but with certain other evidences on different levels of communication, as well as with his own reactions.

The text is a triggering mechanism, whether there is recourse to other sources and evidence or not. Without a doubt the interpreter has much to do with the way he is triggered. He and the text are in a very physical as well as intellectual sense in a common context. That context is also providing stimulation of invisible, subtle sorts. But the interpreter can to some extent vivify the context, the better to determine how it does or *should* affect his "reading."

His job is at least to interpret. His role(s) may require other tasks as well, perhaps decision of some sort in a litigational or other setting requiring other considerations beyond the interpreting problem, very possibly playing into it. As *interpreter*, whatever else he is about, he is involved in (re)constructing relevant contexts which he wants to see as distinct.

Our framework helps him in this job, not only to broaden within limits his range of inquiry but in (re)constructing: (1) the linguistic level context, i.e. locutionary or L_1; and (2) the context at the communicative sorce, i.e. illocutionary or L_2; and (3) the potentially relevant audience contexts *other than his own*, i.e. perlocutionary or L_3. But it is not just a matter of compartmentalizing the differing considerations that thus come to light, but once identifying them in their L_1, L_2, and L_3 contexts, relating them to his own context, which we may wish to consider not only as vivified but enlarged.

It is clear enough that the traditional interpretative terms and distinctions are not adequate to these tasks because they are as much if not more geared to the roles and modes of *persuasion,* blurring the vital perspectives and distinctions. We will discuss "intent" and "purpose" further, but meaning is the most subtle bugaboo of all, for there is a meaning attitude at work whether the word is used or not, even if one insists he will not be charmed by it (as there is a rule attitude at work in statutory interpretation).

J. L. Austin de-emphasized meaning, Wittgenstein virtually abandoned it, but Korzybski slew it. His stress was on the semantic response and his concern with the interpreter, in all conceivable communication situations. Teachers of his view have stressed that meaning is not in words but in people, the interpreters.

Well, it is not anywhere, really. The word "meaning" is not descriptive of any-*thing,* but at best of relationships. (Korzybski's most revealing insights went to the vocabulary and the visualization of relationships and structure.) An observer who would try to chart meanings would be symbolizing relationships between words and people. The more we commit ourselves to *that* sort of reality (relationships are real), the more likely we are not to accept a semantic response sort of meaning judgment as *the* meaning. It is evidence, but only evidence of possible, probable, or maybe desirable meaning judgment.

It is important for the interpreter not to let the meaning attitude charm him into letting "meaning" carry his semantic response right there into the text to appear to be part of it. It is better seen as part of the interpreting context, just as an L_3 semantic response may be for the L_3 context. The semantic response factor in either the L_3 or the interpreter's context may, of course, turn out to be determinative, when *all* the evidence is in and weighed.

Keeping Semantic Response Straight

Different kinds of interpretative problems illuminate the analysis. Consider the matter of judicial interpretation in libel suits, where sensitivity to L_3 factors is particularly important.

Suppose plaintiff alleges that defendant newspaper published an item in which he was described as a "pusher." Whether or not plaintiff has been defamed depends primarily upon L_3 factors, especially the semantic responses of readers of the item. It is conceivable the news item is reporting a speech discussing differing kinds of executive leadership, but if no such explanation is given in the newspaper, then the question becomes, did at least some readers understand "pusher" to mean of drugs.

Whether the newspaper should or should not be legally responsible for semantic responses is the kind of policy question which should not be confused with or smuggled into the purely communications analysis as seems to happen in the libel *per se* pleading rules which puts a premium on being able to bring in a statement which is "on its face" clearly defamatory (a sort of parol evidence rule-approach). But like statutes and contracts, news items trigger differing semantic responses, depending upon the interpretative contexts of each reader. What may appear quite innocent, say that Mrs. Z. Jones just gave birth to triplets, may be harmful if false, at least if readers who know Mrs. Z. Jones also know she is not married.

Note that in this case we are not dealing with "meaning" in the usual senses, but with the implications. Implications are never there *in* texts, but always drawn in, or automatic even. This sort of implication is not an L_1 matter at all. Potential implications are part of the interpretative problem, another reason why concern only with the face of a text, under whatever rule or principle in whatever area, is bound to lead sooner or later to bad results, no matter how well based in policy some particular application might be. *The presumption should not be in favor of such an approach, but against it.*

The L_3 focus is comparatively easy to attain in the defamation situation, much more difficult in interpretations of texts, and especially statutes where it is not at all clear just what persons, *if any*, are in the L_3 context. But take a different sort of interpretation problem, the case of the probate of a will in which we receive further insight into the locutionary, illocutionary, and perlocutionary analysis and also illustration that different sorts of texts sit differently in this framework, and yet further, how other than communications principles come into play to determine resolution of what is a communications dilemma.

It was in Scotland in the earlier part of the century that a Scot left a will with a disposition of a substantial sum of money to the National Society for the Prevention of Cruelty to Children. At the time of probate there was only one organization by that name, and it was in London, of all places. But the representatives of an organization called the Scottish National Society for the Prevention of Cruelty to Children came forth to lay claim to the money, offering extrinsic evidence to support their claim. At this point the "four corners" rule could be invoked to bar the claim. In our terms, the L_1 meaning is clear because there is one sort of expression which is not ambiguous and that is a name, at least where no other object can be identified which has that name. Compare the problem if a provision in a will names as legatee, Jorsine Rapplebitter. In comes Evelyn Brown to claim the sum. Not only presumptively but perhaps conclusively so, such an alteration should not be allowed because in most such instances it just "has to be" scurrilously motivated. Close the barn door good and tight.

But . . . what harm to listen at least through a crack in the door? The whole bit about verbal convention being one thing and private application another helps us here. But we do not necessarily want to be stuck with the Korzybskian semantic response focus. There was evidence that no matter what the words "National Society for the Prevention of Cruelty to Children" now refer to or mean in the L_1 sense, they were not employed that way in the L_2 sense. The testator apparently worked with people in the Scottish Society when its name was also the National Society for the Prevention of Cruelty to Children and was known as the Scottish Branch, with headquarters in London. After the will was executed, the Scottish organization split off from the London group and changed its name. So now we have the problem when does a will speak and to whom? One who drafts his own will may have a fool for a testator but he takes the risk which a lawyer must take as a certainty, of writing to the probate court, ultimately. So far as a communications analysis is concerned, the risk is that there will be none or little. So it was here, for the English court held there was no ambiguity, and Scottish blood still boils.

An interesting aspect is that the only L_3 communicant we have is the court. One could justify a textual meaning approach on both the L_1 and L_3 perspectives, arguing that the ordinary person (L_3) would take these words to mean just what they say (L_1), unlike the libel situation where there should be evidence on that score. In the probate of wills we are not about to hand the matter to the man on the street. But it is a fiction, nonetheless, because the semantic response of the supposed observer-interpreter is what is assigned to the crucial words.

There is the added facet of determining when the will speaks. If it was at the time of drafting, then the London organization may have been the proper recipient in terms of organizational structure. (If there were a corporation, for instance.) If at the time of death, then the disposition, again arguably, is going where its legal purport, if not its testator intent, would take it. If deadhand control is not all that important anyway, then evidence that he knew nothing of the London organization is not important because all it proves is what he was attempting to do with his will. How easy to pass off the resolution in terms of meaning, or for that matter to think that is what *is* conclusive. (The time factor complicates our model but not insurmountably; e.g. in a contract the L_2 context may be a continuing process of interaction.)

Definitional Smuggling

The last example begins to suggest that the Austinian framework is not adequate to our purpose, nor maybe even to his, not that it is all wrong, but that it needs further distinctions.

There are times aplenty when what we call interpretation involves what we might call the assignment of meaning to certain words. If the key words are regarded as ambiguous, then it might seem that a resolution is simply a choice of possible meanings. Here we come to the desirability of recognizing and being sensitive to the technique of rhetorical definition. It is clearly part of the rhetoric of interpretation, so much so that the very distinctions between that rhetoric and the dynamics of communication *qua* interpretation are most difficult, not to make, but to communicate to reader-interpreters.

In the simple instance where we say that "No vehicles are to be driven in the public parks," applies to automobiles, we want to say that we are making a clearly required application because certainly an automobile is a vehicle if anything is. At least that meaning is clear. Talk there of meaning if you must, but recognize also that we are defining vehicles by an intellectual process which could be replicated via the dictionary.

Now what are we doing if we say the bicycles are vehicles within the meaning of the ordinance? We could say that the words can be applied or not applied, take your choice. We can translate that into saying they are ambiguous, having a meaning that includes bicycles and one that does not. But of course that does not exhaust the uses of the word "vehicle" (especially as we consider the word "driven" in the ordinance). If a court holds the application to bicycles valid, surely the court has now (re?) defined some word(s) in the ordinance. The line between defining in accordance with convention and doing it rhetorically or creatively is slippery, that being the very subtlety of the technique of rhetorical definition. Certainly there is a gray area where we may have a chicken-egg situation, but I can tell you when I see a chicken and when I see an egg (even if there is a chicken in the egg or an egg in the chicken).

Almost if not entirely without exception, commentators on the arts and actualities of interpretation show their greatest naïveté or manipulation, whichever if not both, when it comes to sensitivity to rhetorical definition, not only in the objects of commentary but in their own analysis. (See The Right Way in Appendix)

There are numerous examples available, but a timely one involves a statute which reads: "Every person qualified to vote for public office shall be qualified to serve as a juror." Suppose the example of a state where only certain males were allowed to vote, before women suffrage brought about a change in the voting laws. When the change comes, how handle the problem when a defendant in a criminal trial claims foul for lack of liberated women in the jury list? The L_1 interpretation seems to *call* for extension, although an honest appraisal makes it difficult to know whether we are merely applying the "what a reasonable interpreter in the L_3 position would say" and forgetting that legislatures have through the process of most-unusual-word-usages developed new locutionary (L_1) conventions. In short, it is not enough to look only to the man-in-the-street conventions where looking at the L_1 dimension. At least one court confronted with this problem went to great pains, perhaps in manifestation of male ego, but in an interpretational sense legitimately, to show that legislatures often used "person" to mean a lot of other things than "person" in the everyday senses.

This of course opens the door to the L_2 analysis, in terms of purpose and intention, and it is not too hard to show that the legislature "must have meant," or "clearly intended," or "could have had no other purpose but . . ." that only the class of *male* jurors could be enlarged by change in voting qualifications for males. At the time of drafting only that prospect could have been contemplated.

Note that if we were dealing with a Constitutional provision we would have quite a different problem. Not that the L_2 analysis would be different, but the weighing of its significance would be. A constitution is in terms of going or prevalent constitutional interpretation theory a living instrument which speaks perhaps as clearly at the time of interpretation as at the time of drafting, thus necessitating even greater skill with rhetorical definition if the rhetoric seems to call for buttressing in terms of the "meaning at the time of drafting." And there we can call on notions of natural rights and the necessarily human nature of women. Of course women are persons in the eyes of God! Whether a statute is so much a living creature is not so clear. But the rhetoric of interpretation clearly provides for that possibility in terms of the Spirit and Purpose of the Statute.

Is this still a chicken-egg matter, or does the court which says that the statute now applies to admit women to the jury list actually *redefine* the word "persons"? Certainly it defines the word for the future, but maybe a stage beyond the "vehicles"="bicycles" action.

What if the question becomes one of considering to admit eighteen-year-old persons to the jury list because of their admission by law to the polls? Surely that is a different bag of beans if you are thirty or more? (The defense rests.)

But can you take a different stand with respect to women than you do to eighteen-year-olds? Is the first merely interpretation if you say the statute applies to women and something else if you say contra to "boys and girls"? The problem is different in some respects in each case. But rather than try to resolve it at this point observe that somewhere along here we surely have departed from the sort of interpretational problem involved in "applying" the prohibition of vehicles ordinance to *automobiles*.

My chief contention is that when we have so clearly departed from one stage to another, it should be admitted, at least in the context the interpreter (re)constructs for consideration in the dynamics of doing interpretation. It could be admitted more often than it is in the rhetoric of interpretation, say that of a court in its opinion. The major reason it should be admitted during the dynamics of interpreting is that it makes for wiser decision, not only from the perspective of the judicial interpreter, but most certainly from that of any interpreter who is honestly trying to be something other than advocate.

To admit the sort of difference illustrated by the jury-voter statutes is to put in focus the distinctions between the communications analysis and the other factors that necessarily must enter in balance with such communications matters. The concepts of meaning, intent, and purpose serve ideally to obfuscate the problems in the rhetoric of interpretation, allowing, for instance, a court to appear less activist than it is. That of course is what the counter-activism rhetoric of "strict construction" promotes, driving ultimately the wisdom of all kinds of interpretation not only underground and out of sight but completely out of reach. Of course even in times of greater harmony and mutual trust, a court may be hard put to say out loud that it is taking the legislative ball and running with it in a game whose rules and settings are entirely different. "What the legislature has done," proclaims the court in its death knell, "is to create a power of legislation in us: That is one of the risks of legislative legislation."

That's how it is of course. Whether the limits to that power ought to be ascertained not only through the politics of public and legislative reaction but also in reason or at least sincere debate, not only in mass or professional media but also in court, seems at the moment relatively moot in light of the popularity even amongst legislative supremacists of the current rhetoric of interpretation. Of course there are ways of pushing many of the factors that ought to come into consideration in decision making at least part way into the light under the rubrics of interpretation, as the Supreme Court recently showed us in its handling of Adam Clayton Powell's suit against, in effect, the House of Representatives for his dis-memberment from that body.

In that opinion, the last of Chief Justice Warren, he engaged in interpretative rhetoric regarding the Constitutional section which stated that Congress shall be "the Judge of the Qualifications of its own members," relating it to another section that went to matters of age, citizenship, and residency. In stating that these were the only matters which were not reviewable by the Supreme Court, he concluded that historical consideration of the drafting of the provisions (the L_2 factors) gave the needed light to resolve the uncertainty of the meaning of the words (the L_1 factors). In upholding Powell's claim of invalid exclusion, he found this L_2 clarity against a sort of L_3 bit of evidence. His discussion ranged over the possibility that practical construction by the Congress itself might show what the words were intended to mean. (Compare contract interpretation.) In exploring that context, under the reasonable assumption that the Constitution is partly addressed to Congress as well as the Court (L_3 sort of problem), he demonstrated the further assumption that the L_2 action *use* of the words by the drafters took priority. In that process he stated that 19th century examples of a similar Congressional Powell-like exclusion did not save the day for the House of Representatives because that too was invalid. More importantly he raised a great many of the sort of policy considerations that ought to be raised were one to ask simply the question, what ought we to do in light of contemporary considerations. Further, the *decisional* context of interpretation was almost as politically loaded as it could be short of pressures for complete judicial retreat. So we witness a definite advance for interpretative rhetoric, signalling the hope for even greater candidness in some distant Opinion, if the pendulum should swing that way again.

The Fourth Dimension: Exlocution

In the hope that we are not merely blowing in the wind, let us then see where we are in our communications framework analysis. What we are doing on the one hand is exploring more fully the distinction between decision-making from the perspective of a judge or administrator and the like, and on the other, communications analysis. Both sorts of judgment are lumped together under "interpretation."

It becomes clearer that there at least could be a valid distinction made when we look at an interpreter who is not in the judicial *sort* of perspective. Of course if he were merely interested in predicting the judicial decision, then it would be adequate merely to place himself in the judicial perspective. And certainly the distinction is valid from the perspective of those who wish to observe and evaluate interpreters of all sorts. The assumption that this distinction can validly be made is carried into the L_1, L_2, and L_3 framework. But since we have pointed out that the interpreter who wishes to adopt this framework is viewing, as it were, from some *other* vantage point than those of L_1, L_2, or L_3, we need aid in plotting that interpreter's vantage point as well, not only for the observer who has the interpreter in his sights but also for the interpreter himself. He needs aid in the process of vivifying his context, the one that exists around him as he interprets, the one that is most evident to the observer of the interpreter, *but not to the interpreter himself.*

Let us call the interpreter's context *exlocutionary*. This fits the Austin framework, not only in lingo but with respect to communications involvement, especially as it refers to the judicial sort of *action* of extending, extrapolating, executing, and so on, the text in question. And of course symbolically, it is L_4.

Now to the observer at L_4 it may be especially difficult to identify the L_3 factors and context. Remember in the sort of simple communicative behavior situation which Austin was positing, the receiver or reactor was either evident by his presence or apparent from the nature of L_2 sort of speech-act behavior. We saw that the interpretation of a defamation sort of text tended to involve that sort of situation, even if judicial interpreters sometimes underplay the L_3 determining reaction, without which a plaintiff could not be defamed. On the other hand we tend to act as if legislation is meaningful without reference to the L_3 audience, although it becomes clear it is nothing without some sort of audience and even though we have great sorts of ceremony about the need for official printings and all, so that the rules may be visible and available to all who are "covered" by the legislation.

The communicative unreality of thinking of the legislative act as somehow complete in itself, like a work of art, is aided and abetted by the concept of LAW itself. What one does in creating a statute is supposedly to add to the law. Not that the metaphor is simply crude or unworkable, far from it, but we have examined at some lengths in preceding chapters the difficulty of separating metaphoric creativity from conceptual automatism. The metaphor is helpful when we compare again in the rhetoric of purpose: The statute is created with a purpose, a purpose that may become separate from individuals, somehow, as the Purpose of a Cup is for water and not for cigarette ashes, and one can tell that by looking at it.

Of course there are almost always perlocutionary completions of the legislative statutory communicative effort prior to any judicial L_3 action, but the careful observer will discover that there are times when the L_4 interpreter is involved in an L_3 sort of way, maybe even at times when there is some question whether he should be. We have, for instance, said he should not be identifying his position as the L_3 position in the libel text situation. See how easy it would be to do that, for instance in confusing the sort of judgment that is involved in determining what the semantic response of the L_3 newspaper readers was, or likely was, with the evaluation that is involved in determining whether it is defamatory. Whether, for instance, it is defamatory to call a person a hippie is not *just* a question of whether there was a negative reaction, because, for further instance, a court would not call it defamatory of a hardened criminal to say he was a stool pigeon, even though he is hurt among his peers. On the hippie question, there is a sort of evaluation that is certainly communications involved but calling further for a sort of sociological evaluation of the status of hippies. But like so many other socio-moral questions that judges could ask, this one can easily get buried in questions of meaning, intent, and purpose. The risk is that the judge projects his biases into some L_1 interpretation rhetoric, thus, in effect, ignoring the actual L_3 responses which after all constitute some evidence on the sociological question.

Well, judges do not have even that sort of opportunity with respect to statutes, usually. It then becomes especially important for the sincere interpreter, whether judge or not, to identify or evaluate his role, a communications relevant judgment that is very significant in the impact it may have on even "pure interpretation." Thus in the case of a criminal law statute a court may legitimately view its obligation to carry out the legislative purpose as more limited than in other situations. Then it is more apt to weigh in the balance the L_3 factor of notice to the public which in effect downgrades the L_2 factors.

It is not a matter of automatic weighing of one level over another. Questions outside the scope of communications analysis do arise!

Because a statute, for instance, sits as if frozen in the Code, it is more difficult to enliven the L_3 factors in such ways that the interpreter can tell whether he hides them behind his own undelayed responses. Judges often need to exercise insight on this distinction with regard to statutes that create and in various ways empower administrative bodies. It may be that what seems a merely vague phraseology does not call for L_4 judicial response but further L_3 administrative response in the form of regulations and adjudication under those regulations. A judicial decision to that effect in absence of relevant explicit directive in the statute may, of course, be a bit of buck passing, or again an exercise of wise judicial discretion.

But note here that we have confronted one of a great many kinds of instances where we are not necessarily considering meaning, intent, or even purpose, but what the legislature has done. If Congress is said to have created an administrative body, that is a bit of L_3 vocabulary to describe an act that is complete before the judiciary comes along, maybe to intervene, but just as well to augment. This deserves emphasis for those who still have difficulty with what may seem merely metaphor in putting a statute into a behavioral context. So, for further instance, if a legislature follows up some particular judicial decision with a curative statute, we may properly say the legislature has *rejected* the judicial decision, expelled it from the law (completed action). It would be worthwhile to prepare a taxonomy of legislative behavior, and there are parallels regarding other text-acts.

The Values of Interpreting

Someone may object that our exploration model is overly positivistic, not sufficiently value-involved, maybe a-valued.

The real value (s) of the analysis is yet to be exhibited. (Sorry.) Korzybski was in a sense quite positivistic, science-oriented and all, yet he said every observation, and even more any response, involved an evaluation (his term). The assumption here is that any pure observation does involve an evaluation, but it assumes too that there are explicable, ascertainable pieces of behavior that can be evaluated in the reliability fashion dear to science and rigorous analysis, so that we are justified in speaking in terms of descriptions, fact statements (facts), law statements (laws), and so on. One can be empirical about someone else's values, can trust certain judgments about another's likes and dislikes, his preferences, his priorities, his principles, his ideals, his values.

To speak of communications behavior as we have involves a shorthand vocabulary that necessarily posits the premise that someone's *use* of words in speech behavior is a movement toward some end that can be projected and if accomplished also evaluated-observed, whether to inform, amuse, persuade, or what have you. One can be even to some extent taxonomic about communication behavior, certainly to the extent that there are observable similarities and even conventions. There could not be language or communication without such patterns, i.e. L_1, L_2, and L_3 patterns, observables, predictables, having if nothing else communication value. One communicates toward some end or for some purpose (s), some of which are reliably inferable, others that may be hypothesized.

To point out the pattern that backs up a specific speech act is not to remove values at all, simply to take them for granted where they reasonably can be (although one may be mistaken in given instances in taking for granted, of course), and all the better to become sensitive to situations where a piece of seeming pattern-based communication behavior-product should not be taken for granted; e.g. the previous "apology" ("Sorry") for the pun on "value (s)."

The use and other L_2 aspects of our analysis are nicely oriented toward problems of statutory (and other legal text) interpretation, to the extent that the interpreter wants (values the task enough. . .) to see what the legislature was about, what it was trying to do-accomplish, to see what the interpreter or his advisee must do (if that is the attitude) to conform or avoid or what have you. Legislatures create texts which in one sense assert and represent value judgments which are rule-ized, principled, or norm-alized. The job of interpretation includes discovery or recognition of the legislative attitude-value position or posture, the intended or purposed motion of implementation. It requires at its most sincere extreme the considerable effort to assess another body's value position of consensus or agreement (Statute=contract consensus?). The full effort includes attempt to discover one's own value positions, say with respect to this statute and statutes generally, *re* the general problem areas legislatively confronted, the suggested, agreed, or ordered solutions, as well as the particular problem situation which is part of the interpreting context.

The vocabulary and the analysis is suited (!) to the task(s). It happens to suit the vocabulary of the going rhetoric of interpretation, especially regarding the proliferation of purpose(s). Translation from one to the other is not at all difficult, a process which throws light on each, there being an added advantage in having to translate. Since finer distinctions are more consistently called for, the analysis also suits the possibility of comparative analyses, say for one who wishes to interpret, maybe in a value way, the interpreter's articulated justification.

Suppose a judge "interprets" an ordinance: "No vehicle may be driven in a public park," concluding (deciding or interpreting?) that bicycles are prohibited. We see immediately he is (re)defining "vehicle" and also placing some sort of value judgment on the ordinance. If he should say that the purpose of the ordinance is to promote safety in parks, giving no other evidence than the text except maybe *his* reasoning for the assignment of this meaning as an implementation, then we get a glimmering, at least, of *his* attitude *qua* safety of bicycles in parks, and we can say that *his* purpose is to augment the ordinance in this fashion. *He* is *using* the ordinance *too* to further a purpose of the enacting body which is presumptively (is that probably?) there all right. (Maybe the ordinance moves to promote aesthetics or peace and quiet or . . .) Whether or not the ordinance ought to be used this way is not a matter of interpretation purely, or in the pure interpretation$_1$ sense. Of course to *say* ex cathedra, out of a decisional context, that the ordinance prohibits automobiles is about as close as you can get, unless you are using the interpretation to warn somebody not to drive his automobile in the park. (See chapter on Roles, Goals, and Situational Perspectives)

If we follow through on our previous explorations in earlier chapters, we see that a statute itself (what is that?) is not really going to be much of value unless "it" gets *used* in some way(s). The statute is normatively ambiguous, a cryptically fancy way of saying that it gets valued in the use and is used for some end(s) or another by some-body who occupies some position(s) that can be evaluated in terms of status, authority, role, perspective, and so on.

A statute is a function of the situation in which it is interpreted (apply to contract, etc.). The totality of a statute is made up of the text and all the responses to it, and that includes all the statute-talk. Statute-talk (*re* a particular statute) includes but not exclusively the rhetoric of interpretation of courts which interpret them. So, we learn something about statutes (talk) by *interpretation* of statute talk.

When one interprets the rhetoric of interpretation in a judicial opinion, he needs to adjust the framework we have explored to the increased complexity, the further levels of communication that are involved. He is free to place the judicial interpreter (self-avowed, remember, for he is doing something else also, if he has indeed previously interpreted$_1$) in the L_4 position. But he is in the L_4 position as to the judge. Indeed the judge stands behind the opinion in the L_2 position with respect to the analyst of the opinion-dynamics. The judicial opinion drafted by the judge(s) in the L_2 communicative-actions position has L_1 locutionary and L_2 illocutionary dimensions. The analyst might be tempted to place himself in the L_3

addressee position, but then he overlooks the possibilities that the opinion is being written partly to a trial judge (crucial aspect—See analysis earlier of the Garratt Opinion), the parties, the profession, the dissenting judges, and so on. (We have moved from a paper game of tic-tac-toe to a three dimensional model? Well, more than that.)

Not only should he see how, if at all, the judge is conforming or comparing to our structure *in* doing what he purports to be doing (interpreting) in being in the L_4 position of interpreting the statute, but the analyst of this complex of communications dynamics should look to interpret what the judge is doing from his L_2 position in writing the opinion (easier to see than the L_4 perspective of the judge). *Also*, the analyst should place himself in the L_4 position with respect to the statute in order to carry out the job of comparison as best he can through reading the judge's valuations as they appear or are represented or may be reasonably and reliably implied.

Intent and Purpose

For several years now, sophisticated commentary in the field of tort law has taken it for granted that the concept of foreseeability in negligence doctrine is a highly manipulable term. (See Chapter II) Strangely, sophisticated commentators continue to tout the glory of the purpose analysis in matters of statutory interpretation when the purpose concept is manipulable in all respects like foreseeability and in many other ways as well. Of course it needs to be talked about because of its popularity in the rhetoric of interpretation of courts, and it should be in the advocate's bag of tricks. Nor is it *just* a rhetorical device. But at the least its descriptive function should be separated from its persuading and camouflaging functions. That it has these several functions, among others, may well explain why the commentators themselves tend to perpetuate its dominance, for it is a way of expressing what values they have with respect, for instance, to the proper relationships of courts to legislative bodies. And the shift to purpose from plain meaning has been desirable. The de-glamorization of intent is a mixed blessing, but as previously indicated it still appears available in the guise of purpose in ways that make it *seem* less fictional than collegial intent but actually work more mystically yet.

A new vocabulary is needed for communications analysis, but no one can legislate it for courts, the profession, or even the few commentators. Short of that, analysis is needed, to break the covering word-form "purpose" into its family members.

Without regard to its connotative or content aspects, note its use as a device in what we may call the rhetoric of analysis. (One cannot interpret a statute without analysis. Cf. The Right Way.) It allows one to operate at various levels of generality in relating the categories of a statute-like text to the particular situation at hand. If you have apples and oranges, you might want to refer to them as fruit, as might be done in interpreting a health department regulation to the effect "apples, oranges, and other such items may not be brought into the state without inspection." We could thus say the *purpose* was to provide for the inspection of fruit and that bananas are thus included. Of course one could say the purpose was to inspect *produce*, or even all food products not in sealed packages.

The flow of application can be moved in the other direction, as in our statute providing that the jury list shall be made up of "all persons entitled to vote. . ." by saying that "persons" was used for the purpose of reference to the kind of persons who could vote at the time the jury statute was passed. Without more, such analysis almost always begs the question, i.e. whether or not the law in question *should* be applied.

A quite different sort of routing can be accomplished with the purpose analyzer rhetoric, e.g. from the purpose of the legislature in passing the statute to the purpose of the legislature as evidenced over the years in related legislation, or to the purpose of the statute.

Of course there may be value (Sorry) in switching from *the* purpose to *a* purpose or the purposes. One should be careful of this because "the purpose" analytical rhetoric keeps the ball in the possession of the analyst by suggesting there is only one purpose, as one does in saying that the purpose of the courts is to settle disputes and not to promote social reform. But there are times when the shift is necessary. If one wanted to argue that the ordinance prohibiting vehicles from being driven in the park applied to bicycles, for instance, and if he were confronted with some sort of persuasive evidence that the city council had debated or discussed only problems of park air pollution, he might still argue, "Well, that is clearly one of its purposes, but had the council been attacking only that evil, it would have used appropriate wording, so *obviously* there is also the purpose of safety which naturally did not call for debate as being implicit. . . ."

A distinct rhetorical advantage of "purpose" is that the avowed interpreter is allowed the exploration of purpose *qua* intent without the sort of value clarification that would be necessary lest the interpretation-decision seem arbitrary. At this level of concern, the analysis could be in the L_2 context. Remember, when one utters words of apology *under conventional circumstances*, we say he has apologized. We could say he intended to apologize, but ordinarily we would not say that unless we had doubt that he was really sincere in apologizing. To say he intended it is to say "He really *did* it."

When a legislature enacts a statute, it does so conventionally with respect to procedures, etc., or else it has not statutorily acted. It has done that statute. If it statutes that automobiles are prohibited from parks in just those words, and does it in accordance with all the surrounding conventional (Constitutional, legal, etc.) rules, principles, and expectations of various kinds, then we can quite legitimately say it has prohibited automobiles from parks. It would only be if there were some doubt about the matter that we would urge that their intent was (or was not) to prohibit automobiles from parks. There will be circumstances where it seems *likely* that a person has apologized that we might say something about his intent, and so it is with legislative intent. As we know, "intent" is not used in everyday life just to refer to something on one's mind but to his behavior (see Garratt analysis), very often where we do not know or maybe even care what is *really* on his mind. So it is not a far cry to refer to almost clear cases of statutes by the kind of metaphoric use of "intent" which is common to any word you can use (like "use"). *But,* no cheating, please, where the statute is not clear enough. Purpose covers up the cheating a little better.

Suppose Smith picks up a ball and throws it and it hits Jones. Smith says to Jones, "I am sorry you were hit by the baseball," or maybe "I am sorry you could not get out of the way." Jones asks for an apology. Smith might say that such was the purpose of the words. If Jones really wants to *see* the apology, he may say "Say you're sorry." Certainly Jones is justified, having caught Smith cheating.

The ordinance prohibiting "all vehicles from public parks" does not prohibit bicycles, but a court can make it do the job. It would be cheating on intent or purpose *qua* intent ($purpose_1$) to say the enacting body intended to prohibit bicycles, although it would not be so bad to speak of probable intent, but still a little cheat, because *now* the question is being begged. The distinction is subtle, but so is the rhetoric of purpose.

Suppose we back up the Smith-Jones incident to the point where Smith has uttered his non-apology. Green is standing there taking it all in, and Smith runs home to his mother (being only eight). Jones: "He could have said he was sorry." Green: "He did. He did. Didn't you hear him say he was sorry he hit you." Jones: "That wasn't exactly the way he put it." Green: "That was his purpose, all right." And Jones trots home sore but happy to his wife. (We get closer to the statutory sort of scene if Smith ran home before his utterance and later asks Green to tell Jones "That I said I was sorry he could not get out of the way," and Green says to Smith that Jones wanted to apologize and here it is.)

Maybe Green feels consciously (or unconsciously?) that it was wise to be a peace-maker and make Jones feel better too, at no cost to anyone, or that he knows how Jones really feels and that Smith is not very good at that sort of thing or that if he had really thought it all out he would have been clearer about it or that he would have been more apologetic (notice the distinction because that is just what we can do with purpose, extend intent a little bit).

By using purpose we can glide along in metaphors that go further than "intent." Purposes are easier to construct by process of reasonings, inference, and valuation, without having to make distinctions between an inference and a valuation. Thus if Professor Schmidt is preparing a classroom for a lecture, he may say to Brown, "Hey, you'd better get those ashtrays out of here." Brown may assume that Schmidt wants no one to smoke so he might remove the ashtrays and put up a sign saying NO SMOKING. If Schmidt only wanted to discourage smoking without prohibiting it, Brown has gone too far, even though Brown has thought it out in terms of purpose. On the other hand, if Brown fails to remove the paper cups scattered around that have been used as ashtrays, then he is being too literal, unless he turns out to be lucky because Schmidt was only worried that the real ashtrays might get broken. It does not follow that Brown is exercising a policy-value sort of judgment, but a judgment about Schmidt's value-judgments. Still, he might be knowingly going out on his own and deciding that the only way to prevent smoking is to come right out and say it. If he is sure of his relationship to Schmidt, he can explain himself if need be by stating his value judgments. Otherwise he might apologize, but if he does not want to appear stupid and/or he wishes to pass the buck, a bit, then what better than to say, "I only did what you told me," or "I thought that's what you wanted, "or . . had in mind," or even "What other purpose could you possibly have had," a pretty good move to put Schmidt on the spot for failing to be clearer in his instructions.

The examples fit most cases of statutory interpretation that you can find. Commentators like Hart and Sacks, for instance, who have put forth unitary techniques of interpretation that are supposed to be rational and objective tend to talk of a process of reasoning to find out what sort of actions are and what sorts are not covered by a statute to see what makes the best sense. The approach may be wholesome enough in most cases, but still it does not follow that what makes sense to the interpreter is what makes sense to the enactors. This is not to suggest that interpreters should not exercise value judgments in the *decisional* process, but if rationality is valued for itself, and if a unitary scheme of that sort is practicable for the process of *valuation,* then it ought to be seen as just that. But it purports to be "true" interpretation. *The job of decision-making is not limited to that task.* There may even be a time, for instance, even if legislative purpose is discoverable, when it is just possible that it should *not* be carried out. If a court has figured out the most rational purpose-construct it then is a bit difficult to say it should not be implemented.

Still in that last instance, a muddled sort of purpose analysis, muddled from our perspective of this exploration, may be the only way out. To dig into the rhetoric of purpose, for instance, in pursuit of greater clarity and the potential of better reasoning and valuation is not necessarily to say that the purpose *analysis,* as opposed to the rhetoric, should go out the window even though not perfect to the task, even though the associated rhetoric is so highly manipulable. Those who concern themselves with the control of discretion, for instance in administrative or judicial confrontation of statutes, perhaps should be a bit less complacent about the manipulability factor. Those who value wise policy implementation should question whether purpose and associated analytical tools are adequate to *that* task. No doubt, for further related instance, the purpose analysis has a high potential with regard to efficient and adequate communications analysis, but the analyst must take exquisite pains to keep from slipping into other kinds of judgments.

And that is one thing this book is about. There simply is no analysis conceivable that cannot be manipulated, including the sort this chapter has explored as a model. It is put forth as a ball to roll. The roll itself can be manipulated or skewed. But there is this to remember about communication. One has to be a cloudy-headed, minced-brain, mushy-eyed idealist to believe that the fundamental principles of either our society or its legal process put forth communicative sincerity, what we might call "good" communication, as an absolute. Indeed there are times when candidness is despised. Despair we may, but such are the facts *and* the values of life.

CHART #10

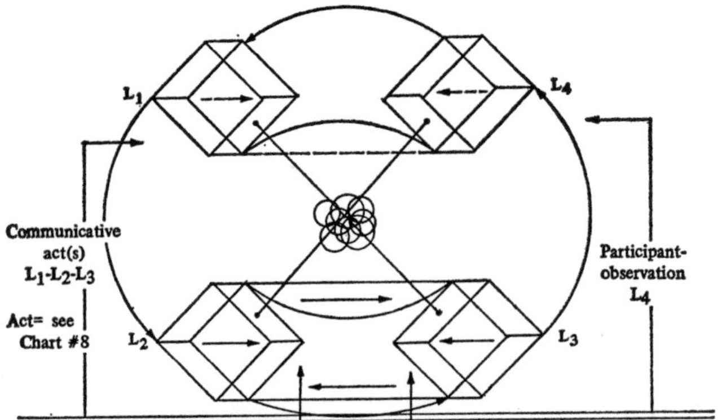

L_1(ocutionary)-act$_1$ linguistic act	(il)L_2(ocutionary)-act$_2$ speech-behavior act	(per)L_3(ocutionary)-act$_3$ behavior-end-act	(ex)L_4(ocutionary) interpreter end-ing
1. It is raining	informing + urging and/or joking and/or . .	B informed + urged not amused	C observes: info urging misfire
2. Get out of here (spoken)	(a) angry tone, frown, waving hands, movement	ordered?–if not rejected.	the order and rejection
	(b) gentle tone, smile, twinkling eyes, etc.	ordered and/or teased	order or teasing
3. No vehicles in park	clues: if ordinance implies regulation	bicycles ordered out?	if only communications analysis: records multi-messages

L_4 obstacles
1. relating L_1 to L_2 ——— distinguishing L_3 from L_4.
2. unmuddling and keeping straight all four contexts, etc.

Highlighting of relations of chapter X to earlier chapters. (See Charts #6-10)

1. LEGALISM: failure to take account of L_2-L_3 stresses rhetoric of meaning & purpose
literalistic; strict construction stresses rules at L_1, i.e., using words "in their way."

Cf. ambiguists: saw L_2 dynamics, but underplayed L_1. Distinguished $L_{3\text{-}4}$ for others but not for selves!

2. RHETORICAL DEFINITION great aid toward L_1-L_2 mobility; from meaning to situational use; help in spotting L_2 clues; attitudinal loadings are relevant as part of the (")act(")

3. WORDS
4. CONSCIOUS-
5. NESS

add contexts consciousness to kinds of Chart #3

LEVELS OF TALK:
each level of talk involves the above dimensions. Level$_3$ (talk talk) picks them out in each of other levels and relates the levels; highlights L_3-L_4

SPLIT SCREENS
feeling for multiple contexts

AMBIGUITY–clarified here, as to structure of, etc.

6. INTENT ANALYSIS
Chap. 6 began to show empirical potential; e.g., intents that are not on the minds.
Cf. intent-purpose analysis in chap. 6 context with chap. 10; add (")meaning("), member of related family.
"Purpose" a very in-word in both interpretation rhetoric and law theory talk (*cf.* Chart #6)

7. FACTS
Fact-finding involves interpr. also, with different sort of source. Chap. 10 kind also requires weighing of evidence, i.e. clues.

Where texts interpr. "relevant facts" close to frozen or hypothetical.

Fact interpr. may require particular effort to distinguish the 4-L stages, esp. L_3 from L_4. Tie-in ACT analysis (Chart # 8)

8. PERSPECTIVES–such stress indispensable to any communications analysis, as is capacity to see all forms (Chart #8)

9. PROCESS of INTERPRETATION –This stress concerns what goes on with the interpreter to vivify the L_4 dimensions (See Chart #9)

APPENDIX

Exhibit I

SHOW ME A RULE

"Show me a rule!" He looked a bit startled. We had been discussing law and order and such things, and he suggested that rules were the heart of law, and I said, "Show me a rule! Go ahead. You feel law is a body of rules and rules are the heart of the law, but I suspect the organism has neither body nor heart."

"You can't have a contract without an offer and acceptance."

"What?"

"I just gave you a rule."

"That's a rule? But all you did was say it. Surely just saying something doesn't make it a rule. I say 'horses have four legs' is a rule, but that doesn't make it a rule let alone legal."

"Well, as a rule horses do have four legs," he said with a trace of a frown. "Now come on, you know I've stated a fundamental rule in contract law."

"It's Greek to me," I said with a wink, "and I'm from Missouri. You've got to show me." As I talked he started leafing through a contract textbook in wide use by law students.

"So, O.K., wise guy. Here it is. See on this page it says that every contract must have an offer and on this later page it says every offer must be accepted before there can be a contract."

I gently reminded him what he had said: "You can't have a contract without an offer and acceptance" and that the book did not bear him out. When he remonstrated that for all purposes it said the same thing, I insisted that certainly a rule had to be a statement that could be written out and have some official status. And I wondered out loud even if the book had said what he said that we could call it, the statement, a rule. It's well known that such statements are not rules but only commentaries on them at best. Or put another way, textbooks are secondary or tertiary sources. "I want the real thing. As far as I am concerned, nothing in that book is a rule."

"Well that's asinine." He looked angry now.

"I'm no expert on contracts, but I can take you through Prosser's Hornbook on Torts and show you a number of places where in one way or another he has exercised some sort of judgment in reading opinions. What he might there call a rule of tort law becomes the Prosser view of it."

He asked me if that meant that I felt I couldn't rely on Prosser. I reminded him that we were only using Prosser's book as an example and that I felt it was one of the best texts on law ever published. It is highly respected in courts and often cited and quoted in opinions. I admitted that I would rather have him on my side than not. Still, in the nature of things, I often find myself in disagreement with him. You have to realize that the rhetoric of law allows all of us to project our wishes for the future into the form of a rule. The temptation would be too great for any of us to resist doing a little persuasion in that way, although for one who is a traditionalist like the good Dean Prosser, the persuasion comes off even better, because he is quite sure that he is stating rules and that any idealism is clearly labeled as such. "But just 'tain't so."

I then noticed a strained look on my friend's face and I realized I had lapsed into lecture number seventeen. I asked him what had started me on that. He said that he had asked if I meant I couldn't rely on Prosser.

"Why, yes, I can rely on Prosser to some considerable extent. I would if I were a lawyer arguing a point of law. I would say, 'The rule is so and so' and say that it was hornbook clear, and so on. What he does is to provide arguments for lawyers, rules of thumb at best. But a rule of thumb cannot be a rule of law."

"Well, would you say that if a court takes something he says and decides a case by it, then we have a rule of law?" He was sitting almost at attention as if listening for some relaxation in my stand.

"Well, now you have another problem—"

"Naturally, naturally. O.K., let's have some more of your sophistry." He sank back in mock boredom. I felt he was deeply interested. Of course you have to think that if you're going to stick to this sort of game.

"This is no sophistry. I'm trying to show you something very important."

"Why don't you just tell me and let me see the flash of light."

"I can't just tell you."

So I went on to explain about "rules" and judicial opinions.

For one thing, it was proven some time ago that courts do not really "decide cases by rules." He laughed when I said that, so I gave him lecture number three, which was pretty much a summary of the legal realists' efforts that demonstrated by means of a kind of communications analysis that judicial opinions did not reveal so much how the case was decided—what determined the outcome—as it showed some of the key stimuli the court was willing to publish. If one could sit through the process of decision where so-called common law rules were involved, he could readily come to appreciate what I was saying. Furthermore, if there really are rules involved in the decisional process, they are derivative of cases, not just *in* opinions.

Put simply, what the courts say are the rules does not serve to explain fully a given decision. One has to look beneath the surface, so to speak, to detect the patterns of behavior of the court over a series of cases. "There's a lot more to this relation, but time will not . . ."

I could see he was shaking his head, so I explained that it would take several lectures and quite a bit of patient work for him to see this, but judicial opinions did not contain rules either. "Look at it this way," I pleaded, "you cannot take any statement that sits in an opinion and preserve its meaning if you take it out of the opinion. This opinion must be understood as a whole. And when you . . ."

"But-but," he butted in, "you are saying that there is no place I can find official forms of common law rules."

I cheered, I clapped, I did a jig. I shook his hand. He saw it, by George, he saw it. "You saw it," I said, "by George, you saw it."

He looked flabbergasted for a moment, then a grin spread slowly over his face. "I do see it. But that doesn't mean I buy it. You'll have to give me an assignment or two." He was quiet for several minutes. So was I for fear of losing him. "So you can't really trust any statement of judicial rules that you see," he mused.

"Not completely, no sir. Of course it isn't as bad as that sounds. You do have your probabilities and all that. You have degrees of reliability. Don't forget, the purport of what we are establishing is simply the impossibility of establishing the finite existence of legal rules."

"Wow!" he exclaimed sarcastically. Suddenly he jumped up.

"I've got you!" He reached for one of the books in my three volume set of official state statutes. "Why, of course, here they are, a whole damned lot of official legal rules. Why in the world didn't I think of that before?"

I slumped back into my chair, putting my head in my hands. I emitted a low moan. "My Lord. Now you *have* regressed. Surely you see where you have gone wrong."

He looked at me quizzically. "Stop that," he said haltingly, as I continued to moan. "Let me give it a try." And by golly he proceeded to give *me* a little lecture. He had recalled a freshman class he had with someone else, where they had read an article which distinguished law on the books from law in action, as it was put. He said that he could certainly find statutes that had never been followed or enforced, or at least were not now enforced. He noted with what seemed a slight blush that certainly you could not say that the statutes prohibiting pre-marital sexual relations were real rules because they hardly were ever used. "More honored in the breach," I recall him saying slyly. "But then," he said with a puzzled tone, "Many of these statutes are followed, enforced, applied, invoked, inveighed, marshalled, and extended." He could see I admired his lawyer's style. "Then, of course, you could say that none of these statutes are the real thing, but only reprints."

"None of these statutes *is* the real thing," I corrected in my best pedagogical sneer. "But we don't want to fall back on that, especially since I must take judicial notice that the official signed legislative bill could be examined. There is a nice question whether it is proper to regard statutes as rules. Generally speaking, courts don't talk that way. It is more apt to be seen as a law, and a law has higher eminence than a rule. Aside from that, even, no given statute is *a* rule. Usually they are a complex of directives, definitions, sanctions, empowerments, and so on. One might want to say something of a statutory rule as contained within a given statute, but it requires interpretation and abstraction to pull it out so that it loses its official seal. You end up with something of the problem we were discussing as to common law rules. A statute has to be decided, in a sense. It was once said by an eminent jurist that a statute was not even law, only a source of law, because it was the courts which gave statutes their real and official meanings. If it isn't law it can hardly be a rule."

"But you said a moment ago . . ."

"That a statute was a law and therefore not a rule." I was really hot now, willing to throw him apparent openings. " 'Law' is a word with many meanings. I just used it in its big L sense, *the* Law, rather than *a* law. Perhaps it would have been clearer had I said it can hardly be a legal rule. If it is not law it cannot be legal. Right?"

He nodded with some weariness. It seemed as good a time as any to call a halt. He said he had enjoyed the exercise. He suggested we might cap the whole thing off with a cocktail since it was "about that time." I assured him I had no liquor in the office, not because I had any compunctions against its use, or even "drinking on the job." "It's simply that it's against the rules."

"Show me the rule," he demanded.

"Well, I don't know that I have anything containing such a rule, but I know there is such a rule. It may not actually be written down in a manual anywhere, but it's more or less implicit, I would say."

"Now—surely now you have proven yourself out of court. Here I thought you were serious before."

"I was and am." I explained that he had not shown me a legal rule and that he never could. I told him the story of the time I had lectured to a high school group on something or other and had the thought that no one had ever seen an electron. A bright young fellow who was deeply involved in science came up afterward and said that he hadn't wanted to embarrass me, but he had seen a picture of an electron. I challenged him to let me see that picture. When next I saw him, he admitted that the picture was not actually of an electron itself, but of the traces the electron had left under certain laboratory conditions.

"I don't know whether that chap got my point, but I certainly hope it doesn't evade you. I didn't then say we shouldn't talk about electrons and I don't now say we shouldn't talk about rules. Our previous conversation put us in a different perspective from the one I am in when I justify my behavior in terms of rules. It would be quite absurd for me to say to the average person—out of my role as teacher to that person—that he could not show me a legal rule. He simply wouldn't get the message. I save that message for the right occasion."

"Well, it's an interesting theory, but not very practical." He said it with a smile as he lifted his hand in goodbye and hurriedly walked away. I knew he was only having the last word, for he had heard lecture number two several times, the one that deals with the manipulative aspects of the theory-practical dichotomy.

"A rule is a rule is a rule," I said softly to myself. That actually made more sense than the line about the rose—if you said it right.

Exhibit II

HAS ANYONE SEEN A FACT?

Has anyone seen a fact?

You can't see facts.

I can see a dog and that is a fact.

If you mean you-can-see-a-dog is a fact, that may be correct; but I cannot see that fact. If you mean the dog is a fact, that is incorrect.

There is a dog in front of me, and that is a fact.

Fine, but I cannot see it.

You can't see the dog?

I can't see the fact that there is a dog there.

All right, look at the following: There is a dog right there.

I see it.

Aha! You see a fact.

Hm?

I put down "there is a dog right there" and that is a fact, and you said you saw it.

The statement is not a fact although what it says is a fact.

And you can't see what it says?

No

Look at it again. It says, "There is a dog right there."

I see that in the sense that I see the statement and I see it in the sense that I understand what it says, but I do not see what it says in the sense of visual perception. I can not see, or touch or do anything to what it says—or to a fact.

You can't do anything to a fact? You can hide them, reveal them, find them . . .

H-m-m. Let's see. Seems to me you do that sort of thing with facts, not *a* fact. I have heard of juries finding facts, but never a fact. Sure, we speak of a finding of fact or a fact finding, but that's a different idea. We could say, "one of the facts that was found," but that does not mean

> the one fact was found; it is a fact among others which were found.

Well look here. Suppose I'm a law teacher. I say, consider the following facts: "Smith threw a rock at Jones, but Jones ducked and the rock hit Brown." Then I say, "Under those facts, Smith is liable for battery to Brown." Then I say, "Now let's change a fact. Let's say that Smith hit Green instead of Brown." I just did something to a fact. I changed it.

> Seems to me you changed the facts, not a fact. But I don't see how you can change a fact. If something is a fact, it is not changeable. You can change what you say about it, but you cannot change *it*.

I think I have you!

> Oh?

You changed the referent on me. The statements I made concerning Smith, Jones, Brown, and Green were facts. You shifted to talking about *things* which are facts. There are statements which are facts and things which are facts.

> There are not things which are facts. It is not the thing which is a fact. A tree, or a dog, or a riot is not a fact.

Wait a minute. I say, "the students are uneasy and about to burn down the building. That's a fact we have to face."

> Well, now that is an interesting . . .

And another thing. You said I cannot change a fact, but you played with the word "it." You said, "If something is a fact, it is unchangeable. But "it" refers to "something" and not to "fact." I can change a fact but not something.

> Nice try, but perhaps "it" refers to both "something" and to "fact." Of course you can change something. You can cut a dog's hair, cut down a tree, and so on. But if something is a fact, then you cannot change it.

Perhaps, but how about that fact you have to face, the student unrest.

> That's a little trickier. I am not facing the student unrest, but the fact *of* student unrest or *that* there is student unrest. "Fact" is referring to state of affairs, or better yet, it's being used in a statement which is just a way of talking.

Well, one last try. Back to my statement about Smith, Jones, Brown, and Green. Is that a fact?

> You can say, "Here are the facts," or "Take these facts," or "These are the facts."

Well, can't you see *them?* Maybe you cannot see *a* fact, but you can see those facts.

> I've never heard anyone talk that way. It just doesn't make sense to talk that way.

But if I were to hand you the statement of facts, I could say, "Look at these facts."

> In that sort of case, you could even say "I saw the facts," but not, I see or saw a fact.

Exhibit III

The following BASIC RULES have been used in seminars on Law and Communication. They are referred to in several places in the text, mainly in connection with matters of interpretation and with regard to the business of teaching law-communication in a seminar sort of situation. It is very possible that the ways these Rules have worked have not been adequately explained. It may not be possible. In any event, they are not presented as *the* model. And further, in no one seminar were we involved with them for more than three sessions. But their impact was in every instance dramatic. We cannot expect that drama in *this* context.

BASIC RULES
(Law and Communication)

PREAMBLE:

Whereas it is our purpose to promote our understanding of law and communication and their interrelationships, the following BASIC RULES have been promulgated after due consideration to take effect when and under such circumstances as herein indicated:

Section 1 Rule of interpretation:
Where it may be appropriate, all ambiguities and inconsistencies shall be resolved in accordance with the above stated goals.

Section 2 Definition:
Where the symbol CL shall appear in these Basic RULES, they shall refer to Professor or such person as he shall designate to carry out his appointed function.

Rule 1. Any member of the class who intentionally does an act which is disruptive of a communication transaction then in process is subject to a fine not to exceed three points. He is also subject to liability to any person who has suffered harm by such a wilful or malicious disruption. Guilt shall be determined by CL and two other persons appointed by him for the purpose. The fine shall be levied by CL. Liability shall be determined by the class as a whole, including Professor, and shall not exceed two points. All decisions shall be made in accordance with procedures governed by Robert's Rules of Order—except that the official rules may not be referred to during a class session.

Rule 2. Other rules not inconsistent with these BASIC RULES and pertaining to classroom decorum may be promulgated by a two-thirds vote of the class subject to approval by CL; or by CL after discussion with other members of the class.

Rule 3. Every member of this class shall start with 20 points, except that Professor will have 50 points. Points may be used as a medium of exchange for whatever purpose desired within the classroom, so long as recorded in the official Registry to be maintained by CL.

Rule 4. At the end of the term, or at such time as these BASIC RULES are repealed by Professor, an accounting will be taken and surplus points may be redeemed by any student for credit on his final grade for the course, on the basis of a 100 point grading scale in effect in the University. This rule is not subject to repeal.

Rule 5. These rules are in operation when so indicated by CL or the student membership as a whole, unless suspended by a two-thirds vote of the class for a time period not to exceed one class hour.

Rule 6. No violation under these BASIC RULES or under any rules promulgated pursuant thereto will be acted upon unless complaint or reparation is initiated by a student member of the class, and at such time as is convenient to CL. A complainant is subject to assessment up to three points for initiating an unsuccessful deliberation.

Rule 7. All points lost by fine shall be transferred to the account of Professor, and CL may allocate points from said account to individual members of the class, so long as he does so for the general welfare of the class.

Rule 8. All decisions are to be governed by notions of due process and fair play as such notions may apply. Each decision shall operate as a binding precedent in the manner known to Common Law. The CL will designate a secretary who shall keep an official record of decisions made under these BASIC RULES to include such notations as are requested by a decisional group, a person fined or assessed, or three members of the class.

Exhibit IV

GARRATT v. DAILEY

Supreme Court of Washington, 1955
46 Wash. 2d 197, 279 P.2d 1091.

HILL, Justice. The liability of an infant for an alleged battery is presented to this court for the first time. Brian Dailey (age five years, nine months) was visiting with Naomi Garratt, an adult and a sister of the plaintiff, Ruth Garratt, likewise an adult, in the back yard of the plaintiff's home, on July 16, 1951. It is plaintiff's contention that she came out into the back yard to talk with Naomi and that, as she started to sit down in a wood and canvas lawn chair, Brian deliberately pulled it out from under her. The only one of the three persons present so testifying was Naomi Garratt. (Ruth Garratt, the plaintiff, did not testify as to how or why she fell.) The trial court, unwilling to accept this testimony, adopted instead Brian Dailey's version of what happened, and made the following findings:

> III. * * * that while Naomi Garratt and Brian Dailey were in the back yard the plaintiff, Ruth Garratt, came out of her house into the back yard. Some time subsequent thereto defendant, Brian Dailey, picked up a lightly built wood and canvas lawn chair which was then and there located in the back yard of the above described premises, moved it sideways a few feet and seated himself therein, at which time he discovered the plaintiff, Ruth Garratt, about to sit down at the place where the lawn chair had formerly been, at which time he hurriedly got up from the chair and attempted to move it toward Ruth Garratt to aid her in sitting down in the chair; that due to the defendant's small size and lack of dexterity he was unable to get the lawn chair under the plaintiff in time to prevent her from falling to the ground. That plaintiff fell to the ground and sustained a fracture of her hip, and other injuries and damages as hereinafter set forth.
>
> IV. That the preponderance of the evidence in this case establishes that when the defendant, Brian Dailey, moved the chair in question *he did not have any wilful or unlawful purpose* in doing so; that *he did not have any intent to injure the plaintiff, or any intent to bring about any unauthorized or offensive contact with her person* or any objects appurtenant thereto; that the circumstances which immediately preceded the fall of the plaintiff establish that the defendant, *Brian Dailey, did not have purpose, intent or design to perform a prank or to effect*

an assault and battery upon the person of the plaintiff. (Italics ours, for a purpose hereinafter indicated.)

It is conceded that Ruth Garratt's fall resulted in a fractured hip and other painful and serious injuries. To obviate the necessity of a retrial in the event this court determines that she was entitled to a judgment against Brian Dailey, the amount of her damage was found to be $11,000. Plaintiff appeals from a judgment dismissing the action and asks for the entry of a judgment in that amount or a new trial.

The authorities generally, but with certain notable exceptions, see Bohlen, "Liability in Tort of Infants and Insane Persons," 23 Mich. L. Rev. 9, state that when a minor has committed a tort with force he is liable to be proceeded against as any other person would be.***

It is urged that Brian's action in moving the chair constituted a battery. A definition (not all-inclusive but sufficient for our purpose) of a battery is the intentional infliction of a harmful bodily contact upon another. The rule that determines liability for battery is given in 1 Restatement, Torts, 29, §13, as:

> An act which, directly or indirectly, is the legal cause of a harmful contact with another's person makes the actor liable to the other, if
>
> (a) the act is done with the intention of bringing about a harmful or offensive contact or an apprehension thereof to the other or a third person, and
>
> (b) the contact is not consented to by the other or the other's consent thereto is procured by fraud or duress, and
>
> (c) the contact is not otherwise privileged.

We have in this case no question of consent or privilege. We therefore proceed to an immediate consideration of intent and its place in the law of battery. In the comment on clause (a), the Restatement says:

> *Character of actor's intention.* In order that an act may be done with the intention of bringing about a harmful or offensive contact or an apprehension thereof to a particular person, either the other or a third person, the act must be done for the purpose of causing the contact or apprehension or with knowledge on the part of the actor that such contact or apprehension is substantially certain to be produced. (See, also, Prosser on Torts 41, §8 [p. 30 in 2d ed.]).

We have here the conceded volitional act of Brian, i.e. the

moving of a chair. Had the plaintiff proved to the satisfaction of the trial court that Brian moved the chair while she was in the act of sitting down, Brian's action would patently have been for the purpose or with the intent of causing the plaintiff's bodily contact with the ground, and she would be entitled to a judgment against him for the resulting damages. Vosburg v. Putney, 1891, 80 Wis. 523, 50 N.W. 403, 14 L.R.A. 226; ***

***After the trial court determined that the plaintiff had not established her theory of a battery (i.e. that Brian had pulled the chair out from under the plaintiff while she was in the act of sitting down), it then became concerned with whether a battery was established under the facts as it found them to be.

In this connection, we quote another portion of the comment on the "character of actor's intention," relating to clause (a) of the rule from the Restatement heretofore set forth:

> It is not enough that the act itself is intentionally done and this, even though the actor realizes or should realize that it contains a very grave risk of bringing about the contact or apprehension. Such realization may make the actor's conduct negligent or even reckless but unless he realizes that to a substantial certainty, the contact or apprehension will result, the actor has not that intention which is necessary to make him liable under the rule stated in this section.

A battery would be established if, in addition to plaintiff's fall, it was proved that, when Brian moved the chair, he knew with substantial certainty that the plaintiff would attempt to sit down where the chair had been. If Brian had any of the intents which the trial court found, in the italicized portions of the findings of fact quoted above, that he did not have, he would of course have had the knowledge to which we have referred. The mere absence of any intent to injure the plaintiff or to play a prank on her or to embarrass her, or to commit an assault and battery on her would not absolve him from liability if in fact he had such knowledge. Mercer v. Corbin, 1889, 117 Ind. 450, 20 N.E. 132, 3 L.R.A. 221. Without such knowledge there would be nothing wrongful about Brian's act in moving the chair and, there being no wrongful act, there would be no liability.

While a finding that Brian had no such knowledge can be inferred from the findings made, we believe that before the plaintiff's action in such a case should be dismissed there should be no question but that the trial court had passed upon that issue; hence, the case should be remanded for clarification of the findings to specifically cover the question of Brian's knowledge, because intent could be inferred therefrom. If the court finds that he had such knowledge the necessary intent will be established and the plaintiff will be entitled to recover, even though there was no purpose to injure or embarrass the plaintiff. *Vosburg v. Putney, supra.* If Brian did not have such knowledge, there was no wrongful act by him and the basic premise of liability on the theory of a battery was not established.

It will be noted that the law of battery as we have discussed it is the law applicable to adults, and no significance has been attached to the fact that Brian was a child less than six years of age when the alleged battery occurred. The only circumstance where Brian's age is of any consequence is in determining what he knew, and there his experience, capacity, and understanding are of course material.***

It is argued that some courts predicate an infant's liability for tort upon the basis of the existence of an estate in the infant; hence it was error for the trial court to refuse to admit as an exhibit a policy of liability insurance as evidence that there was a source from which a judgment might be satisfied. In our opinion the liability of an infant for his tort does not depend upon the size of his estate or even upon the existence of one. That is a matter of concern only to the plaintiff who seeks to enforce a judgment against the infant.***

The cause is remanded for clarification, with instructions to make definite findings on the issue of whether Brian Dailey knew with substantial certainty that the plaintiff would attempt to sit down where the chair which he moved had been, and to change the judgment if the findings warrant it.

It is interesting to note the action taken by the trial judge upon remand of the case. He indicated that he considered the time sequence of events in a way that he had not done previously. He determined that the "arthritic woman had begun the slow process of being seated when the defendant quickly removed the chair and seated himself upon it, and that he knew, with substantial certainty, at that time she would attempt to sit in the place where the chair had been." Plaintiff had judgment which was affirmed in 49 Wash. 2d 499, 304 P. 2d 681 (1956).

Exhibit V

THE ROLES OF INTENT IN THE LAW OF CRIMES AND TORTS

(Delivered by lecture at Oxford, Fall, 1968)

I shall be dealing with examples of situations out of criminal law and tort law. Criminal law is more universally known and discussed outside the legal profession than is the law of torts. Torts concerns what are called civil wrongs, i.e. wrongs for which the remedy is not prosecution and penalty on behalf of the state or the public, but a suit for damages by persons claiming to be harmed. The kinds of harms can be generally classified in terms of (1) injury to person, such as bodily damage; (2) to property; (3) to economic interests, such as fraud; (4) to interpersonal relationships, such as defamation. Running across this classification are such tort categories as assault and battery, false imprisonment, trespass to land, conversion, nuisance, deceit, defamation, and negligence.

The latter kind of tort, negligence, looms largest in the number of cases, but the term "intent" plays various roles across the law of torts. Tort law is said to be largely based on fault, i.e. either intent or negligence. When these criteria are not used as the basis of liability, liability is said to be strict. Strict liability exists in criminal law also. An example of strict liability in tort and of strict responsibility in crimes comes under a statute where sale of impure food or drugs is prohibited regardless of state of mind or of the precautions taken.

Let me point out, however, that there must truly be *some* intent in order for there to be guilt or liability. That is, responsibility is never so strict as to ignore the requirement of a voluntary act in the relevant chain of causation. Voluntariness is seldom discussed, except maybe by way of denial of the claim of intent or by way of defense, say that the act was performed under compulsion or duress. Acting at the point of a gun is in one sense voluntary, but in another it is not.

Not to confuse, but to help set a major theme, let me point out that in one sense of "strict" and of "intent," some of the strictest liability known comes under the heading of intentional torts, such as trespass to land. I shall illustrate shortly.

With that brief survey, I want now to use as a spring-board

some of the ideas and examples that have arisen in the Seminar and several of what seem to me to be the major themes in Dr. Kenny's article on Intent and Purpose (in the Law).

My own intents and purposes are not merely to give an accounting of what the law is. This needs explaining, and I believe the explanation will aid our inquiry. Almost without exception, I find that non-lawyers somehow expect that law is made up of laws which can be taxonomically described. Unfortunately too many lawyers operate under this expectation as well. Any statement of law that is not an *official* statement, say in a judicial opinion, statute, or administrative regulation—also much that appears in official statements,—is normatively ambiguous. I cannot go into a full explanation of normative ambiguity, but it goes first to the necessary indeterminateness of any statement of a rule outside of a specific context of application, in that sense, any general term—and some more than others, such as intent—plays a variety of roles in actual communicative behavior.

Of course Wittgenstein and J. L. Austin did much to explicate that aspect of words as they appear in the language, as opposed to their use in interpersonal relations. But even beyond that analysis of words in general, rules and laws are not just something to be stated or even described. It is usually not indicated whether a statement of a rule is a statement of a controlling norm, an historical account, or a prediction of behavior. One may be prescriptive or descriptive or both in stating a rule or one of its key terms. He may on the other hand be engaging in advocative or critical argument.

For such reason I am not stating what intentional behavior is illegal in the way that Bentham seems to state his taxonomy of intent. If his definitions be seen as merely stipulative, then one could reasonably parallel his efforts in law. I do not thereby suggest scorn of his efforts, rather I suggest they be seen as prescriptive, how conduct ought to be described.

So, doctrinaire as law may seem to the unpracticed eye or ear, I believe the process can with more illumination be approached not just as a collection of laws, rules, and definitions, but as a process of interpretation and decision-making in which terms, doctrines, and other verbalisms—such as those involving intent—are brought into debate and justification, say opinions of courts and comments on courts, in a way that can most expediently be evaluated as dialectical or rhetorical. This is not to say there are no patterns or trends, but they are not necessarily what is seen on the surface of literal expression or to be described in the terms that the courts themselves use.

In Dr. Kenny's splendidly provocative and penetrating article, he jumps off from the 1961 Smith Case (*D.P.P. v. Smith*-1961-A.C. 290). In that case, the defendant was being charged with murder on the ground that he intended to bring great bodily harm to a policeman and that as a result the policeman was killed. The defendant was trying to escape arrest or detention and drove his car wildly with the policeman hanging onto the outside of the car. In its careening progress, the car struck several others and the policeman finally was thrown off to his death as he was struck by another car.

The underlying legal premise was that defendant intended great bodily harm to the policeman, even if he did not want it to occur, so long as he foresaw it. Dr. Kenny seems to question this line of legal reasoning. Apparently, and I stress apparently, it was further premised that the defendant could be found to have had such intent under an objective test. Under the objective test, it is said to be sufficient to find that a reasonable man would have foreseen great bodily harm as a result of the defendant's conduct, whether defendant actually did or not. If the test were to have been subjective, it would be necessary to find that the defendant *did* foresee great bodily harm. I gather that Dr. Kenny probably questions the use of the objective test to determine intent, especially where it is defined in terms of foresight rather than desire or want.

Despite the fact that the Smith Case was heavily criticized, it does not seem to me to do violence to the way that problems of intent have been handled in the Anglo-American law of wrongs. Let me explain.

In court, laws are supposed to operate upon ascertained facts. Outside of court, we think of intent as an ascertainable fact. Certainly we talk that way. As we here know, it has been philosophically as well as psychologically debated as to just where the referents of such expressions as intent may lie. To understand how such terms as intent may be parlayed, one must consider a subtle and important distinction: it is one thing to *assert* that someone has a particular state of mind or intent or purpose. It is quite another to *prove* such an assertion coming in a specific case or situation, such as the intent asserted in the Smith Case. More of this as we proceed.

There is another distinction important to our inquiry and to both law and philosophy generally. That has to do with the assertion of a state of mind in a specific court case as compared to the assertion of a state of mind in a hypothetical fact situation. I stress hypothetical. In court, the assertion is prelude to a trial in which it must be proven. In both a lawyer's and a philosopher's argument, the assertion is a prelude to, or part of, a logical-linguistic process of persuasion. The criteria are quite different in these two kinds of situations, the trial proof and the argumentative proof. More of this also.

Dr. Kenny's main complaint about the Smith Case and criminal law in general is that intent is measured by foresight of caused harm without regard to whether harm is wanted or desired. He may also be objecting that law does not in some way more sophisticated perhaps than the double effect approaches relate findings of intent to ultimate purposes.

I think Dr. Kenny might find the law of torts generally to his dislike also, to the extent that we can say it involves intent analyses that relate moral judgments to suits for damages. Where he is careful in his thoughtful analysis of conduct and its results to make sharp distinctions between one act and another, between the results and the consequences of an act, and to be concerned whether consequences are foreseen and/or wanted, the law of torts is definitely quite sloppy by comparison. In what is known as trespass to land, one may be guilty of trespass if he intentionally does something, say move one foot in front of another, or throw an object, such that he causes his foot or the object to cross over a boundary line, even though he thinks he is still on his own property and is not negligent in thinking so. We say that all the intent that is required is to move from here to there. Yet to be guilty of falsely imprisoning another person, it is not enough to do something intentionally which unexpectedly turns out to be a confinement or total restraint of another person, i.e. unknowingly, locking a person in a room. The intent generally must be to confine. Of course we will say that usually it is enough if the actor knows he will confine another, even if he does not want it. That constitutes intent to confine. There is an interesting aberrational case, involving the business man who locked the door of his store against a group of advancing creditors. The man who was beside him in the store claimed he was thus confined, but the court held the confinement was not intended. What *was* intended was that the creditors be kept out. This seems more in line with the doctrines of double effect than the reasoning of the law of torts, for generally it is said that one intends those results which he knows or believes are substantially certain to occur.

But why does not the law of torts treat false imprisonment problems consistently with trespass to land cases? Why is intent related differently to the range of consequences? I could go so far as to answer that the distinctions lie in historical morality. I think it was made easy to sue for trespass to land because land ownership and right of possession—power to exclude others—was ranked at the very top of socio-legal values. That is further reflected in the rule of damages still existing that if one trespasses on another's property, he is liable for all the proximately caused consequences, whether foreseen or even foreseeable or not. Theoretically, if I walk in good faith on your property and drop a lighted match accidentally, and it burns down your house, I am liable without regard to any other intent or foresight. The law is not so strict as to liberty of movement because historically it did not place so high in value, although its value was high enough to allow an action without any other complaint of damage than "I was restrained."

To be compared with both of these is the law of libel which is very complicated on the matter of intent. For instance, generally speaking, in the United States, it is libelous to write and publish of another person that he is a communist. But suppose a less clear case where A writes of B that he belongs to organization X. If X is a communist organization, or maybe even if radically leftist, then B's reputation can be hurt. Surely it is immoral to harm substantially another's reputation maliciously. That valuation has found its way into the law of torts. But one may still in some situations be liable for libel for something quite less than malice as that term signifies to the layman. Without going into all the complexities, recognize that questions of intent can arise as to whether A intended to say what he said, to mean what his words were taken to say or imply, to publish, to refer to B, to make a false statement, or innuendo and so on. I hesitate to draw any clear picture of the state of the law on these matters, not just because it is so complex, but because it is a crazy quilt which allows if it does not encourage subtle moral and other policy judgments to be made of a certain piece of allegedly harmful conduct. I suggest that many problems are just as complex and open textured in law, but not necessarily with regard to the factor of intent. But more, my claim is that intent is not just a term of analysis which helps to determine *whether* a person has acted illegally or immorally, it is to some extent an expression of judgment that a person *has* acted immorally. Intent is not just something to be described or discovered; or better, the word may vaguely point in that direction, but under some circumstances it points back at the person who is using the word. Logically, the term may seem to be used in a question-begging fashion, yet psychologically it may be coming not from a computer portion of the brain but from the heart or the gut.

Take these examples of intent usage:

(1) If X gets drunk, knowing he will suffer a hangover, we will not say he intended to suffer a hangover.

(2) If Y shot a cannonball at the gate of a fortress, while a person was sitting on top, we might say he intended to harm the person, but if it is a lizard on top, we might argue he did not intend to harm or kill the lizard, or maybe that the demise of the lizard was not part of the act of shooting but some other act, etc.

(3) If Z is a candidate for public office and decides to take an unpopular stand or disclose information which will surely lose for him and he knows it, we do not say he intended to lose the election.

I would suggest to you that we could dream up legal contexts for these examples where we might say otherwise about these intents and where most of you would not be offended at the judgments if you properly considered the workings of law and language, including the difference between asserting something and proving what is asserted.

In any of these cases, how would you go about proving one way or another what X or Y or Z wanted or desired, let alone what he knew or believed? We hypothesize as we must in order to carry out rational arguments, but by that same process we set the odds in our favor. This is one of the most subtle features of language usage and it has not come in for anything like its proper degree of analysis. I'm not giving lawyers any credit when I say they would tell you we do not prove a state of mind in either torts or crimes, but we construct and infer at best. Generally speaking we don't take a defendant's word, but we say that we must judge his intent from the circumstances. I believe that is one good reason why we define intent as we do and also why the so-called subjective test of intent is little short of myth. At best it is a change of emphasis. Whether we use the objective or subjective test, we consider the surrounding circumstances. In neither text do we take the defendant's own self-serving statements at face value. Even when trying to look at his subjectivities we do so objectively by asking what do we think his knowledge and intent must have been, judged by our own experience. Philosophical problems aplenty in this distinction.

In the first or hangover hypothetical, I point out to you that we are not called upon to make a legal judgment about X, nor is there the slightest suggestion that we might or ought to have any moral concern about his hangover. It is otherwise about his drinking, perhaps. He cannot claim that someone else got him drunk—that is his responsibility. But suppose he is a surgeon who is to perform a difficult surgery on the day he has a hangover and suppose he has to withdraw from the operation or that he does not but bungles it. If he uses the hangover as an excuse for not operating and a hearing takes place to decide whether he should be ousted from a medical society, it might even plausibly be argued that he intended to get a hangover. How could he prove that he did not? Someone might say, you did that on purpose.

Suppose I am at a cocktail party and leave a conversation to open a window. Someone says, "That was a clever way to get out of that boring conversation." I say that I merely wanted to freshen the air in the room. I could have had the more complex motivation. The normal routine that guarantees cocktail party mobility is to freshen the drink or to get a bit of food. In these circumstances, contemporary motivational analysis by the man in the street allows him at least to believe that my purposes include getting out of the conversation. We use the word "purpose" that way even to suggest unconscious motivation. But in any event, while we can hypothesize what the intent was one way or the other, if the matter was at issue during a trial, wouldn't it make sense to say that he "knew what he was doing" and that very likely he intended what he knew?

Might someone say that the honest candidate was taking a way out? Of course the candidate has virtue on his side and we are not being asked to judge against him by saying what he intended. In the hypothetical, intent is being used in the want-desire syndrome, not in the make a moral or legal judgment syndromes. In the other hypothetical, the comparison between shooting at a gate with a man on it and shooting at it with a lizard on it, it seems to me to help make my points that moral judgment enters in to the way we use intent and certainly into the way we characterize events and stiuations, as the double effect sophistry illustrates. We continue to develop new ways as the old become exposed. This kind of development is also part of the history of the evolution of legal rules and doctrines.

Now take another hypothetical. A stabs at a curtain behind which a person is apparently standing. A believes it to be his enemy, B. It turns out to be a good friend whom he has thus killed. Now by Dr. Kenny's strict analysis, A obviously did not intend to kill B his friend. Yet there is no doubt that he is guilty of murdering his friend. Lawyers would have no trouble escaping Dr. Kenny's criticism by countering that A did intend to kill the person who was behind the curtain. Or put more generally, he intended to kill someone. There is no doubt, is there, that A is morally wrong, that he showed himself of a murderer's disposition, and so on. And further, I have hypothesized that A did not want to kill his friend, and you have no reason to question my fiat, but how does one really know what A's intents were?

An interesting tort case out of the State of Washington may further our thinking. It involved a 5½-year-old boy who was being sued for assault and battery for damages suffered by an elderly arthritic lady. Her attorney claimed that the boy pulled a chair away in which she was planning to sit. Since she was arthritic, she was unable to recover her balance and fell, doing great damage. In a clear case this will be called a battery. Ordinarily, to batter someone, one hits him intending to do so. To hit a person with an auto ordinarily is merely negligence at worst. But you can also batter a person by intentionally causing his body to be struck by something or to hit the ground. It must be intended, but intent means substantially certain to happen. If I pull out a chair, the person who falls was intended to fall. Of course my timing must be correct; if I pull too soon, he may only stagger. Or I may pull the chair not intending for him to fall but only to stagger. If then he falls I may argue I was only negligent to save me from a claim for punitive damages tacked on top of the compensatory damages for my victim's hurts. But what will be believed about my intent? In court I am not free to control the jury's characterization by self-serving hypothesizing.

Now it is important to know that I could be charged with both intentional wrongdoing and negligence, but a 5½-year-old boy cannot. He is not old enough to be judged by standards of reasonableness. Yet he can be charged with intentional wrongdoing. In California a 4-year-old boy was successfully charged with battering a babysitter. Of course neither could be charged with the crime of battery, not because they lack what might be called the abandoned and malignant heart necessary to mens rea, but because children that age are exempt, are in the eyes of law not old enough to know right from wrong, and all that. Certainly a 4-year-old can have the intent to hit a person. I believe we can make a moral sounding judgment by saying he should not do that. By the time he is 5½, we believe he should know better. We can tell him it is wrong to do that, and we can tell him it is wrong to pull chairs out from people. Indeed, in the Washington case, the evidence revealed that he tried to return to the chair to the plaintiff's underside when he saw what was happening. There is evidence that he acted wrongly or badly.

But is there evidence that he intended the lady to fall down? What was his state of mind? Shall we ask him some time later and shall we believe him or trust his memory? Well, what is the state of mind of a person of that age? Shall we judge by adult standards or have a jury of 5½-year-olds? The fate of the case is now of interest. The trial judge acting without a jury held that the boy did not have any unlawful intent or intent to harm or even to bring about an offensive bodily contact. But his findings of no battery were reversed and the case sent back to him to look again at the record. He was instructed that if the young defendant removed the chair knowing that the plaintiff would attempt to sit down, then he had the requisite intent. The trial judge dutifully found a battery. Most students and lawyers read that case carelessly and assume it is the usual rule: if one knows something is going to happen, then he intends it. But a careful reading shows that the court required even less, it required merely the wrongful impoliteness of knowingly removing a chair from the position where a person would attempt to sit down. The boy might or might not know that an arthritic was likely to lose her balance, but for purposes of the tort suit, it was not necessary to inquire into that maze of mentalism. Still, there is a moral aura to the use of the word "intent." There is still in tort law in this kind of case enough of a criminal law inheritance to require a finding of wrongfulness about conduct which causes unfortunate if unexpected results.

In another battery case from another U.S. jurisdiction about 40 years previously, the use of intent in the way I have suggested is quite clear. The plaintiff was a fourteen-year-old boy who suffered severe damage to his leg as a consequence of being kicked by a boy of twelve. The boys were sitting in a schoolroom and the teacher had formally called the class to order. It is reported that the older boy did not even feel the kick. Because the kick opened up a previous wound, the boy ultimately suffered a paralysis of that leg. It was held that the younger boy was guilty of a tortious battery, even though he intended no harm. Had the kick occurred on the playground, the defendant might well have not been liable. The court reasoned that all that was needed was an unlawful intent and that the intent was unlawful because the act was unlawful because it broke the classroom decorum. I must interpolate that unlawful means wrongful. As strict as a result may seem, it is not as strict as the trespass to land situation, because it is not enough merely to have intended bodily contact. The intent is to be judged in an objective fashion against the circumstances of the situation, by the context of the act, if you will.

When I first taught torts, I used this case as the prime object of my most merciless cynicism regarding the sophistry of early U.S. judicial reasoning, as a prime example of question-begging logic. I finally came to realize especially in that more formalistic period in the United States that the case was an example of the kind of judgmental use of intent that I am now stressing, in aid of lego-moral evaluation of a defendant's conduct as weighed against the resulting consequences and the sanction involved.

It is instructive to compare the Smith case, in which recall, a policeman was thrown from the outside of the defendant's car while he was trying to flee. By a degree of external or objective judgment—inescapable whenever we judge—defendant very likely, not certainly, knew what he was doing bore a very high risk of great bodily harm if not death for the policeman. His act was unlawful. The use of intent from the point of view of one kind of logic or linguistic convention seems strange, but in criminal law the number of conventions are even less than in tort law, and in England they seem to be less in variation than in the multiple jurisdiction complexity of the United States. Necessarily there must be more stretching.

But further, in the tort case, there was a wrong. It may have been a little one, so to speak, but the potential penalty was as compared to the Smith case comparatively light. The wrong in the Smith case may have been a great one. If the court were freer, it might have woven a more acceptable rationale. Where a court is bound on the surface of literal convention, it is not underneath. The result is another prime example of the use of intent to make a lego-moral judgment.

Related to what I have been discussing is the point in Dr. Kenny's article that the legal definition of intent seems to involve a disregard of motive or purpose; i.e. legally speaking it is said that a person intends certain consequences if he foresees them, even though he had some other purpose in mind and did not have those consequences as an end, or a means. (Shooting through another person.) It is generally true that consideration of purpose does not enter into the definition of intent, but it certainly does enter into the broader consideration of guilt or innocence, and whether or not there is liability.

Now let's take a bit closer look at Dr. Kenny's point that it is enough to satisfy the law's intent formula if one merely foresee damage, regardless of purpose. But courts do not tend to speak of one's foreseeing certain consequences when they speak of intent, they speak of knowing with substantial certainty that such and such will occur. I realize that foresee can be and is used by Dr. Kenny in this sense, but I believe he occasionally slips as one almost inevitably must into the sense of foresee which is predominantly used in law.

Foresee is a key term, not in the syntax of intent but that of negligence formulae. In that area, foresight is definitely weighed against purpose in determining whether a person's conduct is blameworthy or reasonable. If one takes a risk of damage, his conduct may not be negligent if it is for a good purpose or serves a protected interest. If damage is foreseeable—not foreseen in the sense of known but foreseen in the sense of possible or probable, maybe the only valid way of using the word—if damage is foreseeable and if the damage occurs, that does not make the actors' conduct negligent in and of itself, and indeed there are some circumstances when harm is foreseen in the sense of known certainty that it is not said to be intended.

Suppose one were driving his car too fast to avoid hitting a group of children running in the road, except that the driver could swerve into a parked car which had occupants. This is a dilemma which has been negligently created by the driver and he will be liable, probably, no matter what happens, but if he swerves into the car, and injures an occupant, we will not say it is a battery, i.e. an intentional tort, or murder, for he did not do it deliberately; his purpose was to avoid the children, one might argue.

Furthermore, foresee is a weasel word which plays many roles in the syntax of negligence. Without elaborating, let me simply say that it serves many of the roles of intent while saving some of the problems of proof. It is in this area, incidentally, that the objective test is most used.

But still, purpose does not enter into the kind of case that we have chosen to consider, so far as the definition of intent is concerned. Even so, it comes in by way of defense, say of one's self or his property.

There may be an advantage in not having purpose as part of the web of intent syntax in the kind of case we have chosen to discuss. In regard to a charge of crime, intent must be alleged and proved by the state, in a tort case, by the plaintiff. Credible evidence of intent creates a presumptive or prime facie case. If defendant is to claim an overriding purpose or justification, then the burden is on *him* to establish its existence. In the Smith case there is actually evidence that defendant had the intent to do great bodily harm and it is really quite impossible for him to bring in evidence of some overriding purpose of social acceptability.

Don't we use the law's approach in everyday life except when we are playing or arguing with hypothetical facts as lawyers or philosophers?? If a man gets out of bed, knowing he will wake the baby, but not wanting to, some would argue there is no intent. If he can give no good reason for getting up, we may feel there is a stroke of meanness which approaches if it is not tantamount to intent. Our criticism of the man may be as heavy, intent or not, but if he shows some acceptable purpose, we sympathize with him by saying he had no such intent. A court can exercise that kind of judgment too—and certainly a jury is always free to do so.

I would conclude by saying that the way the machinery of law and the doctrine of law line up, I doubt that very often a person is found guilty of having a wrongful intent where he proves some higher or acceptable purpose. It is simply that in the face of evidence that defendant is engaged in conduct which shows him to be anti-social, to a great degree in criminal law, to a lesser degree in torts, there is no good reason why he should not be said to have intended the consequences in question.

Note: This lecture was delivered to a seminar on Intent and Morality being reld by Dr. Kenny at Balliol College, Oxford, in the Fall Term, 1968. The article by him referred to in the lecture is "Intention and Purpose in Law," included in *Essays in Legal Philosophy*, at p. 146 (Edited by Summers, Univ. of Calif. Press 1968).

Exhibit VI

THE RIGHT WAY
What To Do With Theory

There are those amongst us who slyly intimate that linguistic analysis does not provide answers to philosophic questions. Still, the *questions* have improved since we became at least a little more word conscious. I hear nobody asking what a right is. Really, it is some improvement to hear it asked instead what a *human* right is, among kinds of rights.

Compare what H. L. A. Hart has done for us. The legal realists had looked at legal rules and because they discovered so much ambiguity and contradiction, they tended to conclude that maybe rules did not really exist. Well, Hart led us to see that there is more than one kind of legal rule. He stopped far short of even a partial taxonomy of legal rules, but what a surprisingly helpful counter move that was. One interesting consequence was the revelation from Hart's most recent sparring partner, Ronald Dworkin. One has to go back at least to the early days of Roscoe Pound to discover what Dworkin has revealed, that our common law is made up not just of rules but also principles.

What are principles? Ah, but one should not ask such a question. Remember? We could ask what *legal* principles are, but no doubt there is more than one kind. Besides, for our purposes it seems to me there is a more interesting question to pursue with respect to Dworkin's revelation.

He does not put it forth as a question. Rather, he asserts it as if it had been there all the time, thus displaying a rhetorical technique shared by lawyers and philosophers and practically all the rest of humanity (maybe this *is* a human right). His theme is as if "Well there they are, principles have been there all the time." Of course *we* know that Dworkin did not invent the word "principle" and he did not invent principles, not even legal principles. Neither did Pound. It is not altogether clear what Dworkin would include within the stable, but his certification procedures would not necessarily be the same as Pound's. Professor Christie has suggested that what Dworkin calls legal principles, some would call rules. Well, he is quite right about that. It is most enlightening to see what judges have done with the potentials lurking in the rhetoric of rules and principles, not to mention maxims, standards, and nowadays, policy. I have seen that standby of early tort law—"one should use his property so as not to injure another"—characterized in all these ways; not all at once, though.

I am still building up to my question, but I must pause to reflect how frightening it must be for laymen to see judges so careless. Imagine not knowing the difference between a rule and a principle—and a maxim. That would rather be like lego-moral theorists not knowing the difference between rights and claims, or the proper relationship of rights to duty, or maybe even worst of all, confusing as is with an ought. We seem to have cleared such hurdles, knowing quite well when we are talking law, or politics, or morality—and I guess humanity.

Lawyers used to be confused about legal rights, mind you, until Hohfeld came along to clarify the matter. Before him Holmes had tried to legislate how we should talk about legal rights and duties, as he put it, in terms of predictions of judicial decisions. But of course Hohfeld was only clarifying. How different from those modern day linguistic analysts who resort to common usage. There is only murkiness in that direction. Some might think Jerome Hall was legislating in suggesting that duty is somehow of greater importance than right, but surely he is only trying to lead us to clearer vision. If I may paraphrase him, the utilitarians and the judges—and I would suppose the lawyers—are looking too hard at the pragmatics of practices. The "ordinary language" analysts in a way do the same thing. Naturally they all get bogged down in diversity and ad hocs, the many, as he says. That is not the way of Theory, which drives toward the One, an all-embracing, all-encompassing Resolution of confused thinking.

Out on the streets lawyers and other people use words in all sorts of ways. Of course the analytical jurists and the legal positivists whom Hall criticizes are somewhat mindful of that. But their mistake is not to see law in three dimensions, especially as they define out the moral-normative aspect. Hall's model of Oneness is not ambiguous, just three sided; not square, but a cube.

But Dworkin and his rule-principle analysis: What is the interesting question? Well, the question is, what is he doing. Why does he want us to see things that way. Hall would tell us that the legal positivists value order and especially the order of law, so they build an edifice solely of law and place it above all other forms of social control. Well, that sort of motivational analysis is fun and I hope Hall does not mind my following his lead. What could we say of Dworkin? His philosophical ambitions do not seem as elaborate as Hall's who would build an intellectual tower from which we could view in three directions and know how Ideas, Facts, and Values coalesce in Law.[1,2,&3] No doubt he is doing something more than that, but Dworkin is a bit simpler for demonstrating my point.

My point is that Dworkin is doing something with words. Of course he is unusual in this regard and worth observing. It is beyond the scope of this paper (as everybody likes to say when they have reached the end of their current thinking) to give a full treatment to what Dworkin is doing, but for our purposes a few brief jabs will do. He does one thing we all too often try to avoid and that is to write rather simply, I mean of course understandably. He does another thing we all must do if we are to be received and that is to knock down other views and/or appear to set up some new ones. In a rather interesting fashion he borrows from legal realism, while scoffing at its nominalists—how philosophically better than calling them rule skeptics—and from legal positivists while sniffing at their simplism—and produces a model which could please tolerant moderates from both camps. What this model allows him to do is to wear the hats of the lawyer, the legal theorist, the moralist, the moral philosopher and potentially stand as critic or draftsman of any view or approach that might conceivably involve the legal process.

And as it turns out, this is what Hart's framework of analysis allows to him also. I believe Hall would do him a discredit if he included Hart as merely valuing *legal* order above others. It seems to me that Hart has nicely set himself as the proper judge of things both legal and moral as well as of the interplay. What more could a theorist ask? But if that is so, why did not Dworkin merely follow his lead? Well, we know that disciples do not get heard in the way they did many years ago. Hart's legal positivism is not acceptable, by and large, in this country. We just do not see law as rules. But compare: rules *and* principles, binding and/or not binding, relevant when significantly related, both quite legal and yet an open door to policy and morality. And maybe the English will now come to see it that way, under new influence. There is a subtle politics in legal philosophy, part of the sociology of knowledge.

But hold on. I am not being *merely* boorish. To say there is a politics is not to say that is all there is or that it is the most important. But it is there, not necessarily conscious. It is one of the dimensions one ought to consider when putting forth a framework of analysis. Nothing radically novel is going to be accepted as either logical or true, or even useful, for instance, unless conceivably it comes from the Mount, and even then it will take much preaching.

In short, at least when it comes to human rights, logic or truth is not enough or even all that relevant. *Persuasion* is the key. Apparently to say to a philosophically oriented theorist that his analysis amounts to rhetoric is to suggest it is somehow wanting, maybe worse than saying it is not really rational. What it means is that he is doing something in public he ought to confine to the study. Having shaped his goals and society's, then he should seek a rhetoric of transcendent principles and claim they sprang from Pure Reason, or from a utilitarian computer.

This *is* the way of it. I happen to agree that at least philosophical analysis as compared to legitimate—not mere—philosophical rhetoric very much requires a special verbal and communications consciousness. I tend to believe it would be particularly fruitful to spread the analysis out on paper because it also involves an actual exploration into social (or legal process) dynamics. But apparently when one "plays with word games," he should close the door. That is what Hart did before he told us there was more than one kind of legal rule. Given his philosophical context, he must know how variously that word "rule" gets used. But to start out the analysis that way would outrage too many people. So, "there *are* several kinds of legal rules." (But really there are more than that.)

It would seem to me that most of the contributors to this conference must have at some time asked themselves something like, (for instance), "What if I use 'right' this way, what happens?" Or, "If I use 'right' in this fashion, is there some correlative way I must use 'duty' "? Some of the contributors seemed to spell some of this thinking out on paper, for instance, Feinberg, Winslade, and Blackstone. But in their public demonstrations, having left out the private explorations, the legitimate philosophical explorations, they mix together analysis with rhetoric. I believe someone has elegantly called this the technique of rational justification.

They are caught in a bind. If one engages in *pure* analysis, he is counted a bore who is not doing anything. You are supposed to take an ethical position, even when you purport to be analyzing or empiricizing. At least your ethics will be assessed, as it legitimately may be in these contributions, if it is only wrapped in analytical cellophane. They try to say they are not moralizing, but a shrewd moralist, like Jerome Hall, will not let them. Of course he has been committed to a lego-moralistic rhetoric for some time. He is sufficiently word conscious to take pot shots at partial efforts, but not sufficiently so to understand what the implications of depth grammar may be, as to why one would be interested in verbs over nouns, for instance, or to see that some effort to rank duty above right could be linguistically explored rather than left at the intuitive level of feeling.

Not that feelings are irrelevant even in philosophy. Why not just admit them and go on from there? Still, Hall's sophisticated arrows may be preferable to a pat on the head from an avowed "instrumentalist" who knows "where it all is" but declines to spell it out. Yet the interesting thing about the "here and now" approach, or the declaration of "manifesto rights," or the juxtaposition à la the absurd, as in the picture of a philosopher telling an almost totally deprived person what his rights are, of all of that, is that it is so obviously and terribly relevant. And yet—it may just be, at least it can be, an escape from the potentials of philosophy.

Just when is one doing philosophy or jurisprudence or political philosophy? Or does it matter? I take it that any one of us could, for instance, try to emulate Noam Chomsky, and write, speak, and in other ways act to promote a radical political view. When *he* does that, is there any connection to his far reaching linguistic theory? I take it his status adds to his influence, although his influence may come to detract from his status (maybe Spock was also wrong about babies?). But I do not think he has to be an ideological activist in his linguistic explorations, although he is certainly a linguistic activist. Well, there is that bind again. Is it that if you are going to do philosophy, or theory, you have got to be doing *something*, something also besides philosophy? What we need is a jobs analysis, or a better awareness of the various roles of theorists, of the hats we may wear—and where.

Beyond the Words

Linguistic analysis can be useful even beyond clarification and discovery, say as a technique for digging out buried social evaluations. But why not go even deeper and to farther horizons? Actually the label "ordinary language analysis" is now a defensive epithet used by the opponents of one sort of philosophy, as academically "semantics" can be a dirty word. What can and ought to be involved is a word consciousness which is not quite aptly reflected in the best dictionary nor caught in the parrot-like question, "What do you mean?"

A better characterization might be "communications analysis." This approach has some relation but does not confine itself to "Oxford philosophy" and semantics. Dictionaries are a tool, but comparative anthologies of linguistic conventions, idioms, and jargons at all levels of communication would be better. Grammar books are relevant, but studies of depth grammar are more subtly significant.

Before the later Wittgenstein and J. L. Austin in England, there was in this country Korzybski and then, among others, Benjamin Lee Whorf to explore the ways that language forms provide maps or spectacles to help focus in certain ways for seeing, knowing, and evaluating, surely matters of theoretical import. What some critics disdain as linguistic analysis does only reveal the top of invisible molds, at least when restrained as it has been. Chomsky sees deeper rules operating as did Wittgenstein (and see Levi—Strauss). There are those who criticize Wittgenstein for dropping off into "mysticism"—he *is* mind-blowing—and they might regard the psychological model of "the unconscious" as similarly "irrational." Chomsky opts for a heightened rationalism back of his exploration of depth grammar, starting from a premise that man is born with a capacity to use language. See what happens if you put Chomsky and Whorf together, re-enforcing some notion perhaps of innate categories of perception and knowing and evaluating. Much of this sort of thing is there in Wittgenstein, but in the lesser dogma of a Socratic monologue—a way of exploring the "secrets" covered in linguistic conventions.

But Wittgenstein offers something more of importance that detractors somehow seem to miss, an appreciation of the metaphoric growth of word references and connotations. (Why do we ignore the function of metaphors?) Rational analysis requires not dogma—that is the proper way at times of legal and other discourses, of propaganda, and as well of moral discourse—it needs keen sensitivity to the history and contemporary facts of communication dynamics: such as (1) a realization that precision comes about through some dictatorial or arbitrary power to stipulate or control symbols, or if democratic conditions exist, only through a preliminary charting midst the pervasive ambiguities of all words, or better, word-forms ("Right" is a word-form that has spawned numerous variations on whatever may have been the main theme); (2) an appreciation that communication never takes place in the abstract, no matter how abstract the words may seem, but in some specific here and now communication setting.

In this respect especially pertinent are the observations of Blackstone regarding "rights-talk" and of Hall regarding tridimensional models. Communication takes place interpersonally and on levels (dimensional). So groups and areas of talk (sub-languages?) develop, not only rights-talk, but law-talk, morality-talk, and so on; i.e. discourses, ways of characterizing, jargons, disciplines, all susceptible to Whorfian insights. Thus, a lawyer may see things differently as he talks of rights than does a moral philosopher, if the lawyer is inhibited by being taught to "think like a lawyer." Yet he may unconsciously learn to moralize through law-talk.

The levels of communication are not so obvious. But an abstract discussion of human rights, for instance, is not just a proof or analysis or whatever, any more than a statement of a legal rule in a lawyer's argument is just a statement of a rule. His form is dogmatic, but we know it to be argumentative. Blackstone's assertion that one's right to respect is a part of being human is indeed eloquent, and it does more than analyze or draw a philosophical road map, if that is the sort of thing it does at all. It sells, it moves—if one feels like buying or moving.

It does also lead to a way of seeing human beings. Whether this is the way we are destined to see, who can say for sure, except it is compelling. Isn't it?

Analysis and Persuasion

Conceptualism is not dead. If it were the rules of rhetoric games would be much different, but it does get in the way of other theory jobs. Awareness that language forms, or surface grammar, are in a sense ambiguous, allows one to realize that "to have rights" is a different sort of having from "to have skin and bones." But a bit deeper down in the grammar (syntax) we see that what we have are "rights-to" and "rights-against." Theorists may want to argue whether it is really one or the other, because it makes a difference to their framework of analysis, their complex models, to the conventions they would like to establish, so obvious with Hohfeld but discoverable in perhaps all legal or moral theory concerned with rights and "other things." Very likely the debaters know full well they are not arguing about tangibles on the object level but relationships of a legal or social kind.

However, when we see it said that claims vary in degree and rights do not, is it as clear as it should be that the descriptive *level* of communication is deserted even if the descriptive *mode* is not? Yet some conventions allow degrees of rights, say a qualified right (one debater might want to say "you mean privilege") as others allow us to speak of questionable facts. Still other conventions speak of facts absolutely. You cannot change a fact, although you can alter a statement of fact *about* something, but the something itself is not a fact even though we may say it is a fact that there is such a something. These latter statements may be confusing because the communicative focus is purposefully changed to cloud the usual deceptive transparency of words. Deeper grammar is exposed, but usually it is unconsciously understood. To solve such seeming conundrums gives insights into word-thing, word-situation, and word-relationship involvements.

There are many words like "fact," "right," "duty," and "rule," which allow—and encourage—expression of fixed relationships or evaluations. No proof there that any appreciated relationship, whether between people, or between words on the one hand and things, people, or relationships on the other, is actually *in nature* fixed, or that it is even "out there" in nature. It only seems so to one who is used to seeing nature through syntax. Nature does not come wrapped with words. Thus, such distinctions as fact-value, is-ought, and law-morality often are conventional distinctions. What we may do with such words as "right" or such syntax as is-ought is to fix a relationship, to freeze it, by putting it under the most convincing and "appropriate" headings. To ignore that only convention is operating, whether that of the "ordinary man" or of a sophisticated discipline, is to put on analytical blinders. This is not to say that some other philosophical or theoretical tasks do not justify blindering.

The analyst is put in a bind by the importance of such words as "right" and "duty" because of their rhetorical strength. Persuasion thrives on ambiguity and metaphor. Rational analysis calls for a skill in separating, for instance, fact from fancy, and is from ought, realizing that an is-ought characterization may itself be fanciful, wistful, or even arbitrary. So hard to *know*.

We must deal with key words such as "right" because they have everyday involvements and perhaps mystical references too. It might seem preferable to set up the relationships in some set of logical symbols and relationships, to avoid emotion and ambiguity. But logical symbols lack in rhetorical strength and metaphorical growth potential. Their communicative versatility is limited. Most moral philosophers will opt for humanitarian discourse and analysts are stuck with it all. Similar problems exist in the interplay of lawyer discourse and theoretical analysis. Besides, it is in the actual involvement with the dynamics of communication that human truths will out, if anywhere.

Now suppose we debate whether rights are really based on or grow out of claims of a certain sort. Why argue about it? Well, for one thing, the word "claim" does not have the rhetorical strength of "right." Perhaps that is why Professor Hall would move to relate rights to duties, since he regards "duty" as even a stronger term. There is indeed a communicative relationship which demonstrates such a stronger link: I may not be convinced to act in a certain way toward you by being told that you have a right to my performance, even if I believe it, but if I am convinced of my duty to perform, what choice have I? I am not so likely to be convinced by hearing that you have a valid or merely a prima facie claim to my performance, or that you need it, or that you need it and *someone* ought to perform.

On the other hand, to tie rights to claims is to invigorate "claims" with the rhetorical strength of "rights." If that door could be opened, at first to the very strongest claims, then the weak might indeed ultimately inherit the earth by claiming it.

Such techniques are basic in persuasion, even if not fully appreciated. The legal realists, for further instance, very much weakened, the persuasive strength of the word "rules," for mostly humanitarian reasons, and to activate the courts. H. L. A. Hart and his followers would prefer legislative activism, if any, so they would recoup the loss in the strength of "rules." Most sophisticated theorists in this country have less respect for "rules," but "principles" come in to absorb some of the loss, even if "neutral principles" do not make it all the way to the top of the hierarchy of controlling verbalisms. "Principle" is not as strong in the control sense as "rule" but it has wider range. If one is committed to a principle, it is just as binding as a rule, but if one is principled, he is perhaps virtuous and just in his actions, not necessarily legalistic. A court which deals in principles balances rather than computes. But according to Dworkin, legal principles are not something to be legislated nor are they court made, at any instant of decision. Beautiful. We know that certain rights are supported by rules, but they are also discoverable in the *interplay* of principles. Intriguing.

This sort of persuasive leadership technique is truly admirable—and inevitable. Still, moral leadership is not the only philosophical job. It falls to some to feel the pulse of society and to articulate the beat, perhaps to remove intellectual obstacles by novel formulations, or subtle reformulations. These jobs can be done in the name of analysis, but exploratory analysis can serve other functions. Communications analysis could even, among other things, conceivably improve understanding if not vision.

I am not saying one should always avoid ethical commitment. It may not even be possible. But analysis can help reveal the hidden commitments.

Note: This exhibit was presented to a conference on Human Rights at the American section of the International Association for Philosophy of Law and Social Philosophy held by Rutgers University, New Brunswick, February 5-7, 1970. But it was written also for inclusion in this book. Reprinted from *Human Rights* (Pollack ed. 1971). Permission granted by Jay Stewart Publications, Inc.

DIRECTORY

Summaries, Previews, Guides, Elaborations

Goals of this Supplement

Some supplemental statements keyed to each chapter. Sensitivity participant should browse through all of these before starting Chapter I, at least those remarks explicitly directed at his level of participation. Those remarks directed respectively at the legal theory level and the communication theory level are not meant to be summarizing so much as suggestive. There is no doubt in the world that the true insights for legal theory simply cannot be summarized. Forgive the undeserved comparison, but the insights of Wittgenstein cannot be summarized. Nor of Korzybski. Nor McLuhan. Nor J. L. Austin. Nor Sensitivity Training. They are the chief inspirations for the explorations entitled as chapters and those called Exhibits in the Appendix.

Why Not Write "Simply"?

Hayakawa, the best known semantics popularizer, has suggested in recent newspaper commentaries that academicians purposely write obtusely. Agreed. But *his* semantics text does not grapple with the guts of written verbal communication. I know from personal experience as a perennial student-reader of obtusities and assignor of some to students that "simplicity" is often merely relative to mood and desire and willingness to try to see things in the author's way(s). Yesterday's profundities are today's simplicities. You cannot grapple at the guts of the bodies of law, language, and communication and not expect to come up bloody!

Order of Exploring

The orderly mind will say this is ridiculous, but it really does not matter to me where one starts in these explorations. Take Chapter X, for instance. As I look it over I can hear someone saying, well this chapter really should have come first. All right, read it first. But I tell you it does not mean as a first chapter-exploration what it means as a tenth. Both the communications theorist and the legal theorist possibly should read it first because it does provide considerable theoretic support for the *previous* explorations (and the Appendix exhibits). I started Chapter X first but finished it after the others! The others lead to it but it leads back to them. Really. Chiefly what it involves is a way of "looking at" communication, as a framework for those who feel wobbly when they get there. It is usable doctrine, but I doubt it will be used as doctrine. Its hope for value is as a visual aid to sensitivity, and aid to the senses, a vivifier of the terrain of interpretation—heuristic. Look through (E) it some time.

That E takes me to Chapter V. It happens to be my favorite (along with the Dialogues) but I could hardly put it first or last. It is meant most of all for the ordered mind, to unorder it, to help re-order it. If you get the hang of the E and use it in your own writing and talking and see where you really can properly (and heuristically) use it, you will never see communication the same way or only one way (even that way) again. Really (E).

And so (,) on.

Exploration I

Shades of Legalism: Some Problems

Sections: Prelude; Ambiguists v. Precisionists; Separations; Realists and Law's Rhetoric; Verbal Power; Beneath the Forms; Spontaneity v. Fixity; Psycholinguistic Magnets; The Neutrality Dilemma; How To Tell A Legalist . . . (. . . but not what).

Mostly at the level of theory talk, at the crossroads of legal theory and communication theory. Something of the history of use of communications analysis by legal theorists and suggestion of the some of the problems that are posed. LEGALISM defined as an attitude toward not only legal rules, but any rules, nor just rules but fixed content-position concepts and verbalisms.

A. SENSITIVITY TRAINING:

Just read for impressions. Get started on thinking of law in non-concrete, non-independent phenomenon way. Read last section on legalism with more care.

B. LEGAL THEORY ANALYSIS:

1. Legal realism and its words-and-rule-skepticism v. H. L. A. Hart and his modest application of Oxford "linguistics."
2. Disputes about reality and ambiguity of rules as having psycho-linguistic implication. So less obviously do disputes about (1) law and morality relationship(s), (2) hierarchy of rule and official authorities, and (3) possibilities of objectivity and rationality.
3. Temporary focus on what people say *re* law as rhetoric, and rhetoric as a species of behavior.
4. Power in words and of people using words.
5. Suggestion that polarity is on surface and does not grapple with psycholinguistic aspects. Partly itself a battle of rhetorics, but deeper issues.
6. Reality looks different at different levels. Words as devices for getting to different levels!

C. COMMUNICATIONS THEORY ANALYSIS:

1. Problems in legal theory and assumptions about law carry assumptions about words and language, and in turn throw light on communication generally.
2. Linguistic and communication theorists have their own debates: different ways of looking at words as rhetoric, media, symbols, analytical routing devices, maps, tools, etc. Disagreement on relationship between words and things, reality of concept of language, significance of surface grammar and other surface forms as related to depth grammar and significance of RULES of these grammars and forms. Precedent system not restricted to law.
3. Those familiar with Wittgenstein, Korzybski, J. L. Austin, Chomsky, McLuhan, etc., should recognize some indebtednesses, even more evidently later on.

Exploration II

An Aspect of Legal Rhetoric

Sections: Introduction of Rhetorical Definitions; Some Kinds of Definitions Compared; Form, Style, and Other Such Factors; Descriptive v. Emotive Words; Emotive and Affect

Terms in Law; Relating Beliefs to Attitudes—Spelling It Out: Syntactic Definitional Complexes.

Of independent significance within that study known as Rhetoric, but also a beginning workout in relationships between meaning, use, and form. Can be seen as a technique of persuasion, but also a technique of analysis and maybe counter-rhetoric. Goes beneath the surface levels of the biggest dictionaries. Focus on single words definition-in-use, but entry through surface syntax into deeper structures of doctrine and idiom. Words grow through subtle metaphoric extension.

A. SENSITIVITY:

1. A good way to words consciousness. Look around in reading, listening, and writing and talking for loaded words. Look at clear descriptors, clear emotors, then at seeming descriptors as emotors also and see how dogmatic assertion, as-if-fact, helps. Definitional technique more complex, but worth watching for and (1) deliberate using and (2) deliberate unloading.
2. Starting an appreciation of subtle ambiguities in every word as it sits in the dictionary, in the pool of words. An important sensitivity to develop, partly to gain tolerance and appreciation.
3. Seems a purely skeptical emphasis. Words consciousness *includes* such skepticism. Balance comes *later*. Ditto *re* law and assertions of and about law! Not intended as a philosophy but an available *skill*.

B. LEGAL THEORY:

1. Relates to current increase of interest in "law as rhetoric": Legal realists, especially F. S. Cohen, but later Lasswell & McDougal, Perleman, J. Stone, and in England, G. Williams—but *not* Hart, because his theory rhetoric more important in his ideology.
2. Critics of an earlier version saw this as superficial theory that law just words, maybe just a piece of radical legal realism. Hold on.
3. Analysis of chapter applicable to legal theory and to this whole book. See this as one way of looking, one view of the elephant.

C. COMMUNICATION THEORY:

1. Taking off from Charles Stevenson's theory of persuasive definitions—philosophical analysis of language of ethics. Highly significant that law language is subject to similar analysis. But it hardly stops there. Wittgenstein, J. L. Austin, *et al.*, and Korzybski did little with this, but actually related. Chapter builds on all of these views.
2. Note the emphasis is not just on rhetoric in the sense of persuasion. Criticism by Gellner (etc.) of English "linguistics" that the stress was conservative, not appreciative of creative uses of words. That door is opened here, suggesting, for elaboration later.
3. See actual relationship to Wittgenstein word-games, word-family relationship which he too actually left *open-ended*, as see elaboration of word-family of word "foreseeable."
4. Getting into depth grammar, through surface of subject-predicate and related surface syntax.
5. Consider a dictionary premised on this view. Look for core or paradigmatic etymological roots, follow precedents in different directions. (See on this, analysis of "intent" in Chapter VI).

Exploration III

Words and Communications Consciousness: Levels of Awareness

Sections: Beyond Just Talking; Who Needs It?; Multi-Dimensionality.

Mainly an exhortation, an excitation to feel the psycholinguistic multi-dimensionality of words, even those in print. The marks and sounds trigger reactions and involvements. Written form meshes psycholinguistically with spoken and with interpersonal behavior. Language is not printed anywhere! Words and word-mapping create barriers to appreciation of the real multi-dimensionality. Almost inevitably what is uttered about or in connection with anything is a choice among alternatives, even in law.

A. SENSITIVITY:

1. A cranking up.
2. Words help and/or inhibit what is perceived and felt.
3. Same event seeable in more than one way *simultaneously*, just for the talking.
4. Levels of awareness, reachable by means of and/or in spite of words. Mobility attainable.
5. Even words in print trigger multiple images, thoughts, etc. Compare split-screen, multi-media involvement.
6. Reading is not just reading, or need not be uni-dimensional.
7. Forms can be deadening. Style and Form need exploration, including mundanes of punctuation, even parentheses.
8. Suggestion: experiment with multiple characterization of single thing, act, and event—to develop flexibility, spontaneity, creativity, levels of awareness.

B. LEGAL THEORY:

1. Not just words analysis, but communications exploration. Involved in an inter-discipline.
2. The emphasis is on talking with the definite intention to imply that written forms are significant as choices among potential alternatives. Legal realists saw this for common law, but more as attack rather than instructive and inevitable mechanism in all communication.
3. Begins the exploration of perspectives, again previously under-explored. Much more later, especially Chapters VIII–X.
4. Any contemporarity "realistic" philosophy or theory must take account not only of language but dynamics of communication.

C. COMMUNICATIONS THEORY:

1. Charles Morris and others stressed need of meta-language for communications exploration. Wittgenstein and J. L. Austin, *et al.*, took a different tack, into the guts of language as it was used. Neither exclusive, but sensitized consciousness, under-rated ingredient. Korzybski stressed, but took negative attitude toward linguistic epistemology.
2. McLuhan demeans written media in favor of dramatizing

others, but it can and must be related to others. See also Hall, *et al.*, on the Silent Language of human behavior and The Hidden Dimension(s) of space, time, etc.

3. Suggesting what is stressed later, "linguistic analysis" mislabelled, also if called "mere philosophy." The term "semantics" is a semantic barrier. Etc. A new empiricism being unfolded, more balanced.

Exploration IV

From Law to Law Talk

Sections: Prelude; Words in Talking: Two Dialogue Analysis; Exploring the Uses of "Law"; Law Talk Explored; Some Further Comment on Talk Talk; Postscript Game: Is it All Just Theoretical?

The word "law," its definitions and uses partially explored, not *theoretically* but as communication. The word has a subtle influence at the level of theory—including that of Joe in the street—to structure how events and situations are perceived. This function of that word infects or relates to all law terminology, in the talk of professionals *and* laymen. Valuable to look at law talk behavior of various kinds, wherein perception, feelings, and values are influenced. The level of law talk is distinguished from that of law-theory and both from our kind of communications exploration, called talk talk. At the latter level, for instance, in law talk behavior, fact talk is better seen as law-fact talk (what the "facts are" depends upon the verbal spectacles through which seen).

Two appendix dialogues on rules and facts explored. Should read again to see what they "say" at this point.

A. SENSITIVITY:

1. Trying to overcome fixed meaning attitude. Stressing sensitivity to variations in word *use* by demonstration through deliberate exposure of rhetorical definition on the page. Sensitizing of participant to immediacy of reading experience (more in later chapters). E.g., Think not of rule and fact out there, but here and now reaction in *this* situation.
2. Indispensable to *jump* into multi-dimensional interpreta-

tion, otherwise flat appearing signals not alive in stereo. Not just intellectual but psycho-logical. Suggestion: Write a dialogue with word "law," maybe borrowing from text. Have fun with it. Play and discover.

3. Think law talk, not law. Forget LAW. Think law talker, law talking, etc.
4. We are not talking about but doing.
5. Learning to be observer, including of self-involvement, to gain skill in participant-observation even in just reading. (Much more coming)
6. Talk talk may sound wild, but *feel* at another level of involvement. Extensive workouts in next two chapters. Chapter II on rhetorical definitions a kind of talk talk, as is checking into dictionary.
7. Try out talk talk, in simple progressive steps.
8. Suggestion: Look at Basic Rules in Appendix. Compare talking *about* them (theory) with using them in a situation where you are involved in applying them, or trying to avoid them, etc. (rule talk). In the process you talk about the words in the rules and about the rules, etc. (talk talk). Explored in some depth in Chapter IX. Better yet, actually try them out.
9. The meanings of a given word (form) do change from situation to situation and certainly from level to level because while the language context may be seemingly the same (at best only similar, often quite different), the *use* is different, the communicative behavior there and then.
10. Not saying that theory talk is impractical. If you observe while participating in theory talk, about Basic Rules for instance, you will witness that the participants are doing many interesting things while seemingly only talking about the rules (which they are doing too—see Chapters VIII-X).

B. LEGAL THEORY:

1. The key to any analysis is its structuralization. All talking structuralizes, law theory often admittedly, but theory rhetoric calls for hiding that facet. (See The Right Way in Appendix) All these chapters in one way or another explore structure(s). Einstein's philosophy-theory looms important here.
2. Law theorists at one level watching, trying to describe,

evaluate, influence, alter, etc., activities on another level and also on their own. Often misleading because either they or their readers fail to take account of relative communications coordinates, goals, and perspectives. (See Chapters VIII and X).

3. Talk talk at a minimum involves a theorist using the language, *understanding it first,* of level he is observing-describing-evaluating-etc., but necessarily at talk talk level rather than closed off theory talk level.
4. For example, the word "law" necessarily gets used differently at theory level than at law talk level, and separate vocabularies with that one word develop whether or not, maybe because, worrying about definition felt futile. Not futile if actual use is first concern, rather than the proper use. Asserting or implicitly postulating "the proper use" (by just doing it) is another game.
5. The move from law to law talk may seem merely an elaboration of the legal realists gambit with regard to common-law talk. However, not a replacement but a necessary move to expanded words and communications consciousness. Not just rhetorical analysis but also situational, behavioral, and valuational. (See Chapters VIII and X) Felix Cohen, Lasswell, and McDougal, *et al.,* worked in this direction, but stopping short to move into rhetorical-persuasion game. Hart stops far short to use word-games analysis to keep law talk separate from morality talk as a socio-political theory (See Chapter V), to *structure* thought and action.

C. COMMUNICATION THEORY:

1. See Sapir-Whorf hypothesis, shared by Korzybski and other structuralists and gestaltists. Any law teacher sensitively attuned can offer clinical experience on impact of law categorizations on perception and thought, can hear the click of the concepts. Good place for research.
2. Participant-observation skill principally from anthropological and psychoanalytical heritage (Third Ear technique), but enriched by words consciousness. Suggestions of such skill at reading level novel (see Chapters IX-X), but Wittgenstein, J. L. Austin, *et al.,* were moving there.

3. Theories of the New Rhetoric (Burke, Richards, Perleman, etc.) need integrating with "new empiricism." (See comments on Chapter X). Political science judicial behaviorists (Schubert, *et al.*) failed to see empiricism in F. S. Cohen because seeming purely verbal, take fact talk of judicial opinions as something other than law talk, the latter being "just rhetoric," thus confusing perspectives, failing to see that what is rhetoric at one level of examination is from the viewpoint of the inside participant some*thing* else again. Learning to law talk *qua* lawyering can be (need not be exclusive) a way of viewing reality. (See Chapter VII further)

Exploration V

(Un)Structuring (")Words(")—Split Screens

Sections: Sensitivities for levels of (")Words(") and (")Rules("); Tolerance to Ambiguities—in Games and Metaphors—E; Coordinating Through Words; Verbal Construct-ing; Socio-Legal Structurings in Theory Talk; Law(s) and Order(s)—Authorities.

Cannot be adequately summarized or paraphrased. Exploration in(to) and through the forms of words, sentences, language, communication—and necessarily law(s). *Not to be read merely literally!* Not poetry, certainly, but not pure prose either. Forced awareness of multiple messages and levels of even the written medium. Hope for appreciation but not intolerance of ambiguity and its pervasiveness—at certain levels, not just of words, or rather lurking under the surface of word-forms, but other surface forms of language and media. Closely inter-meshed with Chapter II, back and forth, not serial, but interlocking. Chapter IX also justifies the sensitizing exploration of this chapter.

A kind of talk talk, but more accurately, write write. Some of the messages come through *only* on written level! Worth thinking about.

A. SENSITIVITY:

1. May call for a non-fretting first go round, then on to Chapter VI, then back again. A sensitizer, but may arouse re-

sentment, intolerance-of-ambiguity anxiety. An elation of liberation equally potential.

2. All writing *can* stimulate multiple levels of awareness, but often repressed, Ditto interpersonal, face-to-face. Chapter VI converts a judicial opinion into something like this chapter. Learn to delay response (Korzybski) to get other messages. Ultimately delay-time is not measurable, seems to happen all at once. (More on semantic response later, especially Chapter X)
3. Try to say "(')Rule(s)(') are ambiguous." Can be translated, as can mathematics, but misses the point of demonstration, that it can be instantaneously appreciated for its multiple, simultaneous messages. Goal is not to learn to write that way (or related ways used), although it can help to communications consciousness—possible in non-written contexts too—but appreciation of multiple messages, sort of multi-media, especially face-to-face, but also here. (You are not "reading" in a vacuum.) This chapter or even the whole book cannot permanently do it to you. Just open the door, so no harm in trying it!
4. Consider multiple messages in following: (1) A is the legal cause of B's death, (2) A is the cause of B's death. Put either in any context! Fully sensitive interpretation requires right now awareness of alternatives. More: (3) You cannot legislate morality, (4) It is a fact that A hit B, (5) This is a legal rule, (6) This is a rule, (7) This is a word, (8) Show me a rule, (9) A dog is not a fact, (10) Etc. (E), (11) (E).
5. Training aids in this chapter, illustrated and used. Not gimmicks. (1) Word games. Consciously playing games leads to sensitivity to serious, subtle games. (Spelled out for "intent" in Chapter VI.) Door opened for various words, by puns, exposure of sub-surface metaphor, fiction, and construct as well as (E) device. (2) The (E) device—use it and see—fun and (")games(")E. (E) does not just equal ambiguous unless you write (E) after ambiguous. (Spelled out in chapter 10 regarding meaning and ambiguity). (3) Hyphens. (4) Quotes. (5) Subscripts—very useful to help keep subtle ambiguities in view—do try it. (6) Parentheses. (7) Commas. (8) The use of Etc. (9) De-

velop your own. Korzybski started this sort of thing, actually exploring linguistic structure, but also as mnemonic aids.

6. Structures being explored: a single word! A sentence. Language. Verbal behavior. Communications media (written, oral, interpersonal, etc.). Levels of Talk. Structures.
7. This new consciousness promotes visualization and feeling non-inhibiting self-involved consciousness, in the sense of locating one's self in the complex. At first a-mazing, but gradually knowable. Reconditioning possible ("Brother Rat").

B. LEGAL THEORY:

1. Law talk (and rule talk, etc.) at $level_1$. Law theory at $level_2$ with respect to $level_1$. Talk talk at $level_3$ with respect to both but also inter-involved with both in ways they are not with each other.
2. View at $level_2$ ($level_1$ also) necessarily involve assumptions about workings of words, language, and comunication (silent epistemology in structures of language).
3. For example, following look different at $level_3$; whether there are legal rules, and if so, what kind(s). Relation of rules to principles. Whether law and morality separate, or how much or when. Whether statement of policy in judicial opinion is extra-legal. The degree of ambiguity in official texts and doctrine.
4. No insult to speak of $level_2$ as rhetoric: not *just* rhetoric, but still . . . $Level_2$ rhetoric has impact at $level_1$. Continuous power struggle at $level_2$ to determine The Right Way of talking at both $levels_{1\&2}$. (Partly by resisting $level_3$ analysis—admit it!)
5. Consider: Much earlier rhetoric stressing logic, precision (Holmes, Hohfeld, and now even Hart) and relevancy (how about from mechanical to computer jurisprudence). Attack by legal realists as camouflage and phony. Attack on them as amoral and overly positivistic. But rhetoric at $level_2$ much changed as result. Hart resists, for his good reasons. All are trying to influence the rhetoric of $level_1$ law talk, because that's "where it's all at."
6. Stability, validity, legal justice, social justice, all impor-

tant criteria, but others too. $Level_3$ exploration clarifies and uncovers more.

7. Important to explore interplay of law talk in official situations with the mechanisms and structures of everyday talk ("language"), including metaphoric change, constructed change, etc. Exploration of relation between (")law(") and (")language(") throws light on all debates and concerns on $level_2$.
8. $Level_3$ analysis has messages that may not be receivable by one who stays at $level_2$, reading and reacting in that fashion (E).

C. COMMUNICATION THEORY:

1. See comments under A&B, *supra.*
2. Much of language theory has been at $level_2$. Wittgenstein and Korzybski broke away, J. L. Austin and others less so. Words consciousness more prevalent in post-semantics era. Will evolve further. Legal education just beginning to show interest. Communications experts can be of considerable aid, even though *that* inter-discipline has been resisted, except by *some legal philosophers.*
3. Query which law talk explorations especially raise: anti-conceptualism important, for words consciousness, empirical pursuits, etc. But conceptualism plays significant part in influence of law talk for needed conformity (See Chapter VIII, further). Form at $level_{1\&2}$ has a seemingly needed magic, and evolution takes place under the cover. Delay to the form possible to avoid deception, etc., still to preserve the magic of symbolism. Magic at $level_3$ as well, the h.i..g...h....e....r one gets, on(in) words. Gain and/or risk? For rule command systems, not just law, but insight and discovery makes pursuit at this level necessary and indispensable. Communications experts should become interested, concerned, involved.
4. Riesman encouraged anthropologists and sociologists to research in lawyers' dens. "Fear not the esoterics of law(yer) talk." Much to be learned about language and communication in there, and culture too (the study of language is study of culture!). Two way street.
5. Other matters deserving of attention: (1) Conscious sen-

sitivity and tolerance to ambiguity: low in significant proportion of professionals, and certainly of laymen. Ideological hook-up, but curable short of pathology. (2) Relation(s) between written media and others, e.g. significance for rule attitudes at both $level_{1\&2}$. Ordinary prose not adequate because phenomenon gets lost between the media. Gets lost in meta-language approach altogether because *meta-language is a different rhetoric.* A major dimension of $Exploration_5$ and others, the more as we go along.
6. Etc.

Exploration VI

(Un)Loaded Concepts—It's All in the Family

Sections: Pre-view from the Bridge; Word-Magic Words; Legalism Writ Large; Intent in Law Talk; Intent in Lay Talk; Intent in Garratt; Conclusion

Conceptualism is legalism writ large, based on assumed rules of word *meaning.* Concepts tend to be overburdened. Unloading reveals a family of less burdened workers under the cover form of the word. Here, piercing intent concept demonstrates one significant technique that reveals important mechanisms of language, showing how legal terminology tied to mother tongue. Seeing how intent works is especially important for over-all communications exploration (see further Chapter X and Exhibit V).

Here the process of interpretation laid out on paper. Usually invisible (see further Chapter IX). Thus "straight" prose of judicial opinion (or other texts) becomes split-screen, like last chapter. Delayed response proven important.

A. SENSITIVITY TRAINING:

1. Attack on word-magic and conceptualism, chief cause *or* excuse for legalism, and so, either curable or exposable, respectively.
2. Important to read and wrestle with assignment of Garratt, before textual analysis.
3. Try to get feel for the inner structures of the *vocabulary of a single word.* Some begun are battery, trespasser,

cause, title, ball, and especially intent. Goal: to have the unapparent structure come to leap out from page or during conversation.

4. Not easy; hard work; psycho-linguistic *defenses*. But short term goals readily attainable, at least to delay response and consider alternative "meanings."
5. Not just chaos in concept shattering—if you do not look just for *meaning* (here of "intent"), but also for doing with the word (spelled out for all interpretation in Chapter X). Tricky at first because it is a different kind of certainty!
6. Even in a dialogue, more than one channel to observe! In reading as well!! Especially in judicial opinion (statute, newspaper editorial, this three-books). In Garratt, court writing not just to you, me, lawyers, but *especially to trial judge!* Imagine you are observing that dialogue. Compare a trial attorney talking to a jury by questioning a witness, a husband "getting at his wife" by scolding his offspring.
7. Try out some home-made efforts, e.g. consider: (1) He hit her with his fist. (2) He hit her with a fish. (3) The car hit the tree. (4) He hit me with a remarkable idea. (5) She hit the audience with her performance. (6) She was the hit of the show. Each meaning of "hit" leads easily into the next. Number six clearly different from one. But do you see difference between one and two, feel it? That's "where it's at!" That's where it begins, and actually much sooner!

B. LEGAL THEORY:

1. Compare Garratt analysis with Law school Socratic case method. Related but not the same. There a less conscious sensitivity emerges through battle. Law teacher would not lay out range of meanings of intent to show what was done, because he is not *that* consciously sensitive to the interplay. Consider the possibility of Socratic monologue (done beautifully by Wittgenstein and J. L. Austin).
2. Legal educators overcome "Well, what is the law in that case?" by putting student in advocate's role and/or engaging in *argument*, which helps him to see the court's use of word(s) is not *necessarily* the "right" one, or only one. But student should additionally be taught other roles (see

Chapters VIII & X), including skills of law talk in various situations, to see how *every* communicator adopts multiple roles, sometimes simultaneously (Chapters VIII & X).

3. Related to the so-called functional analysis of Oliphant, Green, Llewellyn, F. S. Cohen, *et al.*, but not limited to looking at judicial usages and doings. Level$_2$ talk (e.g. legal theory) itself needs to be explored in some such fashion if there is truly interest in being other than purely rhetorical.
4. Law-fact dialectic explored. Still a sacred cow. Why?
5. Debate about the significance of rules, principles, etc., and whether or not they are ambiguous, how much or what kind of discretion there is, etc., is staying too much at level$_2$. The insights come from communications exploration at what is called here level$_3$ (talk talk).
6. Speaking at level$_2$, words, phrases, rules, doctrines, principles, etc., are abstractly indeterminate. There is no linguistic reality in denying this, but in admitting it comes the opportunity of piercing through it at the abstract level of statutes, rules, etc., and getting down to finding a different kind of precision in the doings at the level of *whole* pieces of verbal behavior in the full context of particular communication situations. How generalities (concepts) and specifics relate or are related is to be found *there*, not in level$_2$ theorizing.

C. COMMUNICATION THEORY:

1. Chomsky rightly marvels at and relies upon human capacity to spontaneously understand a combination of words he has never received before—true of almost all verbal communication. He opts for deep structure mechanisms built into human (a la Kant, Descartes), Sounds anti-Whorfian. Compare Roger Brown who in effect argues for a pigeonholing capacity. Analysis of Garratt suggests deep structure *qua* Chomsky does bring a surface *recognition*, because it seems familiar (i.e. regarding the intent of the boy defendant—how deeply is it understood right here on this page?) but not a deeper understanding at all. The experts missed out on Garratt, for instance. This same sort of thing is constantly going on in everyday conver-

sation—recognition for understanding, even though fantastic subtleties are at other times understood. It is not either Chomsky or Whorf! Both.

2. To speak of unloading of conceptuals, rather than merely of emotives, is novel, but word-forms do get over-loaded. Such overloading cannot be prohibited, although it can be derided (As in Korzybski, Ayer, etc.). But sensitization to conceptuals might be best, thus preserving what they are good for.
3. Surely it is misleading to call this sort of exploration merely semantics, or mere linguistic analysis, or merely boring, or tedious, or *merely* anything.
4. Reveals evolutionary process in word-concept growth common to even the esoterics of law-usage. Stare decisis in language process, in the laws of language, as in the other laws that intermix with them.

Exploration VII

(")Fact(s)(")

Sections: Meaningful Interlude: All Together; From Thing Words to Something Words and Back Again; Fact Rankings; Hypothetical Facts (and Rules); Frozen Facts; "Fact" Functions.

Communications exploration of (")fact(s)(") and more subtly of fact-form statements gives insight(s) into interplay of verbal and nonverbal levels of experience and among media of communication. (")Fact(s)(") the open end of rules. "Fact(s)" not merely ambiguous, sitting at one of highest orders of abstract indeterminacy. Facts are verbal, decisional, interpretative *products.* (Juries "find" facts.) Facts are the product of communication dynamics, *functions of the communication situation at hand.* (Especially significant in closed communication situations like jury deliberations.)

In argumentation and reporting alike, dynamics of comunication readily by-passed by mere assertion or statement of hypothetical facts.

Unloading of fact-conceptualism among the most difficult because it is one of the most overburdened, but also inextricably tied up with one's contact with his environment—his world (view) and at the same time, inter-involved with learning (to use) language and vocabularies: to noun, to verb, to adjectivize, to name, etc. Also the way(s) he categorizes. "Fact" operates at *all* orders of abstractness and levels of generality. Operates at a geometric progression of generality because used to collect external, nonverbal experience, and simultaneously to categorize categories.

See further on (")fact(s)("), Chapters IV, VI & IX and Exhibits II & V.

A. SENSITIVITY TRAINING:

1. By now, should readily see what to do with question "What is a fact?" How about, "What does 'fact' mean?" What can be done with "fact?"
2. Need to engage in communications dynamics where some happening, event, etc., being seriously discussed and/or debated, and try to determine why one person favors a certain CHARACTERIZATION over another.
3. Watch and listen for "fact(s)," and be surprised at prevalency and variety of uses.
4. More difficult, but important for law talk and rule talk sensitivity, how are facts and rules dynamicized?

B. LEGAL THEORY:

1. Do legal theorists worry less about facts than one might expect because of reliance on procedures for "fact-finding"? Also on hypothetical and authorities?
2. Distinguish between "hot facts," say those developing in lawyer-client interview, or those during trial before and even during jury deliberations, those hot facts and "cold facts," say those in appellate report or in commentaries, or in hypothetical arguments especially. Very hard to catch hold of by means of written medium of expression. It lies in the interplay of media! (I tried the thought out on Oxford philosopher X, who thought I was accusing X of lying!)
3. If one would take a close look at the communications dy-

namics reflected in an appellate court's evaluation of evidence, say in a negligence case, where the court is determining if the evidence supports the verdict, he gets an excellent opportunity to see the law-fact dialectic at work. Thus see Garratt opinion, and see intent as a term of everyday fact talk, interplaying with its use as a law-fact term and a "pure" law term. And of course the terms "law" (question) and "fact" (question) get involved in allocation of decisional power among the judges and the jury.

4. As significant as the debates about the law-morality dichotomy, the law-fact dichotomy is at least as important. Yet, few besides Jerome Frank have really worried it.
5. Much concern over the is vs. the ought of law. How about a fact assertion as an ought? (See Chapter VIII.)

C. COMMUNICATION THEORY:

1. Think of this: Law(talk) gives lawyers control over facts that come into their dens!
   Or this: Lawyers are expert at translating your facts into their facts. Or this: Sociologists are busy trying to take over certain norm-setting rhetorics by disputing on the *fact* level, and by demeaning the validity of law rhetoric, etc. It *is* a level of rhetoric where LAW(yering) is most vulnerable!
2. Let him who thinks that words are not of equal importance (if not greater) with any other communicative variable consider dealing with facts without words.
3. Korzybski's formulations regarding multiordinality especially significant regarding the word "fact." And of course his structuring of the relationship between the nonverbal level and the verbal levels in terms of the "process of abstraction," and each *order* of verbalism as related to the next.
4. As I think of trying to draw a chart or make a table to comprehend the complexity of just the fact concept, it is at this moment insurmountable. It would have to be done in at least three dimensions, better four, and then . . . .!
5. Remember, I am not suggesting that "fact" is infinitely ambiguous, vague, etc., for it is often situationally determinant, in a functional behavioral sense. And see the Fact

dialogue, Exhibit 2, Appendix again. But some people will still think the dialogue is seriously asking the question whether a fact can be seen in a purely metaphysical sense, whether facts exist, and that sort of thing. This is an interesting question at that level, but it is much more significant at the psycho-linguistic level of consideration. It is a significant point to make, made by Wittgenstein, and suggested in the first page of the chapter, that one cannot get linguistic contact with things outside his skin unless he works within the phylo-linguistic heritage, and within his own vocabularies, because contra to Korzybski, psycho-linguistically, words are *not* separate from things. (cf. Whorf and cf. both with Chomsky)

Exploration VIII

Sections: Prelude; (Un)Muddled Perspectives; Law(yers)' Perspectives; Law(yer) Talk as Camouflage; Doing Things with Words; Doing Things with Laws.

Exploration of law talk in UNOFFICIAL settings.

Of key importance is consideration of the role(s) and perspective(s) of the participants in a given communication transaction, *inter alia,* as a basis for drawing appropriate IMPLICATIONS, the most overlooked dimension(s) of law communications. We pay considerable attention to lawyers' perspective(s), partly as a basis for comparison with other perspectives. The illustrations include reference to murder, breach of contract, Chicago Seven trial, Garratt case, registration of foreign corporations to do business, rights and duties, breaking of law, law-and-order, ownership of property, sanctuaries of family or other social situations including universities, and a state loyalty oath.

Information transmission is significant but far from sole function of communication. Rarely (*if ever*) restricted to that function. Dependent upon implications drawn or drawable by receiver; e.g. (1) as to what sender is doing in sending information (2) what concern to receiver (3) etc. (See Table, end of Chapter VIII.)

Law assertions similarly analyzable. In addition to questions of reliability and credibility (are the facts true, is sender believable; with law assertion, is it valid, etc.) but also other sorts of IMPLICATIONS especially associated with this kind of assertion: e.g. (1) what will be consequences for receiver (or someone). (2) what attitudes of sender implicit: ought to obey, must obey, . . . censure, etc. (See Chart #8.)

If necessary, chapter analysis more than justifies focus on law TALK rather than merely LAW.

A. SENSITIVITY TRAINING:

1. Drawing of implications from any assertion is in some ways a familiar game, going all the way into Freudian motivational depths. We are not going so deeply, because closer to the surface levels are very much under-explored and sensitivity to implications regarding law talk is not generally high.
2. While the semantic emphasis on "What does he mean?" and "How does he know" are as important as ever, additionally we are looking for "What is going on *here*?" (Whether law talk or not.)
3. Goal, to overcome conceptualism-like fascination with this sort of talk: (1) The law is . . . (thus and so) . . . (2) He broke the law . . . . (3) He owns the property. (4) He breached his contract. (5) He has a legal right . . . (to do so and so) . . . . (More in Chapters IX & X.)
4. In short, a law assertion should always be considered to be followed by (E).
5. This is not a subversive approach, not anti-law-and-order, just good communication.
6. What is explored applies to any rule or principle talk. Good to practice observation of non-law rule talk. The difficulty with exploring law talk is knowing what questions to ask, but the chapter is broadly suggestive. The big recommendation is not to be too easily "snowed," but remember "clubs is trumps!" (Hobbes).

B. LEGAL THEORY:

1. Unofficial law talk the most underexplored aspect of legal process.
2. Legal realists opened this door. Their view actually has greatest significance for unofficial law talk, starting with commentaries on THE LAW.

3. They were not sufficiently multi-dimensional for failure to take account of role, perspective, communicative tasks, goals, etc.
4. Legal theory ($Level_2$) into is-ought, normative ambiguity, Northrop's beautiful "The Complexity of Legal and Ethical Experience," values-in-law, law and morality, law and policy, etc., opens the door further, but again the rhetorical axe of this or that theorist usually gets swinging *long before the communications levels are fully explored.*
5. Particular explorations of this chapter increasingly significant in today's pendulum swing toward so-called clinical education. Not only immensely practical but filled with matters very much in need of $level_2$ and naturally $level_3$ analysis (i.e., communications exploration). E.g. consider ethical responsibilities in this or that piece of lawyer talk, far beyond the Canons.
6. Implications for a piece of law talk vary depending upon whether utterer in role of for instance, historian, prophet, advocate (litigational, reform, or what?), decision-maker, interpreter, observer, counselor, interviewer, etc. The IMPLICATIONS can, usually do vary, as well as the criteria of validity, appropriateness, and reliability. Perhaps most important for legal theory of yore is exploration of the implications of law talk and law theory talk of the CRITIC. That was F. S. Cohen's chief concern.
7. Validity remains an important but not exclusive criteria under even Hartian analysis. But even validity should not be measured in two values of yes or no. Rather, as we realize with facts, it is probabilistically measured. Lawyers, then, become risk-assessors and risk-takers. "Moral" questions arise as to when he is "justified" in advising only regarding law risks, and when even that. This is not the bad-man view of Holmes, because that was most unbalanced, even though an important early perception.
8. Compare decision-making theory and situation ethics. These are related concerns, but hardly congruent.
9. Of course there is interplay with sociological and anthropological theories and data and techniques, and rich possibilities for that kind of research enriched by communications-research techniques.
10. Consider this workout for a jurisprudence class, concern-

ing, if you will, the epistemological aspects of *knowing* law. Consider first how one knows what he sees, etc. (Still worthwhile classroom philosophy.) Compare various mechanisms of verifying fact assertions, comparing litigational techniques with those in other parts of legal process, e.g. legislative, administrative, etc., but also those in class, lawyer's office, the home, newspaper reporters, readers, etc. Perform a tort and ask how that is *known*, whether it really is a tort, maybe because of teacher's privilege, etc. Give a hypothetical fact situation with easy legal solution. How is that known, how is *it* verified, etc. What is one doing in making such a legal analysis in the first place, say in a torts class and right here in this jurisprudence class. Consider legal analyses made in a lawyer's office coming out of interview with client (see the chapter generally for further ideas in this connection, being sure not to forget moral overtones, asking whether that sort of thing has anything to do with *knowing* law in that situation). Be sure to come back to the here and now of the classroom and ask how *valid* conclusions can be drawn about what is going on in the hypothetical lawyer's office. Etc.

11. A very interesting example of the possibilities of the union of theory and practicality. I cannot imagine a more practical exploration and yet one proving the importance of theory, and of course communication theory.

C. COMMUNICATIONS THEORY:

1. See earlier portions of this commentary to Chapter VIII.
2. Easier to see how IMPLICATIONS analysis is part of communications analysis generally when dealing with face-to-face, interpersonal communication transactions than it is in reading situations.
3. No doubt some readers will not even yet have seen the implications of my question back in Chapter IV regarding what I was doing, the use I was making of a definition of law (see 1.4 in section of Exploring the Uses of "Law"), right there "on the page," i.e. in the communication transaction with the reader. That jump *has* to be made to appreciate the full ramifications of Chapters IX and X.
4. Somehow considering IMPLICATIONS as *part of* the com-

munication being read seems something other than linguistic. It is, but any linguistic consideration is too. Thus, checking out a word in a dictionary is looking to see what implication is appropriate as to its specific sense or use.

5. This is all associated with the bugaboo of meaning, as being *in* words, and a word having *a* meaning in a specific context. But words are not the only context in which words appear, even *in the reading situation!* Of course meaning had to come early in the history of communication theory and now it has gone these further steps. There need not be any de-meaning of the printed word. It seems to me very possible that this frontier of exploration will bring in insights to be fed back into print-communication that will geometrically enrich it. In academia what obstructs is the compulsion within each discipline of its own forms, styles, and (pecking) orders. If the youth culture would only continue its call for relevancy, knock out the violence, and check its own notions of relevancy, these barriers could fall. It could be a fantastic (r)evolution.
6. If it seems some insights of significance come out of this book(s)' explorations, I cannot imagine what might come of some sort of related explorations of each discipline, field of knowledge, and so on. *Wittgenstein (et al.) was exploring philosophy talk.* He could not help ramify far, far beyond the "doing of philosophy." There is only one Wittgenstein, but the analysis of the doing of psychoanalysis has thrown lights across us all (Consider Reik, Listening With The Third Ear), and while not spelled out pretty obviously pervades these present explorations. I suppose I am suggesting that we are considering not merely an inter-discipline but a supra or super discipline!
7. Charles Morris in Signs, Language, and Behavior was attempting to set up such a super-supra discipline for the behavioral sciences. There is no doubt of the significance of his work. Of course it was mainly at level$_2$ of communication theory *about* communication. The next step is to get in to grapple with the guts of communication in ways which his theory does not encourage but which can certainly be translated into it. (Harold Lasswell has spoken of his heavy reliance on the Morris framework. No further

comment necessary. And in legal theory, his teamwork exploration with Myres McDougal has been monumental—in turn turning things around for this explorer and many others.)

8. J. L. Austin's framework in his little treasury on How To Do Things With Words taken together with his genius in other explorations (see, for instance his Philosophical Papers) is what guides us in this particular chapter as well as Chapter X (but he stopped short of IMPLICATIONS analysis). Compare Chapter IX where the especial influence is Wittgenstein. Those who think one all embracing theory must guide the exploration do not see at all where Wittgenstein was (going). It's in the form(s) of his expression, thinking on paper, exploring (with) (in) the (forms of) words.
9. There is much concern among legal theorists with *values*. Along with this quite understandable emphasis goes a negative attitude toward *analysis*. Analytical theory has not been particularly "in." Of course there is a similar distaste for analysis among some philosophers who have antagonism for the "linguistic analysts." Analysis is thought to be sterile, all that poking around in dingy little corners, when there is so much to be done to change the world, when more data are needed, and ways and means of curing the world's ills, more action and less words certainly, and of course that puts words about words at the lowest level. (E)
10. Well, I have been trying to show here that analysis is inescapable, crypto-analysis grounding every assertion, every articulation, etc. The very use(s) of that word "value(s)" is a case in point. What is called values on the $level_2$ of legal theory (the word is rarely used in law talk at $level_1$!) is some-thing else again at $level_1$ and of course at $level_3$ (communications analysis). (See this chapter and further Chapter X)
11. Of course there is lots wrong with the world and its law(s), and a mere assertion of law must not be allowed to be its own proof and criterion. Lack of sensitivity to that very dimension is one of the big things that are wrong and more generally, it is certainly demonstrable that there are many, many communications gaps around. Not that

talking about communication is going to cure many social ills. But something else again is involved in taking that leap into and then through the jungle (Chapter III). Call it what we may, a deeper sensitivity or, a new consciousness, communications analysis or exploration within, in the guts of communications situations, not only may promote the participants' behavior toward a mutuality of *values* ($level_2$), a "Well, let's do this, then." O.K. ($level_1$) resolution. (Negotiation enriched by built-in mediational techniques!) Each such exploration is a learning experience on the way to the ideal of such mutuality of communications consciousness that the analytical or exploring apparatus is no longer needed! ! ! Certainly there is some considerable value(s) in there.

12. Of course studies of small group behavior and group encounter, sensitivity-training theory, etc., of significance behind this chapter. Those studies and experiences underplay words consciousness. Next two chapters develop further.

Exploration IX

Sections: Prelude; Explorations (of the process of interpretation).

Stress on interpretation of written verbalism but ramifying beyond, showing how interpretation dependent not only upon reading but also sensitivity to words generally, and to interpersonal dynamics of communication. Lack of feedback allows and requires closer attention to psycho-linguistics, including drawing of IMPLICATIONS. Thus important to distinguish process of interpretation from the rhetoric of interpretation. Seeming translation from text to supposedly equivalent words hides the dynamics of interpretation (often being interpretative-rhetorical definitions), as do hypothetical facts not only hide the dynamics of fact production but also of interpretation. Ditto on naming the issues as hiding choice of focus or of weapons.

Communications are of many other kinds in addition to transmission of information, so that query on meaning often a phony issue or a bugaboo, as is plea of or denial of ambiguity.

Interpreter as a sort of participant-observer operating in his own situational context and attempting to replicate those communicatively surrounding and/or relevant to the text.

A. SENSITIVITY TRAINING:

1. Be sure to look over Basic Rules, Exhibit III.
2. Follow along closely and try to answer each question before going on, and introspect, to see what happens in the here-and-now *dynamics of interpreting.*
3. Basic Rules exploration can only tell *about* that sort of experience and cannot give it to you. Fascinating to witness, to be involved and witness, and to see what other participants are DOING in the name of interpreting or applying. (You too if something is at stake.)
4. Play some interpretation games, such that you do an interpretation, and then interact with someone(s), playing different roles, you as the superior in one situation, then reverse, and again as attorney advising, etc. But keep track of what happens between you—tape or video recorder, but at least notes or an observer (you?)—*and* inside your head(s). It's *all* in the act(ing)!
5. Going along on the exploration of the chapter and if possible on the above sort will make the suggestions of the next chapter most meaningful. (E)

B. LEGAL THEORY:

1. Truly significant that certain theorists purport to be experts on interpretation without very much consideration of the nature of the processes, not only jurisprude-types but experts on statutory, contract, and other kinds of areas.
2. Understanding the process of interpretation is of key significance to legal theory because all issues include its nature and problems, even if other matters are additionally also relevant. Here especially is it important to distinguish between $level_2$ theory talk and $level_1$ text talk. Those who write about statutory interpretation and such are mostly on $level_2$.
3. Now of course at what I have called $level_1$ there are further levels of distinction. There is a certain amount of talk-talk ($level_3$) that goes on in any interpretation dynamics, the

guts of law talk, text talk, etc; but talking in terms of meaning, intent, and purpose is not necessarily at the guts of talk talk potential, although it takes place during the dynamics of interpretation and also appears in the rhetoric of interpretation.

4. To see that, we have to get into the meaning and uses of (")meaning(s)("), next chapter (and of course previous chapters).
5. We have already seen that (")ambiguity(") can be used significantly differently at $level_2$ from its use at $level_1$. And intent, purpose, meaning, etc., follow along as well as go off in different directions. There has been some beginning recognition of these matters, but it goes surprisingly slow. Thus the Hart and Sacks theory of interpretation seems to try to discard meaning (no need for that) and put all of its values (E) on purpose.
6. Purpose rhetoric is most use-ful and valu-able. But it is also beautifully normative-ambiguity promoting. It can be used for communications analysis, but just as well for crypto-valuextension. (See next chapter.) These matters simply cannot be seen let alone appreciated by one who confines himself away from $level_3$ communications exploration, even if he moves with fair freedom between the other two levels.
7. Legal education concerns itself quite a bit with problems of interpretation, not just regarding statutes, contracts, and other formal texts, but it really does not teach the skill of interpretation, the sort whose core is communications analysis. Why is that?
8. Well, most legal educators are not themselves trained in these matters and naturally will resist efforts to get it into the curriculum, so it has to be smuggled in. Some people prefer smuggled products, but others get a bit suspicious, or even scared.
9. But further, most theorists, educators, and most just people for that matter, cannot distinguish between their own moving-of-others rhetoric and their own merely observing. We speak of objectivity but rarely come close *in educational situations* because roles, goals, perspectives, and communication contexts are not kept straight, because

one's imagination *too readily* projects him and his audience on the wings of his words out of the here and now situation. Wondrous but mis-leading.

10. Such is the matter with Hart's well intended libertarian model of the legal system, because it encourages mechanistic interpretation, or arbitrary, legalistic, etc. ("there ain't nobody here but us ambiguities.")
11. See Chapter X and comments for further elaboration.
12. But also take a look again at Exhibit VI, The Right Way and other places in previous explorations for the relating of analysis to interpretation.

C. COMMUNICATION THEORY:

1. Of course this whole book is about interpretation and all of it requires the reader-participant to interpret (as all books do), but additionally it often requires the reader-participant to look at what *he* is doing, to sense, feel, and understand the very process, the dynamics of interplay between him and the text. Something has to get him started in listening with the third ear, seeing with the third eye, etc.
2. Strange, because it is so obvious really, but people do not realize at all that what goes on inside their head is part of the communication process, and especially so in reading-interpretation. Probably because there is so often a surface recognition of the word-forms, the sentence-forms, etc., and the deeper understandings possible, coming partly from considerations of the sort suggested in these last two chapters, *are by-passed:* e.g. of the IMPLICATIONS possible, or of the different contexts which are clued or really involved.
3. Group-dynamics sensitivity training is easier to get across, i.e. into, than the kind(s) involved in this chapter and the rest of the book(s). But awareness-sensitivity *qua* what is going on there within-among the group (participants) may take considerable time. Group-dynamics sensitivity does not necessarily bring the analogous sensitivity to written words, *and vice-versa.* But words consciousness involves both kinds of sensitivity!
4. McLuhan's stress on the declining significance of the written form(s) and even of verbal communication may have

been premature, but the kind(s) of consciousness, involvement(s), etc., which he saw happening, what some regard a primitive sort of involvement of young people with their environment(s), is the kind of consciousness which if brought back to words *will lead to radically different theories of interpretation.*

5. I just do not think it is a matter of rationality vs. nonrationality, intellectuality vs. anti-intellectuality, etc. The new consciousness people do not need group-encounter *training,* obviously, but they do need to be shown that it may not all be "just rhetoric." But the rhetoric of interpretation *is* so phony, especially in the mouth or page of a legalist or in a legalistically oriented situation. Yes, tell it like it is, but we have not fully enough realized what "it is" with rules and law and so on. The swing to legalism on the campus, not just with the police but within the dynamics of student discipline and *faculty* discipline, shows in part a lack of capacity to deal with the implications of the NEW CONSCIOUSNESS.
6. Since legal theorists are not willing to explore or discuss the ramifications for law (communications), because defensive, perhaps, communications oriented explorers might be able to do the job(s).
7. There is a second level of new consciousness which people have not yet turned on to, *but* what does this words-communications consciousness (*inevitable*) do to rulism-legalism which has been a bastion of law (talk)? or does that mean "to law?"

Exploration X

Communications Analysis: Prelude to Interpretation

Sections: The Worth of a Model; Why Start with J. L. Austin?; How it Works; Taking the Observer Out of the Act; Meaning, Use, and Ambiguity; Misguides Among Rules and Principles of Interpretation; Context(s), Meaning, and Semantic Reponse; Keeping Semantic Responses Straight; Definitional Smuggling; The Fourth Dimension: Exlocution; The Values of Interpreting; Intent and Purpose.

A sensitizing model or guide or framework or checklist for that sort of interpretation which is at least idealized as approachable if not fully possible, what is called here communications analysis. The stress is on official or formal texts peculiar to law (yering), but the model is usable and useful in *any* communications analysis. It helps the interpreter (in all senses of that word) toward conscious adaptation to appropriate role(s) and perspective(s) as well as to locate himself in his own communication situation relative to other relevant and appropriate contexts *qua* the textual stimuli. The stick-to-the-four-corners of the text approach is exploded for always as generally well "intentioned and meaning" but precisely the wrong emphasis if good communication is to be maximized. It is not necessary when one borrows a leaf from the pages of judicial techniques in evaluating evidence!

A. SENSITIVITY TRAINING:

1. ORDER STARTS IN THE (mind of the) BEHOLDER. As we have seen, words are obviously not *just* mapping devices, but that is one of their significant uses. The mapping of this chapter helps one to experience and maximize the dynamics of interpretation to the order of from 4-6 *dimensions.*
2. See words and feel their stimuli as clues and cues. "Meaning" is a relating term, so that meaning is not in words as atomic items, but in relationships of words as related further to the interpreter and the contexts to which he consciously relates himself. The *forms* (See Chapters V & VI for the complexity just in a text) geometrically perceivable in the text trigger form—ORDER—in the (mind of the) beholder (interpreter).
3. Kinds of clues and cues: (1) locutionary. (2) illocutionary. (3) perlocutionary. (4) exlocutionary. (See Visual Model, p. 289.)
4. (1) Locutionary: how the words of the text relate and are relatable to their linguistic, and surface and depth grammatic heritages. Included here are matters of punctuation, dictionary references, conventional or even certain special usages, etc., what is taken to be the most familiar sense(s) of "meaning."

   (2) Illocutionary: how the words relate and are relatable

to the situation(s) which produced the words of the text, specifically the behavior(s) in that context. Thinking in terms of speech act helps, or communication act. What is the communicator doing in this act of utterance (See Chapter VIII)?

(3) Perlocutionary: how the words relate and are relatable to the situation(s) of the individual(s) or group(s) which constitute the audience(s)—a third sort(s) of context. From the perspective of the observer this aspect constitutes the completion of the communicative act. The actor reaches out in acting. He touches the audience in acting. The audience is touched by the act. What the actor attempts to do in reaching out or touching is one thing, how the audience is touched or otherwise affected may be or may not be what was attempted. (See how intent, purpose, and meaning get in to this act.)

(4) Exlocutionary: how the words relate and are relatable to the observer-interpreter, the communications analyst, as he potentially may perceive the several dimensions as he relates himself in his context to each of the other contexts and as they relate to each other. It is possible for (4) and (3) to coincide, but the job of the analyst is to determine whether that is appropriate, whether he should first adopt (4), for instance, as a means of determining the appropriate completion of the communication *a la* (3).

5. This sort of analysis may seem unfathomable for anyone who has not been working his way along into a position to have this sort of communications involvement!
6. When you are ready, this framework simply has to be tried out. One way is to take it back to previous explorations. NOW move around in Show Me a Rule, for instance, to see how you can move around from level to level, as we called it in Chapters III–V. Try it out on the Garratt opinion. Etc.

B. LEGAL THEORY:

1. Whether law, legal theory, critical commentary, etc., should be concerned less, more, or completely with matters of values turns out to be a loaded sort of question,

because "value" is a very complicated word-form like all the rest, although note *it is primarily a level$_2$ term.* The model set forth should demonstrate that one cannot even *describe* communicative behavior in any value-less way! (When in turn the description is viewed at level$_2$.) in the sort of communications exploration model proposed, the analyst must be value-sensitive at a high level, for one thing to keep his own values in proper perspective, but further to "see what is going on" from the communicator's perspective. (See Directory, comments to Exploration 8.)

2. Morris Cohen and son, F. S. Cohen, agreed that debates in legal theory (and many other places) are either at cross purposes which are not articulated or at different levels so that a by-pass occurs. Previous commentary in text shows up both cross purpose and by-passing. For instance, arguments whether common law rules and statutes are a little, much, or completely ambiguous involves both cross purposes (socio-political theory) and not-coming-to-grips by-passing.
3. Such are the implications properly drawable from the textual analysis of what is wrong with the interpretative approach that says "stick to the four corners" of the text. This problem is explored with respect to kinds of situations: libel, constitutions, statutes and other legislative products, and instruments called wills and contracts.
4. Of course not all debates are thus soluble, nor are all problems of interpretation resolved, even in the narrower sense of communications exploration, but many more of them are soluble in such ways than we presently care to admit.
5. To the extent objectivity is really wanted, then greater candor necessary regarding purposes, goals, values, and what one is trying to do. That must start at level$_2$ commentary, although an increase of candor seems a trend in judicial rhetoric, unless the pendulum swings back in a shock re-action to current events. THE MODEL SUGGESTED PROMOTES CANDOR AND OBJECTIVITY so far as approachable, although not so far as expedience (E) may be concerned!
6. The model is heuristic at least. But it is also usable. Further it demonstrates a major communications-view.

And it provides communications theory (level$_2$!) underpinning for much of the previous textual exploration. Certainly it relates to and justifies a focus on law talk as compared to law, for the purposes of communications analysis. It shows that to look at law talk is related to looking at speech acts and communicative behavior implications. It is not looking at "law as merely rhetoric," but attempting to filter out the rhetoric to see what is left! (or right.)

7. How does talk talk relate to the model? Of course it is part of the candor approach. But see this: talk talk is first a way of getting the kinds of consciousness that makes the heuristic as well as functional model sense-able. But also it forces one to separate for deeper relating the linguistic components from the behavior components, to realize they are both important to communication even when dealing "only with words"—in print. Talk talk definitely involves seeing how meaning in the fairly pure linguistic sense (perhaps the paradigmatic sense?) must be related to *use* (to oversimplify it here). As I have said many times in the previous text, Wittgenstein's analysis of language-games and/or the family of word-uses under the word-form gets one to looking through the word-form of "meaning" to deal with the way words are used no matter what they (seem to) *mean.*
8. Perhaps the best way to see this inter-relating is to turn the model and talk talk techniques back on to legal theory (level$_2$) commentaries to see what can be discovered, then ultimately on one's own theory! Then we could talk more candidly about the tasks of jurisprudence and other sorts of approaches to legal process analysis.
9. Now then, talk talk has its limits of usefulness if all it does is leave one at sea. Remember, it is premised to be a necessary part of getting necessary sensitivities and awareness, a sense of perspectives and roles, for instance (Chapter VIII) in addition to just words *per se* awareness. As the jungle is penetrated, paths are made.
10. Talk talk then becomes a skill within the larger approach, revealing, for instance, alternative possibilities at the locutionary perspective, and further at the speech act or illocutionary coordinates. Then one is ready to take into ac-

count the greater range of communications variables, to see what the choices are, etc., and *then* to make a more considered judgment or decision, if that is the ultimate role-goal. But just because one is a decision-maker or even a pure advocate does not mean that there is not needed a stage in his inquiries where he attempts to approach objectivity. The premise is that we do communicate and the determinacy of much of law(s) is dependent on the desire to find out what the communicator is attempting! Lawyers' dependency on rhetoric blinds them very often to other kinds of communication. Ditto as to legal theorists who are apprehensive to see what sort of communication they are doing, no matter what they thought they were doing!

11. To say it once more, unmuddling of perspectives (Chapter VIII) is a key communications analysis task in the midst of any conceivable kind of communication or effort to communicate. It could be a basis for a complete jurisprudential theory, but at the minimum, it is an indispensable part of *engaging in* the activity of legal theory, being a legal theorist—or any other viewer of and actor in the whole of or some part of legal process. That *is* saying quite a lot.

C. COMMUNICATION THEORY:

1. Building relativity of meaning (meaning 1,2,3 . . . n) into a procedure of communications analysis.
2. Certainly takes into account the unbalance of the logical positivistic sort of view. What is meaningless in the linguistic-context sense (locutionary), or imprecise, or ambiguous, etc., may be quite meaning$_2$-ful, precise$_1$, and concrete$_2$ in a communicative behavior (illocutionary) sense e.g. an atheist not scoffing at "God is love" but looking further into how the participants relate to each other in light of the situational use of the expression. ("But is God *really* love?" may in turn seem a meaningless question to the semanticist, but likely there is another level of significance. Cf. "What is law?")
3. So, a theory of meaning$_{1,2,3 \ldots n}$; or a theory of linguistic analysis taking account of meaning in a limited focus and

in the context of communicative behavior; or a theory of communications analysis, discovery, exploration, etc.

4. Shows how previous claims of a new empiricism are borne out, and how linguistic analysis, so-called, fits into that new empiricism, is part of it.
5. But communications analysts are not just empirically *biased.* "Empiricism" is not a four letter word but the label is primarily a way of relating what we are doing to a way of thinking at a very generalized level. I do not want to stress empiricism to the exclusion of (other) values because I do not think it necessary or desirable. See comment 1. under Legal Theory above, and for that matter all the comments *qua* this chapter.
6. Just to be suggestive, see how this model and the over-all theory involved relate to one behavioral science sort of question. Anthropologists studying primitive tribe to make comparison with our cultures and others on institutions of law. Must a meta-language be used: (1) in the original research, (2) in comparing cultures, (3) in explaining to interested scientists of the home culture, (4) Etc. (See Nader, Law in Culture and Society.)
7. Talk talk apparently must be used in participant-observation of the primitive tribe, i.e. the language must be learned and talk talk in that language used, just to see what is going on and to get in touch with the locutionary, illocutionary, and perlocutionary contexts of *that* culture. Then it would seem to be a matter of translating into the terms of the home culture, but not at the level$_2$ of theory, but at the level of, if it is U.S. for instance, everyday levels of English. Then the focus would be at the illocutionary-perlocutionary contexts. That is, what was observed would have been "described" in the terms of the primitive culture, to be translated as behavioral descriptions in the everyday terms of our culture, and *then* to be assessed within the framework of level$_2$ theory. This is because of the linguistic gap that exists between level$_2$ and level$_1$ in our culture. (Not that we are unusual in that respect.)
8. In any event, it would hardly seem feasible, in terms of our theory analysis, to speak of using a meta-language to explore a country when the likelihood of the map fitting

the terrain is the very question to be asked. It is impossible to work out a meta-language that is not biased to our culture, until there has been enough experience in the new culture to work within its locutionary, illocutionary, and perlocutionary dimensions.

9. Yes, there is a sense in which this model is a meta-language, but here the assumption is, and necessarily it is subject to severe scrutiny, that we *have* learned enough about communication in various cultures to conclude that these *few*, but major, meta-assumptions are justified. It is not the sort of assumption that prejudges whether it these *few*, but major, meta-assumptions which are justified. It is not the sort of assumption that prejudges whether it makes sense to speak of law, or a judicial system, etc., with respect to the culture under exploration.
10. Etc., Etc.

INDEX

Also see the Directory for entry into the text

A

B

C

D

E

F

J

K

L

R

S